Geoff Tibballs is the author of the bestselling *The Mammoth Book of Jokes* and *The Mammoth Book of Dirty Jokes* as well as many other books including *Business Blunders* and *Legal Blunders*. A former journalist and press officer, he is now a full-time writer who lists his hobbies as sport, eating, drinking and avoiding housework. He lives in Nottingham, England.

Also available
The Mammoth Book of 20th Century Science Fiction
The Mammoth Book of Best of Best New SF
The Mammoth Book of Best New Manga 3
The Mammoth Book of Best New SF 21
The Mammoth Book of Best War Comics
The Mammoth Book of Bikers
The Mammoth Book of Boys' Own Stuff
The Mammoth Book of Brain Workouts
The Mammoth Book of Celebrity Murders
The Mammoth Book of Comic Fantasy
The Mammoth Book of Comic Quotes
The Mammoth Book of Cover-Ups
The Mammoth Book of CSI
The Mammoth Book of The Deep
The Mammoth Book of Dickensian Whodunnits
The Mammoth Book of Egyptian Whodunnits
The Mammoth Book of Extreme Fantasy
The Mammoth Book of Fast Puzzles
The Mammoth Book of Funniest Cartoons of All Time
The Mammoth Book of Hard Men
The Mammoth Book of Historical Whodunnits
The Mammoth Book of Inside the Elite Forces
The Mammoth Book of Jacobean Whodunnits
The Mammoth Book of King Arthur
The Mammoth Book of Modern Ghost Stories
The Mammoth Book of Monsters
The Mammoth Book of Mountain Disasters
The Mammoth Book of New Terror
The Mammoth Book of On the Road
The Mammoth Book of Pirates
The Mammoth Book of Poker
The Mammoth Book of Prophecies
The Mammoth Book of Roaring Twenties Whodunnits
The Mammoth Book of Short Spy Novels
The Mammoth Book of Sorcerers' Tales
The Mammoth Book of The Beatles
The Mammoth Book of The Mafia
The Mammoth Book of Vampire Romance
The Mammoth Book of Vintage Whodunnits
The Mammoth Book of Wild Journeys
The Mammoth Book of Zombie Comics

THE MAMMOTH BOOK OF REALLY SILLY JOKES

GEOFF TIBBALLS

RUNNING PRESS
PHILADELPHIA · LONDON

Constable & Robinson Ltd
55–56 Russell Square
WC1B 4HP
www.constablerobinson.com

First published in the UK by Robinson,
an imprint of Constable & Robinson Ltd, 2011

A copy of the British Library Cataloguing in Publication
Data is available from the British Library

UK 978-1-8490-1366-6
1 3 5 7 9 10 8 6 4 2

First published in the United States in 2011 by Running Press Book Publishers,
A Member of the Perseus Books Group

US ISBN 978-3-7624-4272-0
US Library of Congress number: 20010941552

9 8 7 6 5 4 3 2 1
Digit on the right indicates the number of this printing

Running Press Book Publishers
2300 Chestnut Street
Philadelphia, PA 19103-4371

Visit us on the web!
www.runningpress.com

Designed by Mitchell Associates, www.mitch.uk.com

Printed and bound in the UK

CONTENTS

INTRODUCTION

The pulling of Christmas crackers is as much a part of the Yuletide celebrations as Santa Claus, snowmen and newspaper articles about what to do with leftover turkey. Inside the cracker, along with the obligatory ill-fitting paper hat and a novelty gift of dubious use, is the eagerly anticipated joke, printed in festive red on a slip of paper. Usually it is a riddle or an excruciating pun, aimed at kids and guaranteed to draw groans from everyone present. Yet no matter how cringeworthy these jokes may be, they are invariably greeted with warm affection, like old friends.

In many cases they are exactly that. Knock knock jokes, doctor, doctor jokes, elephant jokes and chicken jokes all have their origins in the school playground, the home of silly jokes and arch punsters. Puns are often dismissed as one of the lowest forms of wit – especially if it's sarcasm's day off – but some of the cleverest jokes around have puns at their heart. For example, "Hedgehogs, why can't they just share the hedge?", which was voted the funniest joke at a recent Edinburgh Fringe Festival, is essentially nothing more than a pun, albeit a superior one.

So there's nothing wrong with silly jokes. They rarely offend anyone – except perhaps elephants and chickens – and they provide a welcome dose of silliness in a world in which an alarming number of people take themselves way too seriously.

Thanks to Duncan Proudfoot and Nicky Jeanes at Constable and Robinson and to Gemma Hastilow for the great cartoons.

And a special thanks to my daughter Nicki for her encyclopedic knowledge of chicken jokes.

Geoff Tibballs

AARDVARKS

What is uglier than an aardvark?
Two aardvarks.

What do you call an aardvark outside Buckingham Palace?
A guardvark.

What do you call a pickled aardvark?
A jarredvark.

What do you call an aardvark that's been thrown out of a pub?
A barredvark.

What do you call an aardvark that plays poker?
A cardvark.

What do you call a three-footed aardvark?
A yardvark.

Who is an aardvark's favourite singer?
Barbra Streisant.

What are an aardvark's favourite songs by The Beatles?
I Want To Hold Your Ant and Aard Day's Night.

How do ants hide from aardvarks?
They disguise themselves as uncles.

What do aardvarks eat for breakfast?
Aard-boiled eggs.

Why do aardvarks make undesirable neighbours?
They always have their noses in other people's business.

When is an aardvark jumpy?
When he's got ants in his pants.

Where does the aardvark family always come first?
In the phone book.

Which aardvark holds the world land speed record?
The short-sighted aardvark who wrapped his tongue around a motorcycle.

What do aardvarks like on their pizzas?
Ant-chovies.

Who has a long nose, wears a mask and sits tall in the saddle?
The Lone Aardvark.

Where did the young aardvark learn to tie knots?
In the Boy Snouts.

Did you hear about the household appliance that eats ants and records TV shows?
It's called the VCRdvark.

What has six legs, two arms, four eyes and a tail?
A man holding an aardvark.

Why weren't people scared of the baby aardvark?
Because a little aardvark never hurt anyone.

A man wanted to buy a new aardvark so he looked through the classified ads. He found a phone number offering aardvarks for sale and his call was answered by an old lady.

"How much are your aardvarks?" he asked.

"Thirty dollars each," she replied.

"Did you raise them yourself?" he added.

"Sure did," said the old lady. "Yesterday they were only twenty dollars each."

Why did the aardvark beat the lion in the TV debate about ants?
He stuck to the subject.

What do you call a boxing match between two aardvarks?
A snout bout.

Who loves hamburgers, French fries and ants?
Ronald McAardvark.

What do you call an aardvark that's just lost a fight?
A vark, because he's not aard any more.

An aardvark went on the TV quiz show *Who Wants To Be A Millionaire*? The host, who was very polite, said, "How confident are you of doing well, sir?"

"Quite confident," replied the aardvark. "I'd like to get up to $500,000."

"That's quite a target, sir," smiled the host. "Let's see how we go."

"Oh, before we start," said the aardvark, "I hope you don't mind but I've brought along a supply of ants to eat before I answer each question. I find that eating ants helps stimulate my brain."

"No problem, sir," said the host.

So the aardvark put his snout in his bag of ants for twenty seconds and correctly answered the first question. Then he ate ants for thirty seconds and correctly answered the second question. By the time he'd won $100,000 he was spending up to five minutes eating ants and the host was beginning to grow impatient.

"I must hurry you along, sir," he said. "We're running out of studio time."

"I need my supply of ants," insisted the aardvark. "Otherwise I'll get the question wrong."

Eventually the aardvark reached the $500,000 question.

"Sir," asked the host, "what is the capital of Albania? Is it a) Tirana b) Elbasan c) Ljubljana or d) Durres?"

The aardvark considered the options. "I think it's Tirana," he said, "but I need some more ants before I can be certain."

So he put his snout into the ant bag. On and on he went, guzzling ants for over eight minutes. The host was turning red with rage. "Listen, sir," he said eventually. "I can only give you another twenty seconds. If you're not ready then, we'll have to disqualify you."

At last the aardvark lifted his snout from the bag and the host asked wearily, "Is that your final ant, sir?"

ALIENS

What is an alien's favourite snack?
A Mars bar.

What did the alien say to the gas pump at the service station?
Don't you know it's rude to stick your finger in your ear when I'm talking to you!

Why did the alien think grass was dangerous?

He had heard it was full of blades.

Why does E.T. have such big eyes?
Because he saw his phone bill.

What do you call an alien spaceship that drips water?
A crying saucer.

What did the alien say to the garden?
Take me to your weeder.

Why do Martians suspect that walls keep secrets?
Because they're always meeting in the corner.

What do you get if you cross a baby with an alien spaceship?
An unidentified crying object.

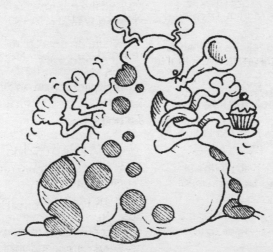

What do you call a fat alien? **An extra cholesterol.**

What is an alien's favourite food?
Martianmallows

How did the aliens hurt the farmer?
They trod on his corn.

What do aliens put on the windows of their spacecraft?
Venutian blinds.

Why was the thirsty alien hanging around the computer?
He was looking for the space bar.

Two Martians from space landed on Earth and spotted their first snake.
The first Martian said, "Don't worry. That's only a little green snake."
"Yes," said the second Martian, "but it might be as dangerous as a ripe one."

Why did the Martian become a bus driver?
So he could tell the Earthlings where to get off.

What's E.T. short for?
Because he's only got little legs.

How do you see flying saucers?
Trip up a waiter.

What did the alien say to the bird?
Take me to your feeder.

ANTS

Where do ants go for their holidays?
Frants.

What do you call a greedy ant?
An anteater.

What do you call an ant who skips school?
A truant.

What do you give a poorly ant?
Antibiotics.

What do you call a 200-year-old ant?
An antique.

Who was the most famous ant scientist?
Albert Antstein.

Why did the ant elope?
Nobody gnu.

Where do ants eat meals?
At a restaurant.

What do you call an ant with frogs' legs?
An antphibian.

How many ants are needed to fill an apartment?
Ten ants.

What kind of ants correct spellings?
Pedants.

What do you call a chic ant?
Elegant.

What do you call an ant that likes to be alone?
Independant.

What is smaller than an ant's mouth?
An ant's dinner.

What kinds of ants are good at maths?
Accountants.

If ants are so busy, how come they always have time to show up at picnics?

ART

Sherlock Holmes and Doctor Watson were doing their usual investigative business one day, when they uncovered an amazing painting.

At first glance, it looked like a picture of normal oak tree, in the middle of a wilderness, but if you looked closer, you could see that it was a surreal painting. The tree's trunk was actually made of fire, and its branches were made of ice, clouds and earth.

"What is it?" asked Watson in awe.

Holmes answered, "It's an element tree, my dear Watson."

Why did the picture go to jail?
Because it had been framed.

Why do statues and paintings of George Washington always show him standing?
Because he would never lie.

What is green and smells like red paint?
Green paint.

Why did the artist stick a stamp on his forehead?
He was a post impressionist.

For his art assignment a student had to draw a picture of William Shakespeare but couldn't decide what pencil to use. He said to himself, "2B or not 2B, that is the question."

What do you get if you cross a famous painter with a famous boxer?
Muhammad Dali.

What do you get if you cross a famous artist with a kebab?
Donner-tello.

What do you call an American drawing?
Yankee doodle.

A man nearly got away with stealing several paintings from a billionaire who had an impressive art collection. However, after planning the crime, and getting in and out past security, he was captured only two blocks away when his Ford Transit ran out of gas. When asked how he could mastermind such a crime and then make such an obvious error, he replied, "I had no Monet to buy Degas to make the Van Gogh."

Why did the nurse go to art school?
To learn how to draw blood.

What did the artist say to the dentist?
Matisse hurt.

Vincent Van Gogh was sitting at a bar when the bartender asked him, "Would you like a drink?"

"No thanks," said Van Gogh. "I've got one 'ere."

A small boy was entertaining himself at home by drawing. His father peered over his shoulder and asked, "What are you drawing, son?"

"I'm drawing God," replied the boy.

"That's quite difficult," said the father, "because nobody knows what God looks like."

The boy said, "They will when I'm finished."

BABIES

What do you get if you cross a mountain with a baby?
A cry for Alp.

What do you get if you cross a baby with soldiers?
Infantry.

Why do we dress baby boys in blue and baby girls in pink?
Because they can't dress themselves.

What are baby witches called?
Halloweenies

Mother: Why is there a strange baby in the crib?
Daughter: You told me to change the baby.

What did the baby corn say to its mother?
Where's pop corn?

How do you get a baby astronaut to sleep?
You rock-et.

What lies in a pram and wobbles?
A jelly baby.

A worried father says, "I see the baby's nose is running again."

His wife says angrily, "Can't you think of anything other than horse racing?"

Why isn't life fair for babies?
Because they always get a bum wrap.

BANANAS

Why did the banana go to the doctor?
Because it wasn't peeling well.

If a crocodile makes shoes, what does a banana make?
Slippers.

Why don't bananas ever get lonely?
Because they go around in bunches.

A man went into a bar with a banana in his ear.

The bartender looked at him suspiciously and said, "Excuse me, do you know you've got a banana in your ear?"

The man said, "I can't hear you. I've got a banana in my ear."

What's yellow and goes bzzzzz?
An electric banana.

What's yellow and goes slam, slam, slam, slam?
A four-door banana.

What's yellow, then green, then yellow, then green?
A banana with a night job as a cucumber.

First man: My wife went on a special banana diet.

Second man: Did she lose weight?

First man: No, but she can sure climb trees!

Why didn't the banana snore?
It was afraid it would wake up the rest of the bunch.

What should you do if you see a blue banana?
Try to cheer it up.

What is yellow and always points to the north?
A magnetic banana.

Why did the man lose his job in a fruit packing firm?
He kept throwing the bent bananas away.

How did the mother banana spoil the baby banana?
She left him out in the sun too long.

Why did the banana put on sun cream?
To keep from peeling.

A man walked into a bar with a banana on his head. As he served him, the bartender said, "I don't know if you're aware of this, but you've got a banana on your head."

"That's okay," said the man. "I always wear a banana on my head on Wednesdays."

"But today's Thursday," said the bartender.

"It's not, is it?" said the man. "Oh, no! I must look a complete fool!"

BATS

Two vampire bats wake up in the middle of the night, thirsty for blood. One says, "Let's fly out of the cave and get some blood."

"We're new here," says the second one. "It's dark out, and we don't know where to look. We'd better wait until the other bats can come with us."

The first bat replies, "Who needs them? I can find blood somewhere." He flies out of the cave and when he returns, he is covered with blood.

The second bat says excitedly, "Where did you get the blood?"

The first bat takes his friend to the mouth of the cave. Pointing into the night, he asks, "See that black building over there?"

"Yes."

"Well," says the first bat, "I didn't."

Why don't bats live alone?
They prefer to hang out with their friends.

How does a girl bat flirt?
She bats her eyes.

What did the mouse say when it saw a bat?
Mom, an angel!

How do bats fly without bumping into things?
They use their wing mirrors.

BEARS

How do you start a teddy bear race?
Ready, teddy, go!

What do you get if you cross a teddy bear with a pig?
A teddy boar.

What should you call a bald teddy?
Fred bear.

How do you hire a teddy bear?
Put it on stilts.

What's small and cuddly and bright purple?
A koala holding its breath.

What do you call a big white bear with a hole in his middle?
A polo bear.

What's a bear's favourite pasta?
Tagliateddy.

A bear walks into a bar. He goes up to the bartender and says, "Please could I have a…" thinks for a moment and continues, "beer."

The bartender replies, "Why the big pause?"

What is a bear's favourite drink?
Coca-koala.

What do you call bears with no ears?
B.

Two men are out hiking. All of a sudden, a bear starts chasing them. They climb a tree, but the bear starts climbing up the tree after them. The first hiker gets his trainers out of his knapsack and starts putting them on. The second hiker asks, "What are you doing?"

The first responds, "I figure

when the bear gets close to us, we'll have to jump down and make a run for it."

The second says, "Are you crazy? Don't you know you can't outrun a bear?"

The first guy says, "I don't have to outrun the bear … I only have to outrun you!"

Why didn't the grizzly wear any shoes?
He wanted to go bear foot.

One day a baby polar bear approaches his mother with a confused expression on his face and says, "Mom? Am I a polar bear?"

His mother replies, "Well, of course you are son!"

The cub says, "You're sure I'm not a brown bear or a black bear?"

"No, of course not. Now run outside and play."

But the baby polar bear is still confused so he approaches his father.

The cub asks, "Dad, am I a polar bear?"

"Why of course son!" he replies.

The cub continues, "Are you sure I don't have any grizzly bear in my bloodlines?"

"No son. I'm a polar bear, your mother is a polar bear, and you too are one hundred per cent purebred polar bear! Why in the world do you ask?"

"Because I'm freezing!"

Why do koalas carry their babies on their back?
Because they can't push a pram up a tree.

A man and a tall brown bear wearing a hat go into a bar. The man says, "I'll have a beer, and the bear will have a large Matabooboo."

The bartender asks, "What's a Matabooboo?"

The bear replies, "Nuttin' Yogi."

What is white, furry and shaped like a tooth?
A molar bear.

What's brown and hairy and can see just as well from either end?
A bear with its eyes shut!

What steps do you take when a bear is chasing you?
Very big ones!

What colour socks do bears wear?
They don't wear socks, they have bear feet.

Why didn't the teddy bear eat his dinner?
Because he was stuffed.

A man was hiking in the woods one day when a bear chased him up a really tall tree. The bear started to climb the tree, so the man climbed even higher. After a while the bear climbed down and went away. The man breathed a sigh of relief and started to climb down the tree.

Suddenly the bear returned and this time he had brought an even bigger bear with him. The two bears climbed the tree, the bigger bear going higher than the smaller bear, but luckily the man was able to climb higher still so that the bears couldn't reach him. Eventually the bears climbed down and went away. The man breathed a huge sigh of relief and started to climb down the tree.

Suddenly the two bears returned – and this time the man knew he was in big trouble. Each bear was carrying a beaver…

What bear hibernates standing on its head?
Yoga Bear.

BEES

Who is a bee's favourite singer?
Sting.

Why do bees have sticky hair?
Because they use honeycombs.

What do bees do with their honey?
They cell it.

Who is a bee's favourite pop group?
The Bee Gees.

Why do bees hum?
Because they've forgotten the words.

What do you call a clumsy bee?
A fumble bee.

What's the best part of a bee?
Its knees.

What do bees do if they want to use public transport?
Wait at a buzz stop.

What do bees chew?
Bumble gum.

What did the bee footballer say after netting a goal?
Hive scored.

How do we know that bees are happy?
Because they hum while they work.

What bee is good for your health?
Vitamin bee.

What does a bee say before it stings someone?
This is going to hurt me a lot more that it will hurt you.

What does a bee order at McDonald's?
A humburger.

What is more dangerous than being with a fool?
Fooling with a bee.

Where do bees go on holiday?
Stingapore.

What does a bee sit on?
Its bee-hind.

Why did the bee start reciting poetry?
He was waxing lyrical.

What are the cleverest bees?
Spelling bees.

What kind of bee talks very quietly?
A mumble bee.

What did the bee say to the bluebottle?
I must fly now but I'll give you a buzz later.

If we get honey from bees, what do we get from wasps?
Waspberry jam.

What did the queen bee say to the naughty bee?
Bee-hive yourself!

Why did the bees go on strike?
Because they wanted more honey and shorter working flowers.

Where did Noah's bees live?
In the Ark-hives.

What did the bee say to the flower?
Hi, honey.

How can you tell if a bee is on the phone?
You get a buzzy signal.

Where do wasps go when they're ill?
To waspital.

The world expert on European wasps and the sounds that they make is taking a stroll through his local town. As he passes by the record shop, a sign catches his eye: "Just Released – New Album – Wasps of the World and the sounds that they make – available now."

Unable to resist the temptation, the man goes into the shop and says to the shop assistant, "I am the world expert on European wasps and the sounds that they make. I'd very much like to listen to the new album you have advertised in the window."

"Certainly, sir," says the young man behind the counter. "If you'd like to step into the booth and put on the headphones, I'll put it on for you."

The man goes into the booth and puts on the headphones.

Three minutes later, he comes out of the booth and announces, "I am the world expert on European wasps and the sounds that they make and yet I recognized none of those."

"I'm very sorry, sir," says the young assistant. "If you'd care to step into the booth again, I can play you another track."

He steps back into the booth and replaces the headphones. Three minutes later, he comes out of the booth shaking his head. "I don't understand it," he says. "I am the world expert on European wasps and the sounds that they make, and yet I still can't recognize any of those!"

"I'm terribly sorry, sir," says the assistant. "Perhaps if you'd like to step into the booth again, you could hear another track?"

Sighing, the man steps back into the booth. Five minutes later, he comes out again, clearly agitated. "I am the world expert on European wasps and the sounds that they make and yet I have recognized none of the wasps on this record."

"I really am terribly sorry," says the young assistant. "I've just realized I was playing you the bee side."

BIRDS

Why do seagulls fly over the sea?
Because if they flew over the bay they would be called bagels.

Why did the owl 'owl?
Because the woodpecker would peck 'er.

What is the definition of robin?
A bird who steals.

When is the best time to buy budgies?
When they're going cheep.

What do you give a sick bird?
Tweetment.

Which bird is always out of breath?
A puffin.

What do you call a penguin in the Sahara?
Lost.

Which birds steal soap from the bath?
Robber ducks.

What language do birds speak?
Pigeon English.

Where do birds invest their money?
In the stork market.

Why don't owls go on dates when it's raining?
It's too wet to woo.

What birds spend all their time on their knees?

Birds of prey.

What kind of birds do you find in prison?
Jail birds.

How much beer can birds with large beaks drink in an evening?
Tou cans.

What did the tree say to the woodpecker?
You bore me.

Two budgies are sat on a perch. One says to the other, "Can you smell fish?"

What do you call a very rude bird?
A mockingbird.

What do pelicans eat?
Anything that fits the bill.

How do you identify a bald eagle?
All his feathers are combed over to one side.

What do you call a woodpecker with no beak?
A headbanger.

Where do penguins vote?
At the South Poll.

A penguin walked into a hotel and asked the receptionist, "Has my wife been in yet?"
"I don't know," said the receptionist. "What does she look like?"

How can you tell when a turkey is done?

He flushes the toilet.

Where do crows go for a drink?
To a crowbar.

What does a baby swan wear on its legs?
A cygnet ring.

Why does an ostrich have a long neck?
Because its head is so far from its body.

What does a bird take with it when it goes skydiving?
A sparrowchute.

What happened when the owl lost his voice?
He didn't give a hoot.

What do you call a bird that digs for coal?
A mynah bird.

After many years of marriage, a husband turned into a couch potato, became completely inattentive to his wife and sat guzzling beer and watching TV all day. The wife was dismayed because no matter what she did to attract her husband's attention, he just shrugged her off with some bored comment.

This went on for months and the wife was going crazy with boredom. Then one day at a pet store, she sees this big, ugly bird with beady eyes and a powerful beak and claws.

The shopkeeper, observing her

fascination with the bird, tells her it is a specially imported Goony bird and it has a very peculiar trait. To demonstrate, he says, "Goony bird! The table!"

Immediately, the Goony bird flies off its perch, attacks the table and smashes it into hundreds of pieces with its powerful beak and claws. To demonstrate some more, the shopkeeper says, "Goony bird! The shelf!"

The Goony bird turns to the shelf and demolishes it in seconds.

"Wow!" says the woman. "If this doesn't attract my husband's attention, nothing will!" So she buys the bird and takes it home.

When she enters the house, the husband is, as usual, sprawled on the sofa guzzling beer and watching the game. "Honey!" she exclaims. "I've got a surprise for you! A Goony bird!"

The husband, in his usual bored tone replies, "Goony bird, my foot!"

What always succeeds?
A toothless budgie.

What bird is grey?
A melted penguin.

What goose once ruled India?
Mohandas Gander.

Why do some sea birds believe everything they are told?
Because they're gull-ible.

A computer programmer, bored with his job, decides to start his own business. Wanting to do something totally different from his current occupation, he buys a pair of rheas, which are like ostriches, and a large tract of land.

His rhea farm is soon doing booming business as there appears to be a great demand for the birds. Not being satisfied with just selling them, the rhea farmer starts researching how the birds are being used. He finds that all parts of the birds are being utilized, except the feathers. Nobody, it seems, wants the plainly coloured rhea feathers.

But the rhea farmer has a plan. He purchases some equipment and chemicals, employs some technical experts and is soon selling pretty coloured rhea feathers. The resulting sales are amazing and make the new feather merchant very happy. There is one small problem. The workers making the coloured feathers are becoming quite ill. The concerned young man calls in a number of doctors to determine the nature of the illness.

It was discovered that the workers had developed a severe case of dye a rhea.

What do you use to help a goose with one leg?
Propagander.

What happens when geese land on a volcano?

Two vultures board an airplane, each carrying two dead raccoons. The flight attendant looks at the vultures and says, "You know the rules, gentlemen – only one carrion allowed per passenger."

They cook their own gooses.

What birds are found in Portugal?
Portu-geese.

What do you call a sick bird of prey?
An illegal.

Two robins are sitting in a tree.
"I'm really hungry," says the first one.

"Me, too," says the second. "Let's fly down and find some lunch."

They fly to the ground and find a nice plot of ploughed land full of worms. They eat and eat until they can eat no more.

"I'm so full I don't think I can fly back up to the tree," says the first robin.

"Me neither. Let's just lay here and bask in the warm sun," says the second.

So they flop down, basking in the sun. No sooner have they fallen asleep than a big fat tabby cat sneaks up behind them and gobbles them up.

As the cat sits washing his face after his meal, he smiles, "I love baskin' robins!"

What birds are always unhappy?
Bluebirds.

Why does a flamingo stand on one leg?
Because if he lifted that leg off the ground he would fall down.

Did you hear the story about

the peacock?
No, but I heard it's a beautiful tale.

What's noisier than a whooping crane?
A trumpeting swan.

What bird is with you at every meal?
A swallow.

Why are birds grouchy in the morning?
Because their bills are over dew.

What's a bird's favourite TV show?
The feather forecast.

What did they call the canary that flew into a pastry dish?
Tweetie Pie.

A petrol attendant is filling a man's car when he notices that a small penguin is sitting in the back seat. The attendant turns to the man and asks what the deal is with the penguin.

"Well," the man says, "I found the little guy a few weeks ago wandering around looking sad. I've been going crazy thinking of things I can do for him."

"There's a zoo just down the road," replies the attendant. "Why don't you take him there?"

The man thanks the attendant, pays and drives off to the zoo.

A few days later the man pulls up to the petrol station and again is met by the attendant who notices that the penguin is still in the back of the car.

"I thought you were taking him to the zoo," says the attendant.

"I did," answers the man. "He loved it, so I'm taking him to the beach today."

What's an owl's favourite subject at school?
Owlgebra.

The rarest bird in the world was called, naturally enough, the Raree Bird. After being hunted to virtual extinction in the nineteenth century, there was just one Raree Bird left on the planet by 1910 and a huge reward was offered for its capture – dead or alive.

That last surviving Raree Bird lived in Africa where it was relentlessly pursued by a hunter eager to claim the reward. After months of tracking the Raree Bird across barren plains and through dense jungle, the hunter finally cornered it in a lone tree. He raised his rifle and took aim but just as he pulled the trigger a fly flew into his face, causing him to miss his target. Nevertheless the shock was enough to send the Raree Bird toppling from its perch, and it fell to the ground with an injured wing.

As the hunter stood ominously above it, the wounded Raree Bird begged, "Please, Mr Hunter, don't kill me like this. Shooting me is not very sporting. Besides, that was your last bullet. What happens if you're attacked by a lion?"

The hunter thought he had better check whether he had any bullets left, and while he was momentarily distracted the Raree Bird took the opportunity to hobble behind a rock. But the hunter spotted a broken feather protruding from behind the rock and fetched a heavy wooden club from his bag.

"Please, Mr Hunter," begged the Raree Bird, "don't kill me like this. If you club me to death, nobody will be able to identify me as a Raree Bird, and you won't be able to claim your reward."

The hunter realized that the Raree Bird had a valid point, so he searched around for another method of killing. While his back was turned, the bird limped off, only to find its progress halted by a steep cliff with a 300-foot drop.

The hunter quickly caught up with the Raree Bird and declared, "I'm going to push you over the cliff and claim the reward. You can't fly so you'll be crushed on the rocks below. Is that a fitting way for the last Raree Bird to die?"

"No, Mr Hunter, please don't," begged the Raree Bird.

"Why, what's wrong this time?" demanded the hunter.

The bird wiped a tear from its eye and sang, "Because it's a long way to tip a Raree…"

BOOKS

CRAZY BOOK TITLES:

Handling Big Cats by Lionel Bite

Transport in Hong Kong by Rick Shaw

Tidiness Around the Home by Anita House

Falling off a Cliff by Eileen Dover

Carpet Fitting by Walter Wall

A Dog's Treat by Nora Bone

The School Truancy Problem by Marcus Absent

Small Green Vegetables by Russell Sprout

Everyday Cooking Utensils by Lydia Saucepan

Building Up by Hedda Steam

Home Furnishings by Chester Drawers

More Home Furnishings by Nesta Tables

Without Warning by Oliver Sudden

Dressing for the Gym by Leo Tard

Islands of the World by Archie Pelago

A Load of Old Rubbish by Stefan Nonsense

The Lehman Brothers Heist by Robin Banks

Bad Cow Jokes by Terry Bull

Keeping Pet Snakes by Sir Pent

Interior Home Decorating by Matt Finish

Security Fences by Barb Dwyer

Battle Axes by Tom A. Hawk

The Housing Problem by Rufus Quick

Confessions of a Gold Digger by Emile Ticket

Hopelessly Lost by Miles Away

A Cowboy's Life by Brandon Irons

Bank Robbery for Beginners by Hans Upp

An Encyclopedia of Explosives by Dinah Mite

Hot Dog by Frank Furter

Puddles In My Bed by I.P. Knightley

A Child's Favourite Candies by Annie Seedball

Candle Vaulting by Jack B. Nimble

Droopy Drawers by Lucy Lastic

Covering Every Eventuality by Justin Case

A Spoonerist's Guide to Caring for Antiques by Christine Pondition

Too Long in Jail by Freda Prisoners

Telephone Problems by Ron Number

Aches and Pains by Arthur Itis

The Peace Process by Olive Branch

My Worst Journey by Helen Back

Christmas, Easter and Thanksgiving by Holly Daze

Falling Trees by Tim Burr

Don't Wake Baby by Elsie Cries

Just Say No by Will Power

Practical Grass Cutting by Moses Lawn

Downpour by Wayne Dwops

Looking Into the Future by Claire Voyant

An Encyclopedia of Plant Eaters by Herb Avore

Into the Danger Zone by Hugo First

I Hate Daytime by Gladys Knight

Practical Vegetable Growing by Tom R. Toe

A History of Scottish Dentistry by Phil McCavity

Decorating Your Mousehole by Minnie Blinds

The Dash for the Train by Willy Makeit and Betty Wont

The Unfortunate Woman by Paul Adey

Military Tactics by Sally Forth

Food on the Table by E. Tittup.

Fade Away by Peter Out

String Instruments by Amanda Linn

The Miracle Drug by Penny Cillin

A Hole in my Roof by Lee King

Bricklaying Skills by Manuel Labour

How to Complain by Mona Lott

Not So Hot by Luke Warm

The Joy of Diamonds by Jules Sparkle

Animal Ailments by Ann Thrax

The Rebounding Bullet by Rick O'Shea

The Telltale Heart by Stefi Scope

Mobile Homes by Winnie Bago

Shotgun Wedding by Marius Quickly

The Haunted House by Major Jump

Neat Shirts by Preston Ironed

The Funeral Guide by Paul Bearer

Bubbles in the Bathtub by

Ivor Windybottom

Artificial Clothing by Polly Ester

Profiting From Divorce by Ali Money

The American Dream by Jason Rainbows

Message Understood by Roger Wilko

Ceiling Lighting by Sean Da Leer

It Won't Work by Mal Function

Italian Pasta Dishes by Ravi Oli

How to Stay Clam by Jill Out

Girl on a Budget by Penny Pincher

Flakes of Scalp by Dan Druff

Keeping Caged Birds by Ken Airey

Preparing Leather by Tanya Hide

Safe Motorcycle Riding by Helmut Wearer

Robbery in the Bar by Nick McGuinness

Snakes of the Amazon by Anna Conda

Don't Mess With Me! by Amanda B. Reckonwith

The Careless Lion Tamer by Claude Bottom

The Welsh Joke Book by Dai Laffin

Target Shooting for Beginners by Mr Completely

Everybody Else by Allan Sundry

Lawn Chairs and Tables by Patty O'Furniture

The Art of Tug of War by Paul Hard

Ready...Set... by Sadie Word

Overpopulation in Paris by Francis Crowded

Flogging in the Army by Corporal Punishment

The Magic of Chlorophyll by Teresa Green

Hertz, Doesn't it? by Lisa Carr

Born with a Silver Spoon in my Mouth by Rich Kidd

The Vanishing Man by Otto Sight

Maintaining Discipline in Society by Laura Norder

Off to Market by Tobias A. Pigg

Collecting Wriggly Creatures by Tina Worms

The Mammoth Book of Mammoths by Ellie Funt

Did you hear about the book on cowardice?
It had no spine.

Did you hear about the book on copyright infringement?
It had legal binding.

Did you hear about the book on fashion?
It had a smart jacket.

Where do books sleep?
Under their covers.

Why did the librarian slip on the library floor?
She was in the non-friction section.

Which book teaches animals how to mate?
The Llama Sutra

A man went into a bookstore and said, "Do you have a book by Shakespeare?"
"Certainly, sir," replied the clerk. "Which one?"
"William, of course."

A man said to his brother, "Do you like the dictionary I bought you for your birthday?"
"Yes," the brother replied. "I just can't find the words to thank you enough."

CANNIBALS

Why don't cannibals eat clowns?
Because they taste funny.

What did the cannibal say when he saw a sleeping missionary?
Oh, yummy! Breakfast in bed!

What do cannibals do at a

wedding?
Toast the bride and groom.

When do cannibals leave the dinner table?
When everyone's eaten.

Did you hear about the cannibal who liked peanut butter?
He ate his son Pat.

What happened when the cannibals ate a comedian?
They had a feast of fun.

What did the cannibal get when he was late for dinner?
The cold shoulder.

Why won't cannibals eat divorced women?
They're very bitter.

What does a cannibal eat with cheese?
Pickled organs.

Why do cannibals prefer eating readers to writers?
Because writers cramp but readers digest.

Did you see the movie about the cannibal who devoured his mother-in-law?
It was called *Gladiator*.

Why did the cannibal decide to become a missionary?
If you can't eat 'em, join 'em.

What did the cannibal mum say to her son who was chasing a missionary?
Stop playing with your food!

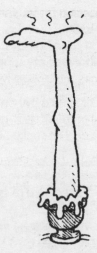

First cannibal: Come and have breakfast in our hut tomorrow.
Second cannibal: What are you having?
First cannibal: Hard-boiled legs.

What do cannibal secretaries do with leftover fingernails?
They file them.

How can you help a starving cannibal?
Give them a hand.

What happened to the cannibal lion?
He had to swallow his pride.

Why did the cannibal eat the tightrope walker?
He wanted a balanced meal.

What happened when the cannibal ate the speaking clock?
It repeated on him.

First cannibal: Who was that lady I saw you with last night?
Second cannibal: That was no lady, that was my supper.

A cannibal arrives home to find his wife chopping up a python and a very small man. "Oh no," groans the cannibal. "Not snake and pygmy pie again!"

"Mom, Mom," said the young cannibal. "I've eaten a missionary and I feel sick."
"Well, that's because it's true what they say – you can't keep a good man down."

Did you hear about the cannibal who loved fast food?
He ordered a pizza with everyone on it.

After eating someone, a cannibal tells his friend, "I'm a vegetarian."
"How can you be a vegetarian?" asks the friend. "I just saw you eat that person."
"That's okay," says the cannibal. "He was a Swede."

"Well, children," said the cannibal cooking teacher. "What did you make of the new history teacher?"
The children replied, "Burgers, ma'am."

What is a cannibal's favourite food?
Baked beings.

Why would the cannibal only eat babies?

He was on a diet.

A young cannibal is sitting at the dinner table. He turns to his mother and says, "I hate grandma."
"Well, leave her on the side of your plate then, dear."

What was the cannibal called who ate his father's sister?
An aunt-eater.

Why did the cannibal have indigestion?
He ate someone who disagreed with him.

A cannibal boy says to his mother, "I've brought a friend home for dinner."
"Put him in the fridge," says the mother, "and we'll have him tomorrow."

What happened when the cannibal crossed the Atlantic on a luxury liner?
He told the waiter to take the menu away and bring him the passenger list.

First cannibal: My wife's really tough.
Second cannibal: You should have left her in the oven for another twenty minutes.

What did the cannibal parents say when their teenaged daughter brought her new boyfriend home?
He's very nice, darling – he looks good enough to eat.

Two missionaries in Africa are captured by a band of cannibals who put them in a large pot of water, build a huge fire under it and leave them there. A few minutes later, one of the missionaries starts to laugh uncontrollably.

His friend couldn't believe it. "What are you laughing at?" he cried. "We're being boiled alive! They're going to eat us! What could possibly be funny at a time like this?"

The laughing missionary says, "I just peed in their soup!"

What happens if you upset a cannibal?
You get into hot water.

What do the cannibals call two skateboarders?
Meals on wheels.

A cannibal visits his neighbour to admire his new refrigerator. "What's the capacity?" he asks.

"I'm not sure," says the neighbour. "But it holds at least the two men who delivered it."

A little cannibal came running into the house saying, "Mom, Dad's fallen on the bonfire!"

His mother said, "Great, we'll have a barbecue."

A cannibal chief was about to stew his latest victim for dinner when the man protested, "You can't eat me, I'm a newspaper editor."

"Well," said the cannibal, "soon you'll be editor in chief."

Two cannibals were having lunch. One said, "Your wife makes a great soup."

"Yes, she does," agreed the other. "I'm going to miss her."

What happened to the comedian who did a show for the cannibal tribe?
He went down really well.

Boy cannibal: Mom says we're having Aunty for Christmas dinner this year.

Girl cannibal: Well, she can't possibly be tougher than last year's turkey!

Why did the cannibal join the police force?
So he could grill suspects.

Why wouldn't the cannibal eat Usain Bolt?
Because he was afraid he would give him the runs.

What happened when the cannibal bit off a missionary's ear?
He had his first taste of Christianity.

What happened after the cannibal discovered religion?
He only ate Catholics on Fridays.

Why was the cannibal expelled from school?
Because he kept buttering up the teacher.

Two cannibals are talking. One says to the other, "I just can't seem to get a tender missionary. I've roasted them, I've grilled them, I've barbecued them, I've baked them, I've stewed them, I've tried everything. But I just can't get them tender."

The second cannibal asks, "What kind of missionary do you use?"

The first cannibal says, "You know, the ones that live in that big house near the woods. They wear those brown cloaks with a rope around the waist and they're sort of bald on top with a funny circle of hair on their heads."

"Ah!" exclaims the second cannibal. "No wonder. Those are friars."

CATS

Little Timmy is in the garden filling in a hole when his neighbour peers over the fence. Interested in what the cheeky-faced youngster is doing, he politely asks, "What are you up to there, Timmy?"

"My goldfish died," replies Timmy tearfully, "and I've just buried him."

The neighbour is concerned. "That's an awfully big hole for a goldfish, isn't it?"

Little Timmy pats down the last heap of earth, then replies, "That's

because he's inside your cat."

What happened when the cat ate a ball of wool?
She had mittens.

What do cat actors say on stage?
Tabby or not tabby.

What did the cat say when he lost all his money?
I'm paw.

What do you call a beautiful cat?
A glamour puss.

What do cats drink from when they're in space?
Flying saucers.

What's furry, has whiskers and chases outlaws?
A posse cat.

A farmer had a sick cat, so he phoned the veterinarian in town to find a cure. After asking the farmer what the problem was, the vet told him to give the animal a pint of castor oil.

"A whole pint?" queried the farmer.

"That's right," said the vet. "That should sort him out in no time."

The next day the vet saw the farmer in town and asked him how the sick calf was getting along.

"You fool!" exclaimed the farmer. "It wasn't a calf. It was a cat!"

"Oh, my goodness!" said the vet in horror. "Did you give it the whole pint of castor oil?"

What do you call a cat with eight legs that likes to swim? **An octopuss.**

"Sure did," replied the farmer.

"What happened?" asked the vet. "Where's the cat now?"

Pointing into the distance, the farmer said, "Last time I saw that cat, he was going over yonder on that hill with five other cats. Two were digging, two were covering up, and one was scouting for new territory."

What do you call a cat that's eaten a lemon?
A sourpuss.

What do cats eat for supper?
Mice Krispies.

What do you get if you cross a cat and a gorilla?
An animal that puts you out at night.

What do you feed an invisible cat?
Evaporated milk.

What flies around your light at night and can bite your arm off?
A tiger moth.

Did you hear about the rebellious circus driver?
He refused to tow the lion.

A man was driving down a country lane when he accidentally ran over and killed a cat. Feeling guilty, he looked at the address on the cat's collar and went to a nearby house to tell the animal's owner what had happened.

A white-haired old lady answered the door.

"I'm really sorry," said the man, "but I'm afraid I've run over your cat. I'd like to replace it."

"Sure," said the old lady. "What are you like at catching mice?"

What is the unluckiest kind of cat to have?
A catastrophe.

Who was the most powerful cat in China?
Chairman Miaow.

What do you call a cat that has just eaten a whole duck?
A duck filled fatty puss.

What do cats read in the morning?
A mewspaper.

How is cat food sold?
Usually purr can.

When is it bad luck to see a black cat?
When you're a mouse.

What happened to the cat who drank seven saucers of milk?
He set a new lap record.

How do cats buy things?
From a catalogue.

Why was the cat afraid of the tree?
Because of its bark.

What works in a circus, walks the tightrope and has claws?
An acrocat.

Why was the cat so small?
Because he only drank condensed milk.

What do you call a cat wearing shoes?
Puss in boots.

If a cat won an Oscar, what would he get?
An Acatemy Award.

How do cats end a fight?
They hiss and make up.

What do you get if you cross a cat with a canary?
Shredded tweet.

Why do you always find the cat in the last place you look?
Because once you've found it, you stop looking.

What is white, sugary, has whiskers and floats on the sea?
A catameringue.

Why did the cat eat cheese?
So he could sit near the mousehole with baited breath.

What does the lion say to his friends before they go out hunting for food?
Let us prey.

What do you call a lion wearing a cravat and velvet pants?
A dandylion.

What happened to the man who tried to cross a lion with a goat?
He had to get a new goat.

When the lion arrived in the jungle, why did all the other animals gather round him?
He was the mane attraction.

How did the lion fare as king of the jungle?
He was a roaring success.

Boy: Did you put the cat out?
Girl: I didn't even know it was on fire.

An English cat, named one two three, and a French cat, called un deux trois, have a swimming race across the English Channel. Which cat wins?

The English cat, one two three, won the swimming race because un deux trois quatre cinq.

What did the lioness say to her cubs when she taught them how to hunt?
Don't go over the road until you see the zebra crossing.

A cat named Ginger is seriously overweight, so his owner decides to take him to the vet to find out if there is anything wrong with him and whether anything can be done about it. She puts him into the kitty-carry box, and drives to the surgery. The vet prescribes a course of pills, and his owner leaves, happy in the knowledge that Ginger will soon be his old slim self again.

But after a few weeks of taking the pills, there is no change. Ginger is as fat as ever. Months go by, and still there is no difference. In fact, if anything, his weight problem is getting worse.

The other problem is the bills from the vet – these pills are costing a fortune.

It soon becomes clear to his owner that Ginger had become a doc-billed fatty-puss.

Why do cats chase birds?
For a lark.

How did a cat take first prize at the bird show?
By reaching into the cage.

If there are ten cats in a boat and one jumps out, how many are left?
None, they were all copycats.

What did the cat say to the fish?
I've got a bone to pick with you.

How are tigers like sergeants in the army?
Both are proud of their stripes.

Why are cats good at video games?
Because they have nine lives.

A missionary was walking in Africa when he heard the ominous padding of a lion behind him. "Oh Lord," prayed the missionary, "grant in thy goodness that the lion walking behind me is a good Christian lion."

In the silence that followed, the missionary heard the lion praying too. "Oh Lord," he prayed, "I thank thee for the food which I am about to receive."

How do you know if your cat has a cold?
He has cat-arrh.

Where do lions get their clothes?
Jungle sales.

Where did the kittens go for a day out?
To a mewseum.

A lion was becoming rather old and was having trouble catching prey. He decided he needed a disguise so that other animals would not know he was a lion and would therefore not run away from him.

He went to a fancy dress shop and bought a gorilla costume. He then went to a nearby watering hole to see if his disguise would work. On the way, he saw three eagles sat on a rock.

One eagle said, "Hello, Mr Lion. Where did you get your gorilla suit?"

The lion was very disappointed. He asked the eagles, "How did you know I was a lion and not a gorilla?"

The eagles began to sing: "You can't hide your lion eyes..."

CHICKENS

Why did the chicken cross the road?
To get to the other side.

Why did the chicken cross the road?
Because he didn't want to go to the barbecue.

Why did the chewing gum cross the road?
It was stuck to the chicken's foot.

Why did the chicken run across the road?
There was a car coming.

Why did the chicken cross the road halfway?
She wanted to lay it on the line.

Why did the rubber chicken cross the road?
She wanted to stretch her legs.

Why did the Roman chicken cross the road?
She was afraid someone would Caesar.

Why did the chicken cross the road?
To prove to the possum it could actually be done.

Why did the chicken cross the road?
Don't ask us, ask the chicken.

Why did the turkey cross the road?
Because it was the chicken's day off.

Why did the chicken cross the playground?
To get to the other slide.

Why did the punk cross the road?
Because he was stapled to the chicken's back.

Why did the dinosaur cross the

road?
Because chickens hadn't evolved yet.

Why did the chicken cross the road, roll in the dirt and then cross the road again?
Because he was a dirty double-crosser.

Why did the rooster run away?
Because he was chicken.

How did the baby chickens dance?
Chick to chick.

What does a rooster say to a hen he likes?
You're one hot chick!

How do chickens book in at the airport?
At the chick-in desk.

A rooster lived on a farm where there were a dozen hens. Naturally he had his favourites, and he was particularly fond of two hens called Tina and Marge. The three shared a lot of happy times and were almost inseparable. But then one day the rooster was loaded onto a truck ready to be taken to a new farm.

His two favourite hens were distraught. "You can't go," they pleaded. "How will we cope without you?"

"You'll be okay," he replied, trying to comfort them. "You'll soon meet a new rooster."

But the two hens were inconsolable and tears began to run down their faces.

As the engine started up, the rooster called out from the back of the truck, "Don't cry for me, Marge and Tina."

Why did the turkey cross the road?
To prove he wasn't chicken.

Why don't chickens like people?
They beat eggs.

What kind of bird lays electric eggs?
A battery hen.

What happened to the chicken whose feathers were all pointing the wrong way?
She was tickled to death.

Why was the chicken sick?
It had people pox.

Why doesn't it take roosters long to pack when they go on vacation?
Because they only have to take a comb.

If a rooster lays an egg on the middle of a slanted roof, on which side will it fall?
Neither side. Roosters don't lay eggs.

A man was driving along a freeway when he noticed a chicken running alongside his car. He was amazed to see the chicken keeping up with him, as he was doing fifty miles per hour.

He accelerated to sixty and the

chicken stayed right next to him. He sped up to seventy-five miles per hour and the chicken passed him. The man noticed that the chicken had three legs.

So he followed the chicken down a road and ended up at a farm. He got out of his car and saw that all the chickens had three legs.

He asked the farmer, "What's up with these chickens?"

The farmer said, "Well, everybody likes chicken legs, so I bred a three-legged bird. I'm going to be a millionaire."

The man asked him how they tasted.

The farmer replied, "I don't know, I haven't caught one yet."

What do you get if you feed gunpowder to a chicken?
Eggs-plosions.

What do you get if you cross a hen with a dog?
Pooched eggs.

What do chicken families do at weekends?
They go on peck-nics.

There was once a chicken farmer who lived in a village in China. One year, his chickens were afflicted with a strange blight that caused them to lose their feathers. The farmer was deeply concerned about this, because winter was coming, and if the chickens had no feathers, he feared they would freeze to death.

So the farmer decided to consult the two wisest men in the land. First he visited Mr Hing, the renowned scholar. Mr Hing leafed through all his agricultural and medicinal texts and pored over books and scrolls well into the night. Finally, he returned to the farmer and told him that if he crushed the leaves of a gum tree into powder, made it into tea and fed it to his chickens, they would be cured.

The farmer then went to Mr Ming, the great seer. Mr Ming cast stones, read tea leaves and poked through entrails until finally he came up with the answer. "As surely as gum causes a shoe to stick to the ground, tea made from gum leaves will cause feathers to stick to chickens."

Now the farmer was ecstatic. The two wisest men in the land had given him exactly the same prescription. So, as soon as he returned home, he took some gum leaves and made tea from them. He mixed this with the chicken feed and fed it to his chickens. But it didn't work. The chickens continued to lose their feathers, and with the onset of winter, they all froze.

The moral of this story is, all of Hing's courses and all of Ming's ken couldn't get gum tea to feather a hen.

What do you call a chicken that eats cement? **A bricklayer.**

What do you get if you cross a chicken and a sergeant major?
A pecking order.

Why does a chicken watch television?
For hentertainment.

How long do chickens work?
Around the cluck.

Why couldn't the chicken find her eggs?
She had mislaid them.

Why did the chicken choose to play a percussion instrument?
Because she already had drumsticks.

Why is a roast chicken like a sofa?
Because they're both full of stuffing.

What do you call a greasy chicken?

A slick chick.

Following the egg hunt on Easter Sunday, a farm boy decided to play a prank. He sneaked into the chicken coop and replaced every egg with a brightly coloured one.

A few minutes later the rooster walked in, saw all the coloured eggs, then stormed outside and beat up the peacock.

Why did the umpire throw the chicken out of the baseball game?
He suspected fowl play.

What is a chicken's least favourite day of the week?
Fry-day.

What do you call a chicken on roller skates?
Poultry in motion.

The farmer's son was returning from market with the crate of chickens his father had entrusted to him when all of a sudden he tripped over a rock, dropped the box and it fell open, scattering chickens everywhere. The boy spent the next hour scouring the neighbourhood, scooping up the wayward birds and returning them to the crate.

Hoping that he had found nearly all of them, he reluctantly made his way home, fearing the worst from his father. "Pa," he confessed sadly, "the chickens got loose, but I managed to find fifteen of them."

"You did real good, son," smiled the father. "You left with ten."

Why did the chick disappoint his mother?
He wasn't what he was cracked up to be.

What did the Spanish farmer say to his chickens?
Oh, lay!

Why can't a chicken coop have more than two doors?
Because if it had four doors it would be a chicken sedan.

Why do roosters never get rich?
Because they work for chicken feed.

A chicken goes into a library and says to the librarian, "Bawk," in a high-pitched chicken's squawk.

The librarian says, "Oh, you want a book?" and gives the chicken a book.

The chicken walks out the door with the book but is back in five minutes, drops the book in front of the librarian, and says, "Bawk, bawk."

The librarian says, "Oh, you want two books?" and gives the chicken two books.

The chicken walks out the door with the two books.

Five minutes later, the chicken is back, drops the books in front of the librarian, and says, "Bawk, bawk, bawk."

The librarian says, "Oh, you want three books now?" and gives the chicken three books.

The chicken walks out with the three books. This time the librarian follows to see where the chicken is going.

The chicken walks down to the pond below the library and drops the books, one at a time, in front of a big bull frog.

The frog looks at the books as they drop and says, in his deep bullfrog voice, "Red-it, red-it, red-it."

CHILDREN

The morning bus was very crowded, and a man on his way to work became more and more annoyed by the little boy next to him who kept sniffing loudly. Eventually he could stand it no longer.

"Haven't you got a handkerchief?" he demanded, irritably.

"Yes," replied the boy. "But I'm not allowed to lend it to strangers."

First boy: Do you always bathe in dirty water?

Second boy: It was clean when I got in.

A little girl was scribbling furiously over some paper with a pencil when her mother asked her what she was drawing.

"I'm not drawing, Mom," she said indignantly, "I'm writing a letter to Billy."

"But you can't write," her mother pointed out.

"That's all right," said the little girl. "Billy can't read."

Timmy was watching his dad build a pine bookshelf. "What are the holes?" asked Timmy.

"They're knot holes," replied his father.

Timmy was puzzled and said, "So what are they if they're not holes?"

Boy: I lost my dog.
Girl: Why don't you put an ad in the newspaper?
Boy: Don't be silly! He can't read.

Mother: Who was that on the phone?

Child: Oh, just a woman saying it was long distance from China. But I told her I already knew that!

How did the child get a flat nose?
His teacher told him to keep it to the grindstone.

First boy: I won twelve goldfish at the fair.
Second boy: Where are you going to keep them?
First boy: In the bath.
Second boy: But what will you do when you want to take a bath?
First boy: Blindfold them.

Why did the invisible mother take her invisible child to the doctor?
To find out why he wasn't all there.

Billy and his sister Jenny were arguing at the dinner table. "You're so stupid!" yelled Billy.

"That's quite enough of that!" said their father. "Now Billy, I want you to apologize to your sister."

"Okay," said Billy. "Jenny, I'm sorry you're stupid."

What did the mother call her identical twin boys?
Pete and Repeat.

Why did the child put his hand in the fuse box when the weather got hot?
He heard that fuses blew.

Girl: What did you get that little medal for?

Boy: For singing.

Girl: What did you get the big one for?

Boy: For stopping!

A young family moved into a house next door to a vacant lot. One day a construction crew turned up to start building a house on the empty land, and inevitably their arrival captured the attention of the family's six-year-old daughter, who soon started chatting to the workmen. They responded by inviting her to join them on their tea breaks and virtually made her one of their gang. They even gave her little jobs to do and rewarded her at the end of the first week by presenting her with her very own pay envelope containing a dollar.

The little girl took the dollar home to her mother, who suggested that they take it to the bank to open a savings account. When they got to the bank, the teller asked the little girl how she had come to earn a dollar at such a young age.

The little girl replied proudly, "I've been working all week with a crew building a house."

"My goodness!" exclaimed the teller. "And will you be working on the house next week, too?"

The little girl replied, "I will if those useless morons at the lumber yard ever bring us the goddam bricks!"

A man had invited the boss and his wife for dinner, and it was little Johnny's job to set the table. But as everyone sat down to eat, Johnny's mother noticed that the boss's wife didn't have any cutlery. She asked Johnny, "Why didn't you give Mrs Smith a knife and fork, dear?"

"I didn't think I needed to," said Johnny. "I heard Dad say she always eats like a horse."

Mother: Why are you crying?

Boy: Because my new sneakers hurt.

Mother: That's because you've put them on the wrong feet.

Boy: But they're the only feet I have!

A little boy came downstairs in tears late one night.

"What's wrong?" asked his mother.

He sobbed, "Is it true, like they said in church, that people turn to dust when they die?"

"Yes, they do," replied his mother.

"In that case," he wailed, "somebody has died under my bed!"

If Mr and Mrs Bigger had a child, who would be the biggest of the three?

The baby, because he's a little Bigger.

A little boy came running into the kitchen. "Dad, Dad," he cried, "there's a man at the door with a really ugly face!"

"Tell him you've already got one," said his father.

Why did the parents call both of their sons Edward?
Because two Eds are better than one.

A little boy rides his bike and stops in front of a church as the priest comes out.

The priest says, "Come inside, I want to show you something."

The little boy says to the priest, "But somebody will steal my bike."

The priest says to him, "Don't worry, the Holy Spirit will watch it."

So the little boy goes inside and the priest says, "Let me show you how to do the sign of the cross. In the name of the Father, the Son and the Holy Spirit, Amen. Now you try it."

So the boy says, "In the name of the Father and the Son, Amen."

The priest asks, "What happened to the Holy Spirit?"

The boy replies, "He's outside, watching my bike."

COMMUNICATION

A man phones a computer helpline and says, "Help, I've pushed a piece of bacon into my computer's disk drive."

The assistant asks, "Has it stopped working?"

The man replies, "No, but there's a lot of crackling."

How do you stop your laptop batteries from running out?
Hide their trainers.

What do prisoners use to call each other?
Cell phones.

How do computers make sweaters?
On the interknit.

Why was the computer in pain?
It had a slipped disk.

Why was the computer so thin?
Because it hadn't had many bytes.

Why did the cat sit on the computer?
To keep an eye on the mouse.

What sits in the middle of the world wide web?
A very, very big spider.

A man went into a store and said, "I bought this computer yesterday and I found a twig in the disk drive."

The sales assistant said, "I'm sorry, sir, you'll have to speak to the branch manager."

What did one keyboard say to the other keyboard?
Sorry, you're not my type.

Why did the boy computer mouse like the girl computer mouse?
They just seemed to click.

What did the mouse say to the webcam?
Cheese.

What do computer experts do at weekends?
Go for a disk drive.

Why did the idiot take his computer to the shoe shop?
Because he had been told to re-boot it.

Did you hear about the email that was circulating saying that swine flu could be caught through tinned pork and ham?
People were advised not to open it because it was just spam.

Which way did the programmer go?
He went data way.

What do you get if you stuff your computer's disk drive with herbs?
A thyme machine.

What does a computer eat when it's hungry?
Chips – one byte at a time.

Two aerials meet on a roof, fall in love and get married. The ceremony was rubbish but the reception was brilliant.

Why are there so many Smiths in the phone book?
They all have phones.

What is a computer's favourite type of music?
Disk-o.

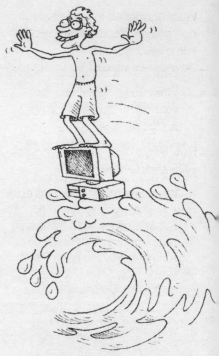

How did the idiot get water in his computer?
He was trying to surf the internet.

Why do tailors love internet forums?
Because they are full of threads.

What is a cursor?
Someone who is getting angry at his computer.

How does the biologist like to communicate?
With his cell phone.

When do computer files blush?
When they're unzipped.

What happened to the telegraph operator who accidentally sent the same message twice?
He was remorseful.

What do you get if you take your computer to an ice rink?
A slipped disk.

How do you fix a broken website?
With stick e-tape.

Why couldn't the apple send an e-mail to the orange?
Because the lime was busy.

Why did the gorilla log on to the internet?
To send chimpanzee-mail.

What goes choo choo choo while online?
Thomas the search engine.

How did the proud computer describe his son?
A microchip off the old block.

Why don't Vikings send e-mails?
They prefer to use Norse code.

Why would an elf use the internet?
To get answers for his gnomework.

How do dolphins send messages?
They use sea-mail.

What did the lumberjack enjoy most about the internet?
Logging on.

Which search engine does Arnold Schwarzenegger use?
Alta Vista baby.

Have you seen the boxing website?
Yes, it really knocked me out.

Have you seen the bus website?
Yes – it's just the ticket.

Have you seen the Dalmatian website?
No – I haven't spotted it yet.

Have you seen the dynamite website?
Yes, it really blew my mind.

Have you seen the goldfish website?
Yes, I was really bowled over.

Have you seen the hypnosis website ?
Yes, but it put me to sleep.

Have you seen the new fishing website?
No, it's not online yet.

Have you seen the new fruitcake website?
Yes – it's my currant favourite!

Have you seen the umbrella website?
Yes, but it went right over my head.

Have you seen the tomato sauce website?
No, I'll ketchup with it later.

Have you heard about the ruler website?
Yes – people are going to great lengths to see it!

Have you heard about the new opticians' website?
Yes, it's a site for sore eyes.

Have you heard that there's a new mountain website?
Really? I must take a peak at it.

Have you seen the history website?
Yes, but it was a long time ago.

Have you seen the dessert website?
Yes, it was a trifle boring.

Have you seen the amnesia website?
I can't remember.

What are the three swiftest means of communication?
Telephone, telegraph and tell-a-secret.

Why was the IT support worker bad-tempered?
Because he had a chip on his shoulder.

A man bought a new computer and after setting it up couldn't wait to try it out. But as soon as he clicked on an icon he was alarmed to see roots suddenly starting to grow out of the screen. These were followed by a huge trunk, branches and finally leaves.

In desperation he phoned the computer helpline. He told them, "All I did was click on an icon and these roots, branches, leaves and a trunk began growing from the screen. They're all over my desk. What's going on?"

"There's no mystery, sir," replied the helpline advisor. "Haven't you heard of the saying from little icons mighty oak trees grow?"

COWS

Why did the bull rush?
Because it saw the cow slip.

What do you call a cow in the Arctic?
An eskimoo.

What happened when the cow jumped over the barbed wire fence?
It was an udder catastrophe.

What do you get if you sit under a cow?
A pat on the head.

What do you get if you cross a cow with a camel?
Lumpy milkshakes.

What do you get from a pampered cow?
Spoiled milk.

Why did the cow cross the road?
To get to the udder side.

Three bulls heard via the grapevine that the rancher was going to bring yet another bull on to the ranch, and the prospect raised a discussion among them.

The first bull said, "Boys, we all know I've been here for five years. Once we settled our differences, we agreed on which hundred of the cows would be mine. Now, I don't know where this newcomer is going to get his cows, but I ain't giving him any of mine."

The second bull said, "That pretty much says it for me, too. I've been here for three years and have earned my right to the fifty cows we've agreed are mine. I'll fight him till I run him off or kill him, but I'm keeping all of my cows."

The third bull added, "I've been here a year, and so far you guys have only let me have ten cows. I may not be as big as you fellows yet but I am young and virile, so I simply must keep all my cows."

They had just finished their big talk when an eighteen-wheeler pulls up in the middle of the pasture with only one animal in it – the biggest bull these guys had ever seen. At 4,700 pounds, each step he took toward the ground strained the steel ramp to breaking point.

The first bull said, "Ahem... You know, it's actually been some time since I really felt I was doing all my cows justice, anyway. I think I can spare a few for our new friend."

The second bull nodded, "I'll have plenty of cows to take care of if I just stay on the opposite end of the pasture from him. I'm certainly not looking for an argument."

They look over at their young friend, the third bull, and find him pawing the dirt, shaking his horns and snorting.

The first bull said to him, "Son, let me give you some advice real quick. Let him have some of your cows and live to tell about it."

The youngest bull replied, "Hey, he can have all my cows. I'm just making sure he knows I'm a bull!"

What did the farmer call the cow that would not give him any milk?
An udder failure.

What is the easiest way to count a herd of cattle?
Use a cowculator.

Where do cows go on a Saturday night?
To the moovies.

Why do they put bells on cows?
Because their horns don't work.

What do you call a sleeping bull?
A bulldozer.

What do you call a bull who tells jokes?
Laugh-a-bull.

If a papa bull eats three bales of hay and a baby bull eats one bale, how much hay will a mama bull eat?
Nothing. There is no such thing as a mama bull.

Two cows are in a field. One goes, "Mooooo."
The other cow says, "I was going to say that."

What is a cow's favourite party game?
Moosical chairs.

What do you call a cow that cuts grass?
A lawn mooer.

What do you get if you cross a cow with a duck?
Cream quackers.

What is the best way to stop milk from turning sour?
Leave it in the cow.

A visitor from the city asked the farmer how long cows should be milked. The farmer replied, "About the same as short ones!"

What has one horn and gives milk?
A milk truck.

What does a cow make when the sun comes out?
A shadow.

Cow: Why don't you shoo those flies?
Bull: No, I'll let them go barefoot.

What do you call cows with a sense of humour?
Laughing stock.

If you had twelve cows and six goats what would you have?
Plenty of milk.

Does running out of a burning barn make cows unusual?
No, only medium rare.

Once there was a cattle rancher who, after two years of trying, finally found a buyer for his oldest bull, Caesar. The new owner was the rancher's closest neighbour and lived on the other side of the river across the valley.

"Well," said the rancher to his cowhands, "it's time to take this bull across the river to his new home."

So the men roped Caesar and walked him down to the river. They were about to put him on the boat when the rancher's son, who had helped to raise Caesar, begged, "Can we just take him for one last munch in his favourite meadow?"

The other hands thought it was a reasonable request and led the bull for a snack in the field. With the sun beating down on them, they forgot all about the job in hand and fell asleep.

Three hours later, the rancher realized that the bull was still on his land. Angrily, he rushed down to the valley and woke up the men.

"What do you think you're doing!" he yelled. "This bull should have been on the boat and across the river hours ago! We've come to ferry Caesar, not to graze him!"

Where do cows go on vacation?
Moo York.

What do you call a cow with no legs?
Ground beef.

What do you call a cow with three legs?
Lean beef.

How did the cow feel after swallowing a hand grenade?
Abombinabull.

A black cow was standing in the middle of the road. A driver came racing around the corner with no lights on but slammed on the brakes just in time to miss the cow. How did the driver see the cow?
It was daytime.

Why is it a waste of time telling a cow a secret?
Because it will just go in one ear and out the udder.

What do you call a cow with holes in it?
Holy cow!

A man climbed over a fence into a field to pick some flowers. Noticing a bull nearby, he said to the farmer, "Is that bull safe?"

The farmer replied, "Well, he's a lot safer than you are right now!"

Why do cows enjoy hearing jokes?
They like to be amoosed.

Why did the farmer buy a brown cow?
Because he wanted chocolate milk.

How do bulls drive their cars?
They steer them.

What kind of car does a cow drive?
A cattelac.

A devout cowboy lost his favourite Bible while he was mending fences out on the range. Three weeks later, a cow walked up to him carrying the Bible in its mouth.

The cowboy couldn't believe his eyes. He took the precious Bible from the cow's mouth, looked up to the heavens and exclaimed, "It's a miracle!"

"Not really," said the cow. "Your name is written inside the cover."

Why did the cow jump over the moon?
Because the farmer had cold hands.

How did the farmer find his lost cow?
He tractor down.

What did the calf say to the silo?
Is my fodder in there?

Teacher: I asked you to draw a cow eating grass, but you've only drawn the cow.

Pupil: Yes, Miss. The cow ate all the grass.

How did cows feel when the branding iron was invented?
They were very impressed.

What goes ooo, oooo, ooooo?
A cow with no lips.

What do you call a bull you can put in the washing machine?
Washable.

A farmer told a neighbour that he had to shoot one of his cows.

"Was it mad?" asked the neighbour.

"Well," said the farmer, "it wasn't too happy about it."

How can you tell a cow is exceptional?
It's out standing in its field.

Where does a cow eat?
In a calf-eteria.

Which two members of the cow family go everywhere with you?
Your calves.

What do you call a cow with a twitch?
Beef jerky.

Why did the farmer take the cow to the vet?
Because she was so mooo-dy.

What happened to the lost cattle?
Nobody's herd.

How do you make a milkshake?
Give a cow a pogo stick.

What kind of milk do you get from a forgetful cow?
Milk of Amnesia.

Why don't cows have any money?

Because farmers milk them dry.

Two cows were chatting over the fence between their fields. The first cow said, "I tell you, this mad cow disease is really pretty scary. They say it is spreading fast. I heard it hit some cows down on the Jones Farm."

The other cow replied, "I'm not worried, it doesn't affect us ducks."

What did the cow wear to the football game?
A jersey.

What do you call a cow that doesn't give milk?
A milk dud.

What do you call a cow that's just had a baby?
De-calfinated.

There were three cows – a black cow, a brown cow and a white cow – all grazing on one side of a twelve-lane superhighway. One day, they realized that they were out of grass and thought to themselves how wonderful it would be if only they could get to the other side of the superhighway where there was sure to be plenty of grass. So the black cow had an idea. She walked over to a telephone pole, climbed up it, walked along the line, which spanned the superhighway, climbed down the other side and started eating the grass.

The brown cow thought that if the black cow could do it, so could she. So she had an idea. She backed away from the highway, took a long run-up, soared into the air, vaulted over all twelve lanes, landed on the other side and started eating the grass.

Left all alone, the white cow thought if the black cow could do it and the brown cow could do it, then so could she. So she had an idea. She calmly walked out on to the superhighway and was immediately run over by a huge truck, dying instantly.

Witnessing this, the black cow turned to the brown cow and said, "Moooooooo."

CREEPY CRAWLIES

What does a caterpillar do on New Year's Day?
He turns over a new leaf.

What pillar doesn't need holding up?
A caterpillar.

Two caterpillars are sitting on a leaf when a butterfly zooms by, startling them. One turns to the other and says, "You'll never get me up in one of those things."

What do you get if you cross a centipede with a parrot?
A walkie talkie.

What do you call two spiders who just got married?
Newlywebs,

What is worse than a giraffe with a sore throat?
A centipede with chilblains.

What do you call a guard with 100 legs?
A sentrypede.

What lies on the ground, a hundred feet in the air?
A dead centipede.

What goes 99-clunk, 99-clunk?
A centipede with a wooden leg.

What did the male centipede say to the female centipede?
Cor, what a nice pair of legs, pair of legs, pair of legs...

What has fifty legs but can't walk?
Half a centipede.

One Saturday afternoon the grasshopper, the snail and the centipede were sitting around the grasshopper's house drinking beer. They ran out of beer before they were ready to quit drinking, so they decided one of them should go out for more cans.

The snail said, "I'd go, but I'm kind of slow. Besides, Grasshopper, this is your neighborhood so you know where to go."

The grasshopper said, "I don't mind going, but my hopping will shake up the beer and we'll get sprayed every time we open a can."

So they decided to send the centipede, and the grasshopper explained how to get to the nearest liquor store.

An hour or so passed and still the centipede hadn't returned, so the snail and the grasshopper decided to go look for him.

They got as far as the front door and found the centipede sitting there still putting on his shoes.

Did you hear about the two silkworms who had a race?
It ended in a tie.

What insect performs daring jumps on a motorbike?
Weevil Knievel.

What is green, sooty and whistles when it rubs its back legs together?

Chimney Cricket.

What do you call a mayfly with a criminal tendencies ?
Baddy longlegs.

What do you call an Irish mayfly?
Paddy longlegs.

Why did the fly fly?
Because the spider spied her.

What insects do cats rest their heads on at night?
Cat-er-pillows.

Boy. Dad, Dad, there's a spider in the bath!

Father: What's wrong with that? You've seen spiders before.

Boy: Yes, but this one is two feet wide and using all the hot water!

What does a spider do when he gets angry?
He goes up the wall.

How do you know if a spider is good with computers?
He has a website.

How did the creepy crawly know his mate was approaching?
He spider.

Two flies were on a cornflake packet. "Why are we running so fast?" asked one.

"Because," said the other, "it says tear along the dotted line."

What are the most faithful insects?

Ticks. Once they find friends, they stick to them.

What did one insect say to the other insect?
Stop bugging me.

What's the difference between a wolf and a flea?
One howls on the prairie and the other prowls on the hairy.

What is a flea's favourite book?
The Itch Hikers Guide To The Galaxy.

Why was the mother flea unhappy?
She thought her children were all going to the dogs.

What did one flea say to the other flea?
Shall we walk or take the dog?

Where do fleas go to surf?
To the microwave.

What did the clean dog say to the insect?
Long time no flea.

How do you find where a flea has bitten you?
Start from scratch.

What's the difference between a dog with fleas and a bored visitor?
One is going to itch and the other is itching to go.

Two flies were buzzing around a room. The first fly said, "For a dare, let's fly at speed through that screen door."

The second fly reluctantly agreed, and the pair flew as fast as they could straight for the door, only to become stuck fast in the screen.

Winded and wounded, the second fly turned to the first fly and said, "This is another fine mesh you've got me into."

Why was the insect thrown out of the forest?
Because he was a litter bug.

What happened to the two bedbugs who fell in love in the winter?
They got married in the spring.

Two cockroaches were munching garbage in a dirty alleyway when one of them started talking about a restaurant that had just opened across the street.

"It's so clean," he said. "The kitchen is spotless and all the floors are gleaming white. There's no dirt or grime anywhere."

"Please," said the other cockroach, frowning. "Not while I'm eating!"

What did the slug say to the other who had hit him and run off?
I'll get you next slime.

What was the snail doing on the highway?
About a mile a week.

What is the definition of a slug?
A snail with a housing problem.

What is the definition of a snail?
A slug in a crash helmet.

What happens when a snail loses its shell?
It looks sluggish.

What is a slug's favourite drink?
Slime cordial.

A sloth is out for a walk when he is mugged by four snails. After recovering his wits, he goes to make a police report.

"Can you describe the snails?" asks the officer.

The sloth replies, "Not really, it all happened so fast."

What do you do when two snails have a fight?
Just leave them to slug it out.

Two slugs were slithering along the road when they saw two snails up ahead.

"Oh, no!" said one slug to the other. "Caravans!"

How do snails get their shells so shiny?
They use snail varnish.

Why is the snail the strongest animal?
Because he carries his house on his back.

Where do you find giant snails?
At the ends of giants' fingers.

How do you keep flies out of the kitchen?
Put a pile of manure in the living room.

A grasshopper walks into a bar and orders a drink. The bartender says, "We've got a drink named after you."

The grasshopper replies, "You've got a drink named Steve?"

What kind of wig can hear?
An earwig.

A snail starts slowly climbing an apple tree. He is watched all the way by a blackbird who can't help laughing at the snail. Eventually, the blackbird says, "Don't you realize there aren't any apples on that tree yet?"

"I know," said the snail, "but there will be by the time I get up there."

Which insect is good at making films?
Steven Spielbug.

What has antlers and sucks blood?
A moose-quito.

What has six legs, sucks blood and talks in code?
A morse-quito.

What's the difference between a mosquito and a fly?
Try doing up the zipper on a mosquito.

What do insects learn at school?
Mothematics.

What is the biggest insect in the world?
A mammoth.

Why was the glow worm unhappy?
Because her children weren't very bright.

What lives underground and is a keen reader?
A bookworm.

What do you call a fly with no wings?
A walk.

What happened to the fly that flew through a sieve?
It strained itself.

Why are glow worms good to carry in your bag?
They can lighten the load.

What did the maggot say to his friend who got stuck in an apple?
Worm your way out of that one.

Why didn't the two worms go on to Noah's Ark in an apple?
Because everyone had to go in pairs.

What is a glow worm's favourite song?
Wake Me Up Before You Glow-Glow.

How do you make a glow worm happy?
Cut off his tail and he'll be delighted.

There was once a snail who was sick and tired of his reputation for being so slow. He decides to get a fast car to make up the difference. After shopping around for a while, he reckons that the Nissan 350Z was the car to get. So the snail goes to the nearest Nissan dealer and says he wants to buy the 350Z, but he wants it repainted 350S.

The dealer asks, "Why 'S'?"

The snail replies, "'S' stands for snail. I want everybody who sees me roaring past to know who's driving."

Well, the dealer doesn't want to lose the unique opportunity to sell a car to a snail, so he agrees to have the car repainted for a small fee.

The snail gets his new car and spends the rest of his days roaring happily down the highway at top speed. And whenever anyone would see him zooming by, they'd say, "Wow! Look at that S-car go!"

DEMONS AND GOBLINS

What is the best way to get rid of a demon?
Exorcise a lot.

What's a devil's picket line called?
A demonstration.

What is the demons' favourite TV sitcom?
Fiends.

Why do demons and ghouls get on so well?
Because demons are a ghoul's best fiend.

What do you call a demon who slurps his food?
A goblin.

What do foreign devils speak?
Devil Dutch.

What did the little goblin do when he bought a house?
He called it Gnome Sweet Gnome.

Why was the demon so good at cooking?
He was a kitchen devil.

What do demons have for breakfast?
Devilled eggs.

What do demons have on holiday?
A devil of a time.

DINOSAURS

What do you call a dinosaur that keeps you awake at night?
Bronto-snore-us.

Why did the pterodactyl catch the worm?
Because it was an early bird.

Why can't you hear a pterodactyl go to the toilet?
Because it has a silent P.

What do you call a dinosaur with no eyes?
Doyouthinkhesaurus.

What do you call a dog belonging to a dinosaur with no eyes?
Doyouthinkhesaurus Rex.

What do you call it when two dinosaurs collide?
Tyrannosaurus wrecks.

What do you call a plated dinosaur when he's asleep?
Stegosnorus.

What does a triceratops sit on?
Its tricerabottom.

How did dinosaurs pass exams?
With extinction.

What do you get when you cross a dinosaur and a pig?
Jurassic Pork.

What do you get if you cross a dinosaur with a wizard?
A Tyrannosaurus hex.

DOCTOR, DOCTOR...

Doctor, Doctor, I swallowed a bone.
Are you choking?
No, I really did!

Doctor, Doctor, I think I need glasses.

You certainly do, sir, this is a fish and chip shop!

Doctor, Doctor, I'm so ugly. What can I do?
Hire yourself out for Halloween parties.

Doctor, Doctor, my son has swallowed my pen, what should I do?
Use a pencil until I get there.

Doctor, Doctor, I've swallowed a whistle.
Here, take this prescription and I don't want to hear another peep out of you.

Doctor, Doctor, I think I'm a bell.
Take these and if it doesn't help give me a ring.

Doctor, Doctor, what can I do to stop my sleepwalking?
Sprinkle tin tacks on your bedroom floor.

Doctor, Doctor, I think I'm suffering from déjà vu.
Didn't I see you yesterday?

Doctor, Doctor, I've got wind. Can you give me something?
Yes – here's a kite.

Doctor, Doctor, how do I stop my nose from running?
Stick your foot out and trip it up.

Doctor, Doctor, I tend to flush a lot.
Don't worry, it's just a chain reaction.

Doctor, Doctor, I keep thinking I'm a bin.
Don't talk rubbish.

Doctor, Doctor, I feel like a bee.
Well buzz off, I'm busy.

Doctor, Doctor, I feel like a spoon.
Sit there and don't stir.

Doctor, Doctor, my eye hurts every time I drink coffee.
Have you tried taking the spoon out?

Doctor, Doctor, I feel like a pack of cards.
I'll deal with you later.

Doctor, Doctor, will this cream clear up my spots?
I never make rash promises.

Doctor, Doctor, I feel like a racehorse.
Take one of these every four laps.

Doctor, Doctor, can I have a second opinion?
Of course, come back tomorrow.

Doctor, Doctor, you have to help me out.
Certainly, which way did you come in?

Doctor, Doctor, my right ear always seems warmer than my left one.
I think you need to adjust your toupée.

Doctor, Doctor, I keep thinking I'm God.

When did this start?
Well first I created the sun, then the earth...

Doctor, Doctor, I keep thinking I'm invisible.
Who said that?

Doctor, Doctor, I feel like an apple.
We must get to the core of this.

Doctor, Doctor, I think I'm a butterfly
Say what you mean and stop flitting about.

Doctor, Doctor, I think I'm an adder.
Great, you can help me with my accounts.

Doctor, Doctor, I'm boiling up.
Just simmer down.

Doctor, Doctor, I keep painting myself gold.
Don't worry, it's just a gilt complex.

Doctor, Doctor, I've broken my arm in two places.
Well don't go back there again.

Doctor, Doctor, I keep thinking I'm a yo-yo.
Stop stringing me along.

Doctor, Doctor, I think I'm a dog.
How long have you felt like this?
Ever since I was a puppy.

Doctor, Doctor, I've just swallowed a roll of film.
Well let's see what develops.

Doctor, Doctor, everyone keeps ignoring me.
Next please!

Doctor, Doctor, some days I feel like a tee-pee and other days I feel like a wig-wam.
You're just too tents.

Doctor, Doctor, whenever I harvest our cornfields I get a really bad headache.
It's migraine.
No, it's not. It's mine!

Doctor, Doctor, I keep thinking I'm a caterpillar.
Don't worry, you'll soon change.

Doctor, Doctor, you've taken out my tonsils, my gall bladder, my varicose veins and my appendix, but I still don't feel well.
That's quite enough out of you.

Doctor, Doctor, I keep seeing an insect flying around in circles.
Don't worry, it's just a bug that's going round.

Doctor, Doctor, I keep thinking I'm a slice of bread.
You've got to stop loafing around.

Doctor, Doctor, I'm having trouble with my breathing.
I'll give you something that will soon put a stop to that.

Doctor, Doctor, I can't get to sleep.
Lie on the edge of the bed and you'll soon drop off.

A man walks into a doctor's office. He has a cucumber up his nose, a carrot in his left ear and a banana in his right ear.
"What's the matter with me?" he asks the doctor.
The doctor replies, "You're not eating properly."

Doctor, Doctor, you've got to help me – I just can't stop my hands shaking.
Do you drink a lot?
Not really – I spill most of it.

Doctor, Doctor, I think I'm a bridge.
What's come over you?
Oh, two cars, a large truck and a coach.

Doctor, Doctor, I've got compulsive Morse code syndrome.
Let me examine you.
You can't – I've got to dash.

Doctor, Doctor, I think I'm an electric eel.
That's shocking.

Patient: I'm in a hospital! Why am I in here?
Doctor: You've had an accident involving a bus.
Patient: What happened?
Doctor: Well, I've got some good news and some bad news. Which would you like to hear first?
Patient: Give me the bad news first.
Doctor: Your legs were injured so badly that we had to amputate both of them.
Patient: That's terrible! What's the good news?
Doctor: There's a guy in the next ward who made a very good offer on your slippers.

Receptionist: Dr Wynazonski is waiting for you.

Patient: Which doctor?
Receptionist: Oh no, he's fully qualified.

Doctor, Doctor, I'm terribly worried. I keep seeing pink striped crocodiles every time I try to get to sleep.
Have you seen a psychiatrist?
No – only pink striped crocodiles.

Doctor, Doctor, will I be able to play the violin after my operation?
Most certainly – you should be able to play it with ease.
That's wonderful – I could never play it before.

Doctor: I have some bad news and some very bad news.
Patient: Well, you might as well give me the bad news first.
Doctor: The lab called with your test results. They said you have twenty-four hours to live.
Patient: Twenty-four hours! That's terrible! What could be worse? What's the very bad news?
Doctor: I've been trying to reach you since yesterday.

Doctor, Doctor, I keep shrinking.
Now settle down, you'll just have to be a little patient.

Doctor, Doctor, I keep thinking I'm a canary.
Perch yourself down and I'll tweet you in a minute.

Doctor, Doctor, I keep thinking I'm a duck.
Why don't you try a quack doctor?

Doctor, Doctor, I keep thinking I'm a frog.
Hop it!

Doctor, Doctor, I keep thinking I'm an owl.
Don't be such a twit.

Doctor, Doctor, I'm in the village band and I swallowed my harmonica. What should I do?
Be grateful that you don't play the piano.

Doctor, Doctor, I'm terrified of squirrels.
You must be nuts.

Doctor, Doctor, I swallowed a clock about eighteen months ago.
Why didn't you come to see me sooner?
I didn't want to alarm anybody.

A doctor says to his patient, "You must take things quietly at night."
The patient replies, "I do, doctor, I'm a cat burglar!"

A doctor says to his patient, "Your cough sounds better today."
The patient replies, "It should, I practised all night."

Doctor, Doctor, I keep thinking I'm a cat.
I've got the purrfect cure for you.

Doctor, Doctor, I think I'm a mouse.
Hard cheese!

Doctor, Doctor, I've just swallowed a sheep.
How do you feel?
Very baa-aaa-d.

Doctor, Doctor, I keep thinking I'm a cow.
Pull the udder one.

Three patients in a mental institution prepare for an examination given by the head psychiatrist. If the patients pass the exam, they will be free to leave the hospital. However, if they fail, the institution will detain them for seven years.

The doctor takes the three patients to the top of a diving board overlooking an empty swimming pool, and asks the first patient to jump.

The first patient jumps head first into the pool and breaks both arms.

Then the second patient jumps and breaks both legs.

The third patient looks over the side and refuses to jump.

"Congratulations! You're a free man. Just tell me why didn't you jump," says the doctor.

The third patient answered, "Well, doctor, I can't swim."

Doctor, Doctor, I can't stop pulling ugly faces.
That's not a serious problem.

Yes, but people with ugly faces don't like it.

Doctor, Doctor, I can't stop sneezing.
Don't worry – it's much achoo about nothing.

Doctor, Doctor, I can't stop trembling.
I'll be with you in a couple of shakes.

Doctor, Doctor, I've got lettuce sticking out of my ear.
Oh dear. I fear that it may be just the tip of the iceberg.

Doctor, Doctor, I feel very flushed.
You must have flu.
No, I walked.

Doctor, Doctor, I keep hearing ringing in my ears.
Nonsense, you're as sound as a bell.

Doctor, Doctor, I keep seeing double.
Just lie down on the couch.
Which one?

Doctor, Doctor, I need something for my kidneys.
Here's some steak – make yourself a pie.

Doctor, Doctor, my hearing aid isn't working properly.
What's wrong with it?
Half-past nine.

Doctor, Doctor, what do you recommend for flat feet?
Try a foot pump.

Doctor: Nurse, how is that little girl doing who swallowed ten quarters last night?
Nurse: No change yet.

Doctor, Doctor, can you treat water on the brain?
Yes, with a tap on the head.

Doctor, Doctor, I swallowed a pillow.
How do you feel?
A little down in the mouth.

As the doctor completed an examination of the patient, he said, "I can't find a cause for your complaint. Frankly, I think it's due to drinking."
"In that case," said the patient, "I'll come back when you're sober."

Nurse: Doctor, there is a man in the waiting room with a glass eye named Brown.
Doctor: What does he call his other eye?

Doctor, Doctor, my stomach keeps getting bigger.
You should diet.
Really? What colour?

Doctor, Doctor, my husband thinks he's a parachutist.
Tell him to drop in and see me sometime.

A man walked into a doctor's office and the receptionist asked him what he had. He said, "Shingles."

So she took down his name, address, medical insurance number and told him to have a seat.

A few minutes later a nurse's aid came out and asked him what he had. He said, "Shingles."

So she took down his height, weight, a complete medical history and told him to wait in the examining room.

Ten minutes later a nurse came in and asked him what he had. He said, "Shingles."

So she gave him a blood test, a blood pressure test, an electrocardiogram, told him to take off all his clothes and wait for the doctor.

Fifteen minutes later the doctor came in and asked him what he had. He said, "Shingles."

The doctor asked, "Where?"

The man replied, "Outside in the truck. Where do you want them?"

Did you hear about the man who was taken to hospital after eating 100 daffodil bulbs?
Doctors say he should be out in the spring.

Doctor: You've got a new disease found in soft butter.
Patient: What is it?
Doctor: I don't know, but it spreads easily.

Grandma was nearly ninety years of age when she won one million dollars in the lottery. Her family were extremely worried about her heart and feared that news of her large win would come as too much of a shock for her.

"I think we had better call in the doctor to tell her the news," suggested the eldest son.

The doctor soon arrived and the situation was explained to him.

"Now, you don't have to worry about anything," said the doctor. "I am fully trained in such delicate matters and I feel sure I can break this news to her gently. I assure you, there is absolutely no need for you to fear for her health. Everything will be quite safe if left to me."

The doctor went in to see the old lady and gradually brought the conversation around to the lottery.

"Tell me," said the doctor, "what would you do if you had a large win on the lottery – say one million dollars?"

"Why," replied the old lady, "I'd give half of it to you, of course."

The doctor fell down dead with shock.

Doctor, Doctor, I'm going on holiday soon. How do I avoid getting diseases from biting insects?
Simple – don't bite any.

Doctor, Doctor, I keep thinking I'm a snooker ball.
Get to the end of the cue.

Doctor, Doctor, I feel like a piano.
I'd better take some notes.

The man looked a little worried when the doctor came in to administer his annual physical, so the first thing the doctor did was to ask whether anything was troubling him.

"Well, to tell the truth, Doctor, yes," answered the patient. "You see, I seem to be getting forgetful. I'm never sure I can remember where I put the car, or whether I answered a letter, or where I'm going, or what it is I'm going to do once I get there – if I get there. So, I really need your help. What can I do?"

The doctor mused for a moment, then answered in his kindest tone, "Pay me in advance."

A paramedic and a nurse were called to the scene of a bad road accident. The paramedic briefly examined the victim and said, "We need to get this man to hospital."

"What is it?" asked the nurse.

"It's a big building with a lot of doctors," said the paramedic, "but that's not important now."

A lady rings her local hospital and says to the receptionist, "Hello, I'd like some information on a patient, Mrs Tiptree. She was admitted last week with chest pains and I

A man told his doctor, "I can't stop deep-frying things in batter. I've deep-fried my laptop, I've deep-fried my mobile phone, I've deep-fried my DVD player, and I've deep-fried all my CDs. All of my possessions are now covered in batter. What's wrong with me?"

The doctor sighed. "Well, I'm afraid it seems to me that you're frittering your life away."

just want to know if her condition has deteriorated, stabilized or improved."

The receptionist asks, "Do you know which ward she is in?"

"Yes, ward P, room 2B."

"I'll just put you through to the nurses' station on that ward."

A nurse picks up the call and says, "Hello, ward P, how can I help?"

The lady says, "I would just like some information on a patient, Mrs Tiptree. I was wondering if her condition had deteriorated, stabilized or improved?"

"I'll just check her notes. I'm pleased to say that Mrs Tiptree's conditioned has improved. She has regained her appetite, her temperature has steadied and after some routine checks tonight, she should be well enough to go home tomorrow."

"Oh that's wonderful news. I'm so happy. Thank you ever so much!"

"You seem very relieved. Are you a close friend or relative?" the nurse asks.

The lady replies, "No, I'm Mrs Tiptree in room 2B. Nobody tells you anything in here."

How did the doctor treat a broken leg?
He took it to the funfair.

A man had been feeling sick for quite some time and finally decided to see a doctor. The doctor came out and told the patient that he had some bad news to share. "You are going to die," he said.

"When will I die?" the patient asked.

"Ten," the doctor replied.

The bewildered patient asked, "Ten what? Years, months, days...? Tell me Doctor, I have to know."

The doctor said, "Nine…"

Why are doctors known as stingy?
First they say they will treat you, and then they make you pay for it.

A doctor had left his stethoscope on the car seat, and on the way to preschool, his little girl picked it up and began playing with it.

"Wonderful!" thought the doctor. "My daughter wants to follow in my footsteps!"

Then the child spoke into the instrument, "Welcome to McDonald's. May I take your order?"

What do you call two doctors?
Paramedics.

Doctor, Doctor, I'm allergic to perfume.
Don't worry, I'll have you scent to a specialist.

Doctor, Doctor, I've got warts and I hate them.
Don't worry, they'll grow on you.

Doctor, Doctor, I'm scared of the high jump.
You'll soon get over it.

Doctor, Doctor, I've got a little sty.
Then you'd better buy a little pig.

Doctor, Doctor, I can't stop climbing mountains.
Don't worry, we'll soon have you in peak condition.

Doctor, Doctor, I can't stop doing crosswords.
What's wrong with that?
I haven't a clue.

Doctor, Doctor, I feel like a needle.
I see your point.

Doctor, Doctor, I feel like a camera.
I'll be with you in a flash.

Doctor, Doctor, I feel like a cup of coffee.
I'll be with you in an instant.

Doctor, Doctor, I feel like a dictionary.
I'll have a word with you later.

Doctor, Doctor, I feel like a racing car.
Now, now – don't exhaust yourself.

Doctor, Doctor, I feel like a kite.
You'll really have to come down to earth.

Doctor, Doctor, I feel like a window.
Tell me where the pane is.

Doctor, Doctor, I keep thinking
I'm a baby.
Now don't get rattled.

Doctor, Doctor, I keep thinking I'm a
barometer.
**Don't worry, you're just a bit
under the weather.**

Doctor, Doctor, I keep thinking
I'm a dumpling.
Don't get into such a stew.

Doctor, Doctor, I keep thinking I'm
a car.
**You must be going round the
bend.**

Doctor, Doctor, I think I've been
bitten by a vampire?
Drink this glass of water.
Will it make me feel better?
**No, but I'll be able to see if
your neck leaks.**

Doctor, Doctor, I keep thinking I'm
a clock.
**Don't worry, you're just a little
wound up.**

Doctor, Doctor, I keep thinking
I'm a watch.
I'll be with you in a tick.

Doctor, Doctor, I keep thinking I'm a
tennis racket.
**Don't worry, you're just highly
strung.**

Doctor, Doctor, I can't stop
singing 'The Green, Green
Grass of Home.'
**That sounds like Tom Jones
Syndrome.**
Is it common?
Well, it's not unusual.

Doctor, Doctor, I keep thinking I'm
an angel.
Don't harp on about it.

Doctor, Doctor, I think I'm going
to die in fifty-nine seconds.
**Hold on, I'll see you in a
minute.**

Doctor, Doctor, I keep thinking I'm a
huge African river.
You're in denial.

Doctor, Doctor, I keep thinking
I'm an elevator.
**You may be coming down
with something.**

Doctor, Doctor, my hair keeps
falling out. Can you give me
something to keep it in?
**Certainly. How about this paper
bag?**

Doctor, Doctor, I keep thinking
I'm a wheelbarrow.
**Don't let people push you
around.**

Doctor, Doctor, I keep thinking I'm a
pair of glasses.
**Stop making a spectacle of
yourself.**

Doctor, Doctor, I keep thinking I'm
an umbrella.
You'll soon be right as rain.

Doctor, Doctor, one day I feel like a knitting needle and the next I feel like a ball of wool.
That's a familiar pattern.

Doctor, Doctor, I keep thinking I'm going to die.
Don't worry, that's the last thing you'll do.

Doctor, Doctor, I keep thinking I'm a ventriloquist.
You're far too old to have a dummy.

Doctor: I can't do anything about your condition. I'm afraid it's hereditary.
Patient: In that case, send the bill to my parents.

Patient: My wife thinks she's a chicken.
Doctor: Have you tried telling her she's not a chicken?
Patient: No. We need the eggs.

Did you hear about the careless plastic surgeon?
He stood in front of a fire and melted.

DOGS

What do you get if you cross a sheepdog with a rose?
A collie-flower.

Where do you find a dog with no legs?
Right where you left him.

What is a dog's favourite city?
New Yorkie.

What dog can jump higher than a tree?
Any dog can jump higher than a tree. Trees don't jump.

What has two thousand eyes and four thousand feet?
A thousand dogs.

Why did the dog cross the road?
To get to the barking lot.

Which gun dogs formed a singing group?
The Pointer Sisters.

Who is a dog's favourite comedian?
Growlcho Marx.

When you catch your dog eating a dictionary, what should you do?
Take the words right out of his mouth.

Where was the dog when the lights went out?
In the dark.

Why did the dog's owner think his

dog was a great mathematician? **When he asked the dog what six minus six was, the dog said nothing.**

What do you get if you cross a dog with an aeroplane?
A jet setter.

What composer is the favourite among dogs?
Poochini.

Two dogs met each other in the street. One dog stopped and said, "My name is Rover. What's yours?"
The other dog thought for a minute and then replied, "I think it's Down Boy."

Why didn't the dog want to play football?
Because it was a Boxer.

Why don't dogs make good dancers?
Because they have two left feet.

What do you get if you take a really big dog out for a walk?
A Great Dane out.

What kind of dog does Dracula have?
A Bloodhound.

What is the only kind of dog you can eat?
A hot dog.

What dog likes to take bubble baths? ***A shampoodle.***

Why wouldn't the dog talk to its foot?
It's not polite to talk back to your paw.

What happens if it rains cats and dogs?
You might step in a poodle.

Why was the male poodle polite to the female gun dog?
Because he didn't want to diss a pointer.

What do dogs eat at the cinema?
Pup-corn.

What kind of dog goes into a corner every time the doorbell rings?
A Boxer.

What happened when the owner bought her pet a new anti-ageing dog lead?
He got a new leash of life.

What did the dog say to the tree?
Bark.

What is the special offer at the pet store this week?
Buy one dog, get one flea.

How many hairs are in a dog's tail?
None. They are all on the outside.

If your dog jumped into a swimming pool, what is the first thing he would do?
Get wet.

What did the dog do when a man-eating tiger followed him?
Nothing. It was a man-eating tiger, not a dog-eating one.

What did the dog get when he multiplied 497 by 684?
The wrong answer.

What do you do with a dog that has no legs?
Take him out for a drag.

What do you call a dog with no legs?
It doesn't matter what you call him, he still won't come.

How do you stop a dog smelling?
Put a peg on its nose.

What is worse than a dog howling at the moon?
Two dogs howling at the moon.

What looks like a dog, sounds like a dog, eats like a dog, but isn't a dog?
A puppy.

When do dogs have sixteen legs?
When there are four of them.

A woman went to the vet to collect her sick Rottweiler. The vet entered the room carrying the dog and said, "I'm really sorry, but I'm going to have to put your dog down."

"Why?" sobbed the woman.

The vet said, "Because he's too heavy."

When is a dog most likely to

enter the house?
When the door is open.

What do you call baby dogs in the snow?
Slush puppies.

How did the little dog feel when he saw a monster?
Terrier-fied.

Why is a lost Dalmatian easily found?
Because he's always spotted.

What kind of dog chases anything red?
A bulldog.

What dog keeps the best time?
A watch dog.

A man walks into a shop and sees a cute little dog. He asks the shopkeeper, "Does your dog bite?"
The shopkeeper says, "No, my dog does not bite."
The man tries to pet the dog and the dog bites him.
"Ouch!" he says. "I thought you said your dog doesn't bite!"
The shopkeeper replies, "That's not my dog."

A man went to visit a friend and was amazed to find him playing chess with his dog. He watched the game in astonishment. "I can hardly believe my eyes!" he exclaimed. "That's the smartest dog I've ever seen!"
"Nah, he's not so smart," his friend replied. "I've beaten him three games out of five."

What do you get if you cross a Cocker Spaniel with a Poodle and a rooster?
A cockerpoodledoo.

What do you get if you cross a Beatle and an Australian dog?
Dingo Starr.

How long are a dog's legs?
Long enough to reach the ground.

Two dog owners bumped into each other in the street. One said, "I'm sick of my dog – he chases anyone on a bike."
"What are you going to do?" asked the other. "Have him put down?"
"No, I think I'll just take his bike away."

What do you give a dog with a fever?
Mustard – it's the best thing for a hot dog.

What do adult dogs say to their yapping pups?
Hush, puppies.

Why do dogs wag their tails?
Because no one else will do it for them.

A man sees a sign in front of a house advertising a talking dog for sale. He rings the bell and the owner tells him the dog is in the back yard. The guy goes into the back yard and sees a mutt sitting there.

"You talk?" he asks.

"Yep," the mutt replies.

"So, what's your story?"

The mutt looks up and says, "Well, I discovered I had this gift pretty young and I wanted to help the government. So I told the CIA about my gift, and in no time they had me jetting from country to country, sitting in rooms with spies and world leaders, because no one figured a dog would be eavesdropping. I was one of their most valuable spies for eight years running. The jetting around really tired me out, and I knew I wasn't getting any younger and I wanted to settle down. So I signed up for a job at the airport to do some undercover security work, mostly wandering near suspicious characters and listening in. I uncovered some incredible dealings there and was awarded a batch of medals. Had a wife, some puppies, and now I'm just retired."

The guy is amazed. He goes back in and asks the owner how much he wants for the dog. The owner says, "Ten dollars."

The guy agrees to buy him and says to the owner, "This dog is amazing. Why on earth are you selling him?"

The owner replies, "He's such a liar."

What's a dog's favourite food? **Anything that's on your plate.**

A woman saw an ad in the newspaper that read: "Purebred Police Dog For Sale $45". Thinking it a bargain, she rang the number and bought the dog, but when the animal was delivered to her home, she found that it was just a scruffy-looking mongrel.

So she phoned the man who had sold her the dog. "How can you possibly call that mangy mutt a purebred police dog?" she complained. "No police force would employ such a dog!"

The man replied, "Don't let his looks deceive you. He's working undercover."

A woman went to the cinema the other day and in the seats in front was an old man with his dog. It was a sad yet funny kind of film. In the sad part, the dog cried his eyes out, and in the funny part, the dog laughed its head off. This happened all the way through the film. After the film had ended, the woman decided to go and speak to the man.

"That's the most amazing thing I've seen," she said. "That dog really seemed to enjoy the film."

The man turned to her and said, "Yeah, it is. He hated the book."

What does a dog get when it graduates from dog school? **A pedigree.**

A man and his dog walk into a bar. The man proclaims, "I'll bet you a round of drinks that my dog can talk."

The bartender looks amused but says, "Yeah, sure. Go ahead."

The man asks his dog, "What covers a house?"

"Roof!" the dog barks.

"How does sandpaper feel?" the man asks.

The dog barks, "Rough!"

The man asks one final question, "Who was the greatest baseball player of all time?"

The dog replies, "Ruth!"

The man says to the bartender, "Pay up, I told you he could talk."

The bartender, annoyed at this point, says, "That dog can't talk, he was just barking." He throws the pair out of the pub.

Sitting on the sidewalk, the dog looks at the guy and says, "Or is the greatest player DiMaggio?"

A butcher is leaning on the counter near the end of the day when a dog with a basket in its jaws pushes open the door.

"What's this then?" he asks. The dog knocks the basket sharply into the butcher's shins, causing the butcher to wince in pain. As he reaches down to smack the dog, he notices a note and a ten-dollar bill in the basket.

The scribble on the note asks for three pounds of his best ground beef. The butcher figures this is too easy. He goes to the window and reaches for the dried-up stuff that's been sitting out all day.

The dog growls at him. The butcher turns around and, glaring at the pup, gets the best meat from the fridge. Weighing out about two and a half pounds, he drops it on the scale with his thumb.

"Hmmmmm, a bit shy. Who'll know?"

Again, the dog growls menacingly so the butcher throws on a generous half pound. He wraps it, drops it in the basket, and adds the change from five dollars. The dog threatens to chew him off at the ankles. Another five goes in the basket.

The butcher is quite impressed and decides to follow the pup home. The dog goes into a high-rise building, enters the lift and pushes the button for the twelfth floor. The dog walks down the corridor and smartly bangs the basket on a door. The door opens and the dog's owner screams at the dog.

"Hey, what are you doing? That's a really smart dog you've got there," says the butcher.

"He's a stupid dog," says his owner. "That's the third time this week he's forgotten his key."

What goes "krab, krab, krab"?
A dog barking in a mirror.

What dog wears contact lenses?
A cock-eyed spaniel.

What did the thirsty Dalmatian say after a nice long drink?
That hit the spots.

Two neighbours had been fighting each other for four decades. Then Bob buys a Yorkshire Terrier and teaches it to use Bill's yard as a bathroom. For one whole year Bill ignores the dog.

So Bob buys a Great Dane and teaches it to use Bill's yard as a bathroom. After about a year and a half of Bob's dogs using Bill's yard as a bathroom, a truck pulls up in front of Bill's house.

Bob runs over and demands to know what's in the truck.

Bill replies, "My new pet elephant."

What did the cowboy say when he saw a bear eat Lassie?
Well, doggone!

What do you get if you cross a terrier with a green vegetable?
A Jack Brussel.

What happened to the dog that was also a skilled blacksmith?
Every time the front door was opened he made a bolt for it.

Why did the cowboy buy a Dachshund?
Because he heard the ranchhand say, "Get along, little doggie."

In a small, out-of-town bar, all the patrons became quite used to the owner's little dog, so were quite upset when one day he died. They got together and decided to cut off his tail and stick it up behind the bar to remind everyone of how the little dog used to wag his tail the whole time.

The little dog went up to heaven and was about to run through the pearly gates when he was stopped by St Peter, who questioned the little dog about where he was going.

The little dog said, "I have been a good dog – so I'm going into heaven where I belong!"

St Peter replied, "Heaven is a place of perfection. You cannot come into heaven without a tail. Where is your tail?"

So the little dog explained what had happened back on earth and St Peter told him to go back down to earth and retrieve his tail. The little dog protested that it was now the middle of the night on earth, but St Peter would not change his mind.

So the little dog went back down to earth and scratched on the door of the pub until the bartender who lived upstairs came down and opened the door.

"My goodness, it's the spirit of the little dog. What can I do for you?" said the bartender.

The little dog explained that he wasn't allowed into heaven without his tail and he needed it back.

The bartender replied, "I would really like to help you, but my liquor license doesn't allow me to re-tail spirits after hours."

Did you hear about the dog that ate nothing but garlic?
His bark was much worse than his bite.

What happened to the blind dog?
He kept barking up the wrong tree.

Why did the man call his dog Camera?
Because it was always snapping.

Why couldn't the Eskimo's dog bark very loudly?
Because he was a little husky.

What dogs are best for sending telegrams?
Wire-haired terriers.

A man arrives for the auditions for a TV talent show with a dog and a cat under each arm. The TV producer watches in amazement as the cat sings a beautiful ballad accompanied by the dog on piano. At the end of the song, the producer applauds wildly and tells the man he definitely wants the piano-playing dog and the singing cat for his show.

The man looks surprisingly glum. "I have a confession to make,' he says. "This act is not quite what it seems."

"How do you mean?" asks the producer.

The man replies, "The dog's a ventriloquist."

A woman walks into an exclusive pet store and says that she wants to buy a blue sweater for her dog. The sales assistant suggests bringing the dog in to ensure a good fit.

"I can't do that," says the customer. "The sweater is a surprise!"

Why was the dog always angry?
It was a cross breed.

Two Dachshunds watching a firework display marvelled as a rocket flashed across the sky.

"Wow!" said the first Dachshund. "I wish I could fly like that."

"You would," said the second Dachshund, "if your tail was on fire!"

In the days of yore, a knight was on his way to do something terribly important, riding his horse into the ground to get to his destination as fast as possible. After being ridden too hard for too long, the horse became lame, and coming to a small town, the knight headed straight for the stables.

"I must have a horse!" he cried. "The life of the King depends upon it!"

The stablekeeper shook his head. "I have no horses," he said. "They have all been taken in the service of your King."

"You must have something – a

pony, a donkey, a mule, anything at all?" the knight asked.

"I have nothing," the stablekeeper said, "apart from a large dog."

"Show me," the knight said.

The stablekeeper led the knight into the stable. Inside was a dog, but no ordinary dog. This dog was a giant, almost as large as the horse the knight was riding. But it was also the filthiest and smelliest dog that the knight had ever seen.

Reluctantly, the knight said, "I'll take it. Where is the saddle?"

The stablekeeper walked over to a saddle near the dog and started gasping for breath, holding the walls to keep himself upright. "I can't do it," he told the knight.

"You must give me the dog!" cried the knight. "Why can't you?"

The stablekeeper said, "I just couldn't send a knight out on a dog like this."

Why did the poor dog chase his own tail?
He was trying to make both ends meet.

Two dogs went into Carnegie Hall and asked for tickets to a concert. The ticket seller looked at them in amazement. "You're dogs!" she exclaimed. "What could you possibly know about classical music?"

"What do you mean?" said one of the dogs. "I Bach and he Offenbach."

How do you keep a dog from barking in your front yard?
Put him in your back yard.

Why do dogs bury bones in the ground?
Because you can't bury them in trees.

Why did the dog say "Miaow"?
He was learning a foreign language.

A woman, carrying a small dog in her arms, boarded a bus in New York City and earnestly begged the conductor to tell her when they reached 42nd Street. As she seemed unusually anxious, he said he would.

At the first stop they made after leaving 72nd Street, she glanced appealingly at the other passengers.

At the next stop she half rose to her feet.

"59th!" called the conductor.

At 50th Street she stumbled forward, but the conductor laid a detaining hand upon her arm.

"Not yet, ma'am. I told you I'd tell you when we get there," he said.

"How soon will we get there?" she asked, breathlessly.

The conductor looked wearily at her. "I'll tell you when we get there," he repeated.

At last, looking pointedly at her, he shouted loudly, "42nd Street! 42nd Street!"

The woman clutched her dog

and, standing up, lifted him to the window.

"Oh, Fido," she said, almost tearfully. "Look, look, Fido! That's 42nd Street, where you were born."

DUCKS

What do you get if you cross a duck with a firework?
A firequacker.

What do you call a crate of ducks?
A box of quackers.

How do you turn a duck into a soul artist?
Put it in the oven until its Bill Withers.

What says "quick quick"?
A duck with hiccups.

Where would you find a duck with no legs?
Where you left it.

What happens to ducks before they grow up?
They grow down.

What time does a duck wake up?
At the quack of dawn.

How do you make a domestic duck wild?
Pull its feathers.

What was the Ugly Duckling after it was five days old?
A six-day-old Ugly Duckling!

A man was sitting at a table in a Chinese restaurant when a duck came over to him with a rose and said, "Your eyes sparkle like the stars, your smile sends my heart all of a flutter.

The man immediately called the waiter over and said, "Excuse me, I ordered aromatic duck!"

Which side of the Ugly Duckling has the most feathers?
The outside!

Why did the Ugly Duckling's parents fly south for the winter?
Because it was too far to walk!

How do you start a book about ducks?
With an intro-duck-tion.

A duck walked into a chemist and said, "Give me some chap stick."

"That's three dollars," said the chemist.

The duck said, "Put it on my bill please."

Why do ducks have webbed feet?
To stamp out forest fires.

Why do elephants have flat feet?
To stamp out burning ducks.

A duck waddles into a bar and hops on to a stool. The grumpy bartender asks, "What do you want?"

The duck said, "Got any grapes?"

The bartender shakes his head and says, "We don't have grapes here, we serve drinks. Now get out."

The duck hops off the stool and waddles out. The next day, the same duck waddles into the same bar, hops on to a stool, looks the bartender in the eye and asks, "Got any grapes?"

The bartender, irritated, says, "I told you yesterday, we don't serve grapes here, we serve drinks, now get out."

The duck hops off the stool and waddles out. The next day, the same duck waddles into the same bar, hops on to a stool, looks at the bartender, and asks, "Got any grapes?"

The bartender, now furious with the duck, pounds his fist on the bar and yells at the duck, "I've already told you twice that we don't serve grapes here, we serve drinks! If you ask me that one more time I'm going to nail your beak to the bar! Now get out!"

With that, the duck shrugs, hops off the stool and waddles out. The next day, the same duck waddles into the same bar, hops on a stool, looks the bartender in the eye and asks, "Got any nails?"

The bartender, puzzled, says, "No."

The duck then looks him square in the eye and says, "Got any grapes?"

EGGS

Why shouldn't you tell an egg a joke?
Because it might crack up.

What is an egg's favourite Broadway musical?
Yolklahoma.

How do you make an egg roll?
Push it down a hill.

What happened to the clown who smashed an egg on another clown's head?
The yolk was on him.

Which Shakespearean character had eggs on his head?
Omelette.

What do you call an egg from outer space?
An unidentified flying omelette.

Why do we paint Easter eggs?
Because it's easier than trying to wallpaper them.

How did the eggs leave the highway?
They went through the eggs-it.

What part did the egg play in the movies?
He was an egg-stra.

What do you call a sleeping egg?
Eggs-austed.

What did the eggs do when the light turned green?
They egg-cellerated.

What do you call an egg from outer space?
An egg-stra terrestial.

Why couldn't the egg family watch TV?
Because their cable was scrambled.

What's red, pink and blue with yellow all over?
An Easter egg rolling down the hill.

What kind of plants do eggs keep?
Eggplants.

A tourist was checking out of a hotel when he noticed a Native American chief sitting in the lobby.

"Who's that?" the tourist asked the hotel manager.

"That's Big Chief Forget Me Not," said the manager. "He's ninety-eight years old and has the most amazing memory. He can remember every single detail of his life, right back to when he was just one year old."

Intrigued, the tourist went over to the chief and tried to strike up a conversation.

"Hi," said the tourist. "I hear you have the most incredible memory. I wonder, can you tell me what you had for breakfast on your eighteenth birthday?"

"Eggs," answered the chief without hesitation.

"Thanks," said the tourist, and he went on his way.

Over the coming months the tourist recounted this story to a number of people and was advised that the proper way to address an Indian chief was not "Hi" but "How". A year later he was staying at the same hotel and to his delight, Big Chief Forget Me Not was still sitting in the lobby.

Remembering the correct etiquette, the tourist went over to him and said, "How?"

"Scrambled," replied the chief.

Why didn't the egg cross the road?
Because he wasn't a chicken yet.

Humpty Dumpty has been found dead. Next of Kinder have been informed.

Did you hear about the eggs that got married?
After a while they separated.

What day does an egg hate the most?
Fry-days.

What happened to the egg when he was tickled too much?
He cracked up.

Why did Humpty Dumpty have a great fall?
To make up for a lousy summer.

Two eggs are sitting on a kitchen table. One of them spots a whisk and asks, "What's that?"
The other egg looks puzzled and replies, "Beats me!"

ELEPHANTS

How do you shoot a blue elephant?
With a blue elephant gun.

How do you shoot a yellow elephant?
Have you ever seen a yellow elephant?

How do you shoot a red elephant?
Hold his trunk shut until he turns blue, and then shoot him with the blue elephant gun.

How do you shoot a purple elephant?
Paint him red, hold his trunk shut until he turns blue, and then shoot him with the blue elephant gun.

How do you put an elephant in a refrigerator?
Step one: Open the door.
Step two: Put the elephant in.
Step three: Close the door.

How do you put a giraffe in a refrigerator?
Step one: Open the door.
Step two: Take the elephant out.
Step three: Put the giraffe in.
Step four: Close the door.

If an elephant and a giraffe had a race, who would win?
The elephant. The giraffe is in the refrigerator.

What do elephants have that nothing else has?
Baby elephants.

What has eight legs, two trunks, four eyes and two tails?
Two elephants.

How many elephants will fit into a Mini?
Four. Two in the front, two in the back.

How do you know there are two elephants in your refrigerator?
You can hear giggling when the light goes out.

How many giraffes will fit into a Mini? **None. It's full of elephants.**

How do you know there are three elephants in your refrigerator?
You can't close the door.

How do you know there are four elephants in your refrigerator?
There's an empty Mini parked outside.

Why is an elephant big, grey and wrinkly?
Because if it was small, white and hard it would be an aspirin.

How can you tell if there's an elephant under your bed?
Your nose touches the ceiling.

Why are golf balls small and white?
Because if they were big and grey they would be elephants.

What's the difference between an elephant and a plum?
Their colour.

What did Tarzan say to Jane when he saw the elephants coming?
Here come the elephants.

What did Jane say to Tarzan when she saw the elephants coming?
Here come the plums; she was colour blind.

What did Tarzan say when he saw the herd of elephants wearing sunglasses?
Nothing, he didn't recognize them.

Why do elephants paint their toenails yellow?
So they can hide upside down in a bowl of custard.

Why did the elephant paint his toenails red?
So he could hide in the cherry tree.

Why did the elephant paint his toenails different colours?

So he could hide in the M&M dish without being seen!

Why are elephants wrinkled?
Have you ever tried to iron one?

Why did the elephant fall out of the tree?
Because it was dead.

Why did the second elephant fall out of the tree?
It was glued to the first one.

Why did the third elephant fall out of the tree?
It thought it was a game.

And why did the tree fall down?
It thought it was an elephant.

How do you know if there is an elephant in the bar?
Its bike is outside.

How do you know if there are two elephants in the bar?
There is a dent in the crossbar of the bike.

How do you know if there are three elephants in the bar?
Stand on the bike and have a look in the window.

How do you get down from an elephant?
You don't, you get down from a duck.

Why can't an elephant ride a bicycle?
Because it doesn't have a thumb to ring the bell.

Why do elephants wear tiny green hats?
To sneak across a pool table without being seen.

Why are elephants grey?
So that you don't confuse them with cherries.

What do you say to an elephant on roller skates?
Don't say anything. Just get out of the way.

What do you call an elephant in a phone box?
Stuck.

What do you give a seasick elephant?
Lots of room.

What is the difference between an elephant and a flea?
An elephant can have fleas but a flea can't have elephants.

Why didn't the elephant go on the Arctic expedition?
Because it was too much of a mammoth task.

Why do elephants have corrugated feet?
To give ants a fifty-fifty chance.

What do you call an elephant that flies?
A jumbo jet.

How does an elephant get up a tree?
He sits on an acorn and waits for it to grow.

How does an elephant get down from a tree?
He sits on a leaf and waits until autumn.

Why were the elephants thrown out of the swimming pool?
They couldn't keep their trunks up.

What do you get if you take an elephant into the city?
Free parking.

What's the difference between a biscuit and an elephant?
You can't dip an elephant into your tea.

What's the difference between a pickle and an elephant?
A pickle always forgets.

What's the difference between a riddle and two elephants sitting on a bun.
One's a conundrum and the other's a bun-under-em.

What's the difference between a sick elephant and a dead bee?
One's a seedy beast and the other's a bee deceased.

What's the difference between a sleeping elephant, and one that's awake?
With some elephants, it's difficult to tell.

What's the difference between a sneezing elephant and a spy?
Nothing – they've both got a code in their trunk.

What's the difference between an elephant and a banana?
Try picking them up – an elephant is usually heavier.

What's the difference between an elephant and a large lettuce?
One is a funny beast, the other is a bunny feast.

How do you raise baby elephants?
With a crane.

What is an elephant's favourite instrument?
A trumpet.

What is as big as an elephant but weighs nothing?
An elephant's shadow.

What is big and grey and bounces?
An elephant on a pogo stick.

Why don't elephants smoke?
They can't fit their butts in the ashtray.

What do you get if a herd of elephants tramples Batman and Robin?
Flatman and Ribbon.

Why are elephants so clever?
They have lots of grey matter.

Why do elephants never forget?
Because nobody tells them anything.

Why did the elephant wear yellow overalls?
Because he split a seam in his blue ones.

Why couldn't the elephants play cards on the Ark?
Because Noah was sitting on the deck.

What time is it when an elephant sits on the fence?
Time to get a new fence.

What did the hotel manager say to the elephant who couldn't pay his bill?
Pack your trunk and get out.

What is grey, beautiful and wears a glass slipper?
Cinderelephant.

What did the grape say when the elephant stood on it?
Nothing, it just gave out a little wine.

How do you know if you've annoyed an elephant?
It says, "Tusk, tusk."

What's the difference between an African elephant and an Indian elephant?
About three thousand miles.

Why don't elephants eat penguins?
Because they can't get the wrappers off.

Why did the elephant eat the candle?
Because he wanted a light snack.

Why don't elephants like playing cards in Africa?
Because of all the cheetahs.

What do you call an elephant that never washes?
A smellyphant.

Why did the elephant stand on the marshmallow?
So he wouldn't fall into the hot chocolate.

What do you get when you cross an elephant and a skin doctor?
A pachydermatologist

Did you hear about the zoo keeper who had to look after the elephants and the walruses?
He was required to multitusk.

What's grey, carries a bunch of flowers and cheers you up when you're ill?
A get wellephant.

What's grey and goes round and round?
An elephant in a washing machine.

Why do elephants have short tails?
Because they can't remember long stories.

What's the difference between an elephant and a piece of paper?
You can't make a paper aeroplane out of an elephant.

What's the difference between an elephant and a banana?
Have you ever tried to peel an elephant?

What's grey and wrinkly and jumps every twenty seconds?
An elephant with hiccups.

Why is a snail stronger than an elephant?
Because a snail carries its house and an elephant just carries its trunk.

A man was standing in the middle of a road with a box of elephant powder in his hands. He was spreading it all over the road when a policeman walked up to him.

The policeman asked him what he was doing and the man replied, "Spreading elephant powder around."

The policeman laughed and said, "There are no elephants round here!"

The man replied, "Well, the powder must be working then!"

How can you tell if an elephant is sitting behind you in the bathtub?
You can smell the peanuts on his breath.

What is grey, has large ears, a trunk and squeaks?
An elephant wearing new shoes.

A lion was walking through the jungle when he came across a deer eating grass in a clearing. The lion roared, "Who is the king of the jungle?"

The deer replied, "Oh, you are, master."

The lion walked off pleased. Soon he came across a zebra drinking at a water hole. The lion roared, "Who is the king of the jungle?"

The zebra replied, "Oh, you are, master."

The lion walked off pleased. Then he came across an elephant. "Who is the king of the jungle?" he roared.

With that the elephant picked up the lion with his trunk and threw him repeatedly at a tree. The lion scraped himself up off the ground and said, "Okay, okay, there's no need to get mad just because you don't know the answer!"

What do you call an elephant who conducts an orchestra?
Tuskanini.

What's the red stuff between an elephant's toes?
Slow pygmies.

What do elephants have for lunch?
An hour, like everyone else.

Did you hear the joke about the prehistoric elephant?
Mastadon.

It was a boring Sunday afternoon in the jungle so the elephants decided to challenge the ants to a game of soccer. The game was going well with the elephants beating the ants ten goals to nil, when the ants gained possession.

The ants' star player was dribbling the ball towards the elephants' goal when the elephants' left back came lumbering towards him. The elephant trod on the little ant, killing him instantly.

The referee stopped the game. "What on earth do you think you're doing? Do you call that sportsmanship, killing another player?"

The elephant replied, "Well, I didn't mean to kill him – I was just trying to trip him up."

How do you know when you've passed an elephant?
You can't get the toilet seat down.

What has two grey legs and two brown legs?
An elephant with diarrhoea.

First man: What have I got in my hands?
Second man: An elephant.
First man: You looked!

ESKIMOS

What do Eskimos get from sitting on the ice too long?
Polaroids.

How often do Eskimos lose their snow pants?
Once in a blue moon.

How do Eskimos stop their mouths from freezing up?
They grit their teeth.

What do you get when you take an Inuit and divide his circumference by his diameter?
Eskimo pi.

First Eskimo: Where does your wife come from?
Second Eskimo: Alaska.
First Eskimo: Don't bother, I'll ask her myself.

What does an Eskimo use to hold his house together?
Iglue.

Despite all their layers of fur, two Eskimos sitting in a kayak were freezing cold. In a desperate

Why do Eskimos eat whale meat and blubber?
You'd blubber too if you had to eat whale meat.

attempt to warm up, they decided to light a fire in the craft but no sooner had they done so than it sank. It just goes to prove that you can't have your kayak and heat it, too.

FAIRY TALES

Aladdin: Get me a fur coat.
  Genie: What fur?
  Aladdin: Fur to keep me warm, that's what fur.

As a child, the wicked magician always wanted to saw people in half.
Was he an only child?
No, he had lots of half-brothers and sisters.

Why did Mickey Mouse buy a telescope?
Because he wanted to see Pluto.

Do you know what's inside Aladdin's lamp?
It would take a genie-us to find out.

A man meets a fairy in an enchanted woodland. The fairy grants him three wishes. Having wished for his most urgent needs, the man decides to use his third wish to ask the fairy to return and give him three more wishes.
  The fairy complies and says, "You can call me whenever you want."

"How can I call you? Please tell me your name," the man says.
  "My name is Nuff," says the fairy.
  "Well," says the man. "That is an odd name. I have never heard of it before."
  The fairy replies, "Fairy Nuff."

What does a magician like to keep up his sleeve?
His arm.

What kind of pet did Aladdin have?
A flying car-pet.

Why did Aladdin's lamp hum?
Because the genie inside it didn't know the words.

"Open Sesame" opened the doors to the robbers' cave. Which piece of jewellery closed it?
A locket.

Ali Baba didn't know it but there were four women locked in the cave with all that jewellery. What were their names?
Ruby, Jade, Coral and Pearl.

What did the Forty Thieves like to drink?
Tea … they were the For Tea Thieves.

What is harder than a diamond?
Paying for it.

Why is Ali Baba's baby like a small diamond?
Because they are both dear little things.

Why couldn't Cinderella use horses to pull the pumpkin coach?
Because they were too busy playing stable tennis.

What do you say when the three bears want to sit down?
Three chairs for the three bears!

What gave Goldilocks a troubled night's sleep?
Night-bears.

What made Goldilocks shiver?
Quaker Oats.

What's brown, furry and has twelve paws?
The three bears.

What's the difference between Mummy Bear's porridge, Daddy Bear's porridge and Baby Bear's porridge?
Well, one is Mummy Bear's, one is Daddy Bear's and one is Baby Bear's.

When Goldilocks spilt the milk, how did she mop it up?
She used a sponge-cake.

Why did Goldilocks stir the porridge so vigorously?
Because Daddy Bear came in and told her to beat it.

Why weren't the porridge bowls round?
Because porridge is a square meal.

After the woodcutter chops a pile of logs, what happens to them at night?
They sleep like humans.

Which is the oldest tree in the forest?
The elder.

What did the woodcutter's wife say to her husband in December?
Not many chopping days left until Christmas.

Why did Hansel eat all the liquorice off the witch's house?
It takes all sorts.

Do giants eat Englishmen with their fingers?
No, they eat their fingers separately.

What seven letters did Old Mother Hubbard say when she opened the cupboard?
O I C U R M T.

How did Jack know how many beans his cow was worth?
He used a cowculator.

Jack stole a golden harp from the giant.
Why couldn't he play it?
Because it took a lot of pluck.

The giant could smell an Englishman a mile away, so he knew that there was an intruder in the castle. The gates were locked, so how had Jack got inside?
Intruder window.

What did the beanstalk say to

Jack?
Stop picking on me.

What do you call a contented giant?
One that's fed up with Englishmen.

What goes: MUF OF EIF IF?
A giant walking backwards.

What is higher than a giant?
A giant's hat.

What is the difference between Jack and the dead giant?
One has beans, the other is a has-been.

Where was the first bean found?
On a beanstalk.

Where was the first beanstalk found?
Growing in the ground.

Which part of an Englishman does a giant find hard to swallow?
His stiff upper lip.

Why did Jack's cow have horns?
Because its bell was broken.

Why did the chicken lay golden eggs?
Because if she dropped them they would dent the floor.

Why didn't the giant have any teeth?
Because he slept with his head under the pillow and the fairies took them.

What did Cinderella say when the chemist lost her photographs?
Some day my prints will come.

Why was there always a conversation going on in the garden?
Because Jack and the beans talk.

What did Little Red Riding Hood say when she saw the big, bad wolf?
There's the big, bad wolf!

Who shouted "Knickers!" at the big, bad wolf?
Little Rude Riding Hood.

What does an elf eat on his birthday?
Shortcake.

Which dance did the little tin soldier take the paper ballerina to?
The Cannon Ball.

What did the sea say to the Little Mermaid?
Nothing, it just waved.

What has beautiful hair, a pretty face, two arms, a fish's tail, looks like a mermaid, but isn't a mermaid?
A photograph of a mermaid.

What is a mermaid's favourite song?
Salmon-chanted Evening.

Which part of a mermaid weighs the most?
The scales.

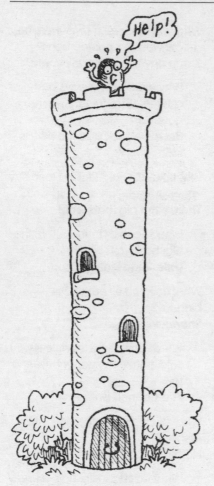

Why was the Little Mermaid embarrassed?
Because she saw the big ship's bottom.

How did the witch know it was exactly twelve midday?
She used her witch watch.

How do we know that Rapunzel went to a lot of parties?
Because she liked to let her hair down.

If you were in Rapunzel's tower during the day, what would be the furthest thing that you could see?
The sun.

If you were in Rapunzel's tower during the night, what would be the furthest thing that you could see?
The curtains … she keeps them closed at night.

Why did Rapunzel live at the top of the tower?
Because she was afraid of depths.

Friar Tuck was a monk, so why did he get involved in a life of crime?
It was his habit.

How did Robin Hood tie his shoelaces?
With a long bow.

What did Robin say when he nearly got hit at the archery contest?
That was an arrow escape.

What's purple and screams from the top of a tower?
A damson in distress.

Why did the Little Mermaid look the other way?
Because the seaweed.

Why did the Little Mermaid ride a sea-horse?
Because she was playing water polo.

What has two holes for the eyes and a slit for the beak?
A Robin Hood.

What is Robin Hood's favourite radio programme?
The Archers.

Where did Robin's Merry Men go to buy their sweets?
The Friar Tuck-shop.

Why couldn't Robin Hood hit the target?
Because his arrows were all in a quiver.

Why did Robin Hood steal from the rich?
Because the poor didn't have anything worth stealing.

Who carries a basket, visits Grandma and steals her jewellery?
Little Red Robin Hood.

The fair had come to Nottingham, so Robin Hood told the Merrie Men that they could go into town and enjoy themselves. There were lots of games and at one booth, you could win a prize by hitting a ten cent silver coin with a lance thrown from twenty paces.

As Friar Tuck was passing the booth, the guy running the game called out to him, "Hey, Brother, can you spear a dime?"

A prince came to a small pool where the most beautiful girl in the world was bathing. On her head was a large, green frog. What was her name?
Why, Lily of course!

What has six legs, four ears and a shining suit of armour?
A prince on horseback.

What is the first thing a king or queen does when they come to the throne?
They sit down.

When does a prince get very wet?
When he becomes the reigning monarch.

When is a piece of wood like a king?
When it's a ruler.

Where do kings and queens get crowned?
On the head.

Where did knights learn to kill dragons?
At knight school.

What did the dragon say when he saw St George in his shining armour?
Oh no, not more canned food!

Why is a well-attended prince like a book?
Because he has so many pages.

Why did Rumpelstiltskin get so angry when the princess guessed his name?
Because being angry was all the rage.

Why would Snow White make a great judge?
Because she's the fairest in the land.

Did you hear about the recent survey?
It shows that six out of seven dwarfs aren't Happy.

What happened when the seven dwarfs applied for another job?
They were put on a short list.

What type of vehicle does Mickey Mouse's girlfriend drive?
A Minnie van.

Why was Cinderella such a bad figure skater?
Because her coach was a pumpkin.

Where does Mother Goose wait before going on stage?
In the wings.

How did the union leader begin his bedtime fairy tale to his young granddaughter?
Once upon a time and a half...

Did you hear about the two-headed ogre who got really angry?
He was beside himself.

What did the ogre get for his birthday?
Another year older.

What do you give an ogre with great big feet?
Lots of space.

What sort of pills do you give to a two-headed ogre?
Aspirin, because they are good for splitting headaches.

What would you call a kind-hearted ogre?
A failure.

Where do ogres dance?
At the odd ball.

Who goes out with an ogre?
His girl-fiend.

Why did everyone laugh when the ogre sat down to play the grand piano?
Because there wasn't a stool.

Why do ogres wear flowery embroidered braces?
To hold their trousers up.

Why did the clever dragon breathe fire?
Because he was a bright spark.

Why do dragons sleep all day?
So that they can fight knights.

FAMILIES

The Smiths were proud of their family tradition. Their ancestors had come to America on the *Mayflower*. Their line had included senators, pastors and Wall Street wizards. Now they decided to compile a family history, a legacy for the children. They hired a fine author. Only one problem arose – how to handle that great-uncle who was executed in the electric chair. But the author said not to worry, he could handle that section of history tactfully.

When the book appeared, the family turned to the section on Uncle George. There, they read: "George Smith occupied a chair of applied electronics at an important government institution, was attached to his position by the strongest of ties. His death came as a real shock."

A little boy greeted his gran with a hug and said, "I'm so happy to see you. Maybe Daddy will do the special trick he has been promising us."

"What trick is that?" she asked.

"Well," said the little boy excitedly, "I heard Daddy tell Mom that he would climb the walls if you came to stay with us again."

A father and his young son went fishing one day. Sitting in the boat for a couple of hours left them with plenty of time for contemplation, so the son started thinking about the world around him. He began to get curious and he asked his father some questions.

"How does this boat float?" he asked.

The father thought for a moment, then replied, "Don't rightly know, son."

The boy returned to his private thoughts, but soon came up with another question.

"How do fish breathe underwater?" he asked.

Once again the father replied, "Don't rightly know, son."

A little later the boy asked his father, "Why is the sky blue?"

Again, the father replied, "Don't rightly know, son."

Worried that he was beginning to annoy his father, he asked, "Dad, do you mind my asking you all of these questions?"

His father immediately assured him, "Of course not, son. If you don't ask questions, you'll never learn anything."

First woman: My grandfather drowned in varnish.
Second woman: What a horrible way to go!
First woman: Yes, but a beautiful finish.

A woman knocked at the door of a house and it was answered by a small boy. "I'm collecting for the old folks' home," she announced.

"Is there anything you would like to give?"

"Who is it?" shouted the boy's mother from the kitchen.

"It's a lady collecting for the old folks' home," replied the boy. "Shall I give her Grandma?"

Boy: Dad, there's a man at the door collecting for a swimming pool.
Father: Give him a glass of water.

A couple were admiring their garden from the kitchen window. The wife said, "One day, you're going to have to make a proper scarecrow to keep the birds off the flower beds."

"What's wrong with the one we've got now?" asked the husband.

"Nothing really," replied the wife. "But mother's arms are getting tired."

A wife phoned her husband at work and asked, "Darling, you know that old family heirloom in the attic?"

"You mean the bureau your mother left you?" he replied.

"Yes, that's the one. Well, I finally got round to unlocking it this morning, and you'll never guess what happened."

"Tell me."

"Ten people fell out!"

"What?! How come?"

The wife said, "It turned out it was a missing persons' bureau."

A frenzied mother was busy trying to prepare dinner for her family and guests when in her haste she accidentally spilled a jar of herbs all over herself.

Her daughter chose that moment to wander into the kitchen and say casually, "Hey, Mom, I need someone to talk to."

The mother replied, "Why would you possibly choose right now to try to talk to me?"

To which the daughter responded, "Well, it looked like you had some thyme on your hands."

Three-year-old Scott had thin fly-away hair, so his mother often wet it to comb it into place. One morning as she applied water and slicked his hair back, she announced it was time for him to get another haircut.

"Mom," Scott replied, "if you'd quit watering it so much, it wouldn't grow so fast!"

One day three-year-old Lauren and her mother were running errands. Everything her mother said or did, Lauren asked, "Why?"

Finally, her mother said, "Lauren, please stop asking me why."

After a short silence, Lauren looked at her mother and asked, "Okay, how come?"

Two sisters arrived home from school crying their eyes out.

"What's the matter with the two

of you?" asked their mother.

"All the kids at school always make fun of my big feet," wailed the first sister.

"Don't let it bother you," comforted the mother. "Your feet aren't that big." She turned her attention to the second sister. "Now why are you crying?"

"My friends invited me to go skiing and I can't find my skis," she cried.

"That's not a problem," the mother said. "You can borrow your sister's shoes."

First boy: My brother's just opened a shop.
Second boy: How's he doing?
First boy: Six months. He opened it with a crowbar.

Four-year-old James was riding with his dad when the dad spotted a flock of geese flying overhead. The dad told James to look out the window so he could see how the geese formed the letter V. James looked up, then asked, "Do geese know the rest of the alphabet too?"

Three rich brothers each wanted to do something special for their elderly mother on her birthday. The first brother bought her a huge house. The second brother gave her a limousine, with a driver. The third brother remembered that his mother used to love to read classic novels but couldn't see well any more, so he got her a specially

trained parrot that could recite any verse from all the classic novels on demand.

Soon, the brothers received thank-you notes from their mother.

The first son's note said: "The house you bought me is much too big! I only live in a small part of it, but I have to clean the whole thing!"

The second son got a note that said: "I rarely leave the house any more, so I hardly use the limousine you gave me. And when I do use it, the driver is so rude!"

The third son's note said: "My darling baby boy, you know just what your mother loves! The chicken you bought me was delicious."

A mother asked her young son, "Why on earth did you swallow the money I gave you?"

The boy replied, "You said it was my lunch money."

Old Aunt Harriet received a letter one morning and on reading it burst into tears.

"What's the matter?" asked her friend.

"It's my favourite nephew," she sobbed. "He's got three feet."

"Three feet?" exclaimed the friend. "Surely that's impossible!"

"Well," said Aunt Harriet, "his mother's just written to tell me that he's grown another foot."

A little girl complained to her father, "Daddy, I wish I had a little sister!"

Trying to be funny, her father joked, "But, honey, you already have a sister."

Confused, the toddler asked, "I do?"

"Sure," her dad said, pulling the kid's chain. "You don't see her because every time you come in the front door, she scoots out the back door."

The confused toddler thought for a moment and then beamed, "You mean just like my other daddy!"

A salesman saw a young boy sitting on the porch of a house and said, "Hi, son. Is your Mom at home?"

"She sure is," replied the boy.

The salesman rang on the doorbell but there was no reply. So he pressed again, and then for a third time. Still there was no reply. Finally, in frustration he turned to the boy and said, "I thought you said your Mom was at home?"

"She is," answered the boy. "But I don't live here."

An Ohio businessman named Henry Lang was part of the wealthiest and most influential family in the district. Everyone around knew of the Langs, and eventually in recognition of all that the family had done for the community, the townsfolk erected a huge sign in front of the train station saying: "Welcome, on behalf of the Langs."

Mother: Why did you put a slug in Grandma's bed?
Boy: Because I couldn't find a snake.

Eventually, Henry moved away to New York, but one New Year's Eve he returned to his Ohio birthplace to see whether the place had changed. He was shocked to see that the townsfolk had taken down the old Lang sign.

Two little boys, aged eight and ten, are excessively mischievous. They are always getting into trouble and their parents know all about it. If any mischief occurs in their town, the two boys are probably involved.

The boys' mother heard that a preacher in town had been successful in disciplining children, so she asked if he would speak with her boys. The preacher agreed, but he asked to see them individually. So the mother sent the eight year old first, in the morning, with the older boy to see the preacher in the afternoon.

The preacher, a huge man with a booming voice, sat the younger boy down and asked him sternly, "Do you know where God is, son?"

The boy's mouth dropped open, but he made no response, sitting there wide-eyed with his mouth hanging open.

So the preacher repeated the question in an even sterner tone, "Where is God?"

Again, the boy made no attempt to answer. The preacher raised his voice even more, shook his finger in the boy's face and bellowed, "Where is God?"

The boy screamed and bolted from the room. He ran directly home and got into his closet, slamming the door behind him.

When his older brother found him in the closet, he asked, "What happened?"

The younger brother, gasping for breath, replied, "We're in big trouble this time. God is missing, and they think we did it!"

FARMS

What do you call a donkey with three legs?
A wonkey.

Which Spanish farm animal fought windmills?
Donkey Oatey.

How do you confuse a stupid farmer?
Put three shovels against a wall and tell him to take his pick.

What did the farmer say to the barren nanny goat?
You must be kidding.

A farmer walked into a bank and asked to see the man who arranged the loans.

"I'm sorry, sir," said the cashier. "The loan arranger is out to lunch."

"Can I speak to Tonto then?" asked the farmer.

A man owned a small ranch in Texas. The Texas Work Force Commission claimed he was not paying proper wages and sent an agent to interview him.

"I need a list of your employees and how much you pay them," demanded the agent.

"Well," replied the rancher, "there's my farm hand who's been with me for three years. I pay him $200 a week plus free room and board. The cook has been here for eighteen months, and I pay her $150 per week plus free room and board. Then there's the half-wit. He works about eighteen hours every day and does about ninety per cent of all the work around here. He makes about ten dollars per week, pays his own room and board, and I buy him a bottle of bourbon every Saturday night. He also sleeps with my wife occasionally."

"That's the guy I want to talk to… the half-wit," says the agent, concerned about how one staff member could be treated so unfairly.

The rancher replied, "That would be me."

Why did the farmer plough his field with a steam roller?
He wanted to grow mashed potatoes.

A farmer was pulling a cartload of horse manure down the lane.

"What are you going to do with that?" asked his dim-witted farmhand.

"I'm going to put it on my strawberries," said the farmer.

"That's odd," said the farmhand. "We put cream and sugar on ours."

How did the farmer mend his pants?
With cabbage patches.

A Texan farmer goes to Australia for a vacation. There he meets an Australian farmer and gets talking. The Aussie shows off his big wheat field and the Texan says, "Oh! We have wheat fields that are at least twice as large."

Then they walk around the ranch a little and the Australian shows off his herd of cattle. The Texan immediately says, "We have longhorns that are at least twice as large as your cows."

The conversation has almost died when the Texan sees a herd of kangaroos hopping through the field. He asks, "And what are those?"

The Aussie asks with an incredulous look, "Don't you have any grasshoppers in Texas?"

What did the farmer say when he lost his tractor?
Where's my tractor?

A farmer and a mathematician were on a train journey. As they passed a flock of sheep in a field, the mathematician declared confidently, "There are 428 sheep in that field."

"That's incredible!" said the farmer. "It so happens I know the owner and that figure is exactly right. Tell me, how did you count them so quickly?"

"It was easy," said the mathematician. "I just counted the number of legs and divided by four."

Why are farmers cruel?
Because they pull corn by the ears.

A farmer kept a donkey in a stable, but the donkey's ears were so long that they repeatedly hit the top of the door, causing the animal to kick out dangerously. So the farmer decided to raise the height of the doorframe.

He spent all day toiling away with his hacksaw. Seeing that he was struggling to complete the task, his neighbour suggested, "Instead of lifting the doorframe, wouldn't it be easier if you simply dug out the ground in the doorway and made it deeper?"

"Don't be stupid," said the farmer. "It's the donkey's ears that are too long, not his legs!"

Why did the scarecrow win an award?
Because he was outstanding in his field.

A farmer says, "I can't decide whether to buy a bicycle or a cow for my farm."

His friend says, "Well, wouldn't you look silly riding a cow?"

"True," says the farmer, "but I'd look even sillier trying to milk a bicycle!"

Why did the farmer bury money in his fields?
Because he wanted the soil to be rich.

Why did the farmer hang a raincoat over his orchard?
Someone had told him he should get an apple mac.

Out in open farming country, there lived a farmer who had a hobby. He collected tractors. He had big ones and small ones, red ones and green ones, and everything in between. And of course, all this machinery took a lot of space, so he had a number of specially constructed buildings.

But slowly, over the years, he got bored with his collection, until one day he decided to get rid of the whole lot, and he set fire to them.

A neighbouring farmer visited him, and found him standing at the entrance to one of the barns, sucking the smoke out of the building to keep the fire burning.

"What's going on?" asked the visitor.

"Well," the farmer replied, "I used to love these machines, but now I've become an ex-tractor fan."

A farmer was ploughing his field when his willing but stupid teenaged son asked if he could help.

"Dad, I'd like to do some ploughing," said the boy.

"I'm not sure, son," replied the farmer. "Ploughing a field requires a steady hand."

"Please! I really want to help."

So the farmer reluctantly agreed and handed the boy the necessary tools but when he came to check the work an hour later, he saw that the ploughed line was crooked.

"Your line is all over the place!" said the farmer.

"But I was watching the plough to make sure that I kept straight," said the boy.

"That's the problem, son. Don't look at the plough. Instead you have to watch where you're going. The trick is to focus on an object at the far end of the field and head straight for it. That way you'll cut a perfect straight line every time."

"Okay, Dad. I'll try that."

While the farmer busied himself with other jobs, the boy set to work once more. An hour later the farmer returned and saw to his horror that the boy had cut the worst row he had ever seen. It went all over the field in loops and circles.

"What the hell happened?" he yelled. "I've never seen a worse looking field in my life. There's not one straight line!"

"But I followed your advice," said the son. "I fixed my sights on that dog playing at the far end of the field."

FISH AND SEA LIFE

Where do fish go to borrow money?
The loan shark.

How could the shrimp afford to buy a house?
He prawned all his possessions.

What do you call a big fish who makes you an offer you can't refuse?
The Codfather.

Why did the fish cross the river?
To get to its school.

Why did the fish cross the sea?
To get to the other tide.

What did the fish say when he hit a concrete wall?
Dam!

*Which fish can perform operations? **The sturgeon.***

How do you make a goldfish age?
Take out the g.

What happened to the shark who swallowed a bunch of keys?
He got lockjaw.

What did Cinderella Dolphin wear to the ball?
Glass flippers.

What fish goes up the river at 100mph?
A motor pike.

What's the difference between a fish and a piano?
You can't tuna fish.

What has eight guns and terrorizes the ocean?
Billy the Squid.

What do you get if you cross an eel with a shopper?
A slippery customer.

Why are fish so clever?
They live in schools.

Where do fish keep their money?
In a river bank.

What do you call a fish with no eyes?
A fsh.

What lives in the ocean, is grumpy and won't speak to its neighbours?
A hermit crab.

Why can't Batman go fishing?

Because Robin eats all the worms.

What do you call a neurotic octopus?
A crazy, mixed-up squid.

What does a squid sheriff form?
An octoposse.

What game do fish like playing the most?
Name that tuna.

Why did the fish miss the call?
Because he was stuck on the other line.

Why do fish live in salt water?
Because pepper makes them sneeze.

Why didn't the lobster share his toys?
Because he was shellfish.

Who held the baby octopus to ransom?
Squidnappers.

Why are fish easy to weigh?
They have scales.

When fish play soccer, who is the captain?
The team's kipper.

What fish do road menders use?
Pneumatic krill.

What did the boy fish say to his girlfriend?
Your plaice or mine?

What does an octopus wear on a cold day?
A coat of arms.

What happened to the man who went to a seafood disco?
He pulled a mussel.

Why did the crab get arrested?
Because he was always pinching things.

There was a sea scout camp near a beach where the dolphins were so friendly they swam into shore at dinner time. The chef used to announce dinner by yelling: "Dinner! For all in tents ... and porpoises."

What lies at the bottom of the sea and quivers?
A nervous wreck.

What do you call a whale that can't keep a secret?
A blubber mouth.

A kipper said to his friend, "Smoking is bad for you."
His friend replied, "It's okay, I've been cured."

What fish swims only at night?
A starfish.

In the window of a seafood restaurant, a man spotted a sign which read: "Lobster Tails $3 each."

Sensing a bargain, he went inside and asked the waitress why they were so cheap. "They must be very short tails for that price," he suggested.

"No," the waitress insisted. "They're normal length."

"Then they must be pretty old," said the man.

"No, they're fresh today."

"The man was not convinced. "There must be something wrong with them."

"No, they're just regular lobster tails."

"Very well," said the man. "For three dollars I'll have one lobster tail."

So the waitress took the man's money, sat him down and said, "Once upon a time, there was a big red lobster ..."

What did the male octopus say to the female octopus?
I want to hold your hand, hand, hand, hand, hand, hand, hand, hand.

What kind of fish is useful in freezing weather?
A skate.

What kind of fish plays a musical instrument?
The double bass.

Why was the shellfish sweating?
Because it was clammy.

Why are sardines the most stupid fish in the sea?
Because they climb into cans, close the lid and leave the key outside.

What is the best way to communicate with a fish?
Drop it a line.

What kind of fish will help you hear better?
A herring aid.

Two fish are in a tank. One says to the other, "Do you know how to drive this thing?"

Where do you weigh whales?
At a whale weigh station.

What kind of money do fishermen make?
Net profits.

How do dolphins reach a decision?
Flipper coin.

How do we know the trout was upset?
Because the fisherman said it was gutted.

What do you get if you cross an abbot with a salmon?
Monkfish.

A man went into a fishmonger's carrying a trout under his arm. "Do you make fishcakes?" he asked.
"Yes, we do," replied the fishmonger.
"Good," said the man. "It's his birthday!"

Why are some fish at the bottom of the ocean?
Because they dropped out of school.

Why do cod swim erratically?
Because cod moves in mysterious ways.

What was the Tsar of Russia's favourite fish?
Tsardines.

What fish eats its victims two by two?
Noah's shark.

A fish walks into a bar. The bartender asks, "What would you like?"
Holding its neck, the fish gasps, "Water."

What happened to the cold jellyfish?
It set.

What do you call someone who sticks his right hand into a shark's mouth?
Lefty.

A boy wanted a new pet and found an ideal one at a local pet shop. It was a brightly coloured fish called a parrot fish. The shop owner told the boy that he would be able to teach the fish to sing like a bird.

After a few weeks, one of his friends came to visit and to see the new pet. The boy said, "I'm a bit disappointed with it, to be honest."

"I can't believe you bought a fish because you thought you would be able to teach it to sing."

"Well, it is called a parrot fish."

His friend said, "You might be able to teach a parrot to sing, but you'll never get anywhere with a parrot fish."

The boy replied, "But he does sing! He sings all through the night. The problem is, he keeps singing off-key. It's driving me mad. Do you know how hard it is to tune a fish?"

Where do fish wash?
In a river basin.

What kind of fish goes well with ice cream?
Jellyfish.

What did the sardine call the submarine?
A can of people.

Why did the trout cross the road?
Just for the halibut.

How do fish set up in business?
They start on a small scale.

Where would you find a down-and-out octopus?
On squid row.

Far away in the tropical waters of the Caribbean, two prawns were swimming around in the sea – one called Justin and the other called Christian. The prawns were constantly being harassed and threatened by sharks that patrolled the area.

One day Justin said to Christian, "I'm bored and frustrated at being a prawn. I wish I was a shark, then I wouldn't have any worries about being eaten."

As Justin had his mind firmly focused on becoming a predator, a mysterious cod appears and says, "Your wish is granted," and lo and behold, Justin turned into a shark. Horrified, Christian immediately swam away, afraid of being eaten by his old friend.

Time went on and Justin found himself becoming bored and lonely as a shark. All his old mates simply swam away whenever he came close to them. Justin didn't realize that his new menacing appearance was the cause of his sad plight.

While out swimming alone one day, he saw the mysterious cod again and couldn't believe his luck. He begged the cod to change him back into a prawn, and after a little hesitation the cod agreed and reversed the transformation. With tears of joy in his tiny little eyes, Justin swam back to his friends and bought them all a cocktail. Looking around the gathering at the reef, he searched for his old pal.

"Where's Christian?" he asked.

The other fish said, "He's at home, distraught that his best friend changed sides to the enemy and became a shark." Eager to put things right again and sort out his friendship, he set off to Christian's house.

As he opened the coral gate the memories came flooding back. He banged on the door and shouted, "It's me, Justin, your old friend, come out and see me again."

Christian replied, "No way man, you'll eat me. You're a shark, the enemy, and I'll not be tricked."

Justin cried back, "No, I'm not. That was the old me. I've changed. I've found cod. I'm a prawn again, Christian."

Which fish go to heaven when they die?
Angelfish.

Why are fish never good tennis players?
They don't like getting close to the net.

Why are fish boots the warmest ones to wear?
Because they have electric 'eels.

Why are dolphins cleverer than humans?
In just three hours they can train a human to stand at the side of a pool and feed them fish.

Some species of fish on the coral reef have adapted to be able to survive the poisonous sting from sea anemones, which gives them a safe place to hide from predators.

One fish decided to be different. One day he swam away from his protective anemone, in search of some other hiding place. At first, he swam into a small gap in the rock, but he very quickly swam out of there when he was chased by

an eel. Then he decided he could hide inside a shell, so he found a nice big one that he liked, but had to retreat from the crab that had got there before him.

Finally, exhausted, he swam into the coral beds, and hid among the brilliant coloured fern-like fronds of the corals.

The next day, when he hadn't come back to the anemone, some of the other fish decided to go out and look for him. They hunted everywhere for him, but they couldn't find him. Eventually, just as they had given up, they heard him calling to them. They looked around, but they couldn't see him anywhere, he was perfectly hidden by the coral.

Finally, he showed himself, and they tried to persuade him to come back home, but he refused as the coral was too good a hiding place to leave.

"After all," he said, "with fronds like these, who needs anemones?"

What did the mermaid do last Saturday night?
She went out with the tide.

What sea creature can add up?
An octoplus.

A man went into a pet store and said, "I'd like to buy a goldfish."

The store owner asked, "Do you want an aquarium?"

The man said, "I don't care what star sign it is."

Where does seaweed look for a job?
In the kelp-wanted ads.

Teacher: Johnny, put some more water in the fish tank, please.
Boy: Why, Miss? I only put some in yesterday and he hasn't drunk that yet!

Where are most fish found?
Between the head and the tail.

What do you call a fish that can't swim?
Dead.

How do fish get to school?
By octobus.

FOOD AND DRINK

A family of three tomatoes were walking downtown one day when the little baby tomato started lagging behind. The big father tomato walked back to the baby tomato, stomped on her, squashing her into a red paste, and said, "Ketchup!"

What is black, white, black, white and green?
Two skunks fighting over a pickle.

What is black, white, green and bumpy?
A pickle wearing a tuxedo.

What do you call cheese that isn't yours?
Nacho cheese.

What kind of coffee was served on the Titanic?
Sanka.

Why did the girl loaf of stale bread slap the boy loaf of stale bread?
Because he tried to get fresh.

Did you hear the joke about the peanut butter?
I'm not telling you. You might spread it.

Why do the French like to eat snails?
Because they don't like fast food.

Which fruit launched a thousand ships?
Melon of Troy.

Why did the fisherman put peanut butter into the sea?
To go with the jellyfish.

What is a porcupine's favourite food?
Prickled onions.

What happened to the American Indian who drank forty cups of tea?
He was found dead the next morning in his tea-pee.

What do you call candy that was stolen?
Hot chocolate.

What kind of nuts always seem to have a cold?
Cashews.

What is green and sings?
Elvis Parsley.

What is green and brown and crawls through the grass?
A Girl Scout who has lost her cookie.

A man went into a bar.

"Good evening, sir," said the bartender. "What would you like to drink?"

"A large whiskey, thank you," said the man.

"That will be three dollars," said the bartender.

"No," said the man. "I distinctly remember you invited me to have a drink. I thought it was very kind of you."

The bartender turned to another customer, who was a solicitor, and asked for his support. The solicitor said that he was very sorry, but the bartender had definitely made an offer and the man had accepted it, so he did not have to pay. The bartender was furious and turned the man out, telling him never to come back again. But about ten minutes later the man reappeared.

"I thought I told you never to come back," the bartender said.

"I've never been here before in my life," said the man.

"Then you must have a double," said the bartender.

The man replied, "Thank you very much, I will, and I'm sure my solicitor friend would like one too."

Why don't you starve in a desert?
Because of all the sand which is there.

Why was the refrigerator afraid?
Because the milk went bad and turned rotten.

What did the potato say after reading the works of Descartes?
I think therefore I yam.

How do you make a walnut laugh?
Crack it up.

In which school do you learn to make ice cream?
Sunday School.

Did you hear about the boy who drowned in a bowl of muesli?
A strong currant pulled him under.

Why did the pie cross the road?
It was meat 'n' potato.

Why shouldn't you tell a secret on a farm?
Because the potatoes have eyes and the corn has ears.

What do you give to a sick lemon?
Lemon aid.

Where is the best place to weigh a pie?

What is a pretzel's favourite dance? **The twist.**

Somewhere over the rainbow ... weigh a pie.

A neutron walks into a restaurant and orders a soda. After finishing the drink the neutron asks the waiter, "How much?"
The waiter replies, "For you, no charge."

Two atoms were sitting in a restaurant.
When they left, the first said, "Wait, I have to go back! I left an electron behind!"
"Are you sure?" asked the other.
"Yes," said the first atom. "I'm positive!"

What do you call a peanut in a spacesuit?
An astronut.

What kind of room has no windows or door?
A mushroom.

What kind of keys do kids like to carry?
Cookies.

What did one kitchen knife say to the other?
Look sharp, the chef is coming.

Are hamburgers male?
Yes, because they're boygers, not girlgers!

Can you name two burgers who are royalty?
Sir Loin and Burger King!

A boy arrived home from school and immediately asked his mother, "Did you get the box of animal crackers?"
"Yes," she replied. "I managed to find the last box in the supermarket."

"Great!" he exclaimed. He then read the wording on the box and tipped the entire contents out over the dining-room table.
"Why have you done that?" his mother asked.
"Because the box says you can't eat them if the seal is broken. So I'm looking for the seal."

What did the mayonnaise say to the fridge?
Close the door, I'm dressing.

Why did the cookie go to the doctor?
Because it felt crummy.

Why did the cabbage win the race?
Because it was a-head!

A man bought a hot dog from a vendor. "Can I have more onions?" he asked.
"No," replied the vendor. "That's shallot."

First man: I know a café where we can eat dirt cheap.
Second man: But who wants to eat dirt?

What is the fastest cake?
Scone!

What does Batman's mother call when she wants him to come in for dinner?
Dinner, dinner, dinner, dinner, dinner, dinner, dinner, dinner, Batman!

Do hamburgers make good vampires?
No, because they always find themselves in ghoulash situations!

Do they really serve burgers in Transylvania?
Very rarely.

How are UFO's related to hamburgers?
Both are Unidentified Frying Objects.

How did the jury find the hamburger?
Grill-ty as charred.

What happened when the lights were too bright at the Chinese restaurant?
The manager decided to dim sum.

How did the man come to be found dead in a tub of cornflakes?
He was the victim of a cereal killer.

What are two things you can't have for breakfast?
Lunch and dinner.

What's the kindest vegetable?
A sweet potato.

What did the toast say to the bread?
Pop up and see me sometime.

How do gossipy hamburgers spend their time?
They chew the fat.

What's eaten with chips and goes dot-dot-dash?
Morse cod.

> Why is it not expensive to feed a giraffe?
> **A little goes a long way.**

How does Bob Marley like his doughnuts?
Wi' jammin'.

> What does Bob Marley say to his friends when he buys doughnuts?
> **Hope you like jammin' too.**

First actor: I was once in a play called Breakfast in Bed.
Second actor: Did you have a big role?
First actor: No, just toast and marmalade.

> What do you call fake pasta?
> **Mockaroni.**

How do you get holy water?
Boil the hell out of it.

Luke Skywalker and Obi-Wan Kenobi were having a meal in a Chinese restaurant. Skilfully using his chopsticks, Obi-Wan dished a large portion of noodles into his bowl and then topped it off with chicken and cashew nuts. All this was performed with the consummate ease that you would expect from a Jedi Master.

However, poor Luke was really struggling with the chopsticks, dropping his food all over the table. Eventually, Obi-Wan looked at him sternly and said, "Use the forks, Luke."

> How do we know burgers love young people?
> **They're pro-teen!**

How do we know hamburgers have high IQs?
They loin fast!

> How do we know that hamburgers love classical music?
> **They're often found at the Meatropolitan Opera House and Cownegie Hall.**

How do you make a cheeseburger sad?
Make it with blue cheese.

> How do you make a hamburger green?
> **Find a yellow cheeseburger and mix it with a blue one.**

A woman phoned a repairman to report that she had a leak in the roof above her dining room.

"When did you first notice the leak?" asked the repairman.

"Last night," she said, "when it took me two hours to finish my soup."

A young boy and his family lived in the country and as a result seldom had guests. Then one evening his father invited two work colleagues home for dinner.

The boy was keen to help his

mother and proudly carried in the first piece of apple pie, giving it to his father who passed it to one of the guests.

Then he came in with a second piece of apple pie and handed it to his father, who, in turn, passed it to the other guest. Seeing this, the boy said, "It's no use, Dad. The pieces are all the same size!"

Why did the baker steal money from the bank?
Because he wanted more dough.

Why do grapes like sunbathing?
It's their raison d'etre.

How does a burger acquire good taste?
With a little seasoning.

How many burgers do you feed a ferocious, fourteen-foot-tall vampire?
As many as it wants.

How was the burger murdered?
It was smothered in mayonnaise.

What's green, red and yellow and wears boxing gloves?
Fruit punch.

What's an aperitif?
A set of dentures.

Which vegetables compete in the Olympics?
Runner beans.

Wife: I baked two kinds of cookies today. Would you like to take your pick?

Husband: No thanks. I'll just use the hammer as usual.

There were three restaurants on the same block. One day one of them put up a sign that said: "The Best Restaurant in the City".

The next day, the largest restaurant on the block put up a larger sign that said: "The Best Restaurant in the World".

On the third day, the smallest restaurant put up a small sign that said: "The Best Restaurant on this Block".

Is there a way to make a hamburger do the Hula?
Sure, order a burger and shake.

What can you say about the six-foot chunk of meat who went into boxing?
The burger they are, the harder they fall!

What did the hamburger say when it pleaded not guilty?
I've been flamed!

What did they say about the burger who went skiing for the first time?
How the meaty have fallen!

What do burgers think when they are surrounded by gherkins?
They think they are in a pickle.

What do hamburger workers say on Monday morning?
Well, it's back to the old grind!

What happens when two burgers fall in love?
They live together in holy meatrimony.

What do meatballs say about mystery stories?
The pot thickens!

Why did the hamburger have to take the first job offered to him?
Because burgers can't be choosers.

What happened to the pilot who flew into a 4,000-pound mountain of meat?
He got grounded!

What is a hamburger's favourite story?
Hansel and Gristle.

What is the hamburger's motto?
If at first you don't succeed, fry, fry, fry again.

What kind of company is a twenty-four-hour hamburger joint?
Fry-by-night.

What kind of girl does a hamburger like?
Any girl named Patty!

What song do burgers sing on the job?
Gristle While You Work!

What food is popular in Transylvania?
Fang-furters.

When can you count on a hamburger in an emergency?
When the chips are down.

When do hamburgers most enjoy watching TV?
During prime time.

When does a hamburger look happiest?
When somebody says "well done".

Where can a burger get a great night's sleep?

On a bed of lettuce.

Where does a burger feel at home?
On the range!

Which burger has four legs, whiskers and a tail?
A cat burger.

Which burger is famous for a long nose?
Cyrano de Burgerac.

Which burgers can tell your fortune?
Medium burgers.

Which dances do the burgers do best?
The burger-loo and the char char.

Which opera is about our meaty friends?
The Barbecue of Seville.

Which type of comedy leaves a hamburger cold?
Biting humour.

Who are the hamburgers' favourite people?
Vegetarians.

Who can beat any burger at golf?
Any links sausage.

Who is the hamburgers' favourite actress?
Candice Berger.

Why aren't burgers very good at basketball?
Too many turnovers.

Why can any hamburger run the mile in under four minutes?
Because it's a fast food!

An overweight lady goes to a health expert and says, "Give me some advice that can reduce my fatness."

The health expert says, "Okay. You must move your head to the right and then the left at a particular time."

The fat lady asks, "At which particular time?"

The health expert replies, "Whenever anybody asks you to eat."

Why did the vampire go crazy at Burger King?
He saw all that ketchup and wanted a transfusion.

Why do hamburgers feel sad at barbecues?
They get to meet their old flames!

What do you call a fast-food snack served at a church fair?
A hymnburger.

Why do hamburgers make good baseball players?
They're great at the plate.

Why do hamburgers make good secret agents?
They won't talk no matter how you grill them.

Why do the hamburgers beat the hot dogs at every sport they play?
Because hot dogs are the wurst.

Why don't meat patties go to many movies?

It's the same old plot – boyger meets grill!

Why was the burger thrown out of the army?
He couldn't pass mustard.

A slice of cheese and a slice of ham were talking in a café, knowing that they would soon be made into a cheese sandwich and a ham roll respectively.

The slice of cheese was sweating at the prospect. "Any moment now I'll be the filling in a sandwich and a huge pair of teeth will sink into me. It's too awful to contemplate."

"It doesn't worry me," said the slice of ham. "Nothing can touch me. I'm on a roll."

How do you make soup golden?
Add twenty-four carrots.

If there were no food left, what could people do?
Country people could eat their forest preserves and city people could have their traffic jams.

Why was the convict not allowed his favourite vegetable at dinner?
The jailer told him, "No peas for the wicked."

What's the difference between boogers and broccoli?
Kids won't eat broccoli.

Which fruit stays up late to study for exams?
A cramberry.

Which dessert was ruined at the Battle of the Little Big Horn?
General Custard.

What cake gives you an electric shock?
A current bun.

What is rhubarb?
Celery with high blood pressure.

Why was the cake so hard?
It was marble cake.

What's bad tempered and goes with custard?
Apple grumble.

Did you hear about the man who went out leaving alphabet soup on the stove?
He was worried it could spell disaster.

What fruits are highly paid and work for the civil service?
Government mandarins.

Two sausages are in a pan. One looks at the other and says, "Gee, it's hot in here."
The other sausage says, "Oh my goodness, it's a talking sausage."

How do you mend a broken tomato?
With tomato paste.

Why did the lettuce cross the road?
To get to the salad bar.

What fruit takes the longest to grow?
A sloe.

How do bakers trade recipes?
On a knead to know basis.

Did you hear about the guy who got hit on the head with a can of soda?
He was lucky it was a soft drink.

A blacksmith who lived in a remote German village was cut off by blizzards during a harsh winter. With the roads impassable, he was unable to get to the shops for essential food supplies. The weather showed no sign of improving and his plight became increasingly desperate. Eventually, with nobody local to turn to, he contacted his brother, who lived over 200 miles away in Berlin and asked him to send a food parcel by helicopter.

"What sort of food do you want me to send?" asked the brother.

The blacksmith said, "Some bread, some milk, oh, and some sausage. Definitely some sausage. It has been weeks since I tasted a good German sausage."

The brother promised to send the parcel as a matter of urgency but three days later it had still not arrived. "I don't know how much longer I can go on like this," wailed the blacksmith. "I am tired and frail, I have no gas or electricity, snow is piled against the front door, and the wurst is yet to come!"

What cheese is made backwards?
Edam.

What's purple and juicy and 5,000 miles long?
The Grape Wall of China.

Why did the raspberry laugh?
Because it saw the strawberry fool.

Why did people think the wedding cake was unhappy?
Because it was in tiers.

Did you hear about the raisin who cheated on his wife?
It was in the newspaper, in the currant affairs section.

How do you make an apple puff?
Chase it round the garden.

How do you make an apple crumble?
Torture it.

How do you make an apple turnover?
Push it down a hill.

Why did the tomato blush?
Because it saw the salad dressing.

What goes with a jacket potato?
Button mushrooms.

A man walked into a bar and ordered a hot dog and a Coke. He drank the Coke, put the hot dog on his head, smashed it with his hand and walked out before the bartender could say a word.

The next day the man returned and again ordered a hot dog and a Coke. The bartender watched in amazement as the man drank the Coke, put the hot dog on his head, smashed it with his hand and walked out.

The man was back again the following day and placed his regular order of a hot dog and a Coke. But this time the bartender decided to catch him out and told him, "We're out of hot dogs."

"Okay," said the man, unfazed. "I'll have a cheeseburger and a Coke."

He drank the Coke, put the cheeseburger on his head, smashed it with his hand and made for the door.

"Hey, wait!" called the bartender, unable to contain his curiosity any longer. "Why did you smash that cheeseburger on your head?"

The man looked at him and replied, "Because you didn't have any hot dogs."

What does the Easter bunny order at a Chinese restaurant? **Hop suey.**

What do you get if you cross a door knocker with some zucchini, tomatoes, onions and garlic? **Rat-a-tat-a-touille.**

What did the plate say to the saucer? **Dinner's on me.**

What is green, round and wears oven gloves?
A cooking apple.

Boy: Dad, do you like baked apples?
Father: Yes, I do. Why?
Boy: The orchard's on fire.

First mushroom: I'm fed up.
Second mushroom: Don't talk to me. I've got truffles enough of my own.

What kind of security systems do fast-food restaurants have?
Burger alarms.

Two young girls were eating their packed lunches in the school yard. One had an apple and the other said, "Watch out for worms, won't you?"

The first girl replied, "Why should I? They can watch out for themselves!"

Why are cooks evil?
Because they whip cream and beat eggs.

Why were the baby strawberries crying?
Because their mother was in a jam.

In the school cafeteria, the lunchlady put up a sign near the pile of apples: "Take Only One. Remember God is watching."

On the pile of candies, a child put up a note: "Take as many as you want. God is watching the apples."

What do you get from a baker with a sense of humour?
Wry bread.

When do you stop at green and go at red?
When you're eating a watermelon.

What's smelly, round and laughs?
A tickled onion.

One day, Bill and Tom went to a restaurant for dinner. As soon as the waiter took out two steaks, Bill quickly picked out the bigger steak for himself. Tom wasn't happy about that. "When are you going to learn to be polite?" he said.

Bill said, "If you had the chance to pick first, which one would you pick?"

Tom replied, "The smaller piece, of course."

"So what are you whining about then?" said Bill. "You've got the smaller piece!"

What did the frog order when he went to McDonald's?
A Hoppy Meal.

Why did the baby cookie cry?
Because his mother was a wafer so long.

Two carrots are crossing the road when one gets run over by a car. His friend calls an ambulance and he is rushed to hospital. After several hours of surgery, the doctor comes out and speaks to his carrot friend.

"I have good news and bad news," the doctor said. "The good news is your friend will live, the bad news is he will be a vegetable for the rest of his life."

Did you hear about the Italian chef who died?
He pasta way last week.

Where are stir-fry cooks never at home?
They're always at wok.

When the waitress in a New York City restaurant brought him the soup du jour, the Englishman was a bit dismayed. "Good heavens," he said. "What is this?"

"Why, it's bean soup," she replied.

"I don't care what it has been," he sputtered. "What is it now?"

Why did the grape go out with the prune?
Because he couldn't find a date.

What do you call a man with jelly in one ear and custard and sponge in the other?
A trifle deaf.

What do you get when two strawberries meet?
A strawberry shake.

Why did the orange stop in the middle of the road?
Because it ran out of juice.

Why do people become bakers?
Because they knead the dough.

A family are having dinner when Johnny, the young son, says, "Daddy, are caterpillars good to eat?"

"I've told you never to mention such things during meals!" his father replies.

His mother says, "Why did you ask that, Johnny?"

Johnny replies, "It's because I saw one on Daddy's lettuce, but now it's gone."

What are apricots?
Where baby monkeys sleep.

What do bakers play on their lunchbreak?
Tic Tac Dough.

What do you call a fake noodle?
An impasta.

First boy: This morning my dad accidentally gave me soap flakes instead of bran flakes for breakfast.
Second boy: I bet you were mad.
First boy: Mad? I was foaming at the mouth!

What did the girl melon say to the boy melon?
We're too young, we can't elope.

What kind of cheese would you hide a horse in?
Mascarpone.

A husband and wife were arguing about who should make the pot of tea in the morning.

She told him, "You should do it because you always get up first, so we won't have as long to wait."

He told her, "You're in charge of cooking, so it's your job. I don't mind waiting."

Flustered, she countered, "No, you should do it because it says in the Bible that it's a man's job to make the pot of tea."

"Where does it say that?" he demanded. "Show me."

So she fetched the Bible, turned to the New Testament and showed him that at the top of several pages it says "Hebrews".

Two oranges go into a bar. One says to the other, "You're round."

Why was the celery scared?
It had a stalker.

What vegetable needs a plumber?
A leek.

"George is so forgetful," the sales manager complained to his secretary. "It's a wonder he can sell anything, and I'm not even sure he'll remember to come back to the office!"

Just then the door flew open, and in bounded George. "You'll never guess what happened!" he shouted. "While I was at lunch I met Old Man Smithers, who hasn't bought anything from us for five years. Well, we got to talking and

he gave me this million-dollar order!"

"See," sighed the sales manager to his secretary. "I told you he'd forget the sandwiches."

What can you make from baked beans and onions?
Tear gas.

Did you hear about the man who decided that becoming a vegetarian was a missed steak?

Why did the mushroom go to the party?
Because he was a fun guy.

If an apple a day keeps the doctor away, what will an onion do?
Keep everyone away!

What can a whole apple do that half an apple can't?
Look round.

Did you hear about the man who was chopping up carrots with the Grim Reaper?
He was dicing with death.

What cake wanted to rule the world?
Attila the Bun.

A stupid guy worked at a doughnut shop. It was his first day there. A customer walked in and said, "How much are these doughnuts?"

The stupid guy answered, "I don't know." So the customer left.

The manager walked in and said, "No, no, you're supposed to say, 'Only a dollar and 25 cents.'"

Another customer walked in and asked, "Are these doughnuts fresh?"

The stupid guy said, "I don't know." So the customer left.

The manager walked in and said, "No, no, you're supposed to say, 'Yes, yes, very fresh.'"

Another customer walked in and said, "Can I buy these?"

And the stupid guy said, "I don't know." So the customer left.

The manager walked in and said, "No, no, you're supposed to say, 'If you don't, somebody else will.'"

The next day a robber walked in to the doughnut shop and said, "How much money you got in that cash register?"

The stupid guy replied, "Only a dollar and 25 cents."

The robber said, "Are you trying to be fresh with me?"

The stupid guy answered, "Yes, yes, very fresh!"

The robber said, "Can I shoot you?"

The stupid guy replied, "If you don't, somebody else will."

Why wouldn't the newspaper reporter leave the mashed potatoes alone?
Because he wanted a scoop.

How should you deal with an angry, 300-pound baked potato?
Just butter him up.

What do you call a potato wearing glasses?
A spec-tater.

What do you call an extremely bossy potato?
A dic-tater.

What do you call a potato that can never decide what to do?
A hezzie-tater.

What do you call a potato that does impressions?
An imi-tater.

What do you call a militant potato?
An agi-tater.

A lady was picking through the frozen turkeys at the grocery store, but couldn't find one big enough for her family.

She asked a stock boy, "Do these turkeys get any bigger?"

The stock boy replied, "No ma'am, they're dead."

A hot dog walked into a bar and ordered a bottle of beer.
The bartender said, "Sorry, we don't serve food here."

What did Lee become when he ate raw onions for a week?
Lone Lee.

Why did the boy eat his homework?
Because his teacher said it was a piece of cake.

What's worse than finding a worm in your apple?

Finding half a worm.

Three prisoners were captured in the war and were about to face a firing squad. Before their execution, they were offered the chance to choose what they would like to eat for their last meal.

The first prisoner asked for a juicy steak. He was served the steak and then taken away to be shot.

The second prisoner requested roast duck. He was served the duck and then taken away to be shot.

The third prisoner asked for strawberries.

"Strawberries?" queried the guards.

"That's right," said the prisoner. "Strawberries."

"But they're out of season!"

"It's okay," said the prisoner. "I'll wait…"

Why does God like Swiss cheese?
Because it's holey.

What did the father say after his son had eaten the last apple?
They don't grow on trees, you know.

> First apple: You look down in the dumps. What's eating you?
> **Second apple: A worm, I think.**

What are the heaviest noodles in the world?
Wanton noodles.

A man approached the cake stall at a fair and asked the woman who was running the stall how much a slice of cake was.

"That's two dollars," she said.

"And how about that cake?" he said, pointing to another slice. "How much is that?"

"That's three dollars," she said.

"Oh!" said the man, surprised. "Why is that more expensive?"

"Because," replied the woman, "that's Madeira cake."

What can you serve but not eat?
A tennis ball.

What kind of bean doesn't grow in your garden?
A jelly bean.

> What is as round as a biscuit, as deep as a cup and not even the Atlantic Ocean can fill it up?
> **A tea strainer.**

A man walks into a bar. Ouch! It was an iron bar.

A man walks into a coffee shop and is given a huge mug, which he takes to his table. But when he tries to drink it, he finds that instead of coffee, the mug contains a pair of beige cotton trousers. So he goes to complain.

The counter staff are not very helpful, so after arguing with them for some time, he eventually gets them to call the shop manager. The manager is very indignant and says, "But it's exactly what you asked for."

"No it isn't!" says the customer. "How can this possibly be what I ordered?"

The manager replies, "It's a cup o' chinos."

When is it dangerous to be hit on the head by a tomato?
When it's still in the can.

How does the gingerbread man make his bed?
With cookie sheets.

How do you know that peanuts are fattening?
Have you ever seen a skinny elephant?

Two men have been lost in the desert for weeks, and they're at death's door. As they stumble on, hoping for salvation in the form of an oasis or something similar, they suddenly spy, through the heat haze, a small tree in the distance.

As they get closer, they can see that the tree is draped with rasher upon rasher of bacon. There's smoked bacon, crispy bacon, life-giving juicy nearly-raw bacon, all sorts.

"Look Dave," says the first man. "It's a bacon tree!"

Dave doesn't wait another second. He runs up to the tree salivating at the prospect of food. But just as he gets to within five feet of the tree, there's the sound of machine-gun fire, and he is shot down in a hail of bullets.

His friend quickly drops down on the sand, and calls across to the dying man, "Dave! Dave! What on earth happened?"

And with his dying breath Dave calls back, "Run! It's not a bacon tree after all. It's a ham bush."

What do you call a gingerbread man with one leg?
Limp biskit.

What's the fastest cake in the world?
Meriiiiiiinnnnnnnngue.

Fork: Who was that ladle I saw you with last night?

Spoon: That was no ladle. That was my knife.

A man walked into a bar and ordered two drinks.

"How about a double instead?" asked the bartender.

"No. I'm drinking with my friend from Denver."

So the bartender gave him the two drinks and he downed them

by alternately sipping from each glass.

Twice a week for the next three months the man came into the bar to drink with his friend from Denver until one day he came in and ordered only one drink.

"Did your friend from Denver die?" asked the bartender.

"No," said the man. "My doctor told me to stop drinking."

A man walked past his refrigerator and heard two onions singing a Bee Gees song. When he opened the fridge door, it was just chives talking.

A man walks into a posh bar and the bartender says, "I'm sorry, I can't serve you here unless you are wearing a tie."

The man says, "Okay, I'll be right back," and goes to his car to find anything he can use for a tie. All he finds is a set of jumper cables, so he ties them around his neck, goes back in and asks, "How's this?"

The bartender replies, "Well, okay, but don't start anything."

What kind of diet involves eating metal paper fastenings?
A staple diet.

What happens when a clock is hungry?
It goes back four seconds.

A man walks into a bar and orders a drink. After sitting for a few minutes, he hears a voice say, "Nice tie." He looks around but doesn't see anybody near him. Some time passes and he hears the same voice say, "Nice shirt." This time he looks everywhere; behind him, up and down the bar, under the chair, behind the bar, everywhere he can think to look, but he doesn't see anyone. A few minutes later he hears, "Nice haircut." He can't stand it any more, so he calls the bartender over and tells him he has been hearing this voice.

The bartender says, "Oh, don't worry, it's just the complimentary nuts."

What would happen if you ate yeast and shoe polish?
Every day you would rise and shine.

Wife: The two things I cook best are meat loaf and apple pie.
Husband: Which is this?

What happened when two peanuts walked down a spooky road at night?
One was assaulted.

A man walks into a bar. The bartender says, "Do you want to play a game? See those two rib-eyes nailed to the ceiling? You get to throw one dart. If you hit one, you get to take them home and I'll give you a free drink."

The man says, "No thanks, the steaks are too high."

A patient sneaks out of the hospital and goes to a nearby bar. He orders a beer and a whiskey, knocks them back and orders the same again. As he drains the last drops, he says to the barman, "I shouldn't be drinking with what I've got."

"What have you got?" the barman asks, looking worried in case the man was about to drop dead.

"About fifty cents," says the patient.

Which Elvis Presley song is a tribute to cake?
In the Gateau.

Which Village People song is about meat stock?
In the Gravy.

There were once two bakeries in a small village. They were in fierce competition, with half the village going to one, and the other half shopping at the other.

One day, one of the bakers bought himself a new device that he found for sale in the city – it was a bread-slicing machine that could slice four loaves at once, using four large blades.

Suddenly, he found himself getting all the business in the town. Nobody went to the other baker's shop any more, and it was forced out of business.

After he had closed the shop for the final time, the second baker went to visit the first, to ask for a job.

"How did you do it?" he asked. "How did you get so much business from me? You just got so much good luck all of a sudden."

"I'm not sure," said the first baker, "but I think it's got something to do with this four-loaf cleaver."

Why did the jelly wobble?
Because it saw the milk shake.

What do you call two rows of cabbages?
A dual cabbageway.

How does Good King Wenceslas like his pizzas?
Deep pan, crisp and even.

William Penn, the founder and mayor of Philadelphia, had two aunts who were skilled in the baking arts. One day, William was petitioned by the citizens of his town because the three bakeries in the town had, during the Revolution, raised the price of pies to the point that only the rich could afford them.

Not wanting to challenge the bakeries directly, he turned to his aunts and asked their advice. But when they had heard the story, the two old ladies were so incensed over the situation that they offered to bake 100 pies themselves, and sell them for two cents lower that any of the bakeries were charging.

It was a roaring success. Their pies sold out quickly, and very soon they had managed to bring down the price of all kinds of pastry in Philadelphia.

In fact, even to this very day, their achievements are remembered as the remarkable pie rates of Penn's aunts.

What's green and writes underwater?
A ballpoint gherkin.

What's red, fruity and mean?
A raspberry with a grudge.

What's red and invisible?
No tomatoes.

What's yellow and dangerous?
Shark-infested custard.

A famous food critic visited Europe last summer. He had a delightful time sampling the cuisine in Italy, France and Germany. On the way home, he stopped off in London and had a great meal of fish and chips at a London pub. He asked the manager of the pub if he could have the recipe for the fish and chips.

The manager confessed that he bought his fish and chips from a nearby monastery and so the critic would have to get the recipe from one of the brothers.

So the food critic quickly ran down the street to the monastery and knocked on the door. When one of the brothers came to the door, he asked, "Are you the Fish Friar?"

The brother replied, "No, I'm the Chip Monk."

FROGS, TOADS AND NEWTS

What is a frog's favourite flower?
Croak-us.

What do you get if you cross a frog and a dog?
A croaker spaniel.

What is a frog's favourite game?
Croak-et.

Why was the frog down in the mouth?
He was unhoppy.

What do toads drink?
Croaka-cola.

When is a car like a frog?
When it is being toad.

What do you get if you cross a science fiction film with a toad?
Star Warts.

What kind of shoes do frogs like to wear in summer?
Open-toad sandals.

Where do tadpoles change into frogs?
In a croakroom

What is green and tough?
A frog with a machine gun.

Why didn't the female frog lay eggs?
Because her husband spawned her affections.

What do you say if you meet a toad?
Wart's new?

What do you call a 100-year-old frog?
An old croak.

What do you get if you cross a frog with some mist?
Kermit the Fog.

What did one frog say to the other?
Time's fun when you're having flies!

What is white on the outside, green on the inside and comes with relish and onions?
A hot frog.

What did the bus conductor say to the frog?
Hop on.

What goes dot-dot-croak, dot-dash-croak?
Morse toad.

What game do Scottish toads play?
Hopscotch.

Why did the toad become a lighthouse keeper?
He had his own frog horn.

What's green and can jump a mile a minute?
A frog with hiccups.

What is a toad's favourite sweet?
Lollihops.

What do you call a frog spy?
A croak and dagger agent.

Which frog became a famous cowboy?
Hopalong Cassidy.

What jumps up and down in front of a car?
Froglights.

What happens when you illegally park a frog?
It gets toad away.

What is green and goes round and round at 100mph?
A frog in a blender.

What is yellow and goes round and round very quickly?
A mouldy frog in a blender.

How do frogs die?
They Kermit suicide.

Where do frogs sit?
On toadstools.

How did the toad die?
Nobody knows, he just croaked.

A frog telephones the Psychic Hotline and is told, "You are going to meet a beautiful young girl who will want to know everything about you."
The frog says, "This is great! Will I meet her at a party, or what?"
"No," says the psychic. "Next semester in her biology class."

Why did the baby salamander feel lonely?
Because he was newt to the area.

A man walks into a bar with a newt on his shoulder.

"Hey," the bartender says. "What's his name?"

"Tiny," the man replies.

"Why call him that?" the bartender asks.

"Because he's my newt."

A frog goes into a bank, and hops up to the loan officer.

The loan officer says, "My name is John Paddywack. Can I help you?"

The frog says, "Yeah, I'd like to borrow some money."

The loan officer finds this a little odd, but gets out a form. He says, "Okay, what's your name?"

The frog says, "Kermit Jagger."

The loan officer says, "Really? Any relation to Mick Jagger?"

The frog says, "Yeah, he's my dad."

The loan officer says, "Okay. Do you have any collateral?"

The frog hands the loan officer a pink ceramic elephant and says, "Will this do?"

The loan officer says, "I'm not sure. Let me go check with the bank manager."

The frog says, "Oh, tell him I said hello. He knows me."

The loan officer goes back to the manager and says, "Excuse me, but there's this frog out there named Kermit Jagger who wants to borrow some money. He claims his dad is Mick Jagger but all he has for collateral is this pink elephant thing.

I don't know what it's for."

The manager says, "It's a knick-knack, Paddywack. Give the frog a loan. His old man's a Rolling Stone."

GEOGRAPHY

Teacher: Johnny, can you find me Australia on the map?
Johnny: There it is, Miss.
Teacher: Now, Mary, who discovered Australia?
Mary: Johnny did, Miss.

What's small, expensive and was built in Greenwich, London?
The Millennium Gnome.

What would the United States be called if everyone in it drove cars?
A car-nation.

What would the United States be called if everyone in it drove pink cars?
A pink car-nation.

What would the United States be called if everyone in it lived in their cars?
An in-car-nation.

Why is Florida so easy to get into?
Because it has many keys.

What is the smartest US state?
Alabama, it has four As and one B.

What stays in the corner, but travels around the world?
A stamp.

Which is the most slippery country in the world?
Greece.

Why are things so expensive to buy in Mexico?
You peso much.

In which Malaysian city do you find koala bears?
Koala Lumpur.

Where do pencils come from?
Pennsylvania.

What did Big Ben say to the Leaning Tower of Pisa?
I've got the time if you've got the inclination.

What do you call an eye doctor living on an island off Alaska?
An optical Aleutian.

What do you call someone with a father from Iceland and a mother from Cuba?
An Ice Cube.

Which English city is the cleanest place to live?
Bath.

What happens if you throw a blue stone into the Red Sea?
It gets wet.

What do you call a party in the Middle East?
An Abu Dhabi do.

What rock group has four men that don't sing?
Mount Rushmore.

Who is the most famous married woman in the United States?
Mrs Sippi.

What is the capital of Washington?
The W.

What did Delaware?
Her New Jersey.

A man lived in California but his watch was always three hours fast. He couldn't fix it so he moved to New York.

What do you say if someone tells a lie in South America?
I don't Bolivia.

What is the fastest country in the world?
Russia.

How do people dance in Saudi Arabia?
Sheikh-to-sheikh.

A little boy was doing his geography homework one evening. He turned to his father, who was reading the newspaper, and said, "Dad, where would I find the Andes?"

"Don't ask me," replied the father. "Ask your mother. She puts everything away in this house."

Why didn't the map grids go to the disco?
Because they were all squares.

An English tourist on a return visit to Turkey was greeted warmly by a local man wearing national costume.

The tourist said, "I'm sorry, I don't remember your name, but your fez is familiar."

What's big, white, furry and always points North?
A Polar Bearing.

Why are people who jump off a bridge in Paris crazy?
Because they are in Seine.

What sort of pudding roams around the Arctic Circle?
Moose.

A man said to his friend, "Where did you go on holiday last year?"

The friend replied, "Spain."
"A cheap place like the Costa Brava?"
"No, very expensive, Costa Fortune."

Which city increases its population two-fold every year?
Dublin.

Why did Eve want to move to New York?
She fell for the Big Apple.

Where can you find an ocean without water?
On a map.

What makes the Leaning Tower of Pisa lean?
It doesn't eat much.

"It's clear," said the schoolteacher to the young boy, "that you haven't studied your geography. What's your excuse?"

"Well," said the boy, "my dad says the world is changing every day. So I decided to wait until it settles down."

A man said to his friend, "My wife's gone to the Caribbean."
"Jamaica?"
"No, she went of her own accord."

A man said to his friend, "My wife's gone to Indonesia."
"Jakarta?"
"No, she went by plane."

A man said to his friend, "I met my wife in a northern Italian city."
"Genoa?"

"Of course I do. I'm married to her, aren't I?"

Which American state is round at each end and high in the middle?
Ohio.

What has four eyes but no face?
Mississippi.

A woman was sitting on the train reading the newspaper. A headline read: "Twelve Brazilian Soldiers Killed".

The woman shook her head at the sad news, turned to the stranger sitting next to her, and asked, "How many is a Brazilian?"

Why did Mickey Mouse go the Sudan?
Because it was full of Khartoum characters.

How many people live in a Polish city?
Lodz.

Teacher: In what part of the world are the people the most ignorant?
Pupil: Hong Kong.
Teacher: Why do you say that?
Pupil: Because the atlas says Hong Kong is where the population is most dense.

How do Minnesotans decide where to retire?
They tie a snow shovel to the back of their RV, drive south, and when people start asking, "What's that thing?" they know they've gone far enough.

If Ireland sank into the sea, which county wouldn't sink?
Cork.

For generations, a woman's family lived on a farm in Manitoba on the border with North Dakota in an area that was in dispute between Canada and the US. One day her grown-up kids came in and told her that the dispute had been settled, the international boundary line ran right through their farm, and the family could choose whether to be Canadians or Americans.

After some thought, the woman declared that they should become Americans. Her reason was that she couldn't stand another Canadian winter.

A burglar went into the bank, pointed a gun at the teller and said, "Give me all your money, or you'll be geography!"

The teller laughed nervously, "You mean history, right?"

The burglar snapped back, "Don't change the subject!"

What tall dessert do they serve in Paris?
The trifle tower.

In which city do Australian women keep their money?
Perth.

Which American state has a friendly greeting for everyone?
Ohio.

First man: Can you tell me what you call someone who comes from Corsica?
Second man: Cors-i-can.

A man and his wife were driving their Recreational Vehicle across Florida and were nearing a town spelled Kissimmee. They noted the strange spelling and tried to figure how to pronounce it – KISS-a-me, kis-A-me, kis-a-ME.

They grew more perplexed as they drove into the town. Since they were hungry, they pulled into a place to get something to eat. At the counter, the man said to the waitress, "My wife and I can't seem to be able to figure out how to pronounce this place. Will you tell me where we are and say it very slowly so that I can understand?"

The waitress looked at him and said, "Buuurrrgerrr Kiiiinnnng."

How do we know that the Earth won't come to an end?
Because it's round.

What does Brazil produce that no other country produces?
Brazilians.

What do John Wayne and a map key have in common?
Both are legends.

Why do maps never win at poker?
Because they always fold.

What do you get if you cross a cowboy with a mapmaker?
A cowtographer.

Two grains of sand were walking together across the Sahara Desert. Suddenly one turned to the other and said, "I think we're being followed."

What do you call the queue of foreign couples outside the Hard Rock Cafe?
The international date line.

Teacher: Is Lapland heavily populated?
Class: No, there are not many Lapps to the mile.

Teacher: What are the Great Plains?
Pupil: 747, Concorde and F-16.

What are the small rivers that run into the Nile?
The juveniles.

Where do bosses come from?
Boston.

Teacher: Where is the English Channel?
Pupil: I don't know, my TV doesn't pick it up.

GHOSTS

What do ghosts eat for breakfast?
Dreaded wheat.

What do ghosts eat for lunch?
Ghoul-ash.

What do ghosts eat for supper?
Spook-etti.

What did the baby ghost eat for dinner?
A boo-loney sandwich.

What do ghosts watch at Christmas?
A phantomime.

How did the beautician style the ghost's hair?
With a scare drier.

Why do you have to wait a long time for a ghost train?
They only run a skeleton service.

How did the ghost song-and-dance act make a living?
By appearing in television spooktaculars.

What happened to the ghost who went to a party?
He had a wail of a time.

What streets do ghosts haunt?
Dead ends.

If you tipped a can of food over a ghoul, what would you get?
Beans on ghost.

Why did the mother ghost take her ghost child to the doctor?
She was worried because he was in such good spirits.

Ghost: Are you coming to my party?
Spook: Where is it?
Ghost: In the morgue. You know what they say, the morgue the merrier.

What is a ghost's favourite fairground ride?
A rollerghoster.

Where do ghosts hang out on a Saturday night?
At all their old haunts.

What do you call a ghostly doctor?
Surgical spirit.

What's got horns and a beard and walks through walls?
Casper the friendly goat.

Why did the ghost go on safari?
He was a big game haunter.

A guest was staying in a haunted house, and in the middle of the night he met one of the ghosts.
The ghost said, "I have been walking these corridors for four hundred years."
"In that case," said the guest, "can you tell me the way to the toilet?"

How do get a ghost to lie perfectly flat?
You use a spirit level.

What do you call a ghost's songbook?
Sheet music.

A woman told her friend, "My daughter has married a ghost!" **"Oh my!" exclaimed the friend. "What possessed her?"**

What did the mother ghost say to the naughty young ghost?
Spook only when you're spoken to.

How can you tell if a ghost is about to faint?
He goes as white as a sheet.

Two ghosts were moaning about their lot. One said, "I don't know what the world's coming to. I just don't seem to have any effect on people these days."

"I know," agreed the other. "For all they care, we might as well be dead."

What did the ghost give his mom for Mother's Day?
A booquet of flowers.

Who did the ghost invite to his party?
Anyone he could dig up.

What kind of pets do ghosts have?
Scaredy cats.

Why is it difficult for a ghost to tell a lie?
Because you can see right through him.

How does a ghost start a letter?
Tomb it may concern…

Why did the ghost work at Scotland Yard?
He was the Chief In-Spectre.

What did the ghost teacher say to her class?
Watch the board and I'll go through it again.

What Central American country has the most ghosts?
Ghosta Rica.

When do ghosts usually appear?
Just before someone screams.

GORILLAS AND CHIMPANZEES

If a cow eats in a calf-eteria, where does a gorilla eat?
Anywhere it pleases.

What did the gorilla call his first wife?
His prime mate.

Two chimps got into a bath. One chimp said to the other, "Oo oo ah ah!"
The other chimp said, "Well, put some cold water in then!"

What does a gorilla eat in Paris?
Apes Suzettes.

Which American president did gorillas like the most?
Ape Lincoln.

Why did the giant ape climb up the side of the skyscraper?
Because the elevator was broken.

An explorer was walking through the jungle when he saw a chimp with a can opener. The explorer said, "You don't need a can opener to peel a banana."

"I know," said the chimp. "This is for the custard."

What is a gorilla's favourite Christmas song?
Jungle Bells.

There was once a young chimp called May who loved to pick fights with bigger animals in the jungle. One day she picked a quarrel with a full-grown lion. The next day was the first of June. Why?

Because that was the end of May.

What did the chimp say when his sister had a baby?
Well, I'll be a monkey's uncle!

If you throw a great ape into one of the Great Lakes, what will it become?
Wet.

What kind of monkey can fly?
A hot air baboon.

Which band do primates go ape over?
The Monkees.

Why do gorillas have big nostrils?
Because they have big fingers.

Why are chimpanzees underpaid?
They work for peanuts.

Why did both Germany and America want to hire apes during World War Two?
Because they are excellent at waging gorilla warfare.

What do you call a 5,000-pound gorilla?
Sir.

What do patriotic monkeys wave on Flag Day?
Star Spangled Bananas.

Fred: Did I ever tell you about the time I came face to face with a very fierce gorilla?
Bert: No, what happened?

Fred: Well, I stood there, without a gun. The gorilla looked at me and snarled and roared and beat his chest. Then it came closer and closer...

Bert: What did you do?

Fred: Oh, I'd had enough, so I moved on to the next cage.

A woman with a baby in her arms was sitting in a station waiting room, sobbing miserably. A porter came up to her and asked her what was the trouble.

"Some people were in here just now and they were so rude about my little boy," she cried. "They all said he was horribly ugly."

"There, there, don't cry," said the porter kindly. "Shall I get you a nice cup of tea?"

"Thank you, that would be nice," replied the woman, wiping her eyes. "You're very kind."

"That's all right. Don't mention it," said the porter. "While I'm at it, by the way, would you like a banana for the chimp?"

No one survived a terrible bus accident except a monkey. As there were no human witnesses, the police decided to interrogate the monkey, which seemed to respond to their questions with gestures.

The police chief asked, "What were the people doing on the bus?"

The monkey shook his head in a condemning manner and started dancing around, meaning the people were dancing and having fun.

The chief asked, "Yeah, but what else were they doing?"

The monkey held his hand to his mouth as if holding a bottle.

The chief said, "Oh! They were drinking! Were they doing anything else?"

The monkey nodded his head and moved his mouth back and forth, meaning they were talking.

The chief lost his patience, "If they were having such a great time, who was driving the stupid bus then?"

The monkey cheerfully swung his arms to the sides as if grabbing a steering wheel.

HISTORY

Why were the early days of history called the Dark Ages?
Because there were so many knights.

What was Camelot?
A place where people parked their camels.

Mother: Why aren't you doing very well in history?

Son: Because the teacher keeps asking about things that happened before I was born.

What was King Arthur's favourite game?
Knights and crosses.

What kind of lighting did Noah use for the ark?
Floodlighting.

Where was the Declaration of Independence signed?
At the bottom.

Did they play tennis in ancient Egypt?
Yes, the Bible tells how Joseph served in Pharaoh's court.

Teacher: What came after the Bronze Age and the Stone Age?
Pupil: The sausage.

First boy: I wish I had been born a thousand years ago.
Second boy: Why is that?
First boy: Just think of all the history that I wouldn't have to learn.

What did 1286BC inscribed on the mummy's tomb mean?
The registration of the car that ran him over.

What has sharp claws, a shell and tried to conquer England in the 16th century?
The Spanish Armadillo.

Who succeeded the first President of the USA?
The second one.

What were the Poles doing in Russia in 1940?
Holding up the telegraph lines.

Why are we sure that Indians were the first people in North America?
Because they had reservations.

A man asked an American Indian what his wife's name was.
The Indian replied, "She called Five Horses."
"That's an unusual name," said the man. "What does it mean?"
The Indian answered, "It old Indian name. It mean... Nag, Nag, Nag, Nag, Nag!"

Where did the pilgrims land when they came to America?
On their feet.

Which US President had a weapon that zapped aliens?
Ronald Raygun.

Which US President was least guilty?
Lincoln. He is in a cent.

Why did Julius Caesar buy crayons?
He wanted to Mark Antony.

Who refereed the tennis match between Julius Caesar and Mark Antony?
A Roman umpire.

Why does history keep repeating itself?
Because we weren't listening the first time.

What was the greatest accomplishment of the early Romans?
Speaking Latin.

*What did Egyptian mummies use to do the washing-up ? **Pharaoh Liquid.***

What did the ruler gain a reputation for during his reign?
Straight talking.

Why did King Arthur have a round table?
So no one could corner him.

Who invented King Arthur's round table?
Sir Cumference.

One day back in the 12th century, the king decided to go hunting. So he gathered up his entourage of servants and set off into the woods in search of deer. After searching for a while, he heard some rustling in the bushes nearby. He drew his longbow and aimed at the bush when suddenly a man came running out, yelling, "Don't shoot! Don't shoot! I'm not a deer!" The king shot him dead.

After a few minutes, one of the king's servants finally mustered the courage to ask the king, "Sire, why did you shoot that man? He said he wasn't a deer."

"Oh!" replied the king. "I thought he said he was a deer!"

Where did Napoleon keep his armies?
Up his sleevies.

Why did Henry VIII have so many wives?
He liked to chop and change.

Why did Henry VIII put skittles on his lawn?
So he could take Anne Boleyn.

Why was the ghost of Anne

Boleyn always running after the ghost of Henry VIII?
She was trying to get ahead.

Which English king was a leading foot doctor ?
William the Corncurer.

When was medicine first mentioned in the Bible?
When Moses received the two tablets.

Which emperor do you get if you throw a grenade into a French kitchen?
Linoleum Blownapart.

Why did the pioneers cross the country in covered wagons?
Because they didn't want to wait forty years for a train.

First Roman Soldier: What is the time?
Second Roman Soldier: XX past VII.

Why did the Romans build straight roads?
So their soldiers didn't go around the bend.

Julius Caesar walked into a bar and asked for a martinus.

The bartender, a little confused, said, "Don't you mean a martini?"

Caesar replied, "If I'd wanted a double, I'd have asked for it."

When a knight in armour was killed in battle, what sign did they put on his grave?
Rust in peace.

What English king invented the fireplace?
Alfred the Grate.

Which English king played a game with chestnuts?
William the Conkeror.

Which English king invented fractions?
Henry the 1/8th.

Why did the Roman Coliseum have to close?
The lions had eaten up all the prophets.

Which pharaoh played the trumpet?
Tooting-khamun.

What was Camelot famous for?
Its knight life.

Who designed Noah's ark?
An arkitect.

Why couldn't Noah catch many fish?
Because he only had two worms.

One fine day in ancient Rome, Julius Caesar turned his attention to a problem that had constantly plagued his mighty empire: laundry. Getting all those white togas clean was a headache to his staff, but to complicate matters Caesar had come up with a theory that if the togas could be made stiff enough, they could act as an additional layer of protection against an assassin's dagger. He figured the best way to achieve this on a large scale was to throw a large quantity of detergent into a tidal pool and then toss in the togas. The gentle motion of the tides would wash the dirt out, after which starch would be thrown in and then the stiff togas could be pulled out to dry.

He assigned the task of implementing this plan to his leading scientists. They followed his instructions, and all went well until they threw in the starch. Suddenly the goddess of nature, angered at the environmental destruction, caused a huge tidal wave to spring up and wash over Caesar's workers. A stiff breeze then dried them off so quickly that they were all frozen into place.

Later that day when Caesar visited the tidal pool with his advisors to see what progress was being made with the toga cleansing, he was alarmed to see his workers stuck rigidly to the spot. He was at a loss to explain what had gone wrong until one of his advisors whispered to him, "Beware the tides of starch."

It is a little known fact that soccer was very popular in ancient Rome. There was a big match planned for one Saturday in the middle of March in the Coliseum, and three famous Romans arranged to meet there. When the day came, Caesar and Cassius met in their favourite bar, but there was no sign of their friend Brutus. So shortly before the kick-off, they gave up and went to their reserved seats to watch the game.

At halftime, Brutus finally arrived. "Sorry I'm late," he said. "The wheel came off the chariot, and I couldn't get it fixed. How's the game going?"

"It's been a fantastic game so far," Caesar replied.

"What's the score, then?"

"Eight-two, Brutus."

Which historical figure was an expert on the springboard?
Lady Good-diver.

Who was the greatest comedian in the Bible?
Samson – he brought the house down.

What do Alexander the Great and Winnie the Pooh have in common?
The same middle name.

How do we know that Joan of Arc was French?
Because she was maid in France.

Which act of the French Revolution was an attempt to obtain fruit sweets?
The Storming of the Pastille.

What did George Washington, Abraham Lincoln and Christopher Columbus have in common?
They were all born on holidays.

Teacher: Why are you reading the last page of your history book first?
Pupil: To see how it ends.

Who was the biggest thief in history?
Atlas, he held up the whole world.

Chief Running Water had two sons. What were their names?
Hot and Cold.

Where was King Solomon's temple?
On his forehead.

HOLIDAYS

Who beats his chest and swings from Christmas cake to Christmas cake?
Tarzipan.

What do you call a snowman in summer?
A puddle.

What did one snowman say to the other snowman?
Can you smell carrot?

How do you know if a snowman has been sleeping in your bed?
You wake up wet.

Boy: Mom, can I have a dog for Christmas?
Mother: No, you can have turkey like everyone else.

What did the big cracker say to the little cracker?
My pop is bigger than yours.

What bird has wings but cannot fly?
Roast turkey.

What's the best thing to put into a Christmas cake ?
Your teeth.

What happens if you eat the Christmas decorations?
You get tinselitis.

What do vampires put on their turkey at Christmas?
Gravey.

Why is a turkey a fashionable bird?
Because he always appears well dressed for dinner.

What disasters could happen if you dropped the Christmas turkey?
The downfall of Turkey, the breakup of China and the overthrow of Greece.

Why is a guitar like a turkey being made ready for the oven?
Because they are both plucked.

What are brown, covered in pastry and sneak around the kitchen at Christmas?
Mince spies.

Where do turkeys go when they die?
The oven.

What do elves learn at school?
The elfabet.

> Why was Santa's little helper depressed?
> **Because he had low elf esteem.**

What do you call Santa's helpers?
Subordinate Clauses.

> What kind of motorbike does Santa ride?
> **A Holly Davidson.**

What do you get when you cross an archer with a gift-wrapper?
Ribbon Hood.

> Why did the elf push his bed into the fireplace?
> **He wanted to sleep like a log.**

What goes ho, ho, swoosh, ho, ho, swoosh?
Santa caught in a revolving door.

> What goes oh, oh, oh?
> **Santa walking backwards.**

Why does Santa Claus go down the chimney on Christmas Eve?
Because it soots him.

> What do you call people who are afraid of Santa Claus?
> **Claustrophobic.**

Why does Scrooge love Rudolph the Red-Nosed Reindeer?
Because every buck is dear to him.

> Why is Christmas just like a day at the office?
> **You do all the work and the fat guy with the suit gets all the credit.**

What do snowmen eat for breakfast? ***Snowflakes.***

Why does Santa enjoy working in the garden?
Because he likes to hoe, hoe, hoe.

What do you get if you cross Father Christmas with a detective?
Santa Clues.

What do the reindeer sing to Santa Claus on his birthday?
Freeze a jolly good fellow.

Why are Christmas trees like bad knitters?
They both drop their needles.

What Christmas carol is heard in the desert?
O Camel Ye Faithful.

What's Christmas called in England?
Yule Britannia.

What did the bald man say when he got a comb for Christmas?
Thanks, I'll never part with it.

What did the fireman's wife get for Christmas?
A ladder in her stocking.

Why does Santa's sled get such good mileage?
Because it has long-distance runners on each side.

What does Santa do with fat elves?
He sends them to an elf farm.

What do you get if you cross an apple with a Christmas tree?
A pineapple.

What do you give a train driver for Christmas?
Platform shoes.

How did Scrooge win the football game?
The ghost of Christmas passed.

What happened when the snowgirl fell out with the snowboy?
She gave him the cold shoulder.

What do snowmen wear on their heads?
Ice caps.

What do snowmen eat for lunch?
Icebergers.

Where do snowmen go to dance?
Snowballs.

What sort of ball doesn't bounce?
A snowball.

Where in a bookstore would you find books about Santa's assistants?
The elf-help section.

What's white and goes up?
A confused snowflake.

A Russian couple were walking down the street in St Petersburg one night, when the man felt a drop hit his nose.

"I think it's raining," he said to his wife.

"No, that felt more like snow to me," she replied.

"No, I'm sure it was just rain," he said.

They were about to have a major argument about whether it was raining or snowing. Just then they saw a minor communist party official walking toward them.

"Let's not fight about it," the man said. "Let's ask Comrade Rudolph whether it's officially raining or snowing."

As the official approached, the man said: "Tell us, Comrade Rudolph, is it officially raining or snowing?"

"It's raining, of course," he answered, and walked on.

But the woman insisted, "I know that felt like snow!"

To which the man quietly replied, "Rudolph the Red knows rain, dear!"

Three men died in a car accident on Christmas Eve, and they all found themselves at the pearly gates, waiting to enter heaven, where they are told they must present something relating to or associated with Christmas.

The first man searched his pocket, and found some mistletoe, so he was allowed in. The second man presented a cracker, so he, too, was allowed in. The third man pulled out a pair of ladies' stockings.

Confused at this last gesture, St Peter asked, "How do these represent Christmas?"

The man replied, "They're Carol's."

What did Adam say on the day before Christmas?
It's Christmas, Eve.

Who delivers presents to baby sharks at Christmas?
Santa Jaws.

What do angry mice send each other at Christmas?
Cross-mouse cards.

How do you make an idiot laugh on Boxing Day?
Tell him a joke on Christmas Eve.

How many chimneys does Father Christmas go down?
Stacks.

It was Christmas and the judge was in a merry mood as he asked the prisoner, "What are you charged with?"

"Doing my Christmas shopping early," replied the defendant.

"That's not an offence," said the judge. "How early were you doing this shopping?"

"Before the store opened."

Why did the boy ask for a broken drum for Christmas?
Because as a present he couldn't beat it.

A football team had just finished its daily practice session when a large turkey came strutting on to the field. While the players looked on in amusement and amazement, the turkey walked up to the head coach and demanded a tryout.

Everyone stared in silence as the turkey caught pass after pass and ran right through the defensive line. When the turkey returned to the sidelines, the coach shouted, "You're terrific! Sign up for the season and I'll make sure you get a huge bonus!"

"Forget the bonus," the turkey said. "All I want to know is, does the season go past Thanksgiving Day?"

It's the day before Thanksgiving and the butcher is just locking up when a man comes and begins pounding on the door.

"Please let me in," the man says. "I forgot to buy a turkey and my wife will kill me if I don't go home with one."

"Okay," says the butcher. "Let me see what I have left." He goes into the freezer and discovers there is just one scrawny turkey left. He brings it out to show the man.

"That one is too skinny," the man says. "What else have you got?"

The butcher takes the bird back to the freezer, waits for a few minutes, and brings the same turkey out to the man.

"Oh no," says the man. "That one doesn't look any better. I'd better take both of them."

Before going on vacation, a man phoned a seaside hotel to check on its exact location. The proprietor said, "It's only a stone's throw from the beach."

"How will I recognize it?" asked the man.

"Easy," said the proprietor. "It's the one with all the broken windows."

Two fortune-tellers were relaxing by the seaside.

"It's a lovely day," said one.

"Yes it is," agreed the other. "This sunny weather reminds me of the summer of 2016."

A man arrived at his holiday guesthouse and met the landlady.

"Can you sing?" she asked.

"No," he said.

"Well, you'd better learn quickly. There's no lock on the bathroom door."

A tourist was travelling with a guide through one of the thickest jungles in South America when he came across an ancient Mayan temple. The tourist was entranced by the temple and asked the guide for details. The guide stated that archaeologists were carrying out excavations and were still finding great treasures. The tourist then queried how old the temple was.

"This temple is 1,503 years old," replied the guide.

Impressed at this accurate dating, the tourist asked how he was able to give this precise figure.

"Easy," replied the guide. "The archaeologists said the temple was 1,500 years old and that was three years ago."

HORSES

Why did the horse cross the road?
To reach his neiggghhhbourhood.

What do you give a horse with a cold?
Cough stirrup.

What did the pony say when he had a sore throat?
Nothing, he was a little horse.

What does it mean if you find a horseshoe?
Some poor horse is walking around in his socks.

Where did the newlywed horses stay?
In the bridle suite.

Where do you take sick ponies?
To the horsepital.

How do you spell hungry horse using only four letters?
MTGG.

When does a horse neigh?
Whinny wants to.

What happens when a pony gets sunburned?
You get a little horsereddish.

What do you call a horse that likes arts and crafts?
A hobby horse.

What is the slowest horse in the world?
A clothes horse.

A miserly horseman went into a saddler's shop and asked for one spur.

"One spur?" said the saddler. "Surely you mean a pair of spurs?"

"No, just one," replied the horseman. "I figure that if I can get one side of the horse to go, the other side is bound to come with it!"

What do you call a horse that eats Indian food ?
An onion bha-gee-gee.

Why didn't the horses' parliament ever pass any legislation?
Because whatever was proposed, they always voted "neigh".

Why didn't the horse draw a cart?
Because he couldn't hold the pencil.

What did one horse say to the other?
Any friend of yours is a palomino.

What do hippie horses eat?
Hay, man.

A horse walks into a bar. The barman says, "Why the long face?"

A stallion and a mare were due to get married, but the stallion didn't turn up at the church. He got colt feet.

How does a horse ride a bicycle?
With stable-izers.

What do you call a horse that plays the violin?
Fiddler on the hoof.

Some race horses were staying in a stable. One of them started to boast about his track record. "In the last 15 races, I've won eight of them!"

Another horse broke in, "Well in the last 27 races, I've won 19!"

"Oh that's good, but in the last 36 races, I've won 28!" said another, flicking his tail.

At this point, they noticed that a greyhound had been sitting there listening. "I don't mean to boast," said the greyhound, "But in my last 90 races, I've won 88 of them!"

The horses were clearly amazed. "Wow!" said one, after a hushed silence. "A talking dog!"

What did the breeder call when his horse was possessed by an evil spirit?
An exhorsist.

What do you call a horse that is more bashful than the others?
A shire horse.

Why is a horse with a sore throat twice as sick as any other animal?
Because he is then a hoarse horse.

The thunder god went for a ride on his favourite horse.

"I'm Thor!" he cried.

The horse replied: "You forgot the thaddle, thilly."

HYENAS

A hyena and a gorilla are talking. The hyena says, "I'm fed up."

"Why's that?" asks the gorilla.

The hyena explains, "Every morning I go for a walk and this lion keeps jumping out of the undergrowth and beating me up."

"That's not very friendly," says the gorilla. "If I ever see that happen, I'll come and help you."

"Thank you," says the hyena.

The next morning, the hyena goes for his usual walk and, sure enough, the lion jumps out, beats him up and runs off. As the hyena lies writhing in agony on the ground, he looks up and sees the gorilla relaxing on the branch of a tree. "Hey," says the hyena, "you said that if you saw the lion beating me up, you'd come and help me."

"I did," says the gorilla, "but you were laughing so much I thought you were winning."

What do you get if you cross a chicken with a hyena?
A creature that laughs at every yolk.

What do you get if you cross a hyena and a Rottweiler?
I don't know, but join in if it laughs.

IDIOTS

Did you hear about the idiot that got an AM radio?
It took him a month to realize he could play it at night.

Why did the idiot scale the chain-link fence?
To see what was on the other side.

How did the idiot die drinking milk?
The cow stepped on him.

A boy walking down the street saw an old idiot sitting on the kerb holding a large sack.

"What's in the sack?" asked the boy.

"I got some pigs in that sack," said the old idiot.

The boy said, "If I can guess how many pigs there are in that sack, can I keep one?"

The old idiot replied, "Boy, if you can guess how many pigs there are in this sack, I'll give you both of 'em!"

Why did the idiot ask his friends to save their burned-out light bulbs?
He needed them for the darkroom he was building.

An idiot said to his brother, "My friend is nuts. He thinks he's Bugs Bunny, but I'm positive he isn't."

"How do you know?" asked the brother.

The idiot said, "Because I am."

An idiot was standing on the very top diving board at a swimming pool when the attendant spotted him.

"Don't dive," shouted the attendant. "There's no water in the pool!"

"That's okay," yelled the idiot. "I can't swim!"

First idiot: Can you telephone from the space shuttle?
Second idiot: Of course I can! The phone's the one with the long cord!

What did the idiot call his pet zebra?
Spot.

Billy and John Boy were fishing in a rowing boat on a lake. Suddenly the spray from a passing speedboat flooded their vessel.

"What shall we do?" asked Billy, panicking.

"Easy," said John Boy. "We just drill a hole in the bottom of the boat to allow the water to drain out."

"Genius!" said Billy.

So the two drilled a hole in the bottom of their boat, but water immediately started rushing in.

"Wait a minute!" exclaimed John Boy. "We need another hole so the water coming in through the first one has a place to go back into the lake!"

Even though it was the middle of summer, an idiot was wearing layers of thick clothes to paint the outside of his house. Seeing the sweat pouring off him, a neighbour asked, "Why are you wearing two jackets in such hot weather to paint your house?"

The idiot replied, "Because the directions on the tin said, 'Put on two coats.'"

Fred's apparent inability to arrive for work on time resulted in him being called to a disciplinary hearing where he was given a chance to explain his lack of punctuality.

He said, "I get up in the morning. I shower, I look in the mirror and try to straighten my hair. Then I sometimes miss the taxi and then I am late."

His boss had a bright idea. He got one of Fred's colleagues to sneak into his bathroom and steal the mirror off the wall, without his knowledge. However, there was no improvement – in fact things got worse. Fred failed to show up at work for the next three days and was summoned to another disciplinary hearing.

Asked why he had been absent from work, Fred explained, "I get up in the morning. I shower, I look in the mirror. I see no Fred so I think Fred must have already left for work."

How do you confuse the village idiot?
Put him in a round room and tell him to go and stand in the corner.

A motorist stopped his car and asked an idiot the quickest way to Halifax, Nova Scotia.

The idiot said, "Are you on foot or in a car?"

"In a car," replied the motorist.

"That's the quickest way," said the idiot.

How did the idiot burn his face?
Bobbing for French fries.

Two idiots were travelling on a cruise ship. One said, "It's awfully quiet on deck tonight – there's nobody around."

His friend said, "That's because everyone will be watching the band tonight."

"There isn't a band playing tonight," said the first.

The second idiot said, "Well, I definitely heard someone say, 'a band on ship'."

What Disney movie is about a stupid boyfriend?
Dumb Beau.

Three guys are stranded on a desert island. One day, they find a magic lantern containing a genie. The genie grants them each one wish.

The first guy says he wishes he was off the island and back home. The genie grants his wish and poof, he is back home.

The second guy wishes the same thing. The genie grants his wish and poof, he is gone too.

The third guy says, "I'm lonely. I wish my friends were back here."

After a visit to the circus, two idiots were discussing the various acts that they had seen.

"I didn't think much of the knife thrower," said one.

"Me neither," said his friend. "He threw all those knives at that girl and he didn't hit her once!"

Two idiot friends were sent to prison. Desperate to keep in contact, they devised a secret code and tapped messages to each other by banging on the hot water pipes with a spoon.

The system worked perfectly for a while but sadly it broke down after they were transferred to separate cells.

Did you hear about the idiot family who froze to death outside a movie theatre?

They had been queuing for three weeks to see Closed For Winter.

A motorist driving along a country lane came to a ford, so he stopped and asked an idiot sitting by the side of the road how deep the water was.

"A couple of inches," replied the idiot.

So the motorist drove into the ford and his car promptly disappeared beneath the surface in a mass of bubbles.

"That's odd," thought the idiot. "The water only goes halfway up on them ducks."

Why can't you tell knock knock jokes to idiots?
Because they leave to answer the door.

Two idiots were on the roof of a house laying tiles when a sudden gust of wind blew their ladder away.

"How are we gonna get down now?" asked one.

"I got an idea," said the other. "I'll throw you down and then you can pick up the ladder."

"Do you think I'm stupid? No, I got a better idea. I'll shine my flashlight and you can climb down on the beam of light."

"What? Do you think I'm stupid? You'll just turn off the flashlight when I'm halfway down!"

Four schoolboys were walking

down the road when they came to a high brick wall. Wondering what was behind it, three of them gave the fourth a leg up so that he could peer over the top.

"It looks like one of them nudist camps," he reported.

"Men or women?" asked the others.

"I can't tell," he said. "They ain't got no clothes on."

An idiot was pulled over by a policeman because he was zig-zagging all over the road.

The police officer asked, "What are you doing? Do you realize how dangerous your driving is?"

The idiot replied, "I swerved because there was a tree in front of me and then there was another one on the other side. They just kept appearing!"

The policeman looked into the car and said, "That is your air freshener."

First idiot: What are you doing?
Second idiot: I'm trying to call Washington!
First idiot: Oh, haven't you heard? He's dead!

Two builders were hammering nails in to the side of a house, but one kept throwing them away.

"Why do you keep throwing them nails away?" asked his fellow worker.

"Because they've got the point at the wrong end."

"You fool! We could use those on the other side of the house!"

Did you hear about the idiot hitchhiker?

He left early to miss the traffic.

Two men were digging a ditch on a very hot day.

One said to the other, "Why are we down in this hole digging a ditch when our boss is up there in the shade of a tree?"

"I don't know," replied the other. "I'll go and ask him."

So he climbed out of the hole and went to his boss. "Why are we digging in the hot sun and you're standing in the shade?" he asked.

"Intelligence," the boss said.

"What's intelligence?" asked the digger.

The boss said, "I'll show you. I'll put my hand on this tree and I want you to hit it with your fist as hard as you can."

The ditch digger took a mighty swing and tried to hit the boss's hand. The boss removed his hand and the ditch digger hit the tree.

The boss said, "That's intelligence!"

The ditch digger went back to his hole.

His friend asked, "What did he say?"

"He said we are down here because of intelligence."

"What's intelligence?" his friend asked.

The ditch digger put his hand on his face and said, "Take your shovel and hit my hand."

Why did the idiot only water half his lawn?
Because he had heard there was a fifty per cent chance of rain.

Why did the idiot give up internet shopping?
Because his shopping cart kept falling off the computer.

Fred's phone rang in the middle of the night.
"Hello?" he said.
"Hello," said a voice. "Is this Tommy?"
"No," said Fred. "You must have the wrong number."
"Oh, sorry," said the caller. "I hope I didn't wake you."
"Oh, that's okay," said Fred. "I had to get up anyway, to answer the phone!"

A stupid glazier was examining a broken window. He looked at it for a while and then said: "It's worse than I thought. It's broken on both sides."

Two idiots met in the street. "Hey!" said one. "How come I don't hear from you no more? Why don't you ever call me?"
"Because," said the other, "you ain't got a phone."
"I know," said the first, "but you have!"

Did you hear about the idiot who couldn't remember how to throw a boomerang?
Eventually it came back to him.

A man wants to cut down some trees in his back yard, so he goes to a chainsaw shop and asks about various chainsaws.

The dealer tells him, "Look, I have a lot of models, but why don't you save yourself a lot of time and aggravation and get the top-of-the-line model? This chainsaw will cut a hundred cords of wood for you in one day."

So the man takes the chainsaw home and begins working on the trees. After cutting for several hours and only cutting two cords, he decides to quit. He thinks there is something wrong with the chainsaw.

"How can I cut for hours and only cut two cords?" the man asks himself. "I will begin first thing in the morning and cut all day."

So the next day the man gets up at four in the morning and cuts and cuts and cuts till nightfall, and still he only manages to cut five cords.

The man is convinced this is a bad saw. He says to himself, "The dealer told me it would cut one hundred cords of wood in a day, no problem. I will take this saw back to the dealer."

The very next day the man

brings the saw back to the dealer and explains the problem. The dealer, baffled by the man's claim, removes the chainsaw from the case. The dealer says, "Hmm, it looks fine."

Then the dealer starts the chainsaw, to which the man responds, "What's that noise?"

What did the idiot builder say when he heard his workmates were striking for shorter hours? **Good for them! I always did think sixty minutes was too long for an hour.**

An idiot barged to the front of the line in a bank.

The teller told him abruptly, "You can't just push in, in front of all these other people who have been waiting patiently. Go to the end of the line, please."

The idiot did as he was told but a few moments later he returned to the teller's window.

"What are you doing back here?" barked the teller. "I thought I told you to go to the end of the line."

"I did," said the idiot. "But someone was already there!"

An idiot went into a watchmaker's shop and said, "I'd like to buy a potato clock, please."

"A potato clock?" queried the watchmaker. "I'm sorry, sir, but I've been in this business for over thirty years and I've never heard of such a thing."

"Well I definitely want a potato clock," confirmed the idiot.

"I don't think I can help you," said the watchmaker. "Where did you hear about it?"

The idiot replied, "I start a new job tomorrow at nine and so my wife said I had to get a potato clock."

Did you hear about the idiot mother who got fed up with putting name tags on her son's shirts? **She legally changed his name to "Machine Washable".**

An idiot was driving through California's apple country when he came to an orchard offering apples for sale.

"How much are your apples?" he asked.

"All you can pick for a dollar," replied the rancher.

"Okay," said the idiot. "I'll take two dollars' worth."

A train was going peacefully along the rail tracks until it suddenly derailed, took a brief detour into nearby fields and then came back on to the tracks. The passengers were horrified.

At the next railway station the driver was questioned by the police about the incident.

He explained that a man had been standing on the tracks and had not moved even after the train's horn had been sounded several times.

"Are you crazy?" asked the police. "Just to save the life of one person you put the lives of so many passengers in danger! You should have run over that person!"

The driver replied, "Exactly, that is what I also decided. But this idiot started running toward the field when the train got close to him..."

Why did the idiot driving in the Indianapolis 500 finish last?
He kept stopping to ask for directions.

An idiot turned up for work one day wearing only one glove.

"Why have you only got one glove?" asked his boss.

"Well," explained the idiot, "I was watching the weather forecast on TV last night, and it said that it was going to be sunny today but on the other hand it could be quite cold."

An idiotic labourer was told by an equally stupid foreman to dig a hole in the roadside.

"What shall I do with the earth?" asked the labourer.

"Use your common sense!" snapped the foreman. "Just dig another hole and bury it."

Two idiots found three hand grenades and decided that they should take them to the nearest police station.

"What if one of the grenades explodes before we get there?" asked one.

"Don't worry," said the other. "We'll just lie and tell them we only found two."

Why did the idiot have his sundial floodlit?
So he could tell the time at night.

A man was standing on his workmate's shoulders trying to measure a flagpole. Seeing their predicament, a passer-by called out, "Why don't you just take down the pole, lay it on the ground and measure it?"

"Leave it to the professionals, pal!" they shouted back. "Anyway we don't want to measure the length, we want to measure the height."

Did you hear about the stupid photographer who asked his friends to give him their burnt-out light bulbs?
He wanted to set up a dark room.

The chief of staff of the US Air Force decided that he would personally intervene in the recruiting crisis affecting the armed services. He directed a new Air Force base to invite all eligible young men and women along to the grand opening.

As he and his staff were standing near a brand new F-15 fighter, twin brothers who looked like they had just stepped off a Marine Corps recruiting poster walked up to them. The chief of staff stuck out his hand and introduced himself.

He looked at the first young man and asked, "Son, what skills can you bring to the Air Force?"

The young man looked at him and said, "Pilot."

The chief of staff excitedly turned to his aide and said, "Get him in today, all the paper work done, everything, do it!"

The aide hustled the young man away. The chief of staff looked at the second young man and asked, "What skills do you bring to the Air Force?"

The young man said, "I chop wood!"

"Son," the chief of staff replied, "we don't need wood choppers in the Air Force. What relevant skills do you have?"

"I chop wood!"

"Young man," huffed the chief of staff, "you are not listening to me! We don't need wood choppers!"

"Well," the young man said, "you hired my brother!"

"Of course we did," said the chief of staff. "He's a pilot!"

The young man rolled his eyes and said, "So what? I have to chop it before he can pile it!"

Did you hear about the idiot who was two hours late for work because the escalator got stuck?

A man bumped into his idiotic friend in the street. "How did you enjoy the play last night at the high school?"

"I saw the first act," replied the idiot, "but not the second."

"Why didn't you stay?"

"It said on the programme 'Two years later' and I couldn't wait that long."

Did you hear about the idiot who thought a fjord was a Norwegian car?

Two idiots bought a truckload of watermelons for a buck apiece. They sold each watermelon for a dollar, but after counting up their cash they realized they'd ended up with the same amount of money they'd started out with.

"See!" said one to the other. "I told you we should have got a bigger truck!"

JOBS

Why did the transplant surgeon quit his job?
His heart wasn't in it.

Why did the tailor quit his job?
He found the work to be just so-so.

Why did the doctor quit his job?
Because he lost his patience.

Why did the banker quit

his job?
He lost interest.

Why did the skydiver quit his job?
Because he fell out with his boss.

Why did the origami teacher quit his job?
Too much paperwork.

Why did the gold prospector quit his job?
It didn't pan out.

Why did the plumber quit his job?
The company was going down the drain.

Why did the man quit his job in the biscuit factory?
Because he went crackers.

Why did the man quit his job designing cul de sacs?
It was a dead-end job.

Why did the man quit his job at Starbucks?
He got sick of the daily grind.

Why did the man quit his job on the farm?
Problems kept cropping up.

Why did the milkmaid quit her job?
She lost her whey.

Why did the man quit his job at the clock company?
He had second thoughts.

Why did the number theorist quit his job?
He was past his prime.

Why did the poker player quit his job?
He was offered a better deal.

Why did the train driver quit his job?
He got sidetracked.

Why did the jockey quit his job?
Business fell off.

Why did the door designer quit his job?
He was looking for a new opening.

Why did the photographer quit his job?
The firm stopped developing.

Why did the skier quit his job?
Everything was going downhill.

Why did the steelmaker quit his job?
He lost his temper.

Why did the food taster quit his job?
He had too much on his plate.

Why did the man quit his job with the history book publisher?
There was no future in it.

Why did the man quit his job in an orange juice factory?
He couldn't concentrate.

Why did the man quit his job selling computer parts?
He lost his drive.

Why did the man quit his job making tablecloths?
The business folded.

Why did the man quit his job as a map designer?
He didn't know which way to turn.

What was Bob the Builder called after he retired?
Bob.

Why did the man quit his job at the swivel chair company?
It made his head spin.

Why did the man quit his job as a professional darts player?
He felt he was aiming too high.

Why did the man quit his job at the balloon factory?
He couldn't keep up with inflation.

Why did the man quit his job as a bell ringer?
It lost its appeal.

Why did the man quit his job as a ploughman?
He was stuck in a rut.

Why did the man quit his job at the travel agency?
It was going nowhere.

Why did the man fire his masseuse?
She rubbed him up the wrong way.

What happened to the man who tried to start a hot-air balloon business?
He couldn't get it off the ground.

Did you hear about the bumper

Why did the man quit his job at the banana company?
He kept slipping up.

car operator who got fired?
He sued his employer for funfair dismissal.

Whose career lies in ruins?
An archaeologist.

How did the hot-dog vendor tackle his new job?
With relish.

How's your job at the clock company?
Only time will tell.

How's your job at the sewing shop?
I'm hanging on by a thread.

How's your job at the crystal ball company?

I'm making a fortune.

How's your job as a shoe cleaner?
I've really taken a shine to it.

How's your job at the bakery?
I spend all day just loafing around.

How's your job as a shipbuilder?
Riveting.

An electrician came home at four in the morning.
"Wire you insulate?" his wife scolded.
"Watts it to you?" he snapped. "I'm ohm, aren't I?"

Did you hear about the man who bought a paper shop?
It blew away.

Once upon a time there was a very large office building in a very large city. This building had 40 levels: level 1, level 2, level 3, level 4, level 5, level 6, level 7, level 8, level 9, level 10, level 11, level 12, level 13, level 14, level 15, level 16, level 17, level 18, level 19, level 20, level 21, level 22, level 23, level 24, level 25, level 26, level 27, level 28, level 29, level 30, level 31, level 32, level 33, level 34, level 35, level 36, level 37, level 38, level 39, and level 40.

One day the owner of the building decided to get a PA system installed on every level, in case there was ever a fire and everyone in the building needed to be contacted at once. The system was installed on every level: level 1, level 2, level 3, level 4, level 5, level 6, level 7, level 8, level 9, level 10, level 11, level 12, level 13, level 14, level 15, level 16, level 17, level 18, level 19, level 20, level 21, level 22, level 23, level 24, level 25, level 26, level 27, level 28, level 29, level 30, level 31, level 32, level 33, level 34, level 35, level 36, level 37, level 38, level 39, and level 40.

One day, an employee named John was doing some paperwork on the 17th level when he saw the pager for the PA system in his boss's office. He could not resist. He picked up the pager, turned it on, cleared his throat, and told a joke. It was the funniest joke anyone in the building had ever heard. They were rolling in the aisles, laughing their heads off. The accountants on level 9 were in tears. The engineers on level 22 were in hysterics. Even the human resources department on level 39 enjoyed it. In fact, workers on every level – level 1, level 2, level 3, level 4, level 5, level 6, level 7, level 8, level 9, level 10, level 11, level 12, level 13, level 14, level 15, level 16, level 17, level 18, level 19, level 20, level 21, level 22, level 23, level 24, level 25, level 26, level 27, level 28, level 29, level 30, level 31, level 32, level 33, level 34, level 35, level 36, level 37, level 38, level 39, and level 40 – could not stop laughing.

He walked out the door of

his boss's office, feeling proud of himself, when who should he run into but his boss.

"John, come with me!" yelled the boss. John reluctantly followed his boss back into his office. His boss looked at him with fury in his eyes. "John," he said, "your joke was very disruptive to the workers in this building! Productivity was decreased on level 1, level 2, level 3, level 4, level 5, level 6, level 7, level 8, level 9, level 10, level 11, level 12, level 13, level 14, level 15, level 16, level 17, level 18, level 19, level 20, level 21, level 22, level 23, level 24, level 25, level 26, level 27, level 28, level 29, level 30, level 31, level 32, level 33, level 34, level 35, level 36, level 37, level 38, level 39, and level 40! You're fired! Clear your desk and get out!"

But then his frown softened and he added, "Still, I have to admit, that joke was funny on so many levels."

KANGAROOS

What did the kangaroo say when her baby went missing?
Help! My pocket's been picked!

What do you call a kangaroo at the North Pole?
Lost.

Two mother kangaroos got talking in the Australian bush.
One said to the other, "I've got seven babies in my pouch."
"Seven?" exclaimed the other in horror.
"Yes, seven! These sleepovers are killing me."

What do you get if you cross a kangaroo with a skyscraper?
A high jumper.

What do you get if you cross a kangaroo with a sheep?
A woolly jumper.

What do you get if you cross a kangaroo with a tiger?
A striped jumper.

What do you get if you cross a kangaroo with a snake?
A jump rope.

What do you get if you cross a kangaroo with an elephant?
Great big holes all over Australia.

What do you get if you cross a kangaroo with a squirrel?
An animal that carries nuts in its pocket.

What do you get if you cross a kangaroo with a lion?
A fur coat with big pockets.

What do you get if you cross a kangaroo with a chicken?
Pouched eggs.

Did you hear about the exhausted kangaroo?
He was out of bounds.

Why didn't the mother kangaroo like her baby watching too much TV?
Because she didn't want him to become a pouch potato.

Why was the mother kangaroo angry with her baby?

She caught him smoking in bed.

What did the baby kangaroo call its mother?
Ma Supial.

KNOCK KNOCK...

Knock Knock
Who's there?
Aardvark!
Aardvark who?
Aardvark a million miles for one of your smiles.

Knock Knock
Who's there?
Aaron!
Aaron who?
Aaron the barber's floor.

Knock Knock
Who's there?
Aaron!
Aaron who?
Aaron the side of caution.

Knock Knock
Who's there?
Abba!
Abba who?
Abba-out turn! Quick march!

Knock Knock
Who's there?
Abba!
Abba who?
Abba banana.

Knock Knock
Who's there?
Abbey!
Abbey who?
Abbey stung me on the nose.

Knock Knock
Who's there?
Abbott!
Abbott who?
Abbott time you opened this door!

Knock Knock
Who's there?
Abby!
Abby who?
Abby birthday to you, Abby
birthday to you...

Knock Knock
Who's there?
Abe!
Abe who?
Abe C D E F G H...

Knock Knock
Who's there?
Abel!
Abel who?
Abel to see you.

Knock Knock
Who's there?
Abel!
Abel who?
Abel seaman.

Knock Knock
Who's there?
Abyssinia!
Abyssinia who?
Abyssinia when I get back.

Knock Knock
Who's there?
Ada!
Ada who?
Ada burger for lunch.

Knock Knock
Who's there?
Adair!
Adair who?
Adair once but I'm bald now.

Knock Knock
Who's there?
Adam!
Adam who?
Adam up and tell me the total.

Knock Knock
Who's there?
Adam!
Adam who?
Adam will burst any minute now.

Knock Knock
Who's there?
Adder!
Adder who?
Adder you get in here?

Knock Knock
Who's there?
Adeline!
Adeline who?
Adeline extra to the letter.

Knock Knock
Who's there?
Adlai!
Adlai who?
Adlai a bet on that.

Knock Knock
Who's there?
Adolf!
Adolf who?
Adolf ball hit me in the mouth.

Knock Knock
Who's there?
Adore!
Adore who?
Adore stands between us, open
up!

Knock Knock
Who's there?
Aesop!
Aesop who?
Aesop I saw a puddy cat.

Knock Knock
Who's there?
Agatha!
Agatha who?
Agatha headache. Do you have an
aspirin?

Knock Knock
Who's there?
Ahab!
Ahab who?
Ahab to go to the toilet now,
quick open the door!

Knock Knock
Who's there?
Ahmed!
Ahmed who?
Ahmed a big mistake coming here.

Knock Knock
Who's there?
Aida!
Aida who?
Aida whole box of chocolate
and I feel really sick!

Knock Knock
Who's there?
Aitch!
Aitch who?
Bless you!

Knock Knock
Who's there?
Al!
Al who?
Al give you a kiss if you open
this door.

Knock Knock
Who's there?
Aladdin!
Aladdin who?
Aladdin the street wants a word
with you.

Knock Knock
Who's there?
Alan!
Alan who?
Alan a day's work.

Knock Knock
Who's there?
Albert!
Albert who?
Albert you don't know who this is!

Knock Knock
Who's there?
Albie!
Albie who?
Albie in the kitchen if you need
me.

Knock Knock
Who's there?
Alda!
Alda who?
Alda time you knew who it was.

Knock Knock
Who's there?
Aldo!
Aldo who?
Aldo anywhere with you.

Knock Knock
Who's there?
Aldous!
Aldous who?
Aldous who want to leave the
room, put your hand up.

Knock Knock
Who's there?
Alec!
Alec who?
Alec-tricity. Isn't that a shock?!

Knock Knock
Who's there?
Alec!
Alec who?
Alec coffee, but I don't like tea.

Knock Knock
Who's there?
Aled!
Aled who?
Aled the ball if you throw it
to me.

Knock Knock
Who's there?
Aleta!
Aleta who?
Aleta from the tax man.

Knock Knock
Who's there?
Aleta!
Aleta who?
Aleta bit of lovin'.

Knock Knock
Who's there?
Alex!
Alex who?
Alex Plain later.

Knock Knock
Who's there?
Alex!
Alex who?
Alex the questions round here.

Knock Knock
Who's there?
Alexander!
Alexander who?
Alexander friend are coming over.

Knock Knock
Who's there?
Alexia!
Alexia who?
Alexia again to open this door.

Knock Knock
Who's there?
Alf!
Alf who?
Alf all if you don't catch me!

Knock Knock
Who's there?
Alfalfa!
Alfalfa who?
Alfalfa you if you fall for me!

Knock Knock
Who's there?
Alfie!
Alfie who?
Alfie you in my dreams.

> Knock Knock
> Who's there?
> Alfie!
> Alfie who?
> Alfie terrible if you leave.

Knock Knock
Who's there?
Alfred!
Alfred who?
Alfred of the dark.

> Knock Knock
> Who's there?
> Alfred!
> Alfred who?
> Alfred the needle if you sew.

Knock Knock
Who's there?
Ali!
Ali who?
Ali-luyah, at last you've opened the door!

> Knock Knock
> Who's there?
> Ali!
> Ali who?
> Ali want to do is have some fun!

Knock Knock
Who's there?
Alice!
Alice who?
Alice forgiven, please come home.

Knock Knock
Who's there?
Alison!
Alison who?
Alison to you if you'll listen to me!

Knock Knock
Who's there?
Alison!
Alison who?
Alison Wonderland.

> Knock Knock
> Who's there?
> Alistair!
> Alistair who?
> Alistairs in this house are broken.

Knock Knock
Who's there?
Allied!
Allied who?
Allied, so sue me!

> Knock Knock
> Who's there?
> Alligator!
> Alligator who?
> Alligator for her birthday was a card.

Knock Knock
Who's there?
Allocate!
Allocate who?
Allocate, how are you dear?

> Knock Knock
> Who's there?
> Alma!
> Alma who?
> Alma candy's gone.

Knock Knock
Who's there?
Alma!
Alma who?
Alma not going to tell you.

Knock Knock
Who's there?
Alma!
Alma who?
Alma-ny knock knock jokes
can you take?

Knock Knock
Who's there?
Almond!
Almond who?
Almond the side of the law.

Knock Knock
Who's there?
Alpaca!
Alpaca who?
Alpaca the trunk, you pack the
suitcase.

Knock Knock
Who's there?
Althea!
Althea who?
Althea later, alligator!

Knock Knock
Who's there?
Alva!
Alva who?
Alva heart.

Knock Knock
Who's there?
Alvin!
Alvin who?
Alvin zis competition - just vait and see!

Knock Knock
Who's there?
Alvin!
Alvin who?
Alvin a great time, how about
you?

Knock Knock
Who's there?
Amahl!
Amahl who?
Amahl shook up.

Knock Knock
Who's there?
Amana!
Amana who?
Amana bad mood.

Knock Knock
Who's there?
Amanda!
Amanda who?
Amanda-rin orange.

Knock Knock
Who's there?
Amanda!
Amanda who?
Amanda the table.

Knock Knock
Who's there?
Amanda!
Amanda who?
Amanda fix the television.

Knock Knock
Who's there?
Amaso!
Amaso who?
Amaso sorry you don't
remember me.

Knock Knock
Who's there?
Amazon!
Amazon who?
Amazon of a doctor. What does
your father do?

Knock Knock
Who's there?
Amber!
Amber who?
Amber-sting to come in.

Knock Knock
Who's there?
Amelia!
Amelia who?
Amelia a package last week - did
you get it?

Knock Knock
Who's there?
Amin!
Amin who?
Amin thing to do.

Knock Knock
Who's there?
Ammon!
Ammon who?
Ammon old hand at picking locks.

Knock Knock
Who's there?
Amory!
Amory who?
Amory Christmas and a Happy
New Year!

Knock Knock
Who's there?
Amos!
Amos who?

Knock Knock
Who's there?
Ammonia!
Ammonia who?
Ammonia little boy who can't
reach the doorbell.

Amos-quito.

Knock Knock
Who's there?
Amour!
Amour who?
Amour you eat, the more you
want.

Knock Knock
Who's there?
Amsterdam!
Amsterdam who?
Amsterdam is like strawberry
jam, but made from hamsters!

Knock Knock
Who's there?
Amsterdam!

Amsterdam who?
Amsterdam hungry I could eat a horse!

> Knock Knock
> Who's there?
> Amy!
> Amy who?
> Amy for the top.

Knock Knock
Who's there?
Amy!
Amy who?
Amy fraid I've forgotten!

> Knock Knock
> Who's there?
> An author!
> An author who?
> An author joke like this and I'm off!

Knock Knock
Who's there?
Anais!
Anais who?
Anais cup of tea!

> Knock Knock
> Who's there?
> Anatole!
> Anatole who?
> Anatole me you'd keep asking questions!

Knock Knock
Who's there?
Anderson!
Anderson who?
Anderson and daughter came too.

Knock Knock
Who's there?
Andrew!
Andrew who?
Andrew all over the wall, and she's in big trouble!

Knock Knock
Who's there?
Andy!
Andy who?
Andy little gadgets to have, door knockers.

> Knock Knock
> Who's there?
> Andy!
> Andy who?
> Andy call it puppy love...

Knock Knock
Who's there?
Anita!
Anita who?
Anita you like I need a hole in the head!

> Knock Knock
> Who's there?
> Anita!
> Anita who?
> Anita use your bathroom!

Knock Knock
Who's there?
Anka!
Anka who?
Anka the ship.

> Knock Knock
> Who's there?
> Ann!
> Ann who?
> Ann-onymous.

Knock Knock
Who's there?
Ann!
Ann who?
Ann Tarctic.

> Knock Knock
> Who's there?
> Anna!
> Anna who?
> Anna-ther brick in the wall.

Knock Knock
Who's there?
Anna!
Anna who?
Anna other thing, how many times
do I have to knock on this door
before you open it?

> Knock Knock
> Who's there?
> Annabel!
> Annabel who?
> Annabel would be useful on
> this door.

Knock Knock
Who's there?
Anne!
Anne who?
Anne apple just fell on my head.

> Knock Knock
> Who's there?
> Anne Dover!
> Anne Dover who?
> Anne Dover your money!

Knock Knock
Who's there?
Annetta!
Annetta who?

Annetta joke like that and I'll never
visit you again!

> Knock Knock
> Who's there?
> Annette!
> Annette who?
> Annette curtain looks good in
> the window.

Knock Knock
Who's there?
Annie!
Annie who?
Annie-versary.

> Knock Knock
> Who's there?
> Annie!
> Annie who?
> Annie one you like!

Knock Knock
Who's there?
Anya!
Anya who?
Anya best behaviour.

> Knock Knock
> Who's there?
> Apple!
> Apple who?
> Apple your hair if you don't let
> me in!

Knock Knock
Who's there?
Arbus!
Arbus who?
Arbus leaves in five minutes.

> Knock Knock
> Who's there?

Arch!
Arch who?
Sounds like you've got the flu!

Knock Knock
Who's there?
Aretha!
Aretha who?
Aretha flowers.

Knock Knock
Who's there?
Argo!
Argo who?
Argo down to the shops.

Knock Knock
Who's there?
Aries!
Aries who?
Aries a reason why I talk this way.

Knock Knock
Who's there?
Arizona!
Arizona who?
Arizona room for one of us in
this town.

Knock Knock
Who's there?
Armageddon!
Armageddon who?
Armageddon out of here!

Knock Knock
Who's there?
Armenia!
Armenia who?
Armenia every word I say.

Knock Knock
Who's there?

Arnie!
Arnie who!
Arnie body home?

Knock Knock
Who's there?
Arnold!
Arnold who?
Arnold friend you haven't seen
for years.

Knock Knock
Who's there?
Arthur!
Arthur who?
Arthur-t you weren't home.

Knock Knock
Who's there?
Arthur!
Arthur who?
Arthur-mometer is good for
measuring the temperature.

Knock Knock
Who's there?
Arthur!
Arthur who?
Arthur any more biscuits in the jar?

Knock Knock
Who's there?
Artichoke!
Artichoke who?
Artichoked when he
swallowed his yo-yo.

Knock Knock
Who's there?
Asia!
Asia who?
Asia sister in?

Knock Knock
Who's there?
Asia!
Asia who?
Asia matter of fact I can't
remember!

Knock Knock
Who's there?
Athena!
Athena who?
Athena reindeer landing on your
roof!

Knock Knock
Who's there?
Atlas!
Atlas who?
Atlas it's the weekend!

Knock Knock
Who's there?
Attila!
Attila who?
Attila no lies!

Knock Knock
Who's there?
Augusta!
Augusta who?
Augusta wind will blow the
house away.

Knock Knock
Who's there?
Aunt Lou!
Aunt Lou who?
Aunt Lou tired of answering this
door?

Knock Knock
Who's there?
Aurora!

Aurora who?
Aurora's just come from a
big tiger.

Knock Knock
Who's there?
Austin!
Austin who?
Austin corrected.

Knock Knock
Who's there?
Auto!
Auto who?
Auto know, but I've forgotten!

Knock Knock
Who's there?
Ava!
Ava who?
Ava good mind to go away now.

Knock Knock
Who's there?
Avenue!
Avenue who?
Avenue learned my name yet?

Knock Knock
Who's there?
Avery!
Avery who?
Avery time I come to your house
we go through this!

Knock Knock
Who's there?
Avon!
Avon who?
Avon you to come and open
this door!

Knock Knock
Who's there?

ACHOO!

Knock Knock
Who's there?
Avocado!
Avocado who?
Avocado cold.

Avon!
Avon who?
Avon to get in!

Knock Knock
Who's there?
Axl!
Axl who?
Axl me nicely and I might just tell you!

Knock Knock
Who's there?
Ayatollah!
Ayatollah who?
Ayatollah you already!

Knock Knock
Who's there?
Bab!
Bab who?
Bab Boon is a real ape.

Knock Knock
Who's there?
Baby Owl!
Baby Owl who?
Baby Owl see you later, maybe I won't.

Knock Knock
Who's there?
Bach!
Bach who?
Bach to school.

Knock Knock
Who's there?
Bacon!
Bacon who?
Bacon a cake for your birthday.

Knock Knock
Who's there?
Baloney!
Baloney who?
Baloney chase you if you're a matador.

Knock Knock
Who's there?
Banana!
Banana who?
Banana split so ice creamed.

Knock knock
Who's there?
Banana!
Banana who?
Knock knock
Who's there?
Banana!
Banana who?
Knock knock
Who's there?

Orange!
Orange who?
Orange you glad I didn't say banana?

Knock Knock
Who's there?
Barack!
Barack who?
Barack-uda bit off my fingers when I went fishing.

Knock Knock
Who's there?
Barack!
Barack who?
Baracks are where soldiers live.

Knock Knock
Who's there?
Barbara!
Barbara who?
Barbara black sheep, have you any wool?

Knock Knock
Who's there?
Bark!
Bark who?
Bark your car on the drive.

Knock Knock
Who's there?
Baron!
Baron who?
Baron mind who you're talking to.

Knock Knock
Who's there?
Barry!
Barry who?
Barry the treasure where no one will find it.

Knock Knock
Who's there?
Bart!
Bart who?
Bart-enders serve drinks!

Knock Knock
Who's there?
Bashful!
Bashful who?
I can't tell you, I'm so embarrassed.

Knock Knock
Who's there?
Bat!
Bat who?
Bat you'll never guess!

Knock Knock
Who's there?
Bea!
Bea who?
Bea-cause I'm worth it.

Knock Knock
Who's there?
Bea!
Bea who?
Bea-t your head against a wall.

Knock Knock
Who's there?
Bean!
Bean who?
Bean working very hard today.

Knock Knock
Who's there?
Beaver E!
Beaver E who?

Beaver E quiet and nobody will find us.

Knock Knock
Who's there?
Becca!
Becca who?
Becca the bus is the best place to sit.

Knock Knock
Who's there?
Beck!
Beck who?
Beck-fast of champions.

Knock Knock
Who's there?
Bee!
Bee who?
Bee quiet.

Knock Knock
Who's there?
Beets!
Beets who?
Beets me, but I just forgot the joke.

Knock Knock
Who's there?
Beezer!
Beezer who?
Beezer black and yellow and make honey.

Knock Knock
Who's there?
Beggar!
Beggar who?
Beggar you don't know.

Knock Knock
Who's there?
Beirut!
Beirut who?
Beirut force.

Knock Knock
Who's there?
Belinda!
Belinda who?
Belinda church steeple.

Knock Knock
Who's there?
Belize!
Belize who?
Belize yourself then.

Knock Knock
Who's there?
Bella!
Bella who?
Bella bottom trousers.

Knock Knock
Who's there?
Bella!
Bella who?
Bella the ball.

Knock Knock
Who's there?
Bella!
Bella who?
Bella not work so I knock on the door.

Knock Knock
Who's there?
Bellows!
Bellows who?
Bellows me some money, can I have it please?

Knock Knock
Who's there?
Ben!
Ben who?
Ben knocking on this door all morning.

Knock Knock
Who's there?
Ben and Anna!
Ben and Anna who?
Ben and Anna split.

Knock Knock
Who's there?
Ben Hur!
Ben Hur who?
Ben Hur an hour – let me in!

Knock Knock
Who's there?
Benjamin!
Benjamin who?
Benjamin the blues.

Knock Knock
Who's there?
Benny!
Benny who?

Benny thing happening?

Knock Knock
Who's there?
Bera!
Bera who?
Bera necessity.

Knock Knock
Who's there?
Berlin!
Berlin who?
Berlin the water for my hard-boiled eggs.

Knock Knock
Who's there?
Bernadette!
Bernadette who?
Bernadette all my dinner and now I'm starving.

Knock Knock
Who's there?
Bertha!
Bertha who?
Bertha-day greetings.

Knock Knock
Who's there?
Bet!
Bet who?
Bet you don't know who's knocking on your door!

Knock Knock
Who's there?
Beth!
Beth who?
Beth wisheth, thweetie.

Knock Knock
Who's there?

Bethany!
Bethany who?
Bethany thing you like you
weren't expecting me!

Knock Knock
Who's there?
Bettina!
Bettina who?
Bettina minute you'll open this door.

Knock Knock
Who's there?
Betty!
Betty who?
Betty doesn't know who I am!

Knock Knock
Who's there?
Betty!
Betty who?
Betty things to do than stand here,
you know!

Knock Knock
Who's there?
Bhuton!
Bhuton who?
Bhuton the other foot.

Knock Knock
Who's there?
Bill!
Bill who?
Bill a better mousetrap and you'll
catch more mice.

Knock Knock
Who's there?
Bingo!
Bingo who?
Bingo-ing to come and see
you for ages.

Knock Knock
Who's there?
Bjork!
Bjork who?
Bjork in the USSR.

Knock Knock
Who's there?
Bjorn!
Bjorn who?
Bjorn in the USA.

Knock Knock
Who's there?
Bless!
Bless who?
I didn't sneeze.

Knock Knock
Who's there?
Blue!
Blue who?
Blue away with the wind.

Knock Knock
Who's there?
Blur!
Blur who?
Blur, it's cold and wet out here!

Knock Knock
Who's there?
Bolivia!
Bolivia who?
Bolivia me, I know what I'm
talking about.

Knock Knock
Who's there?
Boo!
Boo who?
Don't cry, it's only a joke!

Knock Knock
Who's there?
Boris!
Boris who?
Boris with more knock knock
jokes.

Knock Knock
Who's there?
Brad!
Brad who?
Brad news I'm afraid.

Knock Knock
Who's there?
Brazil!
Brazil who?
Brazil support a woman's
chest.

Knock Knock
Who's there?
Brendan!
Brendan who?
Brendan an ear to what I have
to say.

Knock Knock
Who's there?
Bride!
Bride who?
Bride and Prejudice.

Knock Knock
Who's there?
Bryn!
Bryn who?
Bryn waiting for you to answer the
door.

Knock Knock
Who's there?
Buckle!

Buckle who?
Buckle get you a drink but not
much else.

Knock Knock
Who's there?
Bud!
Bud who?
Bud, sweat and tears.

Knock Knock
Who's there?
Buddha!
Buddha who?
Buddha this slice of bread
for me.

Knock Knock
Who's there?
Buddy!
Buddy who?
Buddy-fingers.

Knock Knock
Who's there?
Bullet!
Bullet who?
Bullet all the hay and now he's got nowhere to sleep.

Knock Knock
Who's there?
Bunny!
Bunny who?
Bunny thing is, I've forgotten now!

Knock Knock
Who's there?
Burton!
Burton who?
Burton the hand is worth two in the bush.

Knock Knock
Who's there?
Buster!
Buster who?
Buster tire, can I use your phone?

Knock Knock
Who's there?
Buster!
Buster who?
Buster the leisure centre, please.

Knock Knock
Who's there?
Butch!
Butch who?
Butch your arms around me.

Knock Knock
Who's there?
Butcher!
Butcher who?

Butcher left leg in, your left leg out...

Knock Knock
Who's there?
Butter!
Butter who?
Butter bring an umbrella, it looks like it might rain.

Knock Knock
Who's there?
Button!
Button who?
Button in is not polite.

Knock Knock
Who's there?
Byron!
Byron who?
Byron a new suit.

Knock Knock
Who's there?
Caesar!
Caesar who?
Caesar quickly before she gets away!

Knock Knock
Who's there?
Caesar!
Caesar who?
Caesar jolly good fellow!

Knock Knock
Who's there?
Cain!
Cain who?
Cain you tell?

Knock Knock
Who's there?

Caitlin!
Caitlin who?
Caitlin you my trainers tonight, I'm wearing them.

Knock Knock
Who's there?
Callas!
Callas who?
Callas should be removed by a chiropodist.

Knock Knock
Who's there?
Candice!
Candice who?
Candice get any better?

Knock Knock
Who's there?
Candice!
Candice who?
Candice taste real good.

Knock Knock
Who's there?
Candy!
Candy who?
Candy cow jump over the moon?

Knock Knock
Who's there?
Cannelloni!
Cannelloni who?
Cannelloni some money until next week?

Knock Knock
Who's there?
Canoe!
Canoe who?
Canoe open this door?

Knock Knock
Who's there?
Canon!
Canon who?
Canon open the door then!

Knock Knock
Who's there?
Cantaloupe!
Cantaloupe who?
Cantaloupe with you tonight!

Knock Knock
Who's there?
Canter!
Canter who?
Canter sister come out to play?

Knock Knock
Who's there?
Cargo!
Cargo who?
Cargo beep beep!

Knock Knock
Who's there?
Carl!
Carl who?
Carl get you there quicker than if you walk.

Knock Knock
Who's there?
Carlene!
Carlene who?
Carlene against that wall?

Knock Knock
Who's there?
Carlo!
Carlo who?
Carlo-ad of junk.

Knock Knock
Who's there?
Carlo!
Carlo who?
Carlo because the jack ain't
working.

> Knock Knock
> Who's there?
> Carlotta!
> Carlotta who?
> Carlotta trouble when it breaks
> down.

Knock Knock
Who's there?
Carmen!
Carmen who?
Carmen get it!

Knock Knock
Who's there?
Cassette!
Cassette who?
*Cassette your dinner, I'm
sorry.*

Knock Knock
Who's there?
Carol!
Carol who?
Carol go if you turn the ignition
key.

Knock Knock

Who's there?
Carrie!
Carrie who?
Carrie the bags into the house please.

> Knock Knock
> Who's there?
> Cash!
> Cash who?
> I didn't realize you were some
> kind of nut!

Knock Knock
Who's there?
Cassie!
Cassie who?
Cassie the wood for the trees.

> Knock Knock
> Who's there?
> Cat!
> Cat who?
> Cat you just open this door?

Knock Knock
Who's there?
Catsup!
Catsup who?
Catsup on the roof, do you want
me to go and fetch him?

Knock Knock
Who's there?
Cattle!

Cattle who?
Cattle always purr when you stroke her.

Knock Knock
Who's there?
Cauliflower!
Cauliflower who?
Cauliflower by any other name and it's still a daisy.

Knock Knock
Who's there?
Cecile!
Cecile who?
Cecile the windows. There's a monster out there!

Knock Knock
Who's there?
Celeste!
Celeste who?
Celeste time I lend you money.

Knock Knock
Who's there?
Cellar!
Cellar who?
Cellar car, it can't be repaired.

Knock Knock
Who's there?
Chad!
Chad who?
Chad to make your acquaintance.

Knock Knock
Who's there?
Chair!
Chair who?
Chair you go again, asking more questions!

Knock Knock
Who's there?
Checkmate!
Checkmate who?
Checkmate bounce if you don't have money in the bank.

Knock Knock
Who's there?
Cheese!
Cheese who?
Cheese a jolly good fellow.

Knock Knock
Who's there?
Cherry!
Cherry who?
Cherry-o, see you later!

Knock Knock
Who's there?
Chest!
Chest who?
Chest-nuts for sale.

Knock Knock
Who's there?
Chester!
Chester who?
Chester minute, don't you recognize me?

Knock Knock
Who's there?
Chesterfield!
Chesterfield who?
Chesterfield full of cows, nothing else.

Knock Knock
Who's there?
Chesterfield!
Chesterfield who?

Chesterfield my leg so I
slapped him!

Knock Knock
Who's there?
Chicken!
Chicken who?
Chicken your
pockets, I think your
keys are there.

Knock Knock
Who's there?
Chile!
Chile who?
Chile out tonight.

Knock Knock
Who's there?
Chloe!
Chloe who?
Chloe Encounters of the
Third Kind.

Knock Knock
Who's there?
Choc-ice!
Choc-ice who?
Choc-ice into this glass would
you please?

Knock Knock
Who's there?
Chocs!
Chocs who?
Chocs away!

Knock Knock
Who's there?
Chuck!
Chuck who?
Chuck and see if the door is
locked.

Knock Knock
Who's there?
Claudette!
Claudette who?
Claudette a whole cake.

Knock Knock
Who's there?
Chopin!
Chopin who?
Chopin at the supermarket.

Knock Knock
Who's there?
Chow Mein!
Chow Mein who?
Chow Mein to meet you
my dear!

Knock Knock
Who's there?
Chuck!
Chuck who?
Chuck in a sandwich for lunch.

Knock Knock
Who's there?
Churchill!
Churchill who?
Churchill be the best place for
a wedding.

Knock Knock
Who's there?
Cindy!
Cindy who?
Cindy next one in please.

Knock Knock
Who's there?
Clara!
Clara who?
Clara space on the table.

Knock Knock
Who's there?
Clare!
Clare who?
Clare your throat before you
speak.

Knock Knock
Who's there?
Clarence!
Clarence who?
Clarence sale.

Knock Knock
Who's there?
Clarkson!
Clarkson who?
Clarkson watches tell the time.

Knock Knock
Who's there?
Clive!
Clive who?
Clive every mountain, ford every
stream.

Knock Knock
Who's there?
Closure!
Closure who?
Closure mouth when you eat.

Knock Knock
Who's there?
Clothesline!
Clothesline who?
Clothesline all over the floor end
up creased.

Knock Knock
Who's there?
Cod!
Cod who?
Cod red-handed.

Knock Knock
Who's there?
Cohen!
Cohen who?
Cohen the back door please.

Knock Knock
Who's there?
Colin!
Colin who?
Colin and see me on your
way home.

Knock Knock
Who's there?
Colleen!
Colleen who?
Colleen up your room, it's filthy.

Knock Knock
Who's there?
Cologne!
Cologne who?
Cologne Ranger.

Knock Knock
Who's there?
Cole!
Cole who?
Cole as a cucumber.

Knock Knock
Who's there?
Comb!
Comb who?
Comb on down and I'll tell you.

Knock Knock
Who's there?
Conan!
Conan who?
Conan wafers go well with
ice cream.

Knock Knock
Who's there?
Conga!
Conga who?
Conga on meeting like this.

Knock Knock
Who's there?
Constance Norah!
Constance Norah who?
Constance Norah makes it
difficult to sleep.

Knock Knock
Who's there?
Consumption!
Consumption who?
Consumption be done about all
these knock knock jokes?

Knock Knock
Who's there?
Cook!
Cook who?
I didn't know you were a bird!

Knock Knock
Who's there?
Cousin!
Cousin who?

Cousin stead of opening the door
I'm still stood here!

Knock Knock
Who's there?
Cosmo!
Cosmo who?
Cosmo trouble than you're
worth.

Knock Knock
Who's there?
Courtney!
Courtney who?
Courtney criminals recently?

Knock Knock
Who's there?
Courtney Pine!
Courtney Pine who?
Courtney Pine tables, I need a
new one!

Knock Knock
Who's there?
Cornflakes.
Cornflakes who?
I'll tell you next year, it's a serial...

Knock Knock
Who's there?
Cows go!
Cows go who?
Cows go moo not who!

Knock Knock
Who's there?
Cynthia!
Cynthia who?
Cynthia been away I missed you.

Knock Knock
Who's there?

Cupid!
Cupid who?
Cupid quiet in there.

Knock Knock
Who's there?
Cymbals!
Cymbals who?
Cymbals have horns and
others don't.

Knock Knock
Who's there?
Custer!
Custer who?
Custer a penny to find out.

Knock Knock
Who's there?
Crispin!
Crispin who?
Crispin crunchy is how I like
my apples.

Knock Knock
Who's there?
Cyril!
Cyril who?
Cyril pleasure to meet you
again.

Knock Knock
Who's there?
Czech!
Czech who?
Czech before you open the door!

Knock Knock
Who's there?
Daisy!
Daisy who?
Daisy plays, nights he sleeps.

Knock Knock
Who's there?
Dakota!
Dakota who?
Dakota is too long in the
arms.

Knock Knock
Who's there?
Dale!
Dale who?
Dale come if you ask them.

Knock Knock
Who's there?
Dana!
Dana who?
Dana talk with your mouth full.

183

Knock Knock
Who's there?
Dancer!
Dancer who?
Dancer is simple, it's me!

Knock Knock
Who's there?
Danielle!
Danielle who?
Danielle so loud, I heard you the
first time!

Knock Knock
Who's there?
Danny!
Danny who?
Danny-body home?

Knock Knock
Who's there?
Danzig!
Danzig who?
Danzig in the streets.

Knock Knock
Who's there?
Darius!
Darius who?
Darius a lot I have to tell you.

Knock Knock
Who's there?
Darren!
Darren who?
Darren people go skydiving.

Knock Knock
Who's there?
Daryl!
Daryl who?
Daryl never be another you.

Knock Knock
Who's there?
Datsun!
Datsun who?
Datsun old joke.

Knock Knock
Who's there?
Daughter!
Daughter who?
Daughter be a law against
such bad jokes!

Knock Knock
Who's there?
Dave!
Dave who?
Dave-andalised our home!

Knock Knock
Who's there?
David!
David who?
David the doorbell, so I had to
knock.

Knock Knock
Who's there?
Dawn!
Dawn who?
Dawn leave me out here in the
cold.

Knock Knock
Who's there?
Deanna!
Deanna who?
Deanna-mals are restless so
open the cage.

Knock Knock
Who's there?
Deanne!

Deanne who?
Deanne-swer my friend, is blowin'
in the wind.

> Knock Knock
> Who's there?
> Debbie!
> Debbie who?
> Debbie or not to be, that is the
> question!

Knock Knock
Who's there?
Deceit!
Deceit who?
Deceit of your trousers looks wet.

> Knock Knock
> Who's there?
> Dee!
> Dee who?
> Dee doorbell doesn't appear
> to be working.

Knock Knock
Who's there?
Deepak!
Deepak who?
Deepak of cookies is in the jar.

> Knock Knock
> Who's there?
> Delia!
> Delia who?
> Delia cards and we'll play
> snap.

Knock Knock
Who's there?
Della!
Della who?
Della-catessen.

Knock Knock
Who's there?
Delores!
Delores who?
Delores is on the side of the
good guys.

Knock Knock
Who's there?
Delta!
Delta who?
Delta great hand of cards.

> Knock Knock
> Who's there?
> Demi!
> Demi who?
> Demi why, I don't like
> Mondays.

Knock Knock
Who's there?
De Niro!
De Niro who?
De Niro I am to you, the more I
like you.

> Knock Knock
> Who's there?
> Denise!
> Denise who?
> Denise are above your ankles.

Knock Knock
Who's there?
Dennis!
Dennis who?
Dennis must be the right house?

> Knock Knock
> Who's there?
> Dennis!
> Dennis who?

Dennis says I need to have a tooth out.

Knock Knock
Who's there?
Dennis!
Dennis who?
Dennis anyone?

Knock Knock
Who's there?
Depp!
Depp who?
Depp inside.

Knock Knock
Who's there?
Derek!
Derek who?
Derek of the ship is a big tourist attraction.

Knock Knock
Who's there?
Dermot!
Dermot who?
Dermot may be a way to get you to open this door.

Knock Knock
Who's there?
Des!
Des who?
Des no bell, that's why I'm knocking.

Knock Knock
Who's there?
Dewey!
Dewey who?
Dewey have to keep saying all these jokes?

Knock Knock
Who's there?
Devlin!
Devlin who?
Devlin a red dress.

Knock Knock
Who's there?
Desiree!
Desiree who?
Desiree of sunshine in my life.

Knock Knock
Who's there?
Di!
Di who?
Di Laffin.

Knock Knock
Who's there?
Diana!
Diana who?
Diana thirst, can I have some water please?

Knock Knock
Who's there?
Diego!
Diego who?
Diego before the B in the alphabet.

Knock Knock
Who's there?
Diesel!
Diesel who?
Diesel make you feel better.

Knock Knock
Who's there?
Dill!
Dill who?
Dill we meet again.

Knock Knock
Who's there?
DiMaggio!
DiMaggio who?
DiMaggio yourself on a
desert island.

Knock Knock
Who's there?
Dinah!
Dinah who?
Dinah is served.

Knock Knock
Who's there?
Dino!
Dino who?
Dino the answer?

Knock Knock
Who's there?
Dion!
Dion who?
Dion to come out and play?

Knock Knock
Who's there?
Diploma!
Diploma who?
Diploma to fix the leak.

Knock Knock
Who's there?
Disaster!
Disaster who?
Disaster be my lucky day.

Knock Knock
Who's there?
Disguise!
Disguise who?
Disguise killing me with all these
jokes!

Knock Knock
Who's there?
Dinosaur!
Dinosaur who?
Dinosaur you at the bus stop.

Knock Knock
Who's there?
Disguise!
Disguise who?
Disguise the limit!

Knock Knock
Who's there?
Dishes!
Dishes who?
Dishes your friend, so open the
door!

Knock Knock
Who's there?
Dishwasher!
Dishwasher who?
Dishwasher the way I spoke
before I had false teeth!

Knock Knock
Who's there?
Dismay!
Dismay who?
Dismay be a joke but it doesn't
make me laugh.

Knock Knock
Who's there?
Disney!
Disney who?
Disney make sense.

Knock Knock
Who's there?
Distress!
Distress who?
Distress is brand new.

Knock Knock
Who's there?
Doctor!
Doctor who?
That's right, have you seen my
Tardis?

Knock Knock
Who's there?
Don!
Don who?
Don just stand there, let me in!

Knock Knock
Who's there?
Don Harris!
Don Harris who?
Don Harris me or I won't
come again.

Knock Knock
Who's there?
Donalette!
Donalette who?

Donalette the grass grow under
your feet.

Knock Knock
Who's there?
Donatello!
Donatello who?
Donatello-n me.

Knock Knock
Who's there?
Don Giovanni!
Don Giovanni who?
Don Giovanni talk to me?

Knock Knock
Who's there?
Don Juan!
Don Juan who?
Don Juan to stay out here
forever!

Knock Knock
Who's there?
Donna!
Donna who?
Donna you wanna answer the door?

Knock Knock
Who's there?
Donovan!
Donovan who?
Donovan the door - it's
dangerous!

Knock Knock
Who's there?
Donovan!
Donovan who?
Donovan know your own name!

Knock Knock
Who's there?

Doris!
Doris who?
Doris dropping off its hinges
with all this knocking.

Knock Knock
Who's there?
Dorrie!
Dorrie who?
Dorrie I upset you!

Knock Knock
Who's there?
Doug!
Doug who?
Doug good deeds and you'll
go to heaven.

Knock Knock
Who's there?
Doughnut!
Doughnut who?
Doughnut open the door whatever
you do.

Knock Knock
Who's there?
Douglas!
Douglas who?
Douglas is broken in the
window.

Knock Knock
Who's there?
Dozen!
Dozen who?
Dozen anyone ever answer
the door?

Knock Knock
Who's there?
Dragon!
Dragon who?

Dragon your feet will ruin
your shoes.

Knock Knock
Who's there?
Drew!
Drew who?
Drew you remember the last time
we met?

Knock Knock
Who's there?
Drew!
Drew who?
Drew you a picture while I was
waiting for you to answer
the door.

Knock Knock
Who's there?
Duane!
Duane who?
Duane the bath, I'm dwowning!

Knock Knock
Who's there?
Dublin!
Dublin who?
Dublin up with laughter.

Knock Knock
Who's there?
Duke!
Duke who?
Duke come here often?

Knock Knock
Who's there?
Dumbbell!
Dumbbell who?
Dumbbell doesn't work so I
had to knock.

Knock Knock
Who's there?
Dummy!
Dummy who?
Dummy a favour and go away.

Knock Knock
Who's there?
Duncan!
Duncan who?
Duncan disorderly.

Knock Knock
Who's there?
Duncan!
Duncan who?
Duncan biscuits in your coffee.

Knock Knock
Who's there?
Dunce!
Dunce who?
Dunce-ay another word.

Knock Knock
Who's there?
Dwayne!
Dwayne who?
Dwayne in Spain falls mainly on
the plain.

Knock Knock
Who's there?
Dwight!
Dwight who?
Dwight way and the wrong way.

Knock Knock
Who's there?
Dynamite!
Dynamite who?
Dynamite come out and play if you
ask her nicely.

Knock Knock
Who's there?
Eamonn!
Eamonn who?
Eamonn in the mood for love!

Knock Knock
Who's there?
Ear!
Ear who?
Ear you are, I've been looking
for you.

Knock Knock
Who's there?
Earl!
Earl who?
Earl be glad when you open
this door!

Knock Knock
Who's there?
Ears!
Ears who?
Ears looking at you, kid!

Knock Knock
Who's there?
Edna!
Edna who?
Edna clouds.

Knock Knock
Who's there?
Ed!
Ed who?
Ed like you to let me in now
please.

Knock Knock
Who's there?
Eddie!
Eddie who?
Eddie-body home?

Knock Knock
Who's there?
Edith!
Edith who?
Edith chicken soup, it'll make
you feel better if you have a
cold!

Knock Knock
Who's there?
Edwin!
Edwin who?
Edwin some, Ed lose some.

Knock Knock
Who's there?
Eel!
Eel who?
Eel meet again.

Knock Knock
Who's there?
Effie!
Effie who?
Effie'd known you were coming
he'd have stayed at home.

Knock Knock
Who's there?
Egbert!

Egbert who?
Egbert no bacon please.

Knock Knock
Who's there?
Egg!
Egg who?
Egg-stremely cold waiting for you
to open the door!

Knock Knock
Who's there?
Egypt!
Egypt who?
Egypt a bit off my best china
plate.

Knock Knock
Who's there?
Eight!
Eight who?
Eight me out of house and home.

Knock Knock
Who's there?
Eileen!
Eileen who?
Eileen over backwards to make
you happy.

Knock Knock
Who's there?
Eileen Don!
Eileen Don who?
Eileen Don your bell and broke it.

Knock Knock
Who's there?
Edward!
Edward who?
Edward like to meet you
outside the bus station in half
an hour.

Knock Knock
Who's there?
Eisenhower!
Eisenhower who?
Eisenhower late for school this
morning.

Knock Knock
Who's there?
Elaine!
Elaine who?
Elaine of the freeway.

Knock Knock
Who's there?
Element!
Element who?
Element to tell you that she
can't see you today.

Knock Knock
Who's there?
Elephant!
Elephant who?
Elephant a sizes about being a
Hollywood star!

Knock Knock
Who's there?
Elias!
Elias who?
Elias a terrible thing.

Knock Knock
Who's there?
Eliza!
Eliza who?
Eliza wake at night thinking about
this door.

Knock Knock
Who's there?
Elizabeth!

Elizabeth who?
Elizabeth of knowledge is a
dangerous thing.

Knock Knock
Who's there?
Ella!
Ella who?
Ella-vator. Doesn't that give you
a lift?

Knock Knock
Who's there?
Ella Mann!
Ella Mann who?
Ella Mann-tary, my dear
Watson!

Knock Knock
Who's there?
Ellen!
Ellen who?
Ellen-t you some money, can I have
it back?

Knock Knock
Who's there?
Ellie!
Ellie who?
Ellie Phants never forget!

Knock Knock
Who's there?
Ellis!
Ellis who?
Ellis before M in the alphabet.

Knock Knock
Who's there?
Elsie!
Elsie who?
Elsie you later.

Knock Knock
Who's there?
Elton!
Elton who?
Elton old lady to cross
he road.

Knock Knock
Who's there?
Elvis!
Elvis who?
Elvis-eeing you around soon.

Knock Knock
Who's there?
Emile!
Emile who?
Emile fit for a king.

Knock Knock
Who's there?
Emma!
Emma who?
Emma new neighbour – come
round for tea.

Knock Knock
Who's there?
Emma Dunne!
Emma Dunne who?
Emma Dunne talking to you, I
have to go.

Knock Knock
Who's there?
Emma Freud!
Emma Freud who?
Emma Freud I'll have to ask you to
accompany me to the station.

Knock Knock
Who's there?
Emmanuelle!

Emmanuelle who?
Emmanuelle is what I need to
programme my video.

Knock Knock
Who's there?
Emmett!
Emmett who?
Emmett the back door, not
the front.

Knock Knock
Who's there?
Enid!
Enid who?
Enid some more pocket
money.

Knock Knock
Who's there?
Enoch!
Enoch who?
Enoch and Enoch but no one
answers the door.

Knock Knock
Who's there?
Erda!
Erda who?
Erda room please, it's stuffy.

Knock Knock
Who's there?
Erica!
Erica who?
Erica-d the last sweet.

Knock Knock
Who's there?
Erin!
Erin who?
Erin your lungs.

Knock Knock
Who's there?
Erna!
Erna who?
Erna living.

Knock Knock
Who's there?
Ernie!
Ernie who?
Ernie plenty of money, are you?

Knock Knock
Who's there?
Eryl!
Eryl who?
Eryl shame you didn't answer the
door earlier.

Knock Knock
Who's there?
Eskimo!
Eskimo who?
Eskimo questions and I'll tell
you no lies!

Knock Knock
Who's there?
Esme!
Esme who?
Esme shirt tucked in properly?

Knock Knock
Who's there?
Essen!
Essen who?
Essen it fun to listen to these
jokes?

Knock Knock
Who's there?
Esther!
Esther who?

Esther anything I can do for you?

Knock Knock
Who's there?
Esther!
Esther who?
Esther bunny.

Knock Knock
Who's there?
Ethan!
Ethan who?
Ethan me out of house and home.

Knock Knock
Who's there?
Etta!
Etta who?
Etta way to do it!

Knock Knock
Who's there?
Eugene!
Eugene who?
Eugene, me Tarzan!

Knock Knock
Who's there?
Eugenie!
Eugenie who?
Eugenie from the bottle who
will grant me three wishes?

Knock Knock
Who's there?
Euripedes!
Euripedes who?
Euripedes trousers and you'll pay
for a new pair.

Knock Knock
Who's there?
Europe.

Europe who?
Haha, so are you!

Knock Knock
Who's there?
Europe!
Europe who?
Europe-ning the door too slowly,
hurry up!

> Knock Knock
> Who's there?
> Europe!
> Europe who?
> Europe early this morning.

Knock Knock
Who's there?
Eva!
Eva who?
Eva you're deaf or your doorbell
isn't working.

> Knock Knock
> Who's there?
> Evadne!
> Evadne who?
> Evadne snails to eat? They're
> horrible.

Knock Knock
Who's there?
Evan!
Evan who?
Evan't you heard of answering the
door?

> Knock Knock
> Who's there?
> Evan!
> Evan who?
> Evan and Earth.

Knock Knock
Who's there?
Evans!
Evans who?
Evans about to open up with rain,
let me in quick!

> Knock Knock
> Who's there?
> Eve!
> Eve who?
> Eve-anishes without waiting for
> you to answer the door.

Knock Knock
Who's there?
Everest!
Everest who?
Everest your feet on a table?

> Knock Knock
> Who's there?
> Evie!
> Evie who?
> Evie thing will be fine.

Knock Knock
Who's there?
Ewan!
Ewan who?
Ewan and me should go and play.

> Knock Knock
> Who's there?
> Ewan!
> Ewan who?
> No, just me!

Knock Knock
Who's there?
Ezra!
Ezra who?
Ezra anybody at home?

Knock Knock
Who's there?
Eyes!
Eyes who?
Eyes got loads more knock
knock jokes for you!

Knock Knock
Who's there?
Eyeball!
Eyeball who?
Eyeball my eyes out every time
you go.

Knock Knock
Who's there?
Fajita!
Fajita who?
Fajita another thing I'm going
to be sick!

Knock Knock
Who's there?
Fangs!
Fangs who?
Fangs for letting me in.

Knock Knock
Who's there?
Fanny!
Fanny who?
Fanny body calls, tell them
I'm out.

Knock Knock
Who's there?
Fanny!
Fanny who?
Fanny the way you keep asking
who's there every time I knock.

Knock Knock
Who's there?

Fanta!
Fanta who?
Fanta Claus.

Knock Knock
Who's there?
Fantasy!
Fantasy who?
Fantasy a walk in the park?

Knock Knock
Who's there?
Farley!
Farley who?
Farley the leader.

Knock Knock
Who's there?
Farmer!
Farmer who?
Farmer birthday I'm going to
get a new bike.

Knock Knock
Who's there?
Farmer!
Farmer who?
Farmer people here than there
were last year.

Knock Knock
Who's there?
Farrah!
Farrah who?
Farrah-nough.

Knock Knock
Who's there?
Farrah!
Farrah who?
Farrah a carpenter and you
were a lady…

Knock Knock
Who's there?
Fatso!
Fatso who?
Fatso funny about these knock
knock jokes?

Knock Knock
Who's there?
Faye!
Faye who?
Faye all laughed when your
pants fell down.

Knock Knock
Who's there?
Faye!
Faye who?
Faye Kearings.

Knock Knock
Who's there?
Felicity!

Felicity who?
Felicity getting more polluted
every day.

Knock Knock
Who's there?
Felipe!
Felipe who?
Felipe bath, I need a wash.

Knock Knock
Who's there?
Felix!
Felix who?
Felix-ited about meeting you.

Knock Knock
Who's there?
Felix!
Felix who?
Felix his ice cream it won't melt
as quickly.

Knock Knock
Who's there?
Ferdie!
Ferdie who?
Ferdie last time open this door!

Knock Knock
Who's there?
Ferdinand!
Ferdinand who?
Ferdinand beats two in the bush.

Knock Knock
Who's there?
Fergie!
Fergie who?
Fergie-dness sake let me in!

Knock Knock
Who's there?

Ferris!
Ferris who?
Ferris fair, you win.

Knock Knock
Who's there?
Few!
Few who?
What can you smell?

Knock Knock
Who's there?
Fiddle!
Fiddle who?
Fiddle make you happy, I'll tell you.

Knock Knock
Who's there?
Fiddlestick!
Fiddlestick who?
Fiddlestick out of the bed if the
blanket is too short.

Knock Knock
Who's there?
Fidel!
Fidel who?
Fidel last time open this door!

Knock Knock
Who's there?
Fido!
Fido who?
Fido known you were coming
I'd have left the door open.

Knock Knock
Who's there?
Fido!
Fido who?
Fido I have to wait here?

Knock Knock
Who's there?
Fifi!
Fifi who?
Fifi-ling c-cold, let me in.

Knock Knock
Who's there?
Figs!
Figs who?
Figs the doorbell, it's broken.

Knock Knock
Who's there?
Fish!
Fish who?
Fish-us temper you've got,
calm down.

Knock Knock
Who's there?
Fiona!
Fiona who?
Fiona of the house, I've come to
see if you want new windows.

Knock Knock
Who's there?
Fiona!
Fiona who?
Fiona had something better
to do, do you think I'd be
knocking on this door?

Knock Knock
Who's there?
Fish!
Fish who?
Bless you, do you have a cold?

Knock Knock
Who's there?
Fission!

Fission who?
Fission a bowl are safe from the cat.

Knock Knock
Who's there?
Fitzwilliam!
Fitzwilliam who?
Fitzwilliam better than it fits me.

Knock Knock
Who's there?
Fizzle!
Fizzle who?
Fizzle make you burp!

Knock Knock
Who's there?
Flea!
Flea who?
Flea's a jolly good fellow.

Knock Knock
Who's there?
Flea!
Flea who?
Flea blind mice.

Knock Knock
Who's there?
Fletcher!
Fletcher who?
Fletcher self go.

Knock Knock
Who's there?
Fleur!
Fleur who?
Fleur goodness' sake open the door.

Knock Knock
Who's there?

Flo!
Flo who?
Flo your candles out on your birthday cake.

Knock Knock
Who's there?
Flossie!
Flossie who?
Flossie your teeth everyday.

Knock Knock
Who's there?
Flounder!
Flounder who?
Flounder key on the drive, here you go.

Knock Knock
Who's there?
Foot!
Foot who?
Foot two cents I'd go away now.

Knock Knock
Who's there?
Fonda!
Fonda who?
Fonda you.

Knock Knock
Who's there?
Ford!
Ford who?
Ford he's a jolly good fellow!

Knock Knock
Who's there?
Formosa!
Formosa who?
Formosa the summer I was away on vacation.

Knock Knock
Who's there?
Fossil!
Fossil who?
Fossil last time, open this door!

Knock Knock
Who's there?
Foster!
Foster who?
Foster than a speeding bullet.

Knock Knock
Who's there?
Four Eggs!
Four Eggs who?
Four Eggs ample.

Knock Knock
Who's there?
Fozzie!
Fozzie who?
Fozzie hundredth time, my name is Nathan!

Knock Knock
Who's there?
Fran!
Fran who?
Fran away now you'd never know who was at the door.

Knock Knock
Who's there?
Frances!
Frances who?
Frances hello.

Knock Knock
Who's there?
Francie!
Francie who?
Francie that.

Knock Knock
Who's there?
Francis!
Francis who?
Francis where people eat snails and frogs' legs.

Knock Knock
Who's there?
Francoise!
Francoise who?
Francoise once a great empire.

Knock Knock
Who's there?
Frank!
Frank who?
Frank you for letting me in!

Knock Knock
Who's there?
Franz!
Franz who?
Franz, Romans, Countrymen...

Knock Knock
Who's there?
Fred!
Fred who?
Fred I've got some bad news.

Knock Knock
Who's there?
Fred!
Fred who?
Fred Setter is a breed of dog.

Knock Knock
Who's there?
Freda!
Freda who?
Freda blinda micea.

Knock Knock
Who's there?
Freddie!
Freddie who?
Freddie or not here I come!

Knock Knock
Who's there?
Freddie and Abel!
Freddie and Abel who?
Freddie and Abel to do business.

Knock Knock
Who's there?
Freighter!
Freighter who?
Freighter open the door.

Knock Knock
Who's there?
Fruit!
Fruit who?
Fruit of all evil.

Knock Knock
Who's there?
Fudge!
Fudge who?
Fudge up – there's no room.

Knock Knock
Who's there?
Furlong!
Furlong who?
Furlong time I've wanted to come
and say hello.

Knock Knock
Who's there?
Furry!
Furry who?
Furry's a jolly good fellow!

Knock Knock
Who's there?
Fuzzy!
Fuzzy who?
Fuzzy sake of old times, open ze
door.

Knock Knock
Who's there?
Gail!
Gail who?
Gail of laughter.

Knock Knock
Who's there?
Gala!
Gala who?
Gala-fornia here I come.

Knock Knock
Who's there?
Gandhi!
Gandhi who?
Gandhi come out and play?

Knock Knock
Who's there?
Gary!
Gary who?
Gary on smiling.

Knock Knock
Who's there?
Gaskills!
Gaskills who?
Gaskills if it's not turned off.

Knock Knock
Who's there?
Gay!
Gay who?
Gay Topen, that's how the cows
got out.

Knock Knock
Who's there?
Gazza!
Gazza who?
Gazza kiss.

Knock Knock
Who's there?
Gee!
Gee who?
Gee ken John Peel with his coat
so gay…?

Knock Knock
Who's there?
Geena!
Geena who?
Geena the way to Edinburgh?

Knock Knock
Who's there?
Gene!
Gene who?
Gene and tonic please, senor.

Knock Knock
Who's there?
Ghost!
Ghost who?
Ghost to the shop to get
some milk.

Knock Knock
Who's there?
General Lee!
General Lee who?
General Lee I don't mind school
dinners.

Knock Knock
Who's there?
George!
George who?
George of the Light Brigade.

Knock Knock
Who's there?
Geoff!
Geoff who?
Geoff feel like a drink?

Knock Knock
Who's there?
Gerald!
Gerald who?
Gerald man he played one,
he played knick-knack on my
thumb…

Knock Knock
Who's there?
George!
George who?
George-us lady, give me a kiss.

Knock Knock
Who's there?
Germaine!
Germaine who?
Germaine you don't recognize me?

Knock Knock
Who's there?
Gertie!
Gertie who?
Gertie-sy call.

Knock Knock
Who's there?
Ghoul!
Ghoul who?
Ghoul posts are necessary for
soccer.

Knock Knock
Who's there?
Gilda!
Gilda who?
Gilda fly that sat on the end of
my nose.

Knock Knock
Who's there?
Ginny!
Ginny who?
Ginny'd anything from the shops?

Knock Knock
Who's there?
Gino!
Gino who?
Gino me? If so open the door!

Knock Knock
Who's there?
Giovanna!
Giovanna who?
Giovanna go to a movie?

Knock Knock
Who's there?
Giovanni!
Giovanni who?
Giovanni more biscuits?

Knock Knock
Who's there?
Giselle!
Giselle who?
Giselle-gant and very pretty.

Knock Knock
Who's there?
Gita!
Gita who?
Gita job.

Knock Knock
Who's there?
Giuseppe!
Giuseppe who?
Giuseppe my apology?

Knock Knock
Who's there?
Gladiola!
Gladiola who?
Gladiola door open for me.

Knock Knock
Who's there?
Gladys!
Gladys who?
Gladys the weekend, aren't
you?

Knock Knock
Who's there?
Goat.
Goat who?
Goat to bed.

Knock, knock.
Who's there?
Godfrey.
Godfrey who?
Godfrey tickets to the school
disco. Want to come?

Knock Knock
Who's there?
Godunov!
Godunov who?
Godunov to eat.

Knock Knock
Who's there?
Goose!
Goose who?
Goose who's knocking at
your door.

Knock Knock
Who's there?
Goose!
Goose who?
Goose see a doctor, you don't
look well.

Knock Knock
Who's there?
Gopher!
Gopher who?
Gopher a long walk off a
short pier.

Knock Knock
Who's there?
Gordie!
Gordie who?
Gordie-rectly to jail, do not pass
go, do not collect $200.

Knock Knock
Who's there?
Grace!
Grace who?
Grace your knee when you
fall over.

Knock Knock
Who's there?
Gorilla!
Gorilla who?
Gorilla cheese sandwich for
me and I'll be right over.

Knock Knock
Who's there?
Grace!
Grace who?
Grace your glasses to our good
friend.

Knock Knock
Who's there?
Grady!
Grady who?
Grady Expectations.

Knock Knock
Who's there?
Grammar!
Grammar who?
Grammar is in the old people's
home.

Knock Knock
Who's there?
Granny, knock, knock!
Who's there?
Granny, knock, knock!
Who's there?
Granny, knock, knock!
Who's there?
Granny, knock, knock!
Who's there?
Aunt!
Aunt who?
Aunt you glad Granny's gone?

Knock Knock
Who's there?
Grub!
Grub who?
Grub hold of my hand and let's go.

Knock Knock
Who's there?
Grant!
Grant who?
Grant-stand seats are the best.

Knock Knock
Who's there?
Grant!
Grant who?
Grant you a wish, what is it?

Knock Knock
Who's there?
Grape!
Grape who?
Grape suzette.

Knock Knock
Who's there?
Gravy!
Gravy who?
Gravy Crockett.

Knock Knock
Who's there?
Gray!
Gray who?
Gray Z about you.

Knock Knock
Who's there?
Greece!
Greece who?
Greece my palm and I'll tell you.

Knock Knock
Who's there?
Greta!
Greta who?
Greta balls of fire.

Knock Knock
Who's there?
Greta!
Greta who?
Greta on my nerves.

Knock Knock
Who's there?
Grimm!
Grimm who?
Grimm and bear it.

Knock Knock
Who's there?
Guinevere!
Guinevere who?
Guinevere going to get together?

Knock Knock
Who's there?
Guitar!
Guitar who?
Guitar coats will you, it's raining hard.

Knock Knock
Who's there?
Gus!
Gus who?
That's what you're supposed
to do.

Knock Knock
Who's there?
Gustave!
Gustave who?
Gustave yourself and lose some
weight.

Knock Knock
Who's there?
Guthrie!
Guthrie who?
Guthrie blind mice.

Knock Knock
Who's there?
Gutter!
Gutter who?
Gutter get in, it's snowing out here.

Knock Knock
Who's there?
Gwen!
Gwen who?
Gwen will I see you again?

Knock Knock
Who's there?
Gwenna!
Gwenna who?
Gwenna phone rings, answer it.

Knock Knock
Who's there?
Hacienda!
Hacienda who?
Hacienda the story.

Knock Knock
Who's there?
Gwyn!
Gwyn who?
Gwyn down the shops, wanna
come?

Knock Knock
Who's there?
Haifa!
Haifa who?
Haifa cake is better than none.

Knock Knock
Who's there?
Haiti!
Haiti who?
Haiti see a good thing go to waste.

Knock Knock
Who's there?
Hal!
Hal who?
Hal about Eve.

Knock Knock
Who's there?
Hal!
Hal who?
Hal of a way to run a railroad.

Knock Knock
Who's there?
Hal!
Hal who?
Hal-lelujah!

Knock Knock
Who's there?
Haley!
Haley who?
Haley-en Nation.

Knock Knock
Who's there?
Halibut!
Halibut who?
Halibut letting me in on the
secret?

Knock Knock
Who's there?
Halifax!
Halifax who?
Halifax you if you fax me.

Knock Knock
Who's there?
Hallie!
Hallie who?
Hallie-tosis, your breath stinks!

Knock Knock
Who's there?
Hammond!
Hammond who?
Hammond cheese on toast, please.

Knock Knock
Who's there?
Handel!
Handel who?
Handel with care.

Knock Knock
Who's there?
Handsome!
Handsome who?
Handsome chips through the
letterbox and I'll tell you more!

Knock Knock
Who's there?
Hank!
Hank who?
You're welcome!

Knock Knock
Who's there?
Hannah!
Hannah who?
Hannah clothes out to dry.

Knock Knock
Who's there?
Hannah!
Hannah who?
Hannah partridge in a pear
tree.

Knock Knock
Who's there?
Hansel!
Hansel who?
Hansel freeze out here, let me in!

Knock Knock
Who's there?
Hardy!
Hardy who?
Hardy recognized you, have
you had a haircut?

Knock Knock
Who's there?
Harlow!
Harlow who?
Harlow can you get?

Knock Knock
Who's there?
Harmon!
Harmon who?
Harmon on your side.

Knock Knock
Who's there?
Harmon!
Harmon who?
Harmon animals is very cruel.

Knock Knock
Who's there?
Harmony!
Harmony who?
Harmony knock knock jokes do you expect me to know?

Knock Knock
Who's there?
Harp!
Harp who?
Harp the Herald Angels Sing.

Knock Knock
Who's there?
Harold!
Harold who?
Harold do you think I am?

Knock Knock
Who's there?
Harriet!
Harriet who?
Harriet all my lunch, I'm starving!

Knock Knock
Who's there?
Harriet!
Harriet who?
Harriet up, I've been standing here for ages!

Knock Knock
Who's there?
Harris!
Harris who?
Harris nice to have on the top of your head.

Knock Knock
Who's there?
Harry!
Harry who?
Harry up and answer this door!

Knock Knock
Who's there?
Harry!
Harry who?
Harry you been?

Knock Knock
Who's there?
Harv!
Harv who?
Harv you lonesome tonight?

Knock Knock
Who's there?
Harvey!
Harvey who?
Harvey going to play this game forever?

Knock Knock
Who's there?
Hatch!
Hatch who?
Bless you, do you have a cold?

Knock Knock
Who's there?
Havana!
Havana who?
Havana a wonderful time, wish you were here!

Knock Knock
Who's there?
Havelock!
Havelock who?
Havelock put on your door.

Knock Knock
Who's there?

Hawaii!
Hawaii who?
Hawaii getting on?

> Knock Knock
> Who's there?
> Hawaii!
> Hawaii who?
> Fine, until you kept asking me
> questions!

Knock Knock
Who's there?
Haydn!
Haydn who?
Haydn in this cupboard is boring.

> Knock Knock
> Who's there?
> Hazel!
> Hazel who?
> Hazel mean that you can't
> see far.

Knock Knock
Who's there?
Heart!
Heart who?
Heart to hear you, speak louder.

> Knock Knock
> Who's there?
> Heather!
> Heather who?
> Heather fallen in love with
> someone you shouldn't have
> fallen in love with?

Knock Knock
Who's there?
Heaven!
Heaven who?
Heaven seen you for a long time.

Knock Knock
Who's there?
Heavy!
Heavy who?
Heavy ever been to New York?

Knock Knock
Who's there?
Hedda!
Hedda who?
Hedda ball in goal.

> Knock Knock
> Who's there?
> Heddy!
> Heddy who?
> Heddy-thing but the kitchen
> sink.

Knock Knock
Who's there?
Heidi Clare!
Heidi Clare who?
Heidi Clare war on you.

> Knock Knock
> Who's there?
> Heifer!
> Heifer who?
> Heifer heard so many jokes!

Knock Knock
Who's there?
Heifer!
Heifer who?
Heifer cow is better than none.

> Knock Knock
> Who's there?
> Helen!
> Helen who?
> Helen Earth.

Knock Knock
Who's there?
Henrietta!
Henrietta who?
Henrietta whole cake and now he feels sick.

Knock Knock
Who's there?
Hepburn!
Hepburn who?
Hepburn and indigestion.

Knock Knock
Who's there?
Herman!
Herman who?
Herman dry.

Knock Knock
Who's there?
Herman!
Herman who?
Herman is handsome.

Knock Knock
Who's there?
Hester!
Hester who?
Hester la vista, baby!

Knock Knock
Who's there?
Heywood, Hugh, Harry!
Heywood, Hugh, Harry who?
Heywood Hugh Harry up and open this door?

Knock Knock
Who's there?
Hi!
Hi who?
Hi ho, hi ho, it's off to work we go.

Knock Knock
Who's there?
Hiawatha!
Hiawatha who?
Hiawatha very bad this morning, but it's supposed to brighten up later.

Knock Knock
Who's there?
Hijack!
Hijack who?
Hijack, how's Jill?

Knock Knock
Who's there?
Hip!
Hip who?
Hip-popotamus.

Knock Knock
Who's there?
Hiram!
Hiram who?
Hiram fine, how are you?

Knock Knock
Who's there?
Hobbit!
Hobbit who?
Hobbit letting me in then?

Knock Knock
Who's there?
Hockey!
Hockey who?
Hockey doesn't work, so I had to knock.

Knock Knock
Who's there?
Holland!
Holland who?

Holland you going to make me wait out here?

Knock Knock
Who's there?
Hollis!
Hollis who?
Hollis forgiven, come back home.

Knock Knock
Who's there?
Holly!
Holly who?
Holly absence of door chimes, Batman!

Knock Knock
Who's there?
Holmes!
Holmes who?
Holmes is where the heart is.

Knock Knock
Who's there?
Homer!
Homer who?
Homer-nee times must I ask you to open this door?

Knock Knock
Who's there?
Honda!
Honda who?
Honda the boardwalk.

Knock Knock
Who's there?
Honeydew!
Honeydew who?
Honeydew you want to come out tonight?

Knock Knock
Who's there?
Horace!
Horace who?
Horace-scopes can be fun.

Knock Knock
Who's there?
Horatio!
Horatio who?
Horatio to the end of the street.

Knock Knock
Who's there?
Hosanna!
Hosanna who?
Hosanna Claus gets down the chimney I'll never know!

Knock Knock
Who's there?
Hoss!
Hoss who?
Hoss under the collar.

Knock Knock
Who's there?
House!
House who?
I'm fine thank you, how are you?

Knock Knock
Who's there?
Howard!
Howard who?
Howard I know?

Knock Knock
Who's there?
Howard!
Howard who?
Howard you know unless you open the door?

Knock Knock
Who's there?
Howard!
Howard who?
Howard you like to stand out here
in the cold while some idiot keeps
asking who's there?

> Knock Knock
> Who's there?
> Howard!
> Howard who?
> Howard can it be to guess the
> punchline to a knock knock joke?

Knock Knock
Who's there?
Howard Hughes!
Howard Hughes who?
Howard Hughes like a punch on
the nose?

> Knock Knock
> Who's there?
> Howell!
> Howell who?
> Howell I get in if you don't open
> the door?

Knock Knock
Who's there?
Howie!
Howie who?
Howie Dewin?

> Knock Knock
> Who's there?
> Howie!
> Howie who?
> I'm fine, how are you?

Knock Knock
Who's there?

Howl!
Howl who?
Howl I know when it's dinner time?

> Knock Knock
> Who's there?
> Hubbard!
> Hubbard who?
> Hubbard can sing louder than
> my bird.

Knock Knock
Who's there?
Hubie!
Hubie who?
Hubie-ginning to see the light?

> Knock Knock
> Who's there?
> Huey!
> Huey who?
> Who am I? I'm me!

Knock Knock
Who's there?
Hugh!
Hugh who?
Hello to you too!

> Knock Knock
> Who's there?
> Hugo!
> Hugo who?
> Hugo your way and I'll go
> mine.

Brrring Brrring
Who's there?
Hurd!
Hurd who?
Hurd my hand so couldn't knock
knock.

Knock Knock
Who's there?
Huron!
Huron who?
Huron time for once.

Knock Knock
Who's there?
Hussein!
Hussein who?
Hussein that about
me?

Knock Knock
Who's there?
Hutch!
Hutch who?
Bless you, and I'm right out of
tissues.

Knock Knock
Who's there?
Hyman!
Hyman who?
Hyman the mood for dancing.

Knock Knock
Who's there?
Ian!
Ian who?
Ian his friend have gone bowling.

Knock Knock
Who's there?
Ice cream!
Ice cream who?
Ice cream if you don't let me in.

Knock Knock
Who's there?
Ice cream!
Ice cream who?
Ice cream of Jeannie.

Knock Knock
Who's there?
Hugh!
Hugh who?
Hugh's afraid of the big bad
wolf?

Knock Knock
Who's there?
Ice cream soda!
Ice cream soda who?
Ice cream soda whole world
will know what a nut you are.

Knock Knock
Who's there?
Icy!
Icy who?
Icy you in there, open the door.

Knock Knock
Who's there?
Ida!
Ida who?
Ida know why I love you like I
do.

Knock Knock
Who's there?
Ida!
Ida who?
No, it's Idaho, not Ida-who!

> Knock Knock
> Who's there?
> Ida!
> Ida who?
> Ida face, she's so ugly.

Knock Knock
Who's there?
Ida!
Ida who?
Ida know. Sorry!

> Knock Knock
> Who's there?
> Ida!
> Ida who?
> Ida terrible time getting here.

Knock Knock
Who's there?
Ida!
Ida who?
Ida buy another door
knocker if I were you.

> Knock Knock
> Who's there?
> Idaho!
> Idaho who?
> Idaho-d the whole
> garden but I was
> tired.

Knock Knock
Who's there?
I don't know!
I don't know who?

I told you I don't know. Why don't
you believe me?

> Knock Knock
> Who's there?
> Iglesias!
> Iglesias who?
> Iglesias melting because of
> global warming.

Knock Knock
Who's there?
Iglesias!
Iglesias who?
Iglesias people never do any work.

> Knock Knock
> Who's there?
> Ike!
> Ike who?
> Ike could have danced
> all night.

Knock Knock
Who's there?
Iguana!
Iguana who?
Iguana hold your hand.

Knock Knock
Who's there?
Ilka!
Ilka who?
Ilka-pone.

Knock Knock
Who's there?
Ilona!
Ilona who?
Ilona Ranger.

Knock Knock
Who's there?
Ima!
Ima who?
Ima hungry.

Knock Knock
Who's there?
Imogen!
Imogen who?
Imogen life without these jokes.

Knock Knock
Who's there?
Ina!
Ina who?
Ina minute I'm going to knock this door down.

Knock Knock
Who's there?
Ina Claire!
Ina Claire who?
Ina Claire day, you can see for miles.

Knock Knock
Who's there?
India!
India who?
India summertime I like to go on vacation.

Knock Knock
Who's there?
Innuendo!
Innuendo who?
Innuendo the dinner you get dessert.

Knock Knock
Who's there?
Iona!
Iona who?
Iona a great train set.

Knock Knock
Who's there?
Iowa!
Iowa who?
Iowa you a dollar.

Knock Knock
Who's there?
Ira!
Ira who?
Ira car and we can go on vacation to Florida.

Knock Knock
Who's there?
Iran!
Iran who?
Iran away when you answered before.

Knock Knock
Who's there?
Iraq!
Iraq who?
Iraq of ribs with barbecue sauce.

Knock Knock
Who's there?
Ireland!

Ireland who?
Ireland you some money if you promise to pay me back.

> Knock Knock
> Who's there?
> Irene!
> Irene who?
> Irene and Irene but still no one answers the door.

Knock Knock
Who's there?
Iris!
Iris who?
Iris eyes are smiling.

> Knock Knock
> Who's there?
> Iris!
> Iris who?
> Iris you were here.

Knock Knock
Who's there?
Irish stew!
Irish stew who?
Irish stew in the name of the law!

> Knock Knock
> Who's there?
> Irma!
> Irma who?
> Irma big girl now.

Knock Knock
Who's there?
Isaac!
Isaac who?
Isaac-ly who do think this is?

> Knock Knock
> Who's there?

Isaac!
Isaac who?
Isaac coming out to play?

Knock Knock
Who's there?
Isabel!
Isabel who?
Isabel broken because I had to knock?

> Knock Knock
> Who's there?
> Isabella!
> Isabella who?
> Isabella out of order?

Knock Knock
Who's there?
Isabelle!
Isabelle who?
Isabelle necessary on a bicycle?

> Knock Knock
> Who's there?
> Isadore!
> Isadore who?
> Isadore locked, I can't get in.

Knock Knock
Who's there?
Isaiah!
Isaiah who?
Isaiah again, knock knock!

> Knock Knock
> Who's there?
> Isla!
> Isla who?
> Isla be seeing you.

Knock Knock
Who's there?
Island!

Island who?
Island on your roof with my parachute.

Knock Knock
Who's there?
Issue!
Issue who?
Issue blind? It's me!

Knock Knock
Who's there?
Istvan!
Istvan who?
Istvan to be alone.

Knock Knock
Who's there?
Ivan!
Ivan who?
Ivan my money back now.

Knock Knock
Who's there?
Ivan!
Ivan who?
Ivan idea you don't want to see me.

Knock Knock
Who's there?
Ivan!
Ivan who?
It's not Ivan who, it's Ivanhoe!

Knock Knock
Who's there?
Ivan!
Ivan who?
Ivan U. Hat, do you like it?

Knock Knock
Who's there?
Ivana!

Ivana who?
Ivana be rich.

Knock Knock
Who's there?
Ivanhoe!
Ivanhoe who?
Ivanhoe the garden, please.

Knock Knock
Who's there?
Ivor!
Ivor who?
Ivor sore hand from knocking on your door.

Knock Knock
Who's there?
Ivory!
Ivory who?
Ivory strong like Tarzan.

Knock Knock
Who's there?
Ivy!
Ivy who?
Ivy got you under my skin.

Knock Knock
Who's there?
Izzy!
Izzy who?
Izzy at the door? You'd better answer it then.

Knock Knock
Who's there?
Izzy!
Izzy who?
Izzy come, Izzy go.

Knock Knock
Who's there?

Jack!
Jack who?
Jack Pott!

> Knock Knock
> Who's there?
> Jackson!
> Jackson who?
> Jackson the
> telephone, you'd
> better answer it.

Knock Knock
Who's there?
Jacqueline!
Jacqueline who?
Jacqueline and Hyde.

Ouch!

SIZZLE!

> Knock Knock
> Who's there?
> Jacques!
> Jacques who?
> Jacques of all trades.

Knock Knock
Who's there?
James!
James who?
James people play.

> Knock Knock
> Who's there?
> Janet!
> Janet who?
> Janet has too many holes in it,
> the fish will escape.

Knock Knock
Who's there?
Jasmine!
Jasmine who?
Jasmine like to play the trumpet.

> **Knock Knock**
> **Who's there?**
> **Japan!**
> **Japan who?**
> **Japan is too hot, ouch!**

Knock Knock
Who's there?
Jason!
Jason who?
Jason around after you is tiring me
out.

> Knock Knock
> Who's there?
> Java!
> Java who?
> Java dog in your house?

Knock Knock
Who's there?
Jaws!
Jaws who?
Jaws truly!

Knock Knock
Who's there?
Jean!
Jean who?
Jean-ius, you just don't
recognize it.

Knock Knock
Who's there?
Jeff!
Jeff who?
Jeff in one ear, you'll have
to shout!

Knock Knock
Who's there?
Jeffrey!
Jeffrey who?
Jeffrey time I knock, you ask me
who I am.

Knock Knock
Who's there?
Jenny!
Jenny who?
Jenny-d any help with your
homework?

Knock Knock
Who's there?
Jerome!
Jerome who?
Jerome where you want to.

Knock Knock
Who's there?
Jerry!
Jerry who?
Jerry funny, let me in.

Knock Knock
Who's there?
Jess!

Jess who?
Jess me and my shadow.

Knock Knock
Who's there?
Jess!
Jess who?
I give up, who?

Knock Knock
Who's there?
Jesse!
Jesse who?
Jesse if you can recognize my
voice.

Knock Knock
Who's there?
Jester!
Jester who?
Jester minute, I'm trying to find
my keys.

Knock Knock
Who's there?
Jesus!
Jesus who?
How many do you know?

Knock Knock
Who's there?
Jethro!
Jethro who?
Jethro the boat and stop talking
so much.

Knock Knock
Who's there?
Jewel!
Jewel who?
Jewel know if you open the door!

Knock Knock
Who's there?
Jez!
Jez who?
Jez someone you used to know.

Knock Knock
Who's there?
Jilly!
Jilly who?
Jilly out here, so let me in.

Knock Knock
Who's there?
Jim!
Jim who?
Jim mind if we come in?

Knock Knock
Who's there?
Jimmy!
Jimmy who?
Jimmy a little kiss on the cheek.

Knock Knock
Who's there?
Jiminy!
Jiminy who?
Jiminy roads must a man walk
down before you call him a man?

Knock Knock
Who's there?
Joan!
Joan who?
Joan call us, we'll call you.

Knock Knock
Who's there?
Joanna!
Joanna who?
Joanna answer the door?

Knock Knock
Who's there?
Joanne!
Joanne who?
Joanne tell.

Knock Knock
Who's there?
Joe!
Joe who?
Joe away, I'm not talking to you.

Knock Knock
Who's there?
Joe Namath!
Joe Namath who?
Joe Namath not on the door,
that's why I knocked.

Knock Knock
Who's there?
Joey!
Joey who?
Joey to the world, it's a lovely day.

Knock Knock
Who's there?
Johannes!
Johannes who?
Johannes are cold.

Knock Knock
Who's there?
John!
John who?
John with the wind.

Knock Knock
Who's there?
John!
John who?
John me in a cup of tea.

Knock Knock
Who's there?
Jools!
Jools who?
Jools are a girl's best friend.

> Knock Knock
> Who's there?
> Joplin!
> Joplin who?
> Joplin any time you like.

Knock Knock
Who's there?
Josette!
Josette who?
Josette down and be quiet.

> Knock Knock
> Who's there?
> Juan!
> Juan who?
> Juan to hear some more of
> these jokes?

Knock Knock
Who's there?
Juan!
Juan who?
Juan of these days you'll find out.

> Knock Knock
> Who's there?
> Juan!
> Juan who?
> Juan-der why you keep asking
> me that?

Knock Knock
Who's there?
Juanita!
Juanita who?
Juanita-nother burger?

Knock Knock
Who's there?
Jude!
Jude who?
Jude doubt me, just open the
door.

Knock Knock
Who's there?
Judy!
Judy who?
Judy liver milk still?

> Knock Knock
> Who's there?
> Juice!
> Juice who?
> Juice still want to know?

Knock Knock
Who's there?
Juicy!
Juicy who?
Juicy what I just saw?

> Knock Knock
> Who's there?
> Julian!
> Julian who?
> Julian-d I are going out now.

Knock Knock
Who's there?
Julie!
Julie who?
Julie your door unlocked?

> Knock Knock
> Who's there?
> Juliet!
> Juliet who?
> Juliet all the cookies.

Knock Knock
Who's there?
Juliet!
Juliet who?
Juliet me in or not?

> Knock Knock
> Who's there?
> Julius!
> Julius who?
> Julius just jealous that I know
> all the good jokes.

Knock Knock
Who's there?
July!
July who?
July to me about stealing my
pencil?

> Knock Knock
> Who's there?
> Juno!
> Juno who?
> Of course I do!

Knock Knock
Who's there?
Jupiter!
Jupiter who?
Jupiter hurry, or you'll miss the bus.

> Knock Knock
> Who's there?
> Juno!
> Juno who?
> Juno what time it is?

Knock Knock
Who's there?
Jupiter!
Jupiter who?
Jupiter fly in my soup?

Knock Knock
Who's there?
Kanga!
Kanga who?
No, it's kangaroo not
kanga-who!

Knock Knock
Who's there?
Justice!
Justice who?
Justice I thought, there's no one
home.

> Knock Knock
> Who's there?
> Justin!
> Justin who?
> Justin Quire who is at the door.

Knock Knock
Who's there?
Justin!
Justin who?
Justin time for dinner.

Knock Knock
Who's there?
Kansas!
Kansas who?
Kansas the best way to buy tuna.

Knock Knock
Who's there?
Kareem!
Kareem who?
Kareem of the crop.

Knock Knock
Who's there?
Karen!
Karen who?
Karen the can for you.

Knock Knock
Who's there?
Kathy!
Kathy who?
Kathy you again.

Knock Knock
Who's there ?
Kay!
Kay who?
Kay L, M, N...

Knock Knock
Who's there?
Kay!
Kay who?
Kay sera sera.

Knock Knock
Who's there?
Keanu!
Keanu who?
Keanu let me in, it's cold out here.

Knock Knock
Who's there?
Keith!
Keith who?
Keith your hands off my food!

Knock Knock
Who's there?
Ken!
Ken who?
Ken you answer the door please?

Knock Knock
Who's there?
Kendall!
Kendall who?
Kendall and Barbie doll go together.

Knock Knock
Who's there?
Kenneth!
Kenneth who?
Kenneth little kids play with you?

Knock Knock
Who's there?
Kenny!
Kenny who?
Kenny let me in?

Knock Knock
Who's there?
Kent!
Kent who?
Kent you tell who it is?

Knock Knock
Who's there?
Kenya!
Kenya who?
Kenya guess who's come to see you?

Knock Knock
Who's there?
Kermit!
Kermit who?
Kermit a crime and you'll get locked up.

Knock Knock
Who's there?
Kerry!
Kerry who?
Kerry me up the stairs will you, I ache.

Knock Knock
Who's there?
Khomeini!
Khomeini who?
Khomeini times must I knock on this door?

Knock Knock
Who's there?
Kiki!
Kiki who?
Kiki's stuck in the lock, let me in.

Knock Knock
Who's there?
Kim!

Kim who?
Kim on over to my place.

Knock Knock
Who's there?
King Kong!
King Kong who?
King Kong's now part of China.

Knock Knock
Who's there?
Kipper!
Kipper who?
Kipper hands to yourself.

Knock Knock
Who's there?
Kismet!
Kismet who?
Kismet quick.

Knock Knock
Who's there?
Kitten!
Kitten who?
Kitten the park hit me with a ball.

Knock Knock
Who's there?
Klaus!
Klaus who?
Klaus this door will you.

Knock Knock
Who's there?
Knock, knock!
Who's there?

Knock, knock!
Who's there?
Knock, knock!
I'm sorry, but my mother doesn't allow me to speak to strangers!

Knock Knock
Who's there?
Kristin!
Kristin who?
Kristin the baby in church.

Knock Knock
Who's there?
Kumquat!
Kumquat who?
Kumquat may we'll always be friends.

Knock Knock
Who's there?
Kurt!
Kurt who?
Kurt along the dotted line.

Knock Knock
Who's there?
Kyle!
Kyle who?
Kyle be good if you let me in.

Knock Knock
Who's there?
Kylie!
Kylie who?
Kylie contagious, so keep away!

Knock Knock
Who's there?
Lacey!
Lacey who?
Lacey people can't be bothered to answer the door.

Knock Knock
Who's there?
Lady!
Lady who?
Lady law down.

Knock Knock
Who's there?
Lara!
Lara who?
Lara lara laughs in Liverpool.

Knock Knock
Who's there?
Larry!
Larry who?
Larry Krishna.

Knock Knock
Who's there?
Lass!
Lass who?
That's what cowboys use, isn't it?

Knock Knock
Who's there?
Laurie!
Laurie who?
Laurie load of goodies.

Knock Knock
Who's there?
Laziness!
Laziness who?
Laziness bed all day, when he should be at school.

Knock Knock
Who's there?
Lee!
Lee who?
Lee me alone, I've got a headache.

Knock Knock
Who's there?
Lee King!
Lee King who?
Lee King bucket.

Knock Knock
Who's there?
Lego!
Lego who?
Lego of me and I'll tell you.

Knock Knock
Who's there?
Leif!
Leif who?
Leif me alone with all these
questions.

Knock Knock
Who's there?
Len!
Len who?
Len us five dollars, will you?

Knock Knock
Who's there?
Lena!
Lena who?
Lena little closer and I'll tell you.

Knock Knock
Who's there?
Lettuce!
Lettuce who?
Lettuce in and I'll tell you.

Knock Knock
Who's there?
Lenny!
Lenny who?
Lenny in, I'm hungry.

Knock Knock
Who's there?
Leslie!
Leslie who?
Leslie town now before they
catch us.

Knock Knock
Who's there?
Les!
Les who?
Les go out for a picnic.

Knock Knock
Who's there?
Lester!
Lester who?
Lester-n over a new leaf.

Knock Knock
Who's there?
Leonie!
Leonie who?
Leonie one I love.

Knock Knock
Who's there?
Leon!
Leon who?
Leon me when you're not strong

and I'll be your friend, I'll help you
carry on...

> Knock Knock
> Who's there?
> Letty!
> Letty who?
> Letty it all hang out.

Knock Knock
Who's there?
Lieder!
Lieder who?
Lieder of the pack.

> Knock Knock
> Who's there?
> Lili!
> Lili who?
> Lili brown jug upon my knee.

Knock Knock
Who's there?
Lillian!
Lillian who?
Lillian the garden.

> Knock Knock
> Who's there?
> Lily!
> Lily who?
> Lily house on the prairie.

Knock Knock
Who's there?
Linda!
Linda who?
Linda hand, I can't be expected to
do it all by myself.

> Knock Knock
> Who's there?
> Lionel!

Lionel who?
Lionel get you nowhere, it's
better to tell the truth.

Knock Knock
Who's there?
Lisa!
Lisa who?
Lisa a new car from 99 dollars a
month.

> Knock Knock
> Who's there?
> Lisa!
> Lisa who?
> Lisa you can do is let me in.

Knock Knock
Who's there?
Liszt!
Liszt who?
Liszt of things to do.

> Knock Knock
> Who's there?
> Little old lady!
> Little old lady who?
> I didn't know you could yodel!

Knock Knock
Who's there?
Livia!
Livia who?
Livia me alone.

> Knock Knock
> Who's there?
> Liz!
> Liz who?
> Liz-en to me when I'm talking
> to you.

Knock Knock
Who's there?
Liza!
Liza who?
Liza wrong to tell, even little white ones.

Knock Knock
Who's there?
Llama!
Llama who?
Llama-geddon.

Knock Knock
Who's there?
Lloyd!
Lloyd who?
Lloyd own and I'll give you a massage.

Knock Knock
Who's there?
Lloyd!
Lloyd who?
Lloyd a horse to water but you can't make it drink.

Knock Knock
Who's there?
Lock!
Lock who?
Lock who it is, after all this time.

Knock Knock
Who's there?
Lois!
Lois who?
Lois the limbo dancer.

Knock Knock
Who's there?
Lon!
Lon who?
Lon in the tooth while waiting for you to answer the door.

Knock Knock
Who's there?
Lottie!
Lottie who?
Lottie knock knock jokes I know.

Knock Knock
Who's there?
Louise!
Louise who?
Louise coming to tea today.

Knock Knock
Who's there?
Louisiana!
Louisiana who?
Louisiana boy friend split up.

Knock Knock
Who's there?
Lucille!
Lucille who?
Lucille mean shoe fall apart.

Knock Knock
Who's there?
Lucinda!
Lucinda who?
Lucinda chain, I want to get in.

Knock Knock
Who's there?
Lucinda!
Lucinda who?
Lucinda sky with diamonds.

Knock Knock
Who's there?
Lucretia!
Lucretia who?

Lucretia from the Black Lagoon.

Knock Knock
Who's there?
Luigi!
Luigi who?
Luigi board.

Knock Knock
Who's there?
Luke!
Luke who?
Luke through the keyhole and
see.

Knock Knock
Who's there?
Lydia!
Lydia who?
Lydia teapot is cracked.

Knock Knock
Who's there?
Lyle!
Lyle?
Lyle low until the police have
gone.

Knock Knock
Who's there?
Lyndon!
Lyndon who?
Lyndon ear and I'll tell you.

Knock Knock
Who's there?
Mabel!
Mabel who?
Mabel doesn't ring either.

Knock Knock
Who's there?
Mabel!

Mabel who?
Mabel syrup is lovely on puddings
and pancakes.

Knock Knock
Who's there?
Madame!
Madame who?
Madame finger is caught in
the door.

Knock Knock
Who's there?
Madeleine!
Madeleine who?
Madeleine the water and tell me if
it's cold.

Knock Knock
Who's there?
Madonna!
Madonna who?
Madonna's the worst kebab
I've ever tasted.

Knock Knock
Who's there?
Madrid!
Madrid who?
Madrid you wash my jeans?

Knock Knock
Who's there?
Mae!
Mae who?
Mae be I'll tell you or maybe
I won't.

Knock Knock
Who's there?
Mahatma!
Mahatma who?
Mahatma coat, please.

Knock Knock
Who's there?
Maisie!
Maisie who?
Maisie Grace.

Knock Knock
Who's there?
Major!
Major who?
Major answer, didn't I?

Knock Knock
Who's there?
Malcolm!
Malcolm who?
Malcolm you didn't do your homework?

Knock Knock
Who's there?
Maltesers!
Maltesers who?
Maltesers the girls so much they cry.

Knock Knock
Who's there?
Mandy!
Mandy who?
Mandy lifeboats, the ship is sinking.

Knock Knock
Who's there?
Manny!
Manny who?
Manny people keep asking me that.

Knock Knock
Who's there?
Manuel!

Knock Knock
Who's there?
Maggot!
Maggot who?
Maggot me these new jeans today.

Knock Knock
Who's there?
Maia!
Maia who?
Maia-nimals are like children to me.

Knock Knock
Who's there?
Maida!
Maida who?
Maida cake because I knew you were coming.

Knock Knock
Who's there?
Maine!
Maine who?
Maine I come in now please?

Manuel who?
Manuel be sorry if you don't open this door.

> Knock Knock
> Who's there?
> Maple!
> Maple who?
> Maple the door off its hinges if you don't let me in.

Knock Knock
Who's there?
Mara!
Mara who?
Mara Mara on the wall...

> Knock Knock
> Who's there?
> Marcella!
> Marcella who?
> Marcella is full of water and I'm drowning, help!

Knock Knock
Who's there?
Marcia!
Marcia who?
Marcia glad I stopped by?

> Knock Knock
> Who's there?
> Marcus!
> Marcus who?
> Marcus a book in the Bible.

Knock Knock
Who's there?
Margo!
Margo who?
Margo and fetch Pa off the roof, his ladder just broke.

Knock Knock
Who's there?
Marie!
Marie who?
Marie flexes aren't as quick as they used to be.

Knock Knock
Who's there?
Marilyn!
Marilyn who?
Marilyn is a state north of Virginia.

> Knock Knock
> Who's there?
> Marion!
> Marion who?
> Marion haste, repent at leisure.

Knock Knock
Who's there?
Mark!
Mark who?
Mark my words.

> Knock Knock
> Who's there?
> Mark!
> Mark who?
> Mark the Herald Angels Sing.

Knock Knock
Who's there?
Markus!
Markus who?
Markus down for two tickets will you?

> Knock Knock
> Who's there?
> Marmalade!
> Marmalade who?
> Marmalade me said the little chicken.

Knock Knock
Who's there?
Matt!
Matt who?
**Matt-ador come to fight
the bull.**

Knock Knock
Who's there?
Mars!
Mars who?
Mars-ays you've got to come in
now.

> Knock Knock
> Who's there?
> Martha!
> Martha who?
> Martha them up to the top of
> the hill and then marched them
> down again.

Knock Knock
Who's there?
Martini!
Martini who?
Martini hand is frozen so let me in.

Knock Knock
Who's there?
Marv!
Marv who?
Marv-ellous weather we're having.

> Knock Knock
> Who's there?
> Mary!
> Mary who?
> Mary Christmas.

Knock Knock
Who's there?
Mata!
Mata who?
Mata of life and death.

> Knock Knock
> Who's there?
> Matt!
> Matt who?
> Matt as a hatter.

Knock Knock
Who's there?
Matthew!
Matthew who?
Matthew lace has come undone.

Knock Knock
Who's there?
Mata Hari!
Mata Hari who?
Mata Hari or we will miss the train.

Knock Knock
Who's there?
Matthew!
Matthew who?
Matthew need help with but you're good at English.

Knock Knock
Who's there?
Maude!
Maude who?
Maude at the end of the marina.

Knock Knock
Who's there?
Maude!
Maude who?
Maude-n my job is worth.

Knock Knock
Who's there?
Maura!
Maura who?
Maura these jokes and I'm going home.

Knock Knock
Who's there?
Mauve!
Mauve who?
Mauve over.

Knock Knock
Who's there?
Mavis!

Mavis who?
Mavis be the last time I knock on this door.

Knock Knock
Who's there?
Max!
Max who?
Max-imum security needed around here.

Knock Knock
Who's there?
Max!
Max who?
Max no difference. Open the door!

Knock Knock
Who's there?
Maxie!
Maxie who?
Maxie-mum.

Knock Knock
Who's there?
Maxine!
Maxine who?
Maxine the wave, dude.

Knock Knock
Who's there?
Maxwell!
Maxwell who?
Maxwell call later if you're not going to answer.

Knock Knock
Who's there?
Maya!
Maya who?
Maya best friend?

Knock Knock
Who's there?
Mayonnaise!
Mayonnaise who?
Mayonnaise have seen the
glory of the coming of the Lord.

Knock Knock
Who's there?
McEnroe!
McEnroe who?
McEnroe fast with his own oars.

Knock Knock
Who's there?
Me!
Me who?
I didn't know you had a cat?

Knock Knock
Who's there?
Meg!
Meg who?
Meg your bed before you get any
breakfast.

Knock Knock
Who's there?
Megan!
Megan who?
Megan your mind up.

Knock Knock
Who's there?
Mel!
Mel who?
Mel-ephant's trampling all over
your lawn.

Knock Knock
Who's there?
Meredith!
Meredith who?

Meredith kind of knock knock
jokes and I'm leaving.

Knock Knock
Who's there?
Mercedes!
Mercedes who?
Mercedes your best friend.

Knock Knock
Who's there?
Melita!
Melita who?
Melita chickadee.

Knock Knock
Who's there?
Meter!
Meter who?
Meter at the bus stop at 6p.m.

Knock Knock
Who's there?
Mia!
Mia who?
Mia, Mum, will you let me in.

Knock Knock
Who's there?
Mica!
Mica who?
Mica is double-parked, so hurry up!

Knock Knock
Who's there?
Mia!
Mia who?
Mia, Mama Mia, Mama Mia,
lel me go, Beelzebub has the
devil put aside for me...

Knock Knock
Who's there?

Michael!
Michael who?
Michael lock has stopped ticking.

> Knock Knock
> Who's there?
> Michael!
> Michael who?
> Michael beat you up if you
> don't open this door!

Knock Knock
Who's there?
Michelle!
Michelle who?
Michelle had a big crab inside it.

> Knock Knock
> Who's there?
> Mick!
> Mick who?
> Mick a clean break of it.

Knock Knock
Who's there?
Mickey!
Mickey who?
Mickey is lost so that's why I'm
knocking.

> Knock Knock
> Who's there?
> Midas!
> Midas who?
> Midas well have stayed at
> home for all you care.

Knock Knock
Who's there?
Midas!
Midas who?
Midas be the last knock knock
joke?

Knock Knock
Who's there?
Mike and Angelo!
Mike and Angelo who?
Mike and Angelo's David is a
famous statue.

Knock Knock
Who's there?
Mike!
Mike who?
Mike kind of girl.

> Knock Knock
> Who's there?
> Mikey!
> Mikey who?
> Mikey won't fit in this lock.

Knock Knock
Who's there?
Miles!
Miles who?
Miles away.

> Knock Knock
> Who's there?
> Milo!
> Milo who?
> Milo bed is too uncomfortable.

Knock Knock
Who's there?
Mimi!
Mimi who?
Mimi b-bike is b-broken.

> Knock Knock
> Who's there?
> Mimi
> Mimi who?
> Mimi, me, that's all you ever
> talk about.

Knock Knock
Who's there?
Mine!
Mine who?
Mine U Hat just blew away.

> Knock Knock
> Who's there?
> Minerva!
> Minerva who?
> Minerva-s wrecked from all
> these questions.

Knock Knock
Who's there?
Miniature!
Miniature who?
Miniature open the door, I'll tell
you.

> Knock Knock
> Who's there?
> Minnesota!
> Minnesota who?
> Minnesota old bike to buy new
> clothes.

Knock Knock
Who's there?
Minnie!
Minnie who?
Minnie-mum.

> Knock Knock
> Who's there?
> Minnie!
> Minnie who?
> Minnie people out here
> freezing. Open the door!

Knock Knock
Who's there?
Mint!

Mint who?
Mint to tell you earlier.

> Knock Knock
> Who's there?
> Mira!
> Mira who?
> Mira-dio's broken, can you fix it?.

Knock Knock
Who's there?
Miranda!
Miranda who?
Miranda friend want to come in.

> Knock Knock
> Who's there?
> Mischa!
> Mischa who?
> Mischa a lot when you're
> away.

Knock Knock
Who's there?
Miss!
Miss who?
Miss you too!

> Knock Knock
> Who's there?
> Mistake!
> Mistake who?
> Mistake a pill if you have a
> headache.

Knock Knock
Who's there?
Mister!
Mister who?
Mister last bus home.

> Knock Knock
> Who's there?

Mitzi!
Mitzi who?
Mitzi door shut, you'll never know.

Knock Knock
Who's there?
Moe!
Moe who?
Moe than you bargained for.

Knock Knock
Who's there?
Money!
Money who?
Money is sore since I knocked it on the table leg.

Knock Knock
Who's there?
Monkey!
Monkey who?
Monkey won't fit that's why I knocked.

Knock Knock
Who's there?
Moppet!
Moppet who?
Moppet up before it gets sticky.

Knock Knock
Who's there?
Morrie!
Morrie who?
Morrie tries to kiss me the more I run away.

Knock Knock
Who's there?
Morris!
Morris who?
Morris in the pot, help yourself.

Knock Knock
Who's there?
Modem!
Modem who?
Modem lawns, the grass is getting too long.

Knock Knock
Who's there?
Morrison!
Morrison who?
Morrison, the more suntan.

Knock Knock
Who's there?
Morrissey!
Morrissey who?
Morrissey you the more I want you...

Knock Knock
Who's there?
Mort!
Mort who?
Mort to the point, who are you?

Knock Knock
Who's there?
Mortimer!

Mortimer who?
Mortimer than meets the eye.

Knock Knock
Who's there?
Moscow!
Moscow who?
Moscow home soon.

> Knock Knock
> Who's there?
> Moses!
> Moses who?
> Moses will you come and
> have tea with us?

Knock Knock
Who's there?
Moth!
Moth who?
Moth get mythelf a new key.

> Knock Knock
> Who's there?
> Mountain!
> Mountain who?
> Mountain debts.

Knock Knock
Who's there?
Moustache!
Moustache who?
Moustache you a question, are
you ready?

> Knock Knock
> Who's there?
> Mozart!
> Mozart who?
> Mozart is in museums or
> galleries.

Knock Knock
Who's there?
Muffin!
Muffin who?
Muffin the matter with me, how
about you?

> Knock Knock
> Who's there?
> Murphy!
> Murphy who?
> Murphy, murphy me.

Knock Knock
Who's there?
Murray!
Murray who?
Murray Lee rolling along.

> Knock Knock
> Who's there?
> Murray!
> Murray who?
> Murray me? Not likely!

Knock Knock
Who's there?
Musket!
Musket who?
Musket in, it's urgent.

> Knock Knock
> Who's there?
> Mustafa!
> Mustafa who?
> Mustafa pee, I'm dying for
> the toilet.

Knock Knock
Who's there?
Myth!
Myth who?
Myth you too!

Knock Knock
Who's there?
Nadia!
Nadia who?
Nadia head if you understand
what I'm saying.

Knock Knock
Who's there?
Nana!
Nana who?
Nana your business.

Knock Knock
Who's there?
Nancy!
Nancy who?
Nancy a biscuit?

Knock Knock
Who's there?
Nanny!
Nanny who?
Nanny one at home?

Knock Knock
Who's there?
Nantucket!
Nantucket who?
Nantucket, but she'll have to
give it back.

Knock Knock
Who's there?
Neal!
Neal who?
Neal down and look through the
letterbox.

Knock Knock
Who's there?
Nebraska!
Nebraska who?

Nebraska woman how old
she is.

Knock Knock
Who's there?
Nettie!
Nettie who?
Nettie as a fruitcake.

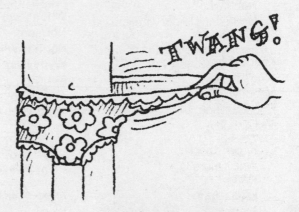

TWANG!

Knock Knock
Who's there?
Nick!
Nick who?
Nick R. Elastic.

Knock Knock
Who's there?
Noah!
Noah who?
Noah good place to eat?

Knock Knock
Who's there?
Noah!
Noah who?
Noah yes, which is it?

Knock Knock
Who's there?
Noah!
Noah who?
Noah body knows the trouble
I've seen.

> Knock Knock
> Who's there?
> Noah!
> Noah who?
> Noah don't know who you
> are either.

Knock Knock
Who's there?
Nobody!
Nobody who?
Just nobody!

> Knock Knock
> Who's there?
> Noel!
> Noel who?
> Noels are too clever by half.

Knock Knock
Who's there?
Noise!
Noise who?
Noise to see you.

> Knock Knock
> Who's there?
> Noleen!
> Noleen who?
> Noleen meat on the beef I
> bought yesterday.

Knock Knock
Who's there?
Noleen!
Noleen who?

Noleen-ing on the lamppost at
the corner of the street in case a
certain little lady comes by.

> Knock Knock
> Who's there?
> Norma Lee!
> Norma Lee who?
> Norma Lee I have my key.

Knock Knock
Who's there?
Norman!
Norman who?
Norman has ever set foot here before.

> Knock Knock
> Who's there?
> Norway!
> Norway who?
> Norway will I leave until you
> open this door.

Knock Knock
Who's there?
Nuisance!
Nuisance who?
What's nuisance yesterday?

> Knock Knock
> Who's there?
> Nurse!
> Nurse who?
> Nurse sense talking to you.

Knock Knock
Who's there?
Oasis!
Oasis who?
Oasis, let your sister in.

> Knock Knock
> Who's there?

Obi Wan!
Obi Wan who?
Obi Wan of the good guys, let me in.

Knock Knock
Who's there?
Oboe!
Oboe who?
Oboe, I've got the wrong address.

Knock Knock
Who's there?
Ocelot!
Ocelot who?
Ocelot of questions, don't you?

Knock Knock
Who's there?
Odette!
Odette who?
Odette can take years to repay.
Always read the small print.

Knock Knock
Who's there?
Odysseus!
Odysseus who?
Odysseus the last straw.

Knock Knock
Who's there?
Ogre!
Ogre who?
Ogre take a flying leap.

Knock Knock
Who's there?
Oil change!
Oil change who?
Oil change my shoes and be back in a minute.

Knock Knock
Who's there?
Ohio!
Ohio who?
Ohio Silver Lining.

Knock Knock
Who's there?
Ohio!
Ohio who?
Ohio feeling?

Knock Knock
Who's there?
Olaf!
Olaf who?
Olaf if you think that it's funny.

Knock Knock
Who's there?
Olaf!
Olaf who?
Olaf you.

Knock Knock
Who's there?
Oldest Son!
Oldest Son who?
Oldest Son shines bright on my old Kentucky home.

Knock Knock
Who's there?
Old King Cole!
Old King Cole who?
Old King Cole, so turn the heating up.

Knock Knock
Who's there?
Ole!
Ole who?
Ole Little Town of Bethlehem.

Knock Knock
Who's there?
Olga!
Olga who?
Olga home if you don't open up.

Knock Knock
Who's there?
Olive!
Olive who?
Olive none of your lip.

Knock Knock
Who's there?
Olive!
Olive who?
Olive across the road.

Knock Knock
Who's there?
Olive!
Olive who?
Olive you too.

Knock Knock
Who's there?
Oliver!
Oliver who?
Oliver, but she doesn't love me.

Knock Knock
Who's there?
Oliver!
Oliver who?
Oliver clothes are getting wet,
it's pouring with rain out here.

Knock Knock
Who's there?
Olivia!
Olivia who?
Olivia me alone.

Knock Knock
Who's there?
Olivia!
Olivia who?
Olivia but I lost the key.

Knock Knock
Who's there?
Ollie!
Ollie who?
Ollie time you do that I want to
scream.

Knock Knock
Who's there?
Oman!
Oman who?
Oman, you are cute.

Knock Knock
Who's there?
Omar!
Omar who?
Omar goodness gracious, I've got
the wrong door!

Knock Knock
Who's there?
Omega!
Omega who?
Omega best man win.

Knock Knock
Who's there?
Omelette!
Omelette who?
Omelette-ing you kiss me.

Knock Knock
Who's there?
Oslo!
Oslo who?
Oslo down, what's the hurry?

Knock Knock
Who's there?
Omelette!
Omelette who?
Omelette smarter than you
think I am!

Knock Knock
Who's there?
Onya!
Onya who?
Onya marks, get set, go!

Knock Knock
Who's there?
Ooze!
Ooze who?
Ooze been sleeping in my
bed?

Knock Knock
Who's there?
Oprah!
Oprah who?
Oprah-tunity, and you thought
opportunity only knocked once.

Knock Knock
Who's there?
Orange!
Orange who?
Orange you even going to
open the door?

Knock Knock
Who's there?
Orange juice!
Orange juice who?
Orange juice sorry you asked?

Knock Knock
Who's there?
Organ!

Organ who?
Organ-ize a party, it's my
birthday!

Knock Knock
Who's there?
Osborn!
Osborn who?
Osborn today – it's my birthday.

Knock Knock
Who's there?
Oscar!
Oscar who?
Oscar silly question, get a silly
answer.

Knock Knock
Who's there?
Oswald!
Oswald who?
Oswald my chewing gum.

Knock Knock
Who's there?
Otis!
Otis who?
Otis is a wonderful day for a
walk in the park.

Knock Knock
Who's there?
Otto!
Otto who?
Otto remember, but I can't.

Knock Knock
Who's there?
Owen!
Owen who?
Owen are you going to let
me in?

Knock Knock
Who's there?
Owl!
Owl who?
Owl I can say is knock, knock.

Knock Knock
Who's there?
Owl!
Owl who?
**Owl be sad if you don't let
me in.**

Knock Knock
Who's there?
Oz!
Oz who?
Oz got something for you.

Knock Knock
Who's there?
Ozzie!
Ozzie who?
Ozzie you later!

Knock Knock
Who's there?
Pablo!
Pablo who?
Pablo your horn.

Knock Knock
Who's there?
Paine!
Paine who?
Paine in the neck.

Knock Knock
Who's there?
Pam!
Pam who?
Pam-per yourself.

Knock Knock
Who's there?
Pammy!
Pammy who?
Pammy the key, the door is
locked.

Knock Knock
Who's there?
Panther!
Panther who?
Panther what you wear on your
legs.

Knock Knock
Who's there?
Paris!
Paris who?
Paris good but I prefer apple.

Knock Knock
Who's there?
Parton!
Parton who?
Parton my French.

Knock Knock
Who's there?
Passion!
Passion who?
Passion by and thought I'd pop in to say hello.

Knock Knock
Who's there?
Pasta!
Pasta who?
Pasta salt please.

Knock Knock
Who's there?
Pasture!
Pasture who?
Pasture bedtime, isn't it?

Knock Knock
Who's there?
Pat!
Pat who?
Pat up your troubles in your old kit bag.

Knock Knock
Who's there?
Patrick!
Patrick who?
Patrick-ed me into coming here.

Knock Knock
Who's there?
Patsy!
Patsy who?
Patsy dog on the head, he likes it.

Knock Knock
Who's there?
Paul!
Paul who?
Paul shook up.

Knock, knock.
Who's there?
Paul.
Paul who?
Paul the rope and raise the drawbridge please!

Knock Knock
Who's there?
Paul and Portia!
Paul and Portia who?
Paul and Portia door to open it.

Knock Knock
Who's there?
Paula!
Paula who?
Paula up the door handle will you and let me in.

Knock Knock
Who's there?
Pecan!
Pecan who?
Pecan work it out.

Knock Knock
Who's there?
Pecan!
Pecan who?
Pecan somebody your own size.

Knock Knock
Who's there?
Peg!
Peg who?
Peg your pardon, I've got the wrong door.

Knock Knock
Who's there?

Pencil!
Pencil who?
Pencil fall down if the elastic goes.

Knock Knock
Who's there?
Penny!
Penny who?
Penny for your thoughts.

Knock Knock
Who's there?
Pepper!
Pepper who?
Pepper pants rustle when you
walk.

Knock Knock
Who's there?
Pepperoni!
Pepperoni who?
Pepperoni makes me sneeze.

Knock Knock
Who's there?
Percy!
Percy who?
Percy Vere and you'll succeed.

Knock Knock
Who's there?
Perry!
Perry who?
Perry well, thank you.

Knock Knock
Who's there?
Personal!
Personal who?
Personal catch their death of cold
out here.

Knock Knock
Who's there?
Pepsi!
Pepsi who?
Pepsi through the keyhole.

Knock Knock
Who's there?
Perth!
Perth who?
Perth your lips and whistle.

Knock Knock
Who's there?
Petal!
Petal who?
Petal fast, it's a steep hill.

Knock Knock
Who's there?
Petunia!
Petunia who?
Petunia and me, there's only a
door.

Knock Knock
Who's there?
Phil!
Phil who?
Phil-y me to the moon, let
me play among the stars, let
me see what spring is like on
Jupiter and Mars.

Knock Knock
Who's there?
Philip!
Philip who?
Philip the tank, I've got a long way
to go.

Knock Knock
Who's there?
Phineas!
Phineas who?
Phineas thing happened on
the way here.

Knock Knock
Who's there?
Phoebe!
Phoebe who?
Phoebe too high for us to pay.

Knock Knock
Who's there?
Phoney!
Phoney who?
Phoney I'd known it was you.

Knock Knock
Who's there?
Phyllis!
Phyllis who?
Phyllis in on the news.

Knock Knock
Who's there?

Piaf!
Piaf who?
Piaf your bills to avoid getting
into debt.

Knock Knock
Who's there?
Pickle!
Pickle who?
Pickle little flower and give it to your
mother.

Knock Knock
Who's there?
Pickle!
Pickle who?
Oh, that's my favourite wind
instrument.

Knock Knock
Who's there?
Pierre!
Pierre who?
Pierre at 6p.m. and I'll tell you.

Knock Knock
Who's there?
Pierre!
Pierre who?
Pierre through the keyhole,
you'll see.

Knock Knock
Who's there?
Pigment!
Pigment who?
Pigment a lot to me and now he's
gone.

Knock Knock
Who's there?
Pill!
Pill who?

Yes please, and a sheet to go with it.

Knock Knock
Who's there?
Pina!
Pina who?
Pina long time since I've seen you.

Knock Knock
Who's there?
Pinafore!
Pinafore who?
Pinafore your thoughts.

Knock Knock
Who's there?
Pinza!
Pinza who?
Pinza needles.

Knock Knock
Who's there?
Pizza!
Pizza who?
Pizza cake would be great right now.

Knock Knock
Who's there?
Plane!
Plane who?
Plane dumb won't save you.

Knock Knock
Who's there?
Plato!
Plato who?
Plato fish and chips please.

Knock Knock
Who's there?
Poker!

Poker who?
Poker and see if she's awake.

Knock Knock
Who's there?
Police!
Police who?
Police open the door. I have to go to the bathroom.

Knock Knock
Who's there?
Polly!
Polly who?
Polly the other one.
Knock Knock

Who's there?
Pollyanna!
Pollyanna who?
Pollyanna bad kid when you get to know her.

Knock Knock
Who's there?
Pop!
Pop who?
Pop over to the shop for me.

Knock Knock
Who's there?
Porpoise!
Porpoise who?
Porpoise of my visit is just to say hello.

Knock Knock
Who's there?
Portia!
Portia who?
Portia the door, it's stuck.

Knock Knock
Who's there?
Porthos!
Porthos who?
Porthos drinks, I'm thirsty.

Knock Knock
Who's there?
Pudding!
Pudding who?
Pudding on your shoes before your trousers is a bad idea.

Knock Knock
Who's there?
Punch!
Punch who?
Don't punch me, I just got here.

Knock Knock
Who's there?
Pyjamas!
Pyjamas who?
Pyjamas around me and hold me tight.

Knock Knock
Who's there?
Pylon!
Pylon who?
Pylon the coats, it's freezing out here.

Knock Knock
Who's there?
Quacker!
Quacker who?
Quacker another bad joke and I'm leaving.

Knock Knock
Who's there?
Quentin!
Quentin who?
Quentin my thirst.

Knock Knock
Who's there?
Quiet Tina!
Quiet Tina who?
Quiet Tina courtroom – the prosecution wants to speak.

Knock Knock
Who's there?
Rabbit!
Rabbit who?
Rabbit up carefully, it's a present

249

Knock Knock
Who's there?
Radio!
Radio who?
Radio not, here I come!

Knock Knock
Who's there?
Ralph!
Ralph who?
Ralph! Ralph! Ralph! I'm a
puppy dog.

Knock Knock
Who's there?
Randy!
Randy who?
Randy four-minute mile.

Knock Knock
Who's there?
Raoul!
Raoul who?
Raoul with the punches.

Knock Knock
Who's there?
Rapunzel!
Rapunzel who?
Rapunzel troubles in your old
kit bag.

Knock Knock
Who's there?
Ray!
Ray who?
Ray drops keep falling on my
head.

Knock Knock
Who's there?
Ray!
Ray who?

Ray-ders of the Lost Ark.

Knock Knock
Who's there?
Ray!
Ray who?
Ray-member me?

Knock Knock
Who's there?
Raymond!
Raymond who?
Raymond me again to buy
some cake.

Knock Knock
Who's there?
Razor!
Razor who?
Razor hands, this is a stick up!

Knock Knock
Who's there?
Red!
Red who?
Red-dy, aim, fire!

Knock Knock
Who's there?
Rena!
Rena who?
Rena this bell doesn't do
any good.

Knock Knock
Who's there?
Renata!
Renata who?
Renata milk, could I borrow some?

Knock Knock
Who's there?
Rene!

Rene who?
Rene way when the bogey man came!

Knock Knock
Who's there?
Reuben!
Reuben who?
Reuben my eyes makes them sore.

Knock Knock
Who's there?
Rhoda!
Rhoda who?
Rhoda boat as fast as you can.

Knock Knock
Who's there?
Rhonda!
Rhonda who?
Rhonda bend.

Knock Knock
Who's there?
Rhoda!
Rhoda who?
Rhoda horse the other day.

Knock Knock
Who's there?
Rhona!
Rhona who?
Rhona boat makes your arms ache.

Knock Knock
Who's there?
Richard!
Richard who?
Richard poor have little in common.

Knock Knock
Who's there?

Ringo!
Ringo who?
Ringo Ringo roses, a pocket full of posies.

Knock Knock
Who's there?
Rio!
Rio who?
Rio-rrange your bedroom please.

Knock Knock
Who's there?
Riot!
Riot who?
Riot on time, here I am.

Knock Knock
Who's there?
Rita!
Rita who?
Rita good book, you might learn something!

Knock Knock
Who's there?
Robin!
Robin who?
Robin the piggy bank again.

Knock Knock
Who's there?
Rocky!
Rocky who?
Rocky bye baby on the tree top…

Knock Knock
Who's there?
Roland!
Roland who?
Roland butter please.

Knock Knock
Who's there?
Roland!
Roland who?
Roland stones gather no moss.

Knock Knock
Who's there?
Rolf!
Rolf who?
Rolf out the barrel.

Knock Knock
Who's there?
Romeo!
Romeo who?
Romeo-ver to the other side of the lake.

Knock Knock
Who's there?
Ron!
Ron who?
Ron the gauntlet.

Knock Knock
Who's there?
Rosa!
Rosa who?
Rosa corn grow in a field.

Knock Knock
Who's there?
Rosina!
Rosina who?
Rosina vase.

Knock Knock
Who's there?
Roxanne!
Roxanne who?
Roxanne pebbles are all over this beach.

Knock Knock
Who's there?
Roxie!
Roxie who?
Roxie horror picture show.

Knock Knock
Who's there?
Royal!
Royal who?
Royal give you a lift if you ask him nicely.

Knock Knock
Who's there?
Rufus!
Rufus who?
Rufus leaking and I'm getting wet.

Knock Knock
Who's there?
Rupert!
Rupert who?
Rupert your left arm in, your left arm out…

Knock Knock
Who's there?
Russell!
Russell who?
Russell up something to eat.

Knock Knock
Who's there?
Russian!
Russian who?
Russian about makes me tired.

Knock Knock
Who's there?
Ruth!
Ruth who?
Ruth is on fire, fetch a bucket!

Knock Knock
Who's there?
Sabina!
Sabina who?
Sabina a long time since I've
seen you.

Knock Knock
Who's there?
Sacha!
Sacha who?
Sacha fuss, just because I knocked
on your door.

Knock Knock
Who's there?
Saddam!
Saddam who?
Saddam and shut up.

Knock Knock
Who's there?
Saddam!
Saddam who?
Saddam waste of a day waiting for
you to answer the door!

Knock Knock
Who's there?
Sadie!
Sadie who?
Sadie ten times table twice.

Knock Knock
Who's there?
Sadie!
Sadie who?
Sadie Pledge of Allegiance.

Knock Knock
Who's there?
Safari!
Safari who?

Safari, so good.

Knock Knock
Who's there?
Sal!
Sal who?
Sal-ong way to Tipperary.

Knock Knock
Who's there?
Sally!
Sally who?
Sally-brate me coming round to
see you.

Knock Knock
Who's there?
Salome!
Salome who?
Salome in please, it's cold out
here.

Knock Knock
Who's there?
Sam!
Sam who?
Sam person who knocked on the
door last time.

Knock Knock
Who's there?
Sam!
Sam who?
Sam Francisco, here I come.

Knock Knock
Who's there?
Sam!
Sam who?
Sam day you'll recognize me.

Knock Knock
Who's there?

Sam and Janet!
Sam and Janet who?
Sam and Janet evening, you
will meet a stranger…

Knock Knock
Who's there?
Samantha!
Samantha who?
Samantha baby have gone to town.

Knock Knock
Who's there?
Sammy!
Sammy who?
Sammy a postcard when you
go on vacation.

Knock Knock
Who's there?
Samson!
Samson who?
Samson you turned out to be.

Knock Knock
Who's there?
Samuel!
Samuel who?
Samuel be famous one day.

Knock Knock
Who's there?
Sandy!
Sandy who?
Sandy locksmith to get this
door open.

Knock Knock
Who's there?
Santa!
Santa who?
Santa email but you
never replied.

Knock Knock
Who's there?
Sarah!
Sarah who?
Sarah doctor in the house?

Knock Knock
Who's there?
Sari!
Sari who?
Sari I was sarong.

Knock Knock
Who's there?
Saul!
Saul who?
Saul the King's horses and all the
King's men…

Knock Knock
Who's there?
Savannah!
Savannah who?
Savannah you going to open
this door?

Knock Knock
Who's there?
Says!
Says who?
Says me, that's who!

Knock Knock
Who's there?
Scissor!
Scissor who?
Scissor and Cleopatra.

Knock Knock
Who's there?
Scold!
Scold who?
Scold enough for snow.

Knock Knock
Who's there?
Scotland!
Scotland who?
Scotland on his head, quick call an ambulance.

Knock Knock
Who's there?
Scott!
Scott who?
Scott nothing to do with you.

Knock Knock
Who's there?
Seamus!
Seamus who?
Seamus you're busy – it would have been a nice day for a picnic.

Knock Knock
Who's there?
Sebastian!
Sebastian who?
Sebastian of the community.

Knock Knock
Who's there?
Senior!
Senior who?
Senior so nosy, I'm not going to tell you.

Knock Knock
Who's there?
Senor!
Senor who?
Senor brother in town half an hour ago.

Knock Knock
Who's there?

Seoul!
Seoul who?
Seoul food.

Knock Knock
Who's there?
Seth!
Seth who?
Seth me, and what I thay goes!

Knock Knock
Who's there?
Seven!
Seven who?
Seven knows.

Knock Knock
Who's there?
Seymour!
Seymour who?
Seymour if you open the door.

Knock Knock
Who's there?
Shaun!
Shaun who?
Shaun sheep look silly.

Knock Knock
Who's there?
Sharon!
Sharon who?
Sharon share alike.

Knock Knock
Who's there?
Sheik!
Sheik who?
Sheik-speare married an Avon lady.

Knock Knock
Who's there?
Sheik and Geisha!
Sheik and Geisha who?
Sheik and Geisha-ll find.

Knock Knock
Who's there?
Shelby!
Shelby who?
Shelby coming round the mountain when she comes...

Knock Knock
Who's there?
Shelley Cohn!
Shelley Cohn who?
Shelley Cohn carne.

Knock Knock
Who's there?
Sherbert!
Sherbert who?
Sherbert Forest is where Robin Hood lived.

Knock Knock
Who's there?
Sherlock!
Sherlock who?
Sherlock your door – someone could break in.

Knock Knock
Who's there?
Sherry!
Sherry who?
Sherry dance?

Knock Knock
Who's there?
Shirley!
Shirley who?
Shirley I don't have to tell you.

Knock Knock
Who's there?
Shoe!
Shoe who?
Shoe, you, you're annoying me.

Knock Knock
Who's there?
Sicily!
Sicily who?
Sicily question.

Knock Knock
Who's there?
Sid!
Sid who?
Sid down and have a cup of tea.

Knock Knock
Who's there?
Sienna!
Sienna who?
Sienna good at putting up shelves?

Knock Knock
Who's there?
Sigrid!

Sigrid who?
Sigrid service – open up!

Knock Knock
Who's there?
Simon!
Simon who?
Simon the other side of the door,
would you please let me in?

Knock Knock
Who's there?
Simon!
Simon who?
Simon the dotted line.

Knock Knock
Who's there?
Sinbad!
Sinbad who?
Sinbad and you'll never get to
heaven.

Knock Knock
Who's there?
Sincerely!
Sincerely who?
Sincerely this morning I've been
waiting for you to open this door.

Knock Knock
Who's there?
Sinead!
Sinead who?
Sineadn't have bothered
answering the door .

Knock Knock
Who's there?
Sinker!
Sinker who?
Sinker swim, it's up to you.

Knock Knock
Who's there?
Sir!
Sir who?
Sir View, right?

Knock Knock
Who's there?
Sis!
Sis who?
Sis any way to treat a friend?

Knock Knock
Who's there?
Sizzle!
Sizzle who?
Sizzle hurt me more than it will
hurt you.

Knock Knock
Who's there?
Sloane!
Sloane who?
Sloane-ly outside, let me in.

Knock Knock
Who's there?
Smee!
Smee who?
Smee, your neighbour.

Knock Knock
Who's there?
Sneezy!
Sneezy who?
Sneezy thing to do, answering
the door.

Knock Knock
Who's there?
Sofa!
Sofa who?
Sofa, so good!

Knock Knock
Who's there?
Soda!
Soda who?
Soda socks, they're full of holes.

Knock Knock
Who's there?
Soldier!
Soldier who?
Soldier bike yet?

Knock Knock
Who's there?
Sonata!
Sonata who?
Sonata such a big deal.

Knock Knock
Who's there?
Sondheim!
Sondheim who?
Sondheim soon we'll meet again.

Knock Knock
Who's there?
Sonia!
Sonia who?
Sonia bird in a gilded cage.

Knock Knock
Who's there?
Sonia!
Sonia who?
Sonia foot, I can smell it from here.

Knock Knock
Who's there?
Sonia!
Sonia who?
Sonia be another year older.

Knock Knock
Who's there?
Sonny!
Sonny who?
Sonny outside, isn't it?

Knock Knock
Who's there?
Sophie!
Sophie who?
Sophie come to ze end of ze lesson.

Knock Knock
Who's there?
Soup!
Soup who?
Soup-erman!

Knock Knock
Who's there?
Spain!
Spain who?
Spain to have to keep knocking on this door.

Knock Knock
Who's there?
Sparkle!
Sparkle who?
Sparkle start a fire if you're not careful.

Knock Knock
Who's there?
Sparrow!
Sparrow who?
Sparrow little change?

Knock Knock
Who's there?
Spectre!
Spectre who?

Spectre Columbo. You're under arrest!

Knock Knock
Who's there?
Sphinx!
Sphinx who?
Sphinx your tie, it's crooked.

Knock Knock
Who's there?
Spice!
Spice who?
Spice, the final frontier.

Knock Knock
Who's there?
Spider!
Spider who?
Spider what everyone says, I like you.

Knock Knock
Who's there?
Stacey!
Stacey who?
Stacey what happens next.

Knock Knock
Who's there?
Stacey!
Stacey who?
Stacey-ted until the bus stops.

Knock Knock
Who's there?
Stalin!
Stalin who?
Stalin for time.

Knock Knock
Who's there?
Spock!
Spock who?
Spock louder.

Knock Knock
Who's there?
Stan!
Stan who?
Stan back, I'm knocking the door down.

Knock Knock
Who's there?
Stan and Della!
Stan and Della who?
Stan and Della-ver!

Knock Knock
Who's there?
Stanton!
Stanton who?
Stanton out here in the cold is no fun.

Knock Knock
Who's there?
Statue!
Statue who?
Statue in there?

Knock Knock
Who's there?
Stella!
Stella who?
Stella no answer at the door.

Knock Knock
Who's there?
Stephanie!
Stephanie who?
Stephanie gas, we're running late.

Knock Knock
Who's there?
Steve!
Steve who?
Steve upper lip.

Knock Knock
Who's there?
Stopwatch!
Stopwatch who?
Stopwatch you're doing right now!

Knock Knock
Who's there?
Stork!
Stork who?
Stork up on ice cream, I'm
coming to stay.

Knock Knock
Who's there?
Stu!
Stu who?
Stu late to ask questions.

Knock Knock
Who's there?
Stubborn!
Stubborn who?
Stubborn your toe really hurts.

Knock Knock
Who's there?
Sturdy!
Sturdy who?
Sturdy pot before dinner burns.

Knock Knock
Who's there?
Sultan!
Sultan who?
Sultan pepper.

Knock Knock
Who's there?
Summer!
Summer who?
Summer good, summer bad.

Knock Knock
Who's there?
Summertime!
Summertime who?
Summertime you will answer
this door.

Knock Knock
Who's there?
Sunday!
Sunday who?
Sunday in the future you'll just
let me in.

Knock Knock
Who's there?
Sven!
Sven who?
Sven Brides for Seven Brothers.

Knock Knock
Who's there?
Swede!
Swede who?
Swede Caroline.

Knock Knock
Who's there?
Sweden!
Sweden who?
Sweden sour is my favourite
Chinese meal.

Knock Knock
Who's there?
Sybil!
Sybil who?
Sybil Simon met a pieman...

Knock Knock
Who's there?
Sybil!
Sybil who?
Sybil-ing rivalry.

Knock Knock
Who's there?
Tad!
Tad who?
Tad's all folks!

Knock Knock
Who's there?
Tailor!
Tailor who?
Tailor head, your call.

Knock Knock
Who's there?
Talbot!
Talbot who?
Talbot too thin.

Knock Knock
Who's there?
Tamara!
Tamara who?
Tamara never comes.

Knock Knock
Who's there?
Tariq!
Tariq who?
Tariq of perfume will put
anyone off.

Knock Knock
Who's there?
Teacher!
Teacher who?
Teacher to go knocking on my door
in the middle of the night.

Knock Knock
Who's there?
Teddy!
Teddy who?
Teddy is the beginning of the
rest of your life.

Knock Knock
Who's there?
Telly!
Telly who?
Telly your friend to come out.

Knock Knock
Who's there?
Tennessee!
Tennessee who?
Tennessee you tonight.

Knock Knock
Who's there?
Tennis!
Tennis who?
Tennis five plus five.

Knock Knock
Who's there?
Termite!
Termite who?
Termite be something wrong
with your glasses – it's me!

Knock Knock
Who's there?
Termite!
Termite who?
Termite's the night.

Knock Knock
Who's there?
Tex!
Tex who?
Tex you ages to open the door.

Knock Knock
Who's there?
Texas!
Texas who?
Texas are getting higher every
year.

Knock Knock
Who's there?
Thatcher!
Thatcher who?
Thatcher could get away with
not opening the door!

Knock Knock
Who's there?
Thayer!
Thayer who?
Thayer thorry and I won't throw
thith pie in your face!

Knock Knock
Who's there?
Thea!

Thea who?
Thea later, alligator!

Knock Knock
Who's there?
Thelonius!
Thelonius who?
Thelonius kid in town has no friends.

Knock Knock
Who's there?
Theodore!
Theodore who?
Theodore wasn't open so I
knocked.

Knock Knock
Who's there?
Theresa!
Theresa who?
Theresa fly in my soup.

Knock Knock
Who's there?
Thermos!
Thermos who?
Thermos be a better knock
knock joke than this!

Knock Knock
Who's there?
Tillie!
Tillie who?
Tillie comes I'm going to wait here.

Knock Knock
Who's there?
Tish!
Tish who?
Have you got a cold?

Knock Knock
Who's there?

Toby!
Toby who?
Toby or not Toby, that is the question.

Knock Knock
Who's there?
Tom Sawyer!
Tom Sawyer who?
Tom Sawyer yesterday
on the bus.

Knock Knock
Who's there?
Too whit!
Too whit who?
I didn't know you had a pet owl.

Knock Knock
Who's there?
Toodle!
Toodle who?
Goodbye!

Knock Knock
Who's there?
Tobias!
Tobias who?
Tobias a pig, that's why I
went to market.

Knock Knock
Who's there?
Torch!
Torch who?
Torch you'd never ask.

Knock Knock
Who's there?
Toucan!
Toucan who?
Toucan play at that game.

Knock Knock
Who's there?
Toyota!
Toyota who?
Toyota be a law against such
awful jokes!

Knock Knock
Who's there?
Tracy!
Tracy who?
Tracy picture with a pencil.

Knock Knock
Who's there?
Tristan!
Tristan who?
Tristan Isolde than his brother.

Knock Knock
Who's there?
Trixie!
Trixie who?
Trixie couldn't do because he was a bad magician.

Knock Knock
Who's there?
Troy!
Troy who?
Troy the bell instead.

Knock Knock
Who's there?
Truman!
Truman who?
Truman and good needed for the jury.

Knock Knock
Who's there?
Turner!
Turner who?
Turner round, what is that behind you?

Knock Knock
Who's there?
Turnip!
Turnip who?

Turnip the heating, it's cold in here!

Knock Knock
Who's there?
Ty!
Ty who?
Ty up loose ends.

Knock Knock
Who's there?
Tyrone!
Tyrone who?
Tyrone shoelaces, I'm fed up of doing them for you!

Knock Knock
Who's there?
Tyson!
Tyson who?
Tyson garlic around your neck to ward off vampires.

Knock Knock
Who's there?
UB40!
UB40 who?
UB40 today, happy birthday!

Knock Knock
Who's there?
UCI!
UCI who?
UCI had to ring because you didn't answer when I knocked!

Knock Knock
Who's there?
Una!
Una who?
No, I don't. Please tell me!

Knock Knock
Who's there?

Unite!
Unite who?
Unite a person, you call
him Sir!

Knock Knock
Who's there?
Urchin!
Urchin who?
Urchin is pointed!

Knock Knock
Who's there?
Utah!
Utah who?
Utah sight, out of mind.

Knock Knock
Who's there?
Value!
Value who?
Value be my Valentine?

Knock Knock
Who's there?
Vanda!
Vanda who?
Vanda you vant me to
come around?

Knock Knock
Who's there?
Vanessa!
Vanessa who?
Vanessa bus due?

Knock Knock
Who's there?
Violins!
Violins who?
Violins is the wrong way to
settle an argument.

Knock Knock
Who's there?
Vanessa!
Vanessa who?
Vanessa time I ring the bell,
you'd better let me in!

Knock Knock
Who's there?
Vaughan!
Vaughan who?
Vaughan day my prince will come.

Knock Knock
Who's there?
Venice!
Venice who?
Venice your mother coming home?

Knock Knock
Who's there?
Vikram!
Vikram who?
Vikram off but I'm still waiting for
you to answer the door.

Knock Knock
Who's there?
Viper!
Viper who?
Viper your nose.

Knock Knock
Who's there?
Viscount!
Viscount who?
Viscount you stop telling jokes?

Knock Knock
Who's there?
Vlad!
Vlad who?
Vlad to meet you!

Knock Knock
Who's there?
Voodoo!
Voodoo who?
Voodoo you think you are?

Knock Knock
Who's there?
Waddle!
Waddle who?
Waddle you give me to make me
go away?

Knock Knock
Who's there?
Wade!
Wade who?
Wade until next time!

Knock Knock
Who's there?
Wah!
Wah who?
Well you don't have to get so
excited about it!

Knock Knock
Who's there?
Waiter!
Waiter who?
Waiter minute while I tie my
shoelaces.

Knock Knock
Who's there?
Waldo!
Waldo who?
Waldo the dishes tomorrow.

Knock Knock
Who's there?
Wallace!
Wallace who?

Wallace about time you
answered the door.

Knock Knock
Who's there?
Wallace!
Wallace who?
Wallace have ears.

Knock Knock
Who's there?
Walnut!
Walnut who?
Walnut too strong, so don't
lean on it.

Knock Knock
Who's there?
Wanda!
Wanda who?
Wanda off and you'll get lost.

Knock Knock
Who's there?
Wanda!
Wanda who?
Wanda buy some cookies?

Knock Knock
Who's there?
Wanda!
Wanda who?
Wanda you want to come to
my house?

Knock Knock
Who's there?
Ward!
Ward who?
Ward do you want?

Knock Knock
Who's there?

Warner!
Warner who?
Warner lift? My car's outside.

Knock Knock
Who's there?
Warner!
Warner who?
Warner you coming out to play?

Knock Knock
Who's there?
Warren!
Warren who?
Warren peace is a famous
Russian novel.

Knock Knock
Who's there?
Watson!
Watson who?
Watson TV this evening?

Knock Knock
Who's there?
Watusi!
Watusi who?
Watusi is what you get!

Knock Knock
Who's there?
Wayne!
Wayne who?
Wayne is coming through the
roof because it's leaking.

Knock Knock
Who's there?
Wayne!
Wayne who?
Wayne are you coming over to my
house?

Knock Knock
Who's there?
Weevil!
Weevil who?
Weevil make you open this
door!

Knock Knock
Who's there?
Wendy!
Wendy who?
Wendy red, red robin comes bob,
bob, bobbin' along.

Knock Knock
Who's there?
Wheelbarrow!
Wheelbarrow who?
Wheelbarrow some money
and go on holiday.

Knock Knock
Who's there?
Who!
Who who?
Bad echo in here, isn't there?

Knock Knock
Who's there?
Wilfred!
Wilfred who?
Wilfred come out and play if
we ask nicely?

Knock Knock
Who's there?
Will!
Will who?
Will you please answer this door!

Knock Knock
Who's there?
Willie!

Knock Knock
Who's there?
Wigwam!
Wigwam who?
Wigwam your head when it's
cold.

Willie who?
Willie be home for dinner?

Knock Knock
Who's there?
Willis!
Willis who?
Willis rain ever stop?

Knock Knock
Who's there?
Wilma!
Wilma who?
Wilma dinner be ready soon?

Knock Knock
Who's there?
Wooden shoe!
Wooden shoe who?
Wooden shoe like to know!

Knock Knock
Who's there?
Woody!
Woody who?
Woody you want?

Knock Knock
Who's there?
Wyn!
Wyn who?
Wyn or lose, it's the taking part
that counts!

Knock Knock
Who's there?
Xavier!
Xavier who?
Xavier your breath, I'm not leaving
until you let me in!

Knock Knock
Who's there?
Xena!
Xena who?
Xena minute!

Knock Knock
Who's there?
Ya!
Ya who?
I didn't know you were a cowboy!

Knock Knock
Who's there?
Yacht!
Yacht who?
Yacht to know me by now!

Knock Knock
Who's there?
Yelp!
Yelp who?
Yelp me, my nose is stuck in
the keyhole!

Knock Knock
Who's there?
Yolande!
Yolande who?
Yolande me a dollar, I'll pay
you back next week!

Knock Knock
Who's there?
You!
You who?
Did you call?

Knock Knock
Who's there?
Yukon!
Yukon who?
Yukon say that again!

Knock Knock
Who's there?
Yvette!
Yvette who?
Yvette helps a lot of sick animals.

Knock Knock
Who's there?
Yvonne!
Yvonne who?
Yvonne to be alone.

Knock Knock
Who's there?
Zeke!
Zeke who?
Zeke and you shall find.

Knock Knock
Who's there?
Zombie!
Zombie who?
Zombies make honey, others are queens.

LIGHT BULBS

How many actors does it take to change a light bulb?
Only one. They don't like to share the spotlight.

How many aerobics instructors does it take to change a light bulb?
Five. Four to do it in perfect synchrony and one to stand there saying: "To the left, and to the left, and to the left, and to the left, and take it out, and put it down, and pick it up, and put it in, and to the right, and to the right, and to the right, and to the right..."

How many aerospace engineers does it take to change a light bulb?
None. It doesn't take a rocket scientist to change a light bulb, you know.

How many people at an American football match does it take to change a light bulb?
Three. One to change it and two to tip the entire contents of the ice bucket over the coach to congratulate him on a successful bulb screwing.

How many American footballers does it take to change a light bulb?
Two. One to screw it in and the other to recover the fumble.

How many archaeologists does does it take to change a light bulb?
Three. One to change it and two to argue about how old the old one is.

How many visitors to an art gallery does it take to screw in a light bulb?
Two. One to do it and one to say, "Huh! My four year old could have done that!"

How many auto mechanics does it take to change a light bulb?
Two. One to screw in all the bulbs he has until he finds one that fits, and the other to tell you he thinks he'll have to replace the whole socket.

How many bankers does it take to change a light bulb?
Four. One to hold the bulb and three to try to remember the combination.

How many cafeteria staff does it take to change a light bulb? **None. They closed eighteen seconds ago, and the manager has just cashed up.**

How many circus performers does it take to change a light bulb? **Four. One for the money, two for the show, three to get ready, and four to go!**

How many country and western singers does it take to change a light bulb? **Four. One to change it, one to sing about how heartbroken he is at the loss of the old one, one to sing about how madly in love she is with the new one, and one to shout "yee-ha!" and throw his hat in the air.**

How many doctors does it take to screw in a light bulb? **Only one, but he has to have a nurse to tell him which end to screw in.**

How many elephants does it take to change a light bulb? **Two, but it has to be a pretty big light bulb.**

How many European ballet dancers does it take to screw in a light bulb? **None, they like Danzig in the dark.**

How many firemen does it take to change a light bulb? **Four. One to change the bulb and three to cut a hole in the roof.**

How many fishermen does it take to change a light bulb? **Four. One to change the light bulb and three to brag about how big the old one was and about the one that they would have changed, but "it got away".**

How many gardeners does it take to change a light bulb? **Three. One to change it and two to have a debate about whether this is the right time of year to be putting in light bulbs or daffodil bulbs.**

How many gas fitters does it take to change a light bulb? **Three. One to turn up the day before when you're out, one to change the switch, and one to bring along the wrong kind of bulb.**

How many grocery store cashiers does it take to change a light bulb? **Are you kidding? They won't even change a five-dollar bill.**

How many health-food freaks does it take to change a light bulb? **Two. One to remove the old one and one to check the ingredients on the new one.**

How many local government officials does it take to change a light bulb?

Fifty. One to change the light bulb and the rest to carry out a fact-finding mission to Barbados to see how they change light bulbs there.

How many lunatics does it take to change a light bulb?
Two. One to change the light bulb and the other to tell him to make sure he sticks his fingers in the socket first, to see if the electricity is switched on.

How many Mafia hitmen does it take to change a light bulb?
Three. One to screw it in, one to watch and one to shoot the witness.

How many magicians does it take to change a light bulb?
It depends on what you want it changed in to...

How many mice does it take to change a light bulb?
One, but you have to cut a hole in the skirting board for it to get in.

How many movie directors does it take to change a light bulb?
Just one, but he wants to do it twenty times, and when he's done, everyone thinks that his last light bulb was much better.

How many musicians does it take to change a light bulb?

How many monkeys does it take to change a light bulb?
Two. One to do it and one to scratch his butt.

SCRATCH

Five. One to change the bulb and four to get in free because they know the guy who owns the socket.

How many mystery writers does it take to screw in a light bulb?
Two. One to screw it almost all the way in and the other to give it a surprising twist at the end.

How many optimists does it take to screw in a light bulb?
None. They're convinced that the power will come back on soon.

How many paranoid people does it take to change a light bulb?
Who wants to know?

How many pessimists does it take to screw in a light bulb?
None. It's a waste of time because the new bulb probably won't work either.

How many philosophers does it take to change a light bulb?
Three. One to change it and two to stand around arguing over whether or not the light bulb exists.

How many politicians does it take to change a light bulb?
Four. One to change it and the other three to deny it.

How many poltergeists does it take to change a light bulb?
Three. One to unscrew the old bulb and drop it on the floor, one to put the new bulb in, and one to move a few more things about just for good measure.

How many procrastinators does it take to screw in a light bulb?
One, but he has to wait until the light is better.

How many psychiatrists does it take to change a light bulb?
Only one, but the light bulb must want to change.

How many punk rockers does it take to change a light bulb?
Two. One to screw in the bulb and the other to smash the old one on his forehead.

How many road workmen does it take to change a light bulb?
Five. One to change the light bulb and four to lean on their shovels and watch the one working.

How many roadies does it take to change a light bulb?
One, two! One, two! One, two!

How many safety inspectors does it take to change a light bulb?
Four. One to change it and three to hold the ladder.

How many schizophrenics does it take to change a light bulb?
Well, he thinks it's five but as we all know it's only him…

How many sheep does it take

to change a light bulb?
Nineteen. One to change it and eighteen to follow him round while he looks for a new one.

How many teenaged girls does it take to screw in a light bulb?
One, but she'll be on the phone for five hours telling all her friends about it.

How many tourists does it take to change a light bulb?
Six. One to hold the bulb and five to ask for directions.

How many university students does it take to change a light bulb?
Two. One to fuse all the electrics while doing something silly, and one to phone the landlord to ask for the light bulb to be changed.

How many waiters does it take to change a light bulb?
None. Even a burned-out bulb can't catch a waiter's eye.

How many WWF wrestlers does it take to change a light bulb?
Five. One to change it and four to fake it.

A man was polishing a light bulb before inserting it into the socket, when there was a big flash and a genie appeared before him.

"I am the genie of the light-bulb," he said. "I will answer any three questions for you, but only three. Do you have three questions you would like to ask?"

"Who? Me?" said the man.

"Yes, you," said the genie. "Now, what is your third question?"

A Frenchman, a German and an Englishman were arguing about which of their respective languages was the best.

The Frenchman said, "French is the language of romance, the most beautiful language in the world."

The German said, "German is the language of science and technology, the language most fitted to the needs of the twenty-first century."

The Englishman said, "Nonsense! There's only one decent language, and that's English. We English say what we mean, no messing about. Take this for instance." He held up a light bulb. "You Frenchmen call it an ampoule. And you Germans call it a Glühlampe. In England, we simply call it a light bulb, which, after all, is precisely what it is."

How does a spoiled rich girl change a light bulb?
She says, "Daddy, I want a new apartment."

How they change the light bulbs in the original Star Trek:
Scotty will report to Captain Kirk that the light bulb in the

Engineering Section is burnt out, at which Kirk will send Bones to pronounce the bulb dead.

Scotty, after checking around, notices that they have no more new light bulbs, and complains that he can't see in the dark to tend to his engines. Kirk must make an emergency stop at the next uncharted planet, Alpha Regula IV, to procure a light bulb from the natives.

Kirk, Spock, Bones, Sulu and three red-shirt security officers beam down. The three security officers are promptly killed by the natives, and the rest of the landing party is captured.

Meanwhile, back in orbit, Scotty notices a Klingon ship approaching and must warp out of orbit to escape detection.

Bones cures the native king, who is suffering from the flu, and as a reward the landing party is set free and given all the light bulbs they can carry.

Scotty cripples the Klingon ship and warps back to the planet just in time to beam up Kirk and the others.

The new bulb is inserted, and the Enterprise continues with its five-year mission.

What did the boy light bulb say to the girl light bulb?
I love you watts and watts.

MILITARY

A general asked his men, "Who likes music?"

Half a dozen soldiers stepped forward straight away.

"Great," said the general. "I just bought a piano. Take it to my apartment on the fourth floor."

What soldiers smell of salt and pepper?
Seasoned troops.

Riding through the forest one day, a medieval duke noticed several archery targets on trees with an arrow smack in the centre of each one. Hugely impressed by such magnificent marksmanship, the duke ordered his followers to find the archer responsible so that he could sign the man up to join his private army. Later that day, they returned with a small boy who was carrying a bow and arrow.

The duke could scarcely believe his eyes. "Do you mean to tell me that this mere boy is the master archer?"

"Yes, sire, it is me," said the boy.

The duke looked at him suspiciously. "Are you sure you didn't just walk up to the targets and then hammer arrows in the centre?"

"No," replied the boy. "I swear on my mother's life that I shot the arrows from one hundred paces."

"Very well," said the duke, "I believe you and hereby admit

you into my service on an annual salary of fifty gold sovereigns for the next ten years. Is that acceptable to you?"

"Yes, sire," answered the boy. "It is most generous of you."

The duke patted the boy on the head and said with a smile, "But you must tell me how you came to be such an outstanding shot."

"It's not difficult," said the boy. "First I fire the arrow at the tree, and then I paint the target around it."

A young soldier went to the army doctor complaining of strange sounds coming from inside his stomach. "I don't know what's happened, doc," he said. "It seems like I've swallowed a watch or a clock or maybe even a bomb."

The army doctor listened to the strange sounds in the soldier's stomach and immediately announced, "I'm going to perform surgery to open you up."

"Why, doc?" asked the soldier.

The doctor replied, "Soldier, I want to see what makes you tick."

Moments before the start of a First World War battle a young recruit said to his sergeant, "I haven't got a rifle, sir."

"No problem, son," said the sergeant. "Here, take this broom. Just point it at the Germans and go, 'Bangety Bang Bang.'"

"But what about a bayonet, sarge?" asked the young soldier.

The sergeant quickly pulled a length of straw from the end of the broom and attached it to the end of the broom handle. "Here, use this. Just go, 'Stabity Stab Stab.'"

Well, the young recruit ended up isolated on the battlefield, holding just his broom. Suddenly a German soldier charged at him. The young recruit pointed the broom at the enemy and went, "Bangety Bang Bang." The German fell dead on the spot.

Then more Germans appeared. The young recruit, amazed by his good fortune, went, "Bangety Bang Bang. Stabity Stab Stab," and mowed down a dozen enemy soldiers.

Finally, the battlefield was clear except for one German walking slowly toward him. The young recruit shouted, "Bangety Bang Bang" but it had no effect. The German kept coming. "Bangety Bang Bang," repeated the young recruit but to no avail. The German was now just a few yards away, so in desperation the young recruit went, "Stabity Stab Stab." The German was unfazed.

Still the German kept coming, slowly but surely. When he reached the young recruit, the German mercilessly stomped him into the ground and said, "Tankety Tank Tank."

Why was William upset when he joined the army?
Because the sergeant ordered the platoon to "fire at will".

With his fort about to be attacked by the Sioux, an army captain sent for his trusty Indian scout. The captain told him, "I want you to use all your legendary tracking skills to give me some idea of enemy numbers."

The Indian scout immediately lay down, put his ear to the ground and reported, "Big war party. Two hundred braves in warpaint. Two chiefs, one on a black horse, one on a white horse. Also medicine man with limp."

"That's incredible!" said the captain. "You can deduce all that information just by listening to the ground?"

"Not really," replied the Indian. "I'm looking under the gate."

Which month do soldiers dislike most?
March.

A young private sought permission from his Commanding Officer to leave camp the following weekend.

"You see," he explained. "My wife's expecting."

"Oh," said the officer, "I understand. Go ahead and tell your wife that I wish her luck."

The following week the same soldier was back again with the same explanation.

"My wife's expecting," he said.

The officer looked surprised.

"Still expecting?" he said. "Well, well, my boy, you must be pretty

bothered. Of course you can have the weekend off."

When the same soldier appeared again the third week, however, the officer lost his temper.

"Don't tell me your wife is still expecting!" he bellowed.

"Yes, sir!" said the soldier resolutely, "She's still expecting."

"What in heaven is she expecting?" cried the officer.

The young soldier replied, "Me."

The sergeant was appalled to discover that ten of his men were late back to army camp following leave. As he waited impatiently at the barracks gates, one man finally ran up to him, panting heavily.

"Sorry, sir, I can explain. You see, I had a date and it ran a little late. I ran to catch the bus but I missed it. So I hailed a cab but it broke down. I managed to find a farm and bought a horse but it dropped dead. In the end, I had to run ten miles, and now I'm here!"

The sergeant was highly sceptical about this explanation, but at least the soldier had made it back eventually, so he let him off this time. A couple of minutes later, eight more of his men ran up to the sergeant, panting. He asked them why they were late. Each told the same story.

"Sorry, sir. I had a date and it ran a little late. I ran to catch the bus but I missed it. So I hailed a cab but it broke down. I managed to find a farm and bought a horse but it dropped dead. In the end, I had to run ten miles, and now I'm here!"

The sergeant eyed them suspiciously but since he had let the first man go, he decided that it was only fair to excuse them, too. A few minutes later, the tenth and last soldier ran up to him, panting heavily.

"Sorry, sir. I had a date and it ran a little late. I ran to catch the bus but I missed it. So I hailed a cab but—"

"Let me guess," interrupted the sergeant. "It broke down."

"No, sir. There were so many dead horses in the road, it took forever to get round them."

Why did the US soldiers storm the necktie store in an English shopping mall?
They'd heard they were invading Tie Rack.

Three American pilots were captured by the Germans during World War Two. The Germans had devised a fiendish way of making their prisoners impart vital information – they made the pilots stand to attention, turn their heads from side to side and say "Tick, tock" over and over.

After three hours of this torture, the first American pilot cracked and began telling the Germans everything he knew.

An hour later, the second pilot cracked under the strain and also disclosed key plans to the Germans.

But the third pilot held on bravely, desperately trying not to crack. He was about halfway cracked and was turning his head to one side only, repeating, "Tick, tick, tick."

The German commanding officer was infuriated by the American's resistance. Finally, he lost his temper, walked over to the pilot and yelled, "Ve haf vays of making you tock!"

A soldier cradled the dying General Custer in his arms at the Little Big Horn. With his last breath, Custer gasped, "I'll never understand Indians. Just a few minutes ago they were singing and dancing…"

MONSTERS

What do you get if you cross an elephant with the Abominable Snowman?
A jumbo yeti.

When should you feed yeti's milk to a baby?
When it's a baby yeti.

Could you kill the Abominable Snowman just by throwing eggs at him?
Of course – he'd be eggs-terminated.

Can the Abominable Snowman jump very high?
Hardly – he can only just clear his throat!

Where are yetis found?
They're so big they're hardly ever lost.

Why shouldn't you dance with a yeti?
Because if it trod on you, you might get flat feet.

How did the yeti feel when he had flu?
Abominable.

What do yetis eat on top of Everest?
High tea.

What kind of man doesn't like to sit in front of the fire?
An Abominable Snowman.

Why was the Abominable Snowman's dog called Frost?
Because Frost bites.

What do Abominable Snowmen call their offspring?
Chill-dren.

Where do Abominable Snowmen go to dance?
To snowballs.

What did one Abominable Snowman say to the other?
I'm afraid I just don't believe in people.

What is the Abominable Snowman's favourite book?
War and Frozen Peas.

Why did the Abominable Snowman send his father to Siberia?
Because he wanted frozen pop.

How does a yeti get to work?
By icicle.

Did you hear the joke about the fierce yeti?
It'll make you roar.

What steps should you take if you see a dangerous yeti on your travels?
Very large ones.

Where do you find wild yetis?
It depends where you left them.

What does a yeti eat for dinner?
Ice-burgers.

What's the difference between Frankenstein and boiled potatoes?
You can't mash Frankenstein.

Did you hear what happened to Frankenstein's monster?
He was stopped for speeding, fined $150 and dismantled for six months.

Igor: Why is Baron Frankenstein such good fun?
Monster: Because he soon has you in stitches.

Why was Baron Frankenstein never lonely?
Because he was good at making fiends.

What should you do if you find yourself in the same room as Frankenstein, Dracula, a werewolf, a vampire and a coven of witches?
Keep your fingers crossed that it's a fancy dress party.

Who brings the monsters their babies?
Frankenstork.

Why did Frankenstein's monster give up boxing?
Because he didn't want to spoil his looks.

What did Frankenstein's monster say when he was struck by lightning?
Great! That was just what I needed.

First monster: The bride of Frankenstein has a lovely face.
Second monster: If you can read between the lines.

What kind of book did Frankenstein's monster like to read?
One with a cemetery plot.

Why did Dr Frankenstein tiptoe past the medicine cabinet?
He didn't want to wake the sleeping pills.

What was the inscription on the tomb of Frankenstein's monster?
Here lies Frankenstein's monster. May he rest in pieces.

Where does the bride of Frankenstein have her hair done?
At the ugly parlour.

What happened to Frankenstein's stupid son?
He had so much wax in his ears that he became a permanent contributor to Madame Tussaud's.

What did one of Frankenstein's ears say to the other?
I didn't know we lived on the same block.

How does Frankenstein sit in his chair?
Bolt upright.

How did Dr Frankenstein pay the men who built his monster?
On a piece rate.

What did Dr Frankenstein get when he put his goldfish's brain in the body of his dog?
I don't know, but it is great at chasing submarines.

How did Frankenstein's monster eat his lunch?
He bolted it down.

What does Frankenstein's monster call a screwdriver?
Daddy.

What do you call a clever monster?
Frank Einstein.

Monster: Someone told me Dr Frankenstein invented the safety match.
Igor: Yes, that was one of his most striking achievements.

Dr Frankenstein: How can I stop that monster charging?
Igor: Why not take away his credit card?

What do you get if you cross King Kong with the Abominable Snowman?
Frostbite.

Why did King Kong join the army?
To learn about gorilla warfare.

What do you do if King Kong sits in front of you at the cinema?
Miss most of the film!

What happened when King Kong swallowed Big Ben?
He found it too time consuming.

What's the best way to get King Kong to sit up and beg?
Wave a two-ton banana in front of his nose.

What do you get if you cross King Kong with a giant frog?
A monster that climbs up the Empire State Building and catches aeroplanes with its tongue.

What's big and hairy and climbs up the Empire State Building in a dress?
Queen Kong.

How can you mend King Kong's arm if he's twisted it?
With a monkey wrench.

If King Kong went to Hong Kong

to play ping pong and died, what would they put on his coffin?
A lid.

King Kong went to Hong Kong to play ping pong and died after being hit on the head. A newspaper reported the story and used the following headline: King Kong Gone, Big Bong on Noggin at Hong Kong Ping Pong Ding Dong.

What is as big as King Kong but doesn't weigh anything?
King Kong's shadow.

What do you get if you cross King Kong with a watchdog?
A terrified postman.

Who is the smelliest, hairiest monarch in the world?
King Pong.

Why didn't King Kong go to Hong Kong?
He didn't like Chinese food.

Why did King Kong paint the bottoms of his feet brown?
So that he could hide upside down in a jar of peanut butter.

What is big, hairy and can fly faster than the speed of sound?
King Koncord.

If King Kong visited England, why would he live in the Tower of London?
Because he's a beef-eater.

What business is King Kong in?
Monkey business.

What would you get if you crossed King Kong with a skunk?
I don't know but it could always get a seat on a bus!

Where does King Kong sleep?
Anywhere he wants to.

What should you do if you are on a picnic with King Kong?
Give him the biggest bananas.

What do you do if you find King Kong in the kitchen?
Just don't monkey with him.

What do you get if King Kong sits on your best friend?
A flat mate.

What do you get if King Kong sits on your piano?
A flat note.

Why is King Kong big and hairy?
So you can tell him apart from a gooseberry.

How do you catch King Kong?
Hang upside down and make a noise like a banana.

What did King Kong say when he rang the wrong number?
King Kong ring wrong.

What do you get if you cross King Kong with a budgie?
A messy cage.

Two policemen in New York were watching King Kong climb up the Empire State Building. One said to the other, "What do you think he's doing?"

"It's obvious," replied his colleague. "He wants to catch a plane."

An explorer in the African jungle heard about a plan to capture the legendary King Kong. And sure enough, when he came to a clearing, there before him, imprisoned in a cage, sat the imposing figure of King Kong.

It occurred to the explorer that he could be the first person ever to touch the great ape and so tentatively he inched towards the cage. Since King Kong appeared quite passive, the explorer thought he would take a chance and reach through the bars to touch him. But as soon as he made contact with the gorilla's fur, King Kong went berserk. He immediately rose to his feet, began beating his chest and with an awesome display of strength, burst through the bars of his cage.

As the explorer ran for his life, King Kong set off in hot pursuit. Instinctively, the explorer headed for the heart of the jungle, hoping that he might be able to hide from his manic pursuer, but wherever he tried to conceal himself, King Kong always managed to find him.

As night began to fall, the explorer prayed that he would be able to lose the gorilla in the darkness but no matter how fast he ran, the sound of King Kong's pounding footsteps was only ever about fifty yards behind.

For three long days and nights, the explorer ran through Africa with King Kong always close behind, occasionally letting out a menacing roar from his vast throat. Eventually, the explorer reached the west coast. There were no ships in sight for an easy escape, so he realized the only option was to dive into the sea and hope that King Kong couldn't swim. But to his horror, the gorilla jumped in straight after him and demonstrated an excellent front crawl.

On and on they swam across the Atlantic – rarely separated by more than thirty yards – until four months later the weary explorer arrived in Brazil. He scrambled ashore with as much energy as he could muster, only to see the mighty King Kong right behind him, still beating his chest ferociously and with steam billowing from his nostrils. Through the streets of Rio they stumbled, explorer and ape equally exhausted, until the explorer took a wrong turn and ended up down a dead end, his escape barred by a twenty-foot-high wall.

With nowhere left to run, he sank to his knees in despair and pleaded to King Kong, "Do whatever you want with me. Kill me, eat me, do what you like, but make it quick. Just put me out of my misery."

King Kong slowly stalked over to the cowering explorer, prodded him with a giant paw and bellowed with a terrifying roar, "You're it!"

Did you hear about the snooker-mad monster? He went to the doctor because he didn't feel well. "What do you eat?" asked the doctor.

"For breakfast I have a couple of red snooker balls, and at lunchtime I grab a black, a pink and two yellows. I have a brown with my tea in the afternoon, and then a blue and another pink for dinner," the monster replied.

"I know why you are not feeling well!" exclaimed the doctor. "You're not getting enough greens."

What do you say to a tetchy monster?
No need to bite my head off.

A man thought he had swallowed a monster, and nothing his doctor said would make him change his mind.

So, finally, the doctor gave him an anaesthetic and put him into a deep sleep. When he woke up, the doctor was standing beside his bed, holding a great big green monster on a lead.

"Nothing more to worry about," the doctor said. "We operated on you and took him out."

"Who are you trying to kid?" said the man. "The monster I swallowed was a blue one."

Where do monsters go for dinner?
To a beastro.

A man was walking behind a hearse with a big monster on a lead. Behind them stretched a long line of mourners.

"What happened?" asked a passer-by.

"The monster bit my wife, and she died of fright."

"Can I borrow it?" the passer-by asked.

The man pointed behind him. "Get in the queue," he said.

Two monsters went duck-hunting with their dogs, but without success.

"I know what it is, Zob," said Grunge. "I know what we're doing wrong."

"What's that then, Grunge?"

"We're not throwing the dogs high enough."

Tarzan climbed to the top of the highest mountain in the jungle. Suddenly, he was surrounded by every kind of hideous, fire-breathing, evil-smelling monster in creation – yetis, goblins, trolls, Martians, mekons, Big Foot, the lot.

Do you know what he said?

"Boy, am I ever in the wrong joke…"

A very posh man was walking around an art gallery, when he stopped by one particular exhibit.

"I suppose this picture of a hideous monster is what you call modern art," he said very pompously.

"No, sir," replied the art gallery assistant. "That's what we call a mirror."

Did you hear about the very well-behaved little monster? **When he was good his father would give him a cent and a pat on the head. By the time he was sixteen he had twenty-five dollars in the bank and his head was totally flat.**

A man's car broke down on a cold and windswept night, near an eerie-looking castle in Transylvania. The wizened old butler invited him to stay the night, and showed him to his room. It was dark and dirty, and the man was scared.

"I hope you'll be comfortable," said the butler. "But if you need anything during the night, just scream."

This little monster boy came home from school one day, crying his eyes out.

"What's the matter, darling?" asked his mother.

"It's all the other monsters at school," he sobbed. "They keep teasing me and saying that I've got a big head."

"Of course you haven't got a big head," said Mrs Monster. "Just ignore them. Now, will you do a little bit of shopping for me? I need a sack of potatoes, ten cartons of orange juice, a dozen loaves of bread, eight cabbages and a cauliflower."

"All right, Mom," said the little monster. "But where's your shopping bag?"

"Oh, that's broken, I'm afraid," said Mrs Monster. "But it doesn't matter – just put the things in your cap."

A man went into a bar with a big, vicious looking monster on a lead.

"Sorry, sir," said the barman. "But that creature looks dangerous. You'll have to tie him up outside."

So the man took the monster outside, and came back and ordered a drink. He was just finishing it when a lady came into the bar and said, "Whose monster is that outside?"

"Mine," said the man, beaming with pride.

"Well, I'm sorry," the lady said. "But my dog's just killed him."

"Killed him! What kind of dog do you have?"

"A miniature poodle," said the lady.

"But how could a miniature poodle kill my great big monster?"

"She got stuck in his throat and choked him."

Three monsters called Manners, Mind-Your-Own-Business and Trouble were on a day's outing from the circus, when all of a sudden Trouble went missing. Being good friends of his, Manners and Mind-Your-Own-Business decided to report Trouble missing.

When they got to the police station, Manners got frightened and decided to stay outside. Mind-Your-Own-Business went in to report the loss. The desk sergeant asked him his name, to which the monster replied, "Mind-Your-Own-Business."

The desk sergeant crossly said, "Where's your manners?"

Mind-Your-Own-Business replied, "Outside."

On hearing such rudeness, the desk sergeant demanded, "Are you looking for trouble?"

Mind-Your-Own-Business quickly replied, "Yes!"

A monster walked into a hamburger restaurant and ordered a cheeseburger, fries and a chocolate milkshake. When he finished his meal he left ten dollars to pay the bill.

The waiter, thinking that the monster probably wasn't very good at adding up, gave him only fifty cents change. At that moment another customer came in.

"Gosh, I've never seen a monster in here before!" he said.

"And you won't be seeing me

First girl: Yesterday I took my boyfriend to see **The Monster From The Swamp** *at the cinema.*
Second girl: What was he like?
First girl: Oh, about ten feet tall, with a horrible, slimey head, and a bolt through his neck.
Second girl: I don't mean your boyfriend, silly. What was the monster like?

again," said the monster furiously. "Not at those prices."

Dr Frankenstein was sitting in his cell when suddenly through the wall came the ghost of his monster, with a rope round his neck.

Frankenstein said, "Monster, monster, what are you doing here?"

The monster said, "Well boss, they hanged me this morning, so now I've come to meet my maker."

Monster: Doctor, doctor, how do I stop my nose from running?
Doctor: Stick out your foot and trip it up.

Patient: Doctor, doctor, you've got to help me – I keep dreaming of bats, creepy-crawlies, demons, ghosts, monsters, vampires, werewolves and yetis.
Doctor: How very interesting! Do you always dream in alphabetical order?

Why did the monster go into hospital?
To have his ghoul-stones removed.

Monster: Doctor, doctor, I need to lose thirty pounds of excess flab.
Doctor: All right, I'll cut your head off.

Monster: Doctor, doctor, what did the X-ray of my head show?
Doctor: Absolutely nothing.

Monster: Doctor, doctor, how long can someone live without a brain?
Doctor: That depends. How old are you?

Monster: Doctor, doctor, I'm a bloodsucking monster and I keep needing to eat doctors.
Doctor: Oh, what a shame. I'm a dentist.

Patient: Doctor, doctor, I keep dreaming there are great, gooey, bug-eyed monsters playing tiddlywinks under my bed. What shall I do?
Doctor: Hide the tiddlywinks.

Patient: Doctor, doctor, I keep thinking I'm the Abominable Snowman.
Doctor: Keep cool.

Doctor: Did the mud pack help your appearance?
Monster: Yes, but it fell off after a few days.

Monster: Where do fleas go in winter?
Werewolf: Search me!

Patient: Can a person be in love with a monster?
Doctor: No.
Patient: Oh. Do you know anyone who wants to buy an extremely large engagement ring then?

What do monsters use to write with?
Ballpoint men.

What do you do with a blue monster?
Try and cheer him up.

What do you do with a green monster?
Wait until it ripens!

Why are monsters' fingers never more than eleven inches long?
Because if they were twelve inches they'd be a foot.

What is the best thing to do if a monster breaks down your front door?
Run out of the back door.

Did you hear about Romeo Monster meeting Juliet Monster?
It was love at first fright.

Why are monsters so forgetful?
Because everything you tell them goes in one ear and out of the others.

The police are looking for a monster with one eye called Cyclops.
What's his other eye called?

What is the best way to speak to a monster?
From a long way away.

Where do space monsters live?
In a far distant terror-tory.

What trees do monsters like best?
Ceme-trees.

Did you hear about the girl

monster who wasn't pretty and wasn't ugly?
She was pretty ugly.

Which monster made friends with three bears?
Ghouldilocks.

What jewels do monsters wear?
Tomb stones.

How can you tell a monster from an elephant?
A monster never remembers.

What's the difference between a monster and a mouse?
A monster makes bigger holes in the skirting board.

Did you hear about the monster who went on a crash diet?
He wrecked three cars and a bus.

Did you hear about the monster who ate a sofa and two chairs?
He had a suite tooth.

What do you get if you cross a tall green monster with a fountain pen?
The Ink-credible Hulk.

Did you hear about the monster with five legs?
His trousers fit him like a glove.

What do you get if you cross a monster's brain with an elastic band?
A real stretch of the imagination.

First monster: That girl over

there just rolled her eyes at me.
Second monster: Well, roll them back, she might need them.

What's big and ugly and goes up and down?
A monster in an elevator.

What's big and ugly and drinks out of the wrong side of the glass?
A monster trying to get rid of hiccups.

What's big and ugly and takes aspirins?
A monster with a headache.

Why did the monster dye her hair yellow?
To see if blondes have more fun.

What's big and ugly and wears sunglasses?
A monster on holiday.

What's big and ugly and found at twenty fathoms?
A monster with an aqualung.

What's big and ugly with red spots?
A monster with measles.

What's big and ugly and has eight wheels?
A monster on roller skates.

Mrs Monster: Will you love me when I'm old and ugly?
Mr Monster: Darling, of course I do.

What's the quickest way to escape from a monster?
Run!

What is a monster who is married with seven children called?
Daddy.

When is a bogey-man most likely to enter your bedroom?
When the door is open.

Boy monster: What would you like for your birthday, sis?
Girl monster: I'd love a frock to match the colour of my eyes.
Boy monster: All right, but where am I going to get a bloodshot dress?

"Here's a good book," said the sales assistant in the book shop to Mrs Monster. "It's called How to Help Your Husband Get Ahead."
"No, thank you," said Mrs Monster. "My husband's got two heads already."

A very tall monster with several arms and legs, all of different lengths, went into a tailor's shop.
"I'd like to see a suit that will fit me," he told the tailor.
"So would I, sir!" said the tailor.

If storks bring human babies, what bring monster babies?
Cranes.

Did you hear about the two-headed monster at the freak show who went on strike for more

money?
He claimed he had an extra mouth to feed.

"Dad, Dad, come quickly! Mother's fighting a horrible twelve-foot monster with two heads and three arms!"
"Don't worry about it, son. I'm sure the monster can look after itself."

What do sea monsters have for dinner?
Fish and ships.

An enormous monster with eight arms and eleven legs walked into a tailor's shop.
"Quick!" shouted the tailor to his assistant. "Hide the 'Free Alterations' sign!"

What is big and hairy and hangs on the line?
A drip-dry monster.

What's big and hairy and goes beep beep?
A monster in a traffic jam.

How do monsters like their shepherd's pie?
Made with real shepherds.

What is a monster's favourite society?
The Consumers' Association.

How can you tell if a monster has a glass eye?
When it comes out in conversation.

Do you know the story about the body-snatchers?
Well, I won't tell you. You might get carried away.

Monster woman: I have the face of a sixteen-year-old girl.
Monster boy: Well you'd better give it back then. You're getting it all wrinkled.

First human boy: I can lift a monster with one hand.
Second human boy: I bet you can't!
First human boy: Find me a monster with one hand and I'll prove it.

What do you get if you cross a bird with a monstrous snarl?
A budgerigrrrrr!

First monster: My sister must be twenty. I counted the rings under her eyes.
Second monster: That's nothing. My sister's tongue is so long, she can lick an envelope after she's posted it.

How did the midget monster get into the police force?
He lied about his height.

Igor: Your monster was making a terrible noise last night.
Frankenstein: Yes, I know. Ever since he ate Madonna, he thinks he can sing.

Monster teacher: If I had two people beside me, and you had

two people beside you, what would we have?
Monster pupil: Lunch!

How do monsters tell the future?
With horrorscopes.

Teacher: What would you do if you saw a big monster?
Pupil: Hope it didn't see me!

Girl: What shall I do? My teacher says I've got to write an essay on a monster.
Boy: Well first, you're going to need a very big ladder...

Monster: Did you ever see anyone like me before?
Human girl: Yes, once. But I had to pay admission.

What is a monster called after it is one year old?
A two-year-old monster.

How can you get your teeth pulled out for free?
Smack a monster.

What do you get if you cross a monster with a boy scout?
A monster that scares old ladies across the street.

Why is the monsters' football pitch wet?
Because the players keep dribbling on it.

What is the best way to see a monster?
On television.

First monster: I'm going to a party tonight.
Second monster: Oh, are you?
First monster: Yes, I must go to the graveyard and dig out a few old friends.

How do you raise a baby monster that has been abandoned by its parents?
With a forklift truck.

What's the difference between a biscuit and a monster?
Have you ever tried dunking a monster?

Can a monster jump higher than a lamp post?
Yes – lamp posts can't jump.

Boy 1: I'm going to keep this monster under my bed.
Boy 2: But what about the smell?
Boy 1: He'll just have to get used to it.

What do you do if a monster feels sick?
Stand well back!

Why does a barber never shave a monster with a forked tongue?
Because it's easier with a razor.

What do you get if you cross a monster with a flea?
Lots of very worried dogs.

Did you hear about the monster that has pedestrian eyes?
They look both ways before they cross.

Mr Monster: Hurry up with my supper! I'm hungry!
Mrs Monster: Oh, do be quiet. I've only got three pairs of hands.

What do you get if you cross a biscuit with a monster?
Crumbs.

What do you get if you cross a monster with a pig?
Large pork chops.

What do you get if you cross a monster with peanut butter?
A monster that sticks to the roof of your mouth.

What's green and wrinkled?
The Incredible Hulk's granny.

What's green, seven feet tall and mopes in the corner?
The Incredible Sulk.

What is big, slimy, ugly and very blue?
A monster holding its breath.

What do you get if you cross a monster with a pigeon?
Lots of very worried pedestrians.

What do you get if you cross a monster with a skunk?
A big, ugly smell!

If you saw nine monsters outside the pharmacist's with blue socks and one monster outside Wal-Mart with red socks, what would that prove?

That nine out of ten monsters wear blue socks.

Slimy monster: What would I have to give you to get a little kiss?
Beautiful girl: Chloroform.

Two monsters are preparing for a visit from relatives. Mrs Monster says to her husband, "Try to be nice to my mother when she visits us this weekend, dear. Fall down when she hits you."

Boy to woman monster: Is that your real face or are you wearing a gas-mask?
Woman monster: I didn't come here to be insulted.
Boy: Oh, where do you usually go?

What's big and ugly and red all over?
An embarrassed monster.

Brother monster: Don't look out of the window, you'll confuse people.
Sister monster: What do you mean?
Brother monster: They'll think Hallowe'en is early this year.

Girl monster: You remind me of my favourite boxer.
Boy monster: Mike Tyson?
Girl monster: No, his name is Fido.

Girl monster: Do you think I should let my hair grow?

Boy monster: Yes right over your face.

Boy monster: You remind me of the ocean.
Girl monster: Oh, romantic, wild, untamed and restless?
Boy monster: No, you make me sick.

Female monster: I wish I had a pound for every boy that has asked me to marry him.
Male monster: Would that be enough for you to buy a bag of crisps?

First monster: I throw myself into everything I do.
Second monster: Then why don't you go and dig yourself a nice big hole?

First monster: I think my brother was born upside down.
Second monster: Oh, why is that?
First monster: His nose runs, and his feet smell.

What happened to the monster who ran away with the circus?
The police made him bring it back.

How do you make a monster fly?
Start with a ten-foot zip.

What do you get if you cross a monster with a watchdog?
Very nervous postmen!

How do you get a monster into a matchbox?

Take all the matches out first.

What time is it when a monster puts his left foot on your right foot?
Time to call an ambulance.

What happens when monsters hold beauty contests?
Nobody wins.

What does a monster do when he loses a hand?
He goes to a second-hand shop.

What do you get if you cross a Scottish monster with a hamburger?
A Big Mac.

What kind of horse would a headless horseman ride?
A nightmare.

Johnny: Dad, what has a purple body with yellow spots, eight hairy legs and big slimy eyes on stalks?
Dad: I don't know. Why?
Johnny: Because one's just crawled up your trouser leg.

What weighed twenty stone and terrorized Paris?
The Fat-Tum of the Opera.

What's blue and hairy and goes round and round?
A monster on a turntable.

How do you make a monster float?
Take two scoops of ice-cream, a glass of Coke and add one monster...

On which day do monsters eat people?
Chewsday.

Why did the monster eat candles?
For light refreshment.

First monster: I had a nice man to dinner last night.
Second monster: So you enjoyed having him?
First monster: Oh yes. He was delicious.

What's a monster's favourite soup?
Scream of tomato.

How do monsters like their eggs?
Terror fried.

Monster wife: I don't know what to make of my husband.
Friend: How about a hotpot?

What is a monster's favourite drink?
Demonade.

Which monster eats the fastest?
The goblin.

Why do some monsters eat raw meat?
Because they don't know how to cook.

What does a monster mother say to her kids at dinnertime?
Don't talk with someone in your mouth.

What did the monster want to eat in the restaurant?
The finger bowl.

Monster: And how much for a couple of legs as well?
First monster: Am I late for dinner?
Second monster: Yes, everyone's been eaten.

What did the monster say when he saw a rush-hour train full of passengers?
Oh good! A chew-chew train!

What do monsters like eating most in restaurants?
The waiters!

Where do greedy monsters feed their babies?
Under the guzzle-berry bush.

Monster mother: How many times have I told you not to eat with your fingers? Use the spade like everyone else.

Little monster: I've finished. Can I leave the table?

Mother monster: Yes, I'll save it for your tea.

Why do waiters prefer monsters to flies?
Have you ever heard anyone complaining of a monster in their soup?

Mother monster: Don't eat that uranium.
Little monster: Why not?
Mother monster: You'll get atomic-ache.

What happened to Ray when he met the man-eating monster?

What do they have for lunch at Monster School?
Human beans, boiled legs, pickled bunions and eyes-cream.

What did the monster eat after its teeth were pulled out?
The dentist.

What do nasty monsters give each other for breakfast?
Smacks in the mouth.

What's the hardest part of making monster soup?
Stirring it.

What did the monster say when he ate a herd of gnus?
And that's the end of the gnus.

Monster: How much do you charge for dinner here?
Waiter: Twenty dollars a head, sir.

He became an ex-Ray.

What happened when the ice monster ate a curry?
He blew his cool.

What makes an ideal present for a monster?
Five pairs of gloves – one for each hand.

Why did the monster walk over the hill?
It was too much bother to walk through it.

First monster: We had burglars last night.
Second monster: Oh, did you?
First monster: Well, it made a change from slime on toast.

What sort of soup do monsters like?
One with plenty of body in it.

Father monster: Johnny, don't make faces at that man. I've told you before not to play with your food.

What do you get if you cross a giant, hairy monster with a penguin?
I don't know but it's a very tight-fitting dinner suit.

What do you get if you cross a long-fanged, purple-spotted monster with a cat?
A town that is free of dogs.

Which is the most dangerous animal in the northern hemisphere?
Yak the Ripper.

How can you tell the difference between a rabbit and a red-eyed monster?
Just try getting a red-eyed monster into a rabbit hutch.

Why did the monster paint himself in rainbow colours?
Because he wanted to hide in the crayon box.

What's big, heavy, furry, dangerous and has sixteen wheels?
A monster on roller-skates.

Why did the monster have green ears and a red nose?
So that he could hide in rhubarb patches.

Why was the big, hairy, two-headed monster top of the class at school?
Because two heads are better than one.

What happened when a purple-headed monster took up singing?
He had a frog in his throat.

Why do monsters have lots of matted fur?
Because they'd look silly in plastic macs.

What do you get if you cross a plum with a man-eating monster?
A purple people-eater.

Cross-eyed Monster: When I grow up, I want to be a bus driver.
Witch: Well, I won't stand in your way.

What do you call a mouse that can pick up a monster?
Sir.

What does a polite monster say when he meets you for the first time?
Pleased to eat you!

Why did the monster-breeder call his monster Fog?
Because he was grey and thick.

How do you tell a good monster from a bad one?
If it's a good one you will be able to talk about it later!

Why didn't the monster use toothpaste?
Because he said his teeth weren't loose.

How do you stop a monster digging up your garden?
Take his spade away.

What happened when two huge monsters ran in a race?
One ran in short bursts, the other ran in burst shorts.

What kind of monster can sit on the end of your finger?
The bogeyman.

What can a monster do that you can't do?

Count up to twenty-five on his fingers.

Why did the monster cross the road?
He wanted to know what it was like to be a chicken.

How do you know if there's a monster in your bed?
By the M on his pyjamas.

How do you get six monsters in a biscuit jar?
Take the biscuits out first.

What's the difference between a monster and a fly?
Quite a lot really.

What happened when the dumb monster went shoplifting?
He stole a free sample.

What happened when the nasty monster stole a pig?
The pig squealed to the police.

What happened when the big, black monster became a chimney sweep?
He started a grime wave.

What do you call a huge, ugly, slobbering, furry monster with cotton wool in his ears?
Anything you like – he can't hear you.

What aftershave do monsters wear?
Brute.

What did one of the monster's

eyes say to the other?
Between us there is something that smells.

What happened when a monster fell in love with a grand piano.
He said, "Darling, you've got lovely teeth."

How do you talk to a giant?
Use big words.

How do you know that there's a monster in your bath?
You can't get the shower curtain closed.

Why couldn't Swamp Thing go to the party?
Because he was bogged down in his work.

What happened when the monster fell down a well?
He kicked the bucket.

How did the world's tallest monster become short overnight?
Someone stole all his money.

How do you greet a three-headed monster?
Hello, hello, hello.

Why was the monster standing on his head?
He was turning things over in his mind.

What happened when the monster stole a bottle of perfume?
He was convicted of fragrancy.

How do you address a monster?
Very politely.

When do banshees howl?
On Moanday night.

First monster: I've just changed my mind.
Second monster: Does it work any better?

Mother monster: Did you catch everyone's eyes in that dress, dear?
Girl monster: Yes, Mom, and I've brought them all home for Cedric to play marbles with.

Mother monster: What are you doing with that saw and where's your little brother?
Young monster: Ha! Ha! He's my half-brother now.

First monster: I have a hunch.
Second monster: I thought you were a funny shape.

First monster: I was in the zoo last week.
Second monster: Really? Which cage were you in?

First monster: What is that son of yours doing these days?,
Second monster: He's at medical school.
First monster: Oh, what's he studying?
Second monster: Nothing, they're studying him.

The police are looking for a monster with one eye.

Why don't they use two?

Girl: Mom, Mom, a monster's just bitten my foot off.
Mom: Well, keep out of the kitchen, I've just washed the floor.

How did the monster cure his sore throat?
He spent all day gargoyling.

Did you hear about the monster who sent his picture to a lonely hearts club?
They sent it back saying they weren't that lonely!

Did you hear about the monster who lost all his hair in the war?
He lost it in a hair raid.

Did you hear about the monster who had eight arms?
He said they came in handy.

Did you hear about the man who took up monster-baiting for a living?
He used to be a teacher but he lost his nerve.

How do you keep an ugly monster in suspense?
I'll tell you tomorrow…

How do man-eating monsters count to a thousand?
On their warts.

What do you call a one-eyed monster who rides a bike?
Cycle-ops.

What game do ants play with monsters?

Squash.

What do young female monsters do at parties?
They go around looking for edible bachelors.

Monster: I've got to walk twenty-five miles to get home.
Ghost: Why don't you take a train?
Monster: I did once, but my mother made me give it back.

How can you tell the difference between a monster and a banana?
Try picking it up. If you can't, it's either a monster or a giant banana.

A female monster walked into the rent office with a five dollar note stuck in one ear and a ten dollar note in the other.
You see, she was fifteen dollars in arrears.

Did the bionic monster have a brother?
No, but he had lots of trans-sisters.

Did you hear about the monster burglar who fell in the cement mixer?
Now he's a hardened criminal.

Why did the monster have to buy two tickets for the zoo?
One to get in and one to get out.

What did the monster say when he saw Snow White and the Seven Dwarfs?
Yum, yum!

What kind of monster has the best hearing?
The eeriest.

Why did the cyclops apply for half a television licence?
Because he only had one eye.

Did you hear about the stupid monster who hurt himself while he was raking up leaves?

Monster: I'm so ugly.
Ghost: It's not that bad!
Monster: It is! When my grandfather was born they passed out cigars. When my father was born they just passed out cigarettes. When I was born they simply passed out.

Why did the monster take a dead man for a drive in his car?
Because he was a car-case.

What did they say about the aristocratic monster?
That he was born with a silver shovel in his mouth.

Why did the monster drink ten litres of antifreeze?
So that he didn't have to buy a winter coat.

What's the best way of stopping a monster sliding through the eye of a needle?
Tie a knot in his neck.

A little monster was learning to play the violin. "I'm good, aren't I?" he asked his big brother.
"You should be on the radio,"

Why was the scary-looking monster called Isaiah?
Because one eye's 'igher than the other.

said the brother.
"You think I'm that good?"
"No, I think you're terrible, but if you were on the radio, I could switch you off."

What is the difference between a huge smelly monster and a sweet?
People like sweets.

Why did it take the monster nine months to finish a book?
He wasn't very hungry.

What is big, red and prickly, has three eyes and eats rocks?
A big, red, prickly, three-eyed rock eater.

First monster: Every time we meet, you remind me of a famous film star.
Second monster: Really, which one? Meryl Streep? Meg Ryan? Raquel Welch?
First Monster: No, E.T.

Why are monsters green?
Because they didn't take their travel sickness pills.

Why do monsters wear glasses?
So they don't bump into other monsters.

What is twenty metres long, ugly, and sings "Scotland the Brave"?
The Loch Ness songster.

What do you get if you cross a Scottish sea creature and a skunk?
The Loch Ness pongster.

What followed the Loch Ness monster?
A whopping big tail.

What did the Loch Ness monster say to his friend?
Long time no sea.

What do you call a Scottish sea monster who hangs people?
The Loch Noose monster.

What do you get if you cross a fashion designer with a sea monster?
The Loch Dress monster.

What is large, yellow, lives in Scotland and has never been seen?

The Loch Ness canary.

Which is the unluckiest monster in the world?
The Luck Less monster.

Boy: Mom, why can't I swim in Loch Ness?
Mother: Because there are monsters in it.
Boy: But dad's swimming there.
Mother: That's different. He's insured.

What do you get if you cross the Loch Ness monster with a shark?
Loch jaws.

MONSTER BOOK TITLES

Never Make a Girl Monster Angry by Sheila Tack

The Bad-Tempered Werewolf by Claudia Armoff

The Greediest Monster in the World by Buster Butt

The Monster Hanging off the Cliff by Alf Hall

Tracking Monsters by Woody Hurt

The Vampire's Victim by E. Drew Blood

The Omen by B. Warned

Foaming at the Mouth by Dee Monic

Creature From Mars by A. Lee-En

Frankenstein's Experiments by Tess Tube

The Story of Dracula by Pierce Nex

A History of Poltergeists by Eve L. Spirit

In the Monster's Jaws by Mandy Ceased

Late-night Horror Story by Denise R. Knockin

Ghosts and Ghoulies by Sue Pernatural

When to go Monster Hunting by Mae B. Tomorrow

Bungee Jumping with Monsters by Wade R. Go

A Very Hungry Giant by Ethan D. Lot

I Caught the Loch Ness Monster by Janet A. Bigwun

What did the monster say when he ate Aesop?
Make a fable out of that then!

MUSIC

A tourist in Vienna is going through a graveyard and all of a sudden he hears some music. No one is around, so he starts searching for the source.

He finally locates the origin and finds it is coming from a grave with a headstone that reads: Ludwig van Beethoven, 1770–1827. Then he realizes that the music is the Ninth Symphony and it is being played backwards. Puzzled, he leaves the graveyard and persuades a friend to return with him. By the time they arrive back at the grave, the music has changed. This time it is the Seventh Symphony, but like the previous piece, it is being played backwards.

Curious, the men go to visit a music scholar. When they return with the expert, the Fifth Symphony is playing, again backwards. The expert notices that the symphonies are being played in the reverse order from that in which they were composed, the Ninth, then the Seventh, then the Fifth.

By the next day word has spread and a throng has gathered around Beethoven's grave. They are all listening to the Second Symphony being played backwards.

Just then the graveyard's caretaker ambles up to the group. Someone in the crowd asks him if he has an explanation for the music.

"Oh, it's nothing to worry about," says the caretaker. "He's just decomposing."

What's the definition of a gentleman?
Somebody who knows how to play the accordion, but doesn't.

What's the difference between an accordion and an onion?
Nobody cries when you chop up an accordion.

A violinist was auditioning in 2010 for the Halle orchestra in England. After his audition he was talking with the conductor. "What do you think about Brahms?" the conductor asked.

"Great guy!" enthused the violinist. "Real talented musician. As a matter of fact, he and I were playing some duets together only last week."

"And what about Mozart?" said the conductor.

"One of my favourites," gushed the violinist. "He and I had dinner together last month. Terrific company."

Then the violinist looked at his watch and said he had to leave to catch the two o'clock train to London.

Afterwards, the conductor was discussing the violinist with the members of the orchestra board. The conductor confessed, "I feel very uneasy about hiring this violinist because there appears to me to be a serious credibility gap. I know for a fact that there is no two o'clock train to London."

Why do bagpipers walk when they play?
To get away from the noise.

What's the difference between a bagpipe and a trampoline?
You take your shoes off when you jump on a trampoline.

If you were lost in the woods, who would you trust for directions, an in-tune bagpipe player, an out-of-tune bagpipe player, or Santa Claus?
The out-of-tune bagpipe player. The other two indicate you have been hallucinating.

What's the difference between a banjo and an anchor?
You tie a rope to the anchor before you throw it overboard.

What's the best way to tune a banjo?
With wirecutters.

What's the difference between a banjo and a South American macaw?
One is offensive and noisy, and the other is a bird.

How do you annoy Lady Gaga?
Poker face.

What happened when Fred Astaire went out to dinner?
He got pudding on his top hat, pudding on his white tie and pudding on his tails.

Bono and The Edge were trying to think of a name for their rock band.
The Edge said, "I like the sound of The Hype. I think it's got something to it. That's what we should call ourselves."
"No way," said Bono. "It's a terrible name."
Just then Adam Clayton walked into the room and said, "I think we should call ourselves The Hype."
"Not you too!" groaned Bono.
And Larry Mullen Jr exclaimed, "That's it!"

How do you make a bandstand?
Take their chairs away.

What do you get from a poorly piano?
A sick note.

What is the name of Britney Spears' tasty brother?
Broccoli Spears.

What did the overweight ballet dancer perform?
The Dance of the Sugar Plump Fairy.

At the floral disco, what did the girl roses say about the boy rose?
Look at the hips on that!

A man goes on vacation to a tropical island. As soon as he gets off the plane, he hears drums. He thinks, "Wow, this is cool."

He goes to the beach, he hears the drums, he eats lunch, he hears drums, he goes to bed, he hears drums. He tries to go to sleep, yet he hears drums.

This goes on for several nights, and gets to the point where the guy can't sleep at night because of the drums. Finally, he goes down to the front desk.

When he gets there, he asks the manager, "What's with these drums. Don't they ever stop? I can't get any sleep."

The manager says, "No! Drums must never stop. It's very bad if drums stop."

"Why?"

"When drums stop…bass solo begins."

Why is a bassoon better than an oboe?
A bassoon burns for longer.

Why did Mozart get rid of his chickens?
They kept saying, "Bach, Bach".

What did the boy say when it was time for his violin lesson?
Oh, fiddle!

What type of guitar did the pool player own?
A-cue-stick.

Why couldn't the athlete listen to her music?
Because she broke the record.

Stevie Wonder was playing his first-ever concert in Beijing and twenty minutes into the show, in a bid to strike up a rapport with his audience, he asked if anyone had any requests. At this, an old Chinese man in the front row shouted out, "Play a jazz chord! Play a jazz chord!"

Stevie was impressed that the old man knew about the jazz influences in his career, and so he responded by playing an E minor scale before embarking on a complicated jazz melody that went on for over fifteen minutes.

When he finished, the rest of the audience applauded wildly, but the old man in the front row shouted out again, "No, no, play a jazz chord! Play a jazz chord!"

Irritated that this one person was calling his jazz credentials into question, Stevie immediately launched into a brilliant jazz improvisation with his band around the B flat minor chord. Ten minutes later, he received a standing ovation – except from the old man in the front row who again shouted out, "No, no. Play a jazz chord! Play a jazz chord!"

This was too much for Stevie to take. So he called out to the old man in the front row, "Okay then, if you think you can do better, come up here and show everyone."

The old man climbed slowly up on to the stage, tottered over to the microphone and started to sing, "A jazz chord to say I love you…"

What type of music are balloons scared of?
Pop music.

What makes music on your head?
A head band.

What do you get when you put an ice bucket on the CD player?
The coolest music around.

What part of the turkey is musical?
The drumstick.

What do you get if you cross a koala and a harp?
A bear-faced lyre.

What has forty feet and sings?
The school choir.

Why did the girl sit on the ladder to sing?
She wanted to reach the high notes.

There's a five-dollar note on the floor. Out of a thrash metal guitarist, a drummer who keeps good time, and a drummer who

What happened to the classical string quartet who couldn't sell tickets to their concerts?
They went baroque.

How do you clean a tuba?
With a tuba toothpaste.

What kind of paper likes music?
Rapping paper.

What is the most dangerous kind of dancer?
A breakdancer.

What did Cher call the act when she appeared on stage with a Cher impersonator?
Cher and Cher Alike.

What is a rock's favourite band?
The Rolling Stones.

Did you hear about the pianist who kept banging his head against the keys?
He was playing by ear.

What do you get when you drop a piano on an army base?
A flat major.

What do you get when you drop a piano down a mine shaft?
A flat miner.

Why was the man in no fit state to play his stringed instrument?
He was harpist.

What's the difference between a guitarist and a savings bond?
Eventually the savings bond will mature and earn money.

Why was the guitar upset?
Because he was tired of being picked on.

keeps bad time, who picks it up?
The drummer who keeps bad time. The other drummer doesn't exist, and the thrash guitarist doesn't care about notes anyway.

What kind of phone can make music?
A saxophone.

Why did the music teacher get locked out of the classroom?
The keys were in the piano.

How do you get four cellos in tune?
Shoot three of them.

Why were the string section of the orchestra dissatisfied with their overnight accommodation?
Because they were staying at a vile inn.

A violist is sitting in the front row, crying hysterically. The conductor asks, "What's wrong?"

The violist answers, "The second oboe player loosened one of my tuning pegs."

The conductor replied, "I admit, that seems a little childish, but nothing to get so upset about. Why are you crying?"

To which the violist replied, "He won't tell me which one!"

A man went into a music store and said, "I want to buy a violin."

The proprietor asked, "Do you want a bow?"

The man said, "No, don't bother wrapping it."

Why are an organist's fingers like lightning?
Because they rarely strike the same place twice.

What do you call a rock band made up of animal doctors?
Vet, Vet, Vet.

Two musicians are walking down the street. One says to the other, "Who was that piccolo I saw you with last night?"
The other replies, "That was no piccolo, that was my fife."

Why did the tenor break into song?
Because he couldn't find the key.

Why did the soprano go on a cruise?
So she could hit the high Cs.

Why is a slippery pavement like music?
If you don't C sharp, you'll B flat.

An orchestra was rehearsing a contemporary symphony in which there was a particularly difficult jazz trumpet riff. However, none of the trumpet players could play it. One trumpet player suggests they hire in a jazz trumpeter.

The conductor says, "No, no, no. Jazz musicians are irresponsible, can't play in tune, and are not real musicians!"

Finally, they talk him into it. The next night at 7:57 the jazz musician shows up for the 8:00 rehearsal, carrying his trumpet in a paper bag. The conductor decides to wait until after to yell at him. But he plays the riff perfectly the first time. The conductor tries to thank him after rehearsal, but the jazz trumpeter is gone.

The next couple of rehearsals go pretty much the same way, with the trumpeter actually playing the entire first trumpet part perfectly.

Finally, the conductor grabs him after rehearsal and says, "You know, at first I didn't want to hire you because I thought jazz musicians were irresponsible and couldn't play in tune, but I must say you have changed my mind. Thank you."

The jazz trumpeter replies, "Well, I figure it's the least I could do since I can't make the gig."

Why doesn't a guitar work?
Because it only knows how to play.

Why was the guitar player nervous?
He was always fretting about something.

What do a cello and a lawsuit have in common?
Everyone is happy when the case is closed.

How can you tell which child in a playground is the son of a trombonist?
He doesn't know how to use the slide, and he can't swing.

Two girls are walking along the street when they hear a voice say, "Hey! Down here!" They both look down and see a frog sitting beside the road.

The frog says to them, "Hey, if you kiss me, I'll turn into a world famous drummer and make you both rich and famous!"

The two girls look at each other, and one of them reaches down, grabs the frog and stuffs it in her pocket.

The other girl says, "What did you do that for? Why didn't you kiss him?"

The first replies, "I'm not stupid. I know a talking frog is worth heaps more than a famous drummer any day!"

What happens if you sing country music backwards?
You get your job and your wife back.

Did you hear about the man who was crushed to death by a piano?
His funeral was very low key.

What do you call a bunch of guys who break into a music store and help themselves to some of the stringed instruments?
Luters.

A cowboy and a biker are on Death Row and are to be executed on the same day. The day comes, and they are brought out together. The warden asks the cowboy if he has a last request, to which the cowboy replies, "I sure do, warden. I'd be mighty grateful if you'd play *Achy Breaky Heart* for me before I go."

"Sure enough, we can do that," says the warden. He turns to the biker, "And you, what's your last request?"

The biker replies, "That you kill me first."

What's musical and useful in a supermarket?
A Chopin Liszt.

NIGHT

Did you hear about the idiot who found a feather in his bed?
He thought he had chicken pox.

Did you hear about the man who heard a mouse squeaking one night?
He got up to oil it.

Did you hear about the man who plugged his electric blanket into the toaster?
He kept popping out of bed all night.

Did you hear about the New Yorker who slept under an old tractor?
He wanted to wake up oily in the morning.

Did you hear about the parents who called their baby daughter Caffeine?
She kept them awake all night.

How can you shorten a bed?
Don't sleep long on it.

What noise wakes you up in the morning?

The crack of dawn.

How do you know when someone is sleeping like a log?
When you hear them sawing.

A man says to his friend, "I want a divorce."

"Why?" his friend asks.

"My wife smokes in bed."

"It's not that bad, is it?"

"Yes it is. She smokes kippers."

A man walks into a bed shop and says to the sales assistant, "I'd like to buy a new bed, please."

"Certainly, sir. Would you like a spring mattress?"

"Oh, no. I'd like to use it all the year round."

A man complains to his friend, "My bed's too short and every night my feet freeze because they stick out from under the covers."

"Why don't you curl up so you can put your feet under the covers?"

"What? I'm not putting those cold things in bed with me!"

Shall I tell you the joke about the bed?
I can't. It hasn't been made up yet.

What did Sir Lancelot wear to bed?
A knight-gown.

What does one good turn do for you?
Gives you all the blankets.

What happened when a boy dreamed he was eating a giant marshmallow?
When he woke up, his pillow had gone.

What has four legs, but only one foot?
A bed.

What horse sleeps only at night?
A nightmare.

What is the softest bed for a baby to sleep on?
Cot-on wool.

What overpowers you without hurting you?
Sleep.

What question can never be answered with "yes"?
Are you asleep?

What should you do if you find an elephant asleep in your bed?
Sleep somewhere else.

Why did the man run around his bed?
To catch up on his sleep.

What side of the bed do you sleep on?
The top side.

What's huge and grey and sends people to sleep?
A hypno-potamus.

What's the best advice to give a worm?
Sleep late.

Where do strawberries sleep?
In strawberry beds.

What's the difference between a feather bed and a poor man?
One is soft down, the other is hard up.

What's the laziest letter of the alphabet?
E – because it's always in bed.

What purrs along the road and leaves holes in your lawn?
A Moles Royce.

When is it proper to go to bed with your shoes on?
When you're a horse.

A manager says to his employee, "Why are you late for work?"
The employee says, "There are eight of us in the family, but the alarm clock was set for seven."

Why did the idiot put his bed in the fireplace?
Because he wanted to sleep like a log.

Why did the idiot take his bicycle to bed with him?
Because he didn't want to walk in his sleep.

Why did the idiot throw away his alarm clock?
It kept going off when he was asleep.

Why did the bed spread?
Because it saw the pillow slip.

Why did the composer work in bed?
He wrote sheet music.

Why did the gangster cut the legs off his bed?
He wanted to lie low for a while.

Why did the idiot take a tape measure to bed with him?
To see how long he slept.

Why did the girl put sugar under her pillow?
She wanted sweet dreams.

Why isn't it safe to sleep on trains?
Because they run over sleepers.

Why did the jockey take hay to bed?
To feed his nightmares.

Why did the man climb on to the chandelier to go to sleep?
Because he was a light sleeper.

Why do people go to bed?
Because the bed won't go to them.

A boy asked his vain and stupid girlfriend, "Why do you comb your hair before going to bed?"
She replied, "To make a good impression on the pillow."

Why is a river lazy?
It never leaves its bed.

Why is breakfast in bed so easy?
It's just a few rolls and a turnover.

Why is the ocean always restless?
It has so many rocks in its bed.

Did you hear about the girl who was so keen on road safety that she always wore white at night?
Last winter she was knocked down by a snow plough.

Did you hear about the idiot who sat up all night wondering where the sun had gone?
The next morning it dawned on him.

Did you hear about the man who drove his car into the lake one night?
He was trying to dip his headlights.

Did you hear about the night-owl who installed a skylight so he could watch the stars?
The people in the apartment above were furious…

Did you hear about the wolves' all-night party?
It was a howling success.

How can you go without sleep for seven days and not be tired?
Sleep at night.

How did Noah see in the dark?
By ark-lights and flood-lights!

How did the dog get into the locked cemetery at night?
He used a skeleton key.

How did the glow-worm feel when it backed into a tree?
De-lighted.

If we breathe oxygen in the daytime, what do we breathe at night?
Nitrogen.

A man says to his friend, "I've been on my computer all night!"
His friend replies, "Don't you think you'd be more comfortable on a bed like everyone else?"

Two stupid drunks were staggering home one night. One looked up at the sky and said, "Is that the sun or the moon?"
"I don't know," said the other. "I don't live round here either."

What night-loving animal has wooden legs?
A timber wolf.

What dance can you see in the night sky?
The moon walk.

What did Mrs Wolf say to Mr Wolf?
The baby's howling again.

What did one bat say to another?
Let's hang around.

What did one glow-worm say to the other when his light went out?
Give me a push, my battery is dead.

What did one shooting star say to the other?
Pleased to meteor.

What did one shooting star say to the other?
Do you comet here often?

What did the big star say to the little star?
You're too young to go out at night.

What do bats do at night?
Aerobatics.

What do you call a clever glow-worm?
A bright spark.

What do you call the longest night of the year?
A fortnight!

What do you get if you cross a glow-worm with a python?
A very long strip-light that can squeeze you to death.

What do you get if you cross a wolf with a cockerel?
An animal that howls when the sun rises.

What game do cats play at night?
Trivial Purr-suit.

What is an astronomer?
A night watchman with a college education.

Which is farther away, Australia or the moon?
Australia, because you can see the moon at night.

What is there more of the less you see?
Darkness.

What kind of car do wolves drive?

A Wolfswagen.

What makes a glow-worm glow?
It eats light meals.

What time is it when a knight looks at his belly button?
It is the middle of the night.

What was the most dangerous time for knights?
Nightfall.

What's big and bright and silly?
A fool moon.

When does a bed grow longer?
At night, because two feet are added to it.

A pastor asked a little boy if he said his prayers every night.
    "Yes, sir," the boy replied.
    "And, do you always say them in the morning, too?" the pastor asked.
    "No, sir," the boy replied. "I'm not scared in the daytime."

Where are starfish found?
In a planet-arium.

Where was the cat when the lights went out?
In the dark.

Which stars go to jail?
Shooting stars.

A man went to see his doctor. "Doctor, you've got to help me," he said. "I keep having this same dream night after night. There's this door with a sign on it, and I push and push the

door but I just can't get it open."
"I see," said the doctor.
"What does the sign on the door say?"
"Pull."

Who's tall and dark and goes to discos all night long?
Darth Raver.

Why are false teeth like stars?
They come out at night.

Why are wolves like cards?
They come in packs.

Miguel Rodriguez suffered from such bad insomnia that he rarely slept for more than two hours a night. He had consulted numerous physicians in his native Mexico but none had been able to help him. Even the strongest sedatives were unable to give him a good night's sleep.

Then one day he met and fell in love with a beautiful senorita by the name of Esta Gomez and his sleeping problems were cured overnight. Now whenever he needs to sleep he just looks at her picture, reminding him of what his parents always told him as a child: when you see Esta, you sleep.

Why can't it rain for two nights in a row?
Because there is a day between.

Why does Father Time wear bandages?
Because day breaks and night falls.

Why is a cat longer at night than in the morning?
Because it's let out at night and taken in again in the morning.

Why was night baseball started?
Because bats like to sleep in the daytime.

Why was the glow-worm sad?
Because it didn't know if it was coming or glowing.

PANDAS

A giant panda walked into a bar. The bartender took one look at him and said: "I'm sorry I don't want you in here. You'll cause trouble."

"I'm just here for a quiet drink," protested the panda. "What do you mean I'll cause trouble?"

"You're always getting into fights," said the bartender.

"No, I'm not," answered the panda. "What makes you think that?"

"Well, look at the state of you," said the bartender. "Somebody's already given you two black eyes."

A giant panda escapes from the zoo in New York. Eventually, he makes his way downtown and walks into a restaurant, where he finds a seat at an empty table. The waiter, being a native New Yorker, figures he's seen stranger things than this, so he takes the panda's order. In due course the panda's meal arrives and he eats.

After he finishes his dinner he stands up, calmly pulls out a gun and blows away several customers. Then he turns around and walks toward the door.

Naturally, the waiter is horrified. He stops the panda and demands an explanation.

The panda says to him, "What do I look like to you?"

The waiter answers, "Well, a giant panda, of course."

"That's right," says the panda. "Look it up," and he walks out.

The waiter calls the police. When they arrive, he relates the whole story to them, including the panda's comment about looking it up. So the chief detective sends a rookie to get an encyclopedia.

He eventually returns so the detective looks up "panda", and there's the answer: "Giant panda, lives in China, eats shoots and leaves."

What's black and white and as hard as a rock?
A panda that's fallen in cement.

Why was the cub so spoiled?
Because his mother panda'd to his every need.

Why do pandas have fur coats?

Because they'd look silly wearing denim jackets.

What do pandas cause when they become agitated?
Panda-monium.

Why do pandas like old movies?
Because they're in black and white.

PARROTS

What is a polygon?
A dead parrot.

Which side of a parrot has the prettiest feathers?
The outside.

What is a plastic parrot made of?
Polystyrene.

Why did the caged bird join the Air Force?
He wanted to be a parrot trooper.

An elderly lady, recently widowed, decides to see if a pet will ease her loneliness and goes to the pet store. She decides against a puppy or kitten and is about to leave the store when she hears a voice saying, "My, do you look lovely this afternoon, madam."

She turns around quickly to see who has spoken, but there is no one. All she sees is a big green parrot, resting on his perch in his cage. "Did you say that?" she asks.

"Why, yes, I did!" he replies. "And may I add that dress is a very nice colour for you."

The lady suddenly realizes how nice it would be not only to have a talking parrot, but one that gives such nice compliments. So she pays for him and takes him home. On the way, she says, "You know, I am so proud of you that I believe I'll take you out for dinner! Would you like that?"

The parrot says, "Why yes, that would be delightful. I know a charming place on Main Street."

So they arrive home and the lady goes upstairs to her apartment to change for dinner, bringing the parrot along, of course. When they go in, the parrot begins complaining, swearing, and even biting her.

Well, the lady is flabbergasted! She grabs the parrot by the throat, marches down the stairs into the basement, and stuffs the parrot in the freezer. She leaves him there for five long minutes before taking him back out. The parrot is very cold.

She says, "Well? Have you learned your lesson? I will not tolerate such language in my house!"

The parrot says, "Okay, okay, I promise it won't happen again. I am deeply sorry."

Within five minutes, he is cursing again and bites her once on the arm and once on the finger.

The lady is absolutely stunned. She rips the parrot out of his cage, goes down the stairs, into the cellar, and hurls him into the freezer. This time, she leaves him in there for fifteen minutes.

When she finally takes him out, the parrot is one step away from death. He is shivering and has light frost on the beak. "I swear it will never ever happen again! I will never insult you again! I promise!" As he thaws, he looks up at the lady and says, "I do have one question, though. That turkey in there, what on earth did he do?"

Mrs Peterson phoned the repairman because her dishwasher had stopped working. He couldn't accommodate her with an evening appointment and, since she had to go to work, she told him, "I'll leave the key under the mat. Fix the dishwasher, leave the bill on the counter, and I'll mail you a cheque. By the way, I have a large Rottweiler. His name is Killer but he won't bother you. I also have a parrot, and whatever you do, do not talk to the bird!"

Well, sure enough the dog, Killer, totally ignored the repairman, but the whole time he was there, the parrot cursed, yelled, screamed, and drove him nuts.

As he was ready to leave, he couldn't resist saying, "You stupid bird, just shut up!"

To which the bird replied, "Killer, get him!"

*Two idiots were standing on a cliff with their arms outstretched.
One had some budgies lined up on each arm, the other had
parrots lined up on his arms.
After a couple of minutes, they both leaped off the cliff and fell to
the ground.
Laying next to each other in intensive care at the hospital,
one idiot said to the other, "I don't think much of this budgie
jumping."
The other idiot replied, "Yeah, I'm not too keen on this parrot
gliding either."*

What do you call a parrot wearing a raincoat?
Polyunsaturated.

A magician on a cruise ship specialized in sleight of hand tricks, but night after night his act was ruined by the ship's parrot shouting, "It's up his sleeve!" or "It's in his pocket!"

The magician got so fed up with this that he threatened to kill the parrot if it interrupted his act again. But that evening right at the finish of his act, just as the magician was about to disappear in a spectacular puff of smoke, the ship hit an iceberg and sank in a matter of seconds.

The magician and the parrot were the only survivors of the shipwreck. Lying dazed on a piece of driftwood that was floating on the sea, the magician eventually opened his eyes and saw the parrot staring at him.

"Okay," said the parrot. "I give up. What did you do with the ship?"

Where does a parrot go to improve its education?
A polytechnic.

What material was the parrot's coat made of?
Polyester.

A lady was expecting the plumber, who was supposed to come at ten o'clock. Ten o'clock came and went, no plumber. Eleven o'clock, twelve o'clock, one o'clock and still no plumber. She concluded he wasn't coming, and went out to do some errands. While she was out, the plumber arrived.

He knocked on the door and the lady's parrot, who was in a cage by the door, said, "Who is it?"

He replied, "It's the plumber."

He thought it was the lady who had answered and waited for her to come and let him in. When this didn't happen he knocked again, and again the parrot said, "Who is it?"

He said, "It's the plumber!"

He waited, and again the lady didn't come to let him in. He knocked again, and again the parrot said, "Who is it?"

He was growing increasingly annoyed and shouted, "It's the plumber!"

Again he waited; again she didn't come; again he knocked; again the parrot said, "Who is it?"

The plumber flew into a rage and pushed the door in and ripped it off its hinges. He suffered a heart attack and he fell dead in the doorway.

The lady came home from her errands, only to see the door ripped off its hinges and a corpse lying in the doorway. "A dead body!" she exclaimed. "Who is it?"

The parrot said, "It's the plumber."

What's orange and sounds like a parrot?
A carrot.

What do you call a box of parrot food?
Polly filla.

Where do parrots make films?
Pollywood.

A preacher is buying a parrot.

"Are you sure it doesn't scream, yell, or swear?" asked the preacher.

"Oh absolutely. It's a religious parrot," the storekeeper assures him. "Do you see those strings on his legs? When you pull the right one, he recites the Lord's Prayer, and when you pull on the left he recites the 23rd Psalm."

"Wonderful!" says the preacher. "But what happens if you pull both strings?"

"I fall off my perch, you stupid fool!" screeched the parrot.

A man bought a parrot from a pet shop but was disappointed when it showed no inclination to talk. So he went back to the pet shop and told the shop owner, "I've had this parrot for three months but he hasn't said a word. What should I do?"

"Try getting him a mirror," suggested the shop owner. "They love to look at their own reflections. You wait – soon he won't stop talking."

So the man bought a mirror, but still the parrot refused to talk. Two weeks later, the man returned to the pet shop.

"Try buying him a ladder," advised the pet shop owner. "Parrots love to climb. You wait – you won't be able to shut him up once he's got a ladder."

So the man bought a ladder, but the parrot remained silent. Two weeks later, the man was back at the pet shop.

"Try getting him a bell," said the pet shop owner. "That will definitely work. You wait – music will bring out the talker in him."

So the man bought a bell. Two weeks later, he returned to the pet shop.

"At last my parrot said something!" he exclaimed. "He looked in his mirror, climbed up his ladder, rang his bell, said a few words, then dropped dead off his perch."

"Oh, no!" said the pet shop owner. "What did he say?"

"He said, 'Doesn't that shop sell bird seed?'"

On reaching his airplane seat a man is surprised to see a parrot strapped in next to him. He asks the stewardess for a coffee at which point the parrot squawks, "And get me a whisky, you fool!" The stewardess, flustered, brings back a whisky for the parrot and forgets the coffee.

When this omission is pointed out to her, the parrot drains its glass and screeches, "And get me another whisky, you idiot." Quite upset, the girl comes back with another whisky but still no coffee.

Unaccustomed to such slackness the man tries the parrot's approach. He says to the stewardess, "I've asked you twice for a coffee, go and get it now or I'll kick you."

The next moment, both he and the parrot have been pulled out of their seats and thrown out of the emergency exit by two burly stewards. As they plunge to the ground, the parrot turns to the man and says, "For someone who can't fly, you complain too much!"

What do you get if you cross a parrot with a woodpecker?
A bird that talks in Morse code.

What flies through the jungle singing light opera?
The parrots of Penzance.

A burglar has just crept into the house he's intending ransacking, and he's looking around for swag to steal. All of a sudden, a little voice pipes up, "I can see you, and so can Jesus!"

Startled, the burglar looks around the room. No one there at all, so he goes back to his business.

The voice repeats, "I can see you, and so can Jesus!"

The burglar jumps again, and takes a longer look around the room. Over in the corner by the window, almost obscured by curtains, is a cage in which sits a parrot, who pipes up again, "I can see you, and so can Jesus!"

"So what," says the burglar. "You're only a parrot!"

To which the parrot replies, "Maybe, but Jesus is a Rottweiler!"

PIGEONS

What do you call a pigeon with a machine gun?
A military coo.

What do you get if you cross a carrier pigeon with a woodpecker?
A bird that knocks before delivering a message.

Worried about having to fly a long distance, a baby pigeon said to his mother, "I can't do it. I'll get tired."

"Don't worry," said the mother pigeon. "I'll tie one end of a piece of string to one of your legs and the other end to mine."

The baby pigeon immediately started to cry.

"What's wrong?" asked the mother pigeon.

The baby said, "I don't want to end up being pigeon towed."

Two pigeons were sitting chatting on the roof of a house.

"I'm bored," said one.

"Me, too," said the other.

"I know. Why don't we fly over to that new car showroom and put a deposit on a Rolls-Royce?"

Two pigeons arranged a date to meet on the ledge outside the ninth floor of a tower block. The female was there on time but the male arrived over an hour late.

"Where have you been?" asked the female pigeon. "I've been worried sick."

"Sorry," said the male. "But it was such a nice day I decided to walk."

PIGS

How do you fit more pigs on your farm?
Build a sty-scraper.

What do you give a sick pig?
Oinkment.

What is a pig's favourite ballet?
Swine Lake.

Who is a pig's favourite painter?
Pigcasso.

What was the name of the hog who was knighted by King Arthur?
Sir Lunchalot.

How do you take a pig to hospital?
By hambulance.

What did the fat pig say when the farmer dumped corn mash into the trough?
I'm afraid that's all going to waist.

What happened to the pig who had driving lessons?
He became a crashing boar.

Why is getting up a four o'clock in the morning like a pig's tail?
Because it's twirly.

What do you call a pig with three eyes?
A piiig.

What game do pigs hate to play?
Backgammon.

What kind of story is the story about the three little pigs?
A pigtail.

Which monster scares pigs?
Frankenswine.

What do you call a posh pig delivering newspapers?
Bacon rind.

What do get if you cross a pig with Johnny Depp?
A ham actor.

Why do pigs never recover from

illnesses?
Because you have to kill them before you cure them.

What do you call a pig who has been arrested for dangerous driving?
A road hog.

What do you call a pig with no clothes on?
Streaky bacon.

What are pigs warned to look out for in New York?
Pigpockets.

What did the pig call his manuscript?
A shoat story.

What pig meets foreign dignitaries and lives in luxury five-star accommodation?
The English Hambassador.

What part of New York do pigs like best?
Central Pork.

First piglet: How do you know your boyfriend loves you?
Second piglet: He finishes his texts with hogs and kisses.

Why did the farmer feed his pigs sugar and lemons?
He wanted sweet and sour pork.

Why did the three little pigs leave home?
Because their father was a big boar.

What do you call a pig that

travelled by plane?
Swine flu.

What do you call a pig that's not a professional?
A hamateur.

Why was the pig grateful to the butcher?
Because he saved his bacon.

Where does a hog look when he can't spell very well?
The pigtionary.

What happens to pigs who break the law?
They get sent to the pen.

What do you call a pig that's lost its voice?
Disgruntled.

Why do pigs scratch themselves?
Because they're the only ones who know where they itch.

When pigs have a party, who jumps out of the cake?
Nobody. The pigs all jump in.

What did one pig say to the other?
Let's be pen friends.

A man was out for a walk one day and on his travels he wandered through a farm. Strangely, he saw a pig with a wooden leg. This intrigued him so much he found the farmer and quizzed him about it.

"This be no ordinary pig,"

What do you call a pig that knows karate? **A pork chop.**

said the farmer. "For example, only two days ago there was a fire in the chicken shed when I was away from the farm. The pig noticed this and immediately went and let all the chickens out into the yard. He then phoned for the fire brigade and came straight back to hold the fire until they arrived. And a few weeks ago, I was driving my tractor down a steep hill, when I lost control and the vehicle overturned and knocked me unconscious. The pig saw this, phoned for the ambulance and then rushed to the tractor and pulled me clear of the cab just before it caught fire."

The farmer was just about to launch into another tale when the man said, "Yes yes, but what about the wooden leg?"

"Well," said the farmer.

"When you've got a pig as good as that, you don't eat it all at once."

What song do pigs sing on New Year's Eve?
Auld Lang Swine.

Did you hear about the piglets who wanted to do something special for Mother's Day?
They threw a sowprize party.

Which sporting event do pigs look forward to the most?
The Olympigs.

Where do pigs go on sunny days?
They go on pignics.

What would happen if pigs could fly?
Bacon would go up.

When the pig opened a pawnbroker's shop, what did he call it?
Ham Hocks.

When the pig opened a launderette, what did he call it?
Hog Wash.

Did you hear about the pig who began hiding garbage in November?
She wanted to do her Christmas shopping early.

A city child was on a school visit to a farm. After studying the pigs, she ran up to her teacher and said, "No wonder that mother pig is so big! There's a bunch of little pigs blowing her up!"

What kind of vehicle do pigs drive?
Pig-up trucks.

What kind of tie does a pig wear?
Pigs' tie.

What did the pig naval captain shout as his ship left port?
Oinkers away!

Why did the pig join the Army?
He heard they ate in a mess.

Why did the pig go to the casino?
To play the slop machine.

A man from the city visited a small farm and during this visit he saw a farmer feeding pigs in a most extraordinary manner. The farmer would lift a pig up to a nearby apple tree and the pig would eat the apples off the tree directly. The farmer would move the pig from one apple to another until the pig was satisfied, then he would start again with another pig.

The city man watched this activity for some time with great astonishment. Finally, he could not resist saying to the farmer, "This is the most inefficient method of feeding pigs that I can imagine. Just think of the time that would be saved if you simply shook the apples off the tree and let the pigs eat them from the ground."

The farmer looked puzzled and

replied, "What's time to a pig?"

PIRATES

How do pirates make their money?
By hook or by crook.

Which pirate's parrot sat on his shoulder squawking, "Pieces of four! Pieces of four!"
Short John Silver.

Why did the pirate give his ship a coat of paint?
Its timbers were shivering.

What do pirates use to blow their noses?
Anchor-chiefs.

What has seven legs and seven eyes?
Seven pirates.

Why did the pirate refuse to say, "Aye, aye, captain."
Because he only had one eye.

Why does a pirate's phone go beep beep beep beep?
Because he left it off the hook.

Which Star Wars character is really a pirate?
Aaaaaarrrrrrgh-2 D-2!

What does a pirate believe happens when the world ends?
Aaaaarrrrrghmageddon.

Where do pirates store their gym clothes?
Davy Jones locker.

"Where did you get that nose ring?" one pirate asked another. "It makes you look more evil than ever. I want one just like it."

"I bought it last time we were ashore. In a place in the old town."

"And how much did it cost you?"

"More than I could afford. I paid through the nose for it."

What did the pirate order when he went to a fish restaurant?
Pieces of skate.

What do you call a pirate who skips class?
Captain Hooky.

Where on a ship can you find a pirate's bathroom?
The poop deck.

Why do pirates have both ears pierced?
Because it only costs them a buck an ear.

Why couldn't the twelve-year-old American kid watch the pirate movie?
Because it was Aaaaaaaarrrgh-rated.

Why wasn't the pirate any good at golf?
Because he had an awful hook.

Which pirate drools continuously?
Long John Saliva.

How much did the pirate pay for

his hook and his peg leg?
An arm and a leg.

A pirate walked into a bar, and the bartender noticed that he had a peg leg, a hook and an eye patch.

"How did you end up with the peg leg?" asked the bartender.

The pirate said, "We were in a fearful storm at sea and I was swept overboard into a school of sharks. Just as my men were pulling me out, this huge shark bit off my leg."

"Wow!" said the bartender. "What about your hook? How did you get that?"

The pirate replied, "We were boarding an enemy ship and fighting with swords. One of the enemy cut off my hand."

"Amazing!" said the bartender. "So how did you get the eye patch?"

The pirate said, "A seagull dropping fell into my eye."

"You lost your eye to a seagull dropping?" asked the bartender incredulously.

"Well," said the pirate, "it was my first day with the hook."

Why are pirates so popular?
They just aaaarrrrrggh.

POLICE AND CRIMINALS

How do you join the police?
Handcuff them together.

Why did the police officer carry a pencil and a piece of thin paper?
He wanted to trace someone.

Detective: Your first two wives died after eating poisoned ham sandwiches, and your third has just broken her neck after falling off the roof. It's all rather suspicious, isn't it?
Husband: Not really. She wouldn't eat the poisoned sandwiches.

What did the policeman say to his tummy?
You're under a vest.

A traffic cop stopped a motorist for speeding and told him, "When I saw you driving down the road I guessed sixty at least."

"You're wrong, officer," replied the motorist. "It's only my hat that makes me look that old."

Police chief: Why did you arrest that doctor?
Rookie cop: I heard someone say he was trying to take that woman's purse.
Police chief: No, you idiot! He was trying to take her pulse!

Why did the criminal attach a strip of barbed wire to the neck of his shirt?

Because he didn't want to have his collar felt.

A driver pulled up to the kerb and asked a policeman, "Can I park here?"

"No,' replied the officer.

"What about all these other cars?" the driver protested.

"They didn't ask."

A man was caught for speeding and went before the judge.

The judge said, "What will you take – thirty days or thirty dollars?"

The man said, "I think I'll take the money."

Why was the man arrested for waiting in the Big Top?
He was loitering within tent.

How do you know policemen are strong?
Because they can hold up traffic.

Three rookie cops were training to become detectives. To test their skills in recognizing a suspect, the chief of detectives showed each trainee a picture for five seconds and then hid it.

Showing the picture to the first rookie, he said, "This is your suspect. How would you recognize him?"

"That's easy," said the first rookie. "We'd catch him straight away because he's only got one eye."

"Uh, that's because the picture shows his profile," explained the chief.

Baffled by the first rookie's response, the chief turned to the second trainee. Showing him the same picture for five seconds, the chief said, "This is your suspect. How would you recognize him?"

"No problem," said the second rookie confidently. "He'd be easy to catch because he's only got one ear."

The chief threw up his hands in dismay. "What's the matter with you two idiots?" he raged. "Of course only one eye and one ear are showing – that's because it's a picture of his profile! Is that the best answer you can come up with?"

Despairing of the quality of the candidates, the chief turned to the third rookie, showed him the same picture and said testily, "This is your suspect. How would you recognize him? And please don't give me another stupid answer."

The third rookie studied the picture intently for a minute or two and then declared, "The suspect wears contact lenses."

The chief was impressed by the answer and said, "Wait while I check his file to see if he does wear contact lenses." The chief then checked on the computer. "Hey, how about that!" he beamed. "It's true. The suspect does wear contact lenses. That's a brilliant piece of deduction. How did you work it out just from looking at the picture?"

The third rookie replied, "It was easy. He can't wear regular glasses because he only has one eye and one ear."

How did the belt break the law? **It held up some pants.**

What type of sentence would you get if you broke the law of gravity? **A suspended sentence.**

What happened when an eight-foot-tall convict and a three-foot-tall convict escaped from jail together? **Police officers searched high and low for them.**

Why did the police officers spend hours in a restaurant? **They were on a steak out.**

Before a burglary trial, the judge explained to the defendant, "You can either let me try your case or you can elect to be judged by a jury of your peers."

The defendant thought for a moment and then asked, "What are peers?"

"They're your equals," replied the judge. "They're people just like you."

"Forget it!" exclaimed the defendant. "I don't want to be tried by a bunch of thieves!"

Who is the strongest thief? **A shoplifter.**

Did you hear about the three-fingered thief? **He only steals bowling balls.**

Why are burglars such good tennis players? **Because they spend so much time in courts.**

Two prisoners were involved in a fight in jail. A warden rushed in to break it up.

"Okay, that's enough," he said, pulling the two men apart. "Right, what's all this about?"

One of the prisoners said, "He called me a dirty number, warden."

When did the criminal get smart? **When the judge threw the book at him.**

What kind of robbery is not dangerous? **A safe robbery.**

A man was given a job as a security guard at a factory where there had been a series of thefts by workers on the night shift. So every morning when the night-shift workers passed through his gate, he had to check their bags and pockets to make sure that nothing was being stolen.

On his first night on duty, everything was quiet until a man pushing a wheelbarrow full of newspapers arrived at the gate. The guard's suspicions were aroused immediately. Convinced that something of value was concealed beneath the newspapers, he conducted a thorough search of the wheelbarrow but, to his dismay, found nothing. Even so, he still thought the worker was acting oddly, so he questioned him further about the cargo.

The worker explained, "I get a little extra money from recycling newspapers, so I go into the canteen and collect all the ones that people have discarded."

The guard accepted the explanation, but made a mental note to keep a close eye on the man in future.

Night after night, week after week, it was the same story. The same guy would push the wheelbarrow of newspapers past the guard's checkpoint. The guard would always check the contents of the wheelbarrow but find nothing untoward. Then one night, six months into the job, the guard reported for duty as usual but found a message ordering him to go straight to the supervisor's office. As soon as he walked through the door of the office, the supervisor told him, "You're fired!"

"Fired?" asked the guard, bemused. "Why? What have I done wrong?"

The supervisor raged, "It was your job to prevent theft from this factory, and you have failed miserably. So you're fired."

"What do you mean, failed?" protested the guard. "Nobody has stolen anything from this place during the six months I have been on duty."

"Oh really?" said the supervisor sarcastically. "Then how do you account for the fact that there are 182 missing wheelbarrows?"

What did the burglar say to the watchmaker as he tied him up? **Sorry to take so much of your valuable time.**

There were six murders in a neighbourhood, and a knitting needle was found at each crime scene. The police said they were looking for some sort of pattern.

Did you hear about the prisoner in the electric chair who asked the executioner to reverse the charges?

Customer: Any news on the robbery?
Store owner: Yes, the police are looking for a man with one eye.
Customer: Why don't they use two?

What is a prisoner's favourite punctuation mark? **A full stop, because it marks the end of his sentence.**

After burglars broke into a boss's house and stole money from his safe, he made everyone at work feel guilty. They protested, "But it wasn't our vault!"

What do you call a policeman with blond hair? **A fair cop.**

What happened when the

Did you hear about the kleptomaniac's daughter?

She took after her mother.

police station toilet was stolen?
The police had nothing to go on.

What did the police officer say to the icicle?
Freeze!

Did you hear about the rookie cop who handed out thirty-one parking tickets before he realized he was at a drive-in movie?

What diploma do criminals get?
The third degree.

Why was the sword swallower sent to prison?
He coughed and killed two people.

Motorist: Why are you crying after giving me that ticket?
Police officer: It was a moving violation.

What does a police officer use when he arrests a pig?
Ham cuffs.

Judge: Is this the first time that you have been up before me?
Defendant: I don't know, your honour. What time do you get up?

A stupid bank robber rushed into a bank, pointed two fingers at the clerk and said, "This is a muck-up!"

"Don't you mean a stick-up?" said the clerk.

"No," replied the robber. "It's definitely a muck-up. I've forgotten my gun!"

What do you call four burglars?
Two pairs of sneakers.

Harry: Where did you get that gold watch, Joe?
Joe: I won it in a race.
Harry: How many people were in this race?
Joe: Three – a policeman, the owner of the watch and me!

Why must judges be good at spelling?
They have to follow the letter of the law.

What did Winnie the Pooh say when he carried out a robbery?
Give me your honey!

Criminal: Why don't you hire the twins for the robbery, boss?

Criminal boss: I'm afraid of a double-cross.

Police officer: I'm afraid I'm going to have to lock you up for the night.
Man: What's the charge?
Police officer: Oh, there's no charge. It's all part of the service.

Police chief: Why are you putting handcuffs on that building?
Police officer: I'm making a house arrest.

Police detective: Do you think I should put on the cuffs?
Criminal: Why? You look good in short sleeves.

Police detective: Why did you dump those vegetables on my desk?
Criminal: You said it was time to spill the beans.

A shoplifter was caught red-handed trying to steal a watch from an exclusive jewellery store. "Listen," he said to the store manager, "I know you don't want the hassle of notifying the police and going to court, so how about we settle this amicably? Why don't I just buy the watch and we forget all about it?"

"Very well," said the store manager, and he wrote out the sales slip.

The criminal looked at the slip and said, "This is a bit more than I intended to spend. Can you show me something less expensive?"

The cross-eyed judge looked at the three defendants in the dock and said to the first one, "How do you plead?"

"Not guilty," said the second defendant.

"I wasn't talking to you," shouted the judge.

"I never said a word," replied the third defendant.

A police patrol-car driver out of his usual area was surprised to see an inspector on traffic duty.

"It's Inspector Brown, isn't it?" asked the patrol-car driver.

"Not any longer. It's just Constable Brown these days."

"Why? What happened?" said the patrol-car driver. "I didn't know you had been demoted."

"My downfall," sighed Brown wearily, "was arresting a judge on his way to a fancy dress party. How was I to know that his convict suit was only a costume?"

"I guess that's a lesson for us all," said the patrol-car driver. "Never book a judge by his cover."

Two burglars were robbing an apartment block when they heard the sound of approaching police car sirens.

"Quick!" said one of the burglars. "Jump out of the window!"

"But we're on the thirteenth floor," protested his accomplice.

The first burglar said, "This is no time to be superstitious!"

How did the police find a suspect standing on a set of bathroom scales?
He gave himself a weigh.

Three men were beaten to death with pictures by Picasso. Police are looking for a surreal killer.

Why did the robber take a bath before stealing cash from the bank?
He wanted to make a clean getaway.

Once upon a time, long long ago, in a land far far away, there lived a woman who was just too busy! She decided to make a clone of herself so she could get twice as much work done. Well, the clone helped her a lot, but it also gave her a bad reputation because the clone constantly swore. One day, the woman couldn't take her clone's foul mouth any more, so she took it to the top of a building and pushed it off. Soon after, the woman was arrested by the police for making an obscene clone fall.

A driver who was weaving erratically over the road was pulled over by a traffic cop.

As he opened the door and smelled the driver's breath, the cop snarled, "You're drunk!"

"Thank goodness for that!" said the driver. "I thought the steering had gone."

A hillbilly was driving across Texas when a traffic cop ordered him to stop.

"Got any ID?" asked the patrolman.

"'Bout what?" replied the hillbilly.

What were the gangster's last words?
Who put that violin in my violin case?

A police officer knocked on the door of a house and said to the woman who answered the door: "I'm looking for a man with one leg called Johnson."
The woman said, "What's his other leg called?"

Why did the police officer ticket the computer?
It was speeding along the information highway.

Woman: Officer, please help me. I've lost my wig.
Police officer: Certainly, madam. We'll comb the area.

Two Alabama State Troopers were pursuing a stolen car along the interstate highway toward Georgia. When the suspect crossed the state line into Georgia, the trooper who was driving pulled over immediately.

"Why did you stop, sarge?" asked the other trooper.

The sergeant replied, "He's in Georgia now. They're an hour ahead of us, so we'll never catch him."

Police chief: Why do you spend all your time trying to hit flies?
Police officer: You assigned me to the swat team, didn't you?

A woman was driving down the highway when a police patrol car pulled up alongside. The officer shouted to her, "Pull over."
"No," replied the woman, "it's a cardigan actually, but thank you for noticing."

RABBITS

Who is the Easter Bunny's favourite movie actor?
Rabbit De Niro.

What's pink, has five toes and is carried by the Easter Bunny?
His lucky people's foot.

What would you get if you crossed the Easter Bunny with an over-stressed person?
An Easter basket case!

Why does Peter Cottontail hop down the bunny trail?
Because his parents wouldn't let him borrow the car!

Why did the Easter Bunny have to fire the duck?
Because he kept quacking all the eggs!

What is the Easter Bunny's favourite state capital?
Albunny, New York!

How do you catch a rabbit?
Hide behind a tree and make carrot noises.

What do you call rabbits that marched in a long sweltering Easter parade?
Hot, cross bunnies.

How do you make a rabbit stew?
Make it wait for three hours.

When is rabbit soup not so good?
When there's a hare in it.

What do you call spending the afternoon with a cranky rabbit?
A bad hare day.

What's the difference between a rabbit and a lumberjack?
One chews and hops and the other hews and chops.

How could you tell the rabbit was angry?
He was hopping mad.

Why couldn't the rabbit fly home for Easter?
He didn't have the hare fare.

How many chocolate bunnies can you put into an empty Easter basket?

One. After that the basket won't be empty.

Why did the rabbit cross the road?
Because the chicken had his Easter eggs.

How do you catch a unique rabbit?
Unique up on him.

What do you call a rabbit dressed up as a cake?
A cream bunny.

What do you get if you cross a rabbit with a shallot?
A bunion.

What do rabbits use to keep their fur in place?
Hare spray.

A man went into a butcher's shop and asked for half a rabbit.
"Sorry," said the butcher, "but I don't want to split hares."

What do you get when you give a rabbit a perm?
Curly hare.

What do you call a rabbit with loads of money?
A millionhare.

What do you call a dumb bunny?
A hare brain.

What was the rabbit's favourite TV cop show?
Starsky and Hutch.

Rabbit: Are you sure this bottle

of special carrot juice will cure me?

Doctor: Absolutely. No rabbit has ever come back for a repeat prescription.

What happened when a man broke into a pet shop and stole a rabbit?

He made a run for it.

How far can a rabbit run into the woods?

Halfway. After that he's running out of the woods.

Where do rabbits go after their wedding?

On bunnymoon.

How do you know that carrots are good for your eyes?

Have you ever seen a rabbit wearing glasses?

How can you tell which rabbits are the oldest in a group?

Just look for the grey hares.

Why did the rabbit have trouble hopping?

Because he kept one foot in his pocket for good luck.

Why did the rabbit cross the road?

To get to the hopping centre.

A man was driving along the highway, and saw a rabbit hopping across the middle of the road. He swerved to avoid it, but unfortunately the rabbit jumped in front of the car and was hit. The driver, being a sensitive man as well as an animal lover, pulled over to the side of the road and got out to see what had become of the rabbit. Much to his dismay, the rabbit was dead. The driver felt so awful he began to cry.

A woman driving down the highway saw the man crying on the side of the road and pulled over. She stepped out of her car and asked the man what was wrong.

"I feel terrible," he explained. "I accidentally hit this rabbit and killed it."

The woman told the man not to worry. She knew what to do. She went to her car trunk and pulled out a spray can. She walked over to the limp, dead rabbit, and sprayed the contents of the can on to the rabbit. Miraculously, the rabbit came to life, jumped up, waved its paw at the two humans and hopped down the road. Fifty feet away the rabbit stopped, turned around, waved at the two again, hopped down the road another fifty feet, turned, waved, and hopped another fifty feet.

The man was astonished. He couldn't figure out what substance could be in the woman's spray can. He ran over to the woman and asked, "What was in your spray can? What did you spray on to that rabbit?"

The woman turned the can around so that the man could read the label. It said, "Hair spray. Restores life to limp hair. Adds permanent wave."

How does the Easter Bunny stay healthy?
He gets lots of eggsercise, particularly hareobics.

When does a rabbit go as fast as a train?
When it's on the train.

Which rabbits were famous bank robbers?
Bunny and Clyde.

What did the rabbit say when he found he only had a thistle to eat?
Thistle have to do.

Why did the rabbit eat the wedding ring?
He heard it was eighteen carrots.

Two rabbits running away from a group of foxes hid in a haystack. One rabbit turned to the other and said, "Okay, we can either run for it or we can stay here and outnumber them."
"We're going to run for it, you idiot," said the other rabbit. "I'm your brother!"

How is a rabbit like a plum?
They're both purple, except for the rabbit.

What did the bunny want to do when he grew up?
Join the hare force.

What do you call a rabbit who works in a bakery?
A yeaster bunny.

What did the customer say to the pet-shop owner after buying a bunny?
Rabbit up nicely, it's a present.

What do you call an egg-laden rabbit who jumps off bridges?
The Easter Bungee.

What's a rabbit's favourite car?
Any make – so long as it's a hutchback.

What must a police officer have before searching a rabbit's home?
A search warren.

What do you get when you cross a rabbit with a spider?
A harenet.

What do you call an ugly rabbit that sits on someone's forehead?
Unsightly facial hare.

Baby rabbit: Mommy, where did I come from?
Mother rabbit: I'll tell you when you're older.
Baby rabbit: Oh, Mommy, please tell me know.
Mother rabbit: Oh, very well. If you must know you were pulled from a magician's hat.

Which rabbit was a famous female aviator? **Amelia Harehart.**

What's a rabbit's favourite dance?
The bunny hop.

What's a rabbit's favourite TV show?
Hoppy Days.

What did the rabbit bride get on her wedding day?
A twenty-four-carrot ring.

Why are rabbits like calculators?
They both multiply a lot.

A baby rabbit was orphaned, but fortunately a family of squirrels took him in and raised him as one of their own. However, the adoption resulted in the rabbit displaying unusual behaviour, notably a tendency to scurry up trees like his step-siblings instead of hopping along the ground like other rabbits. Eventually, the young rabbit, realizing that he was different, became so confused about his role in the animal kingdom that he decided to discuss the problem with his adoptive parents.

"Am I a rabbit or am I squirrel?" he asked.

"You must be true to your roots," they advised. "You must start behaving like a rabbit."

"You mean…?"

"Yes," they said, bursting into song. "Don't scurry. Be hoppy."

Why did the rabbits go on strike?
They wanted a better celery.

What do you call a chocolate

Easter bunny that was out in the sun too long?
A runny bunny.

Why was the Energizer Bunny arrested?
He was charged with battery.

A lady opened her refrigerator and saw a rabbit sitting on one of the shelves.
"What are you doing in there?" she asked.
The rabbit replied, "This is a Westinghouse, isn't it?"
The lady confirmed, "Yes."
"Well," the rabbit said. "I'm westing."

What did the magician say when he made his rabbit disappear?
Hare today, gone tomorrow.

What do you call a rabbit who is real cool?
A hip hopper.

What do you call a rabbit with no clothes on?
A bare hare.

What do you call mobile homes for rabbits?
Wheelburrows.

REINDEER

What do reindeer say before telling you a joke?
This one will sleigh you.

How do you make a slow reindeer fast?
Don't feed it.

What is the wettest animal?
A raindeer.

Teacher: Name an animal that lives in Lapland.
Pupil: A reindeer
Teacher: Good, now name another.
Pupil: Another reindeer.

First boy: How come you never hear anything about the tenth reindeer, Olive?
Second boy: Olive?
First boy: Yeah, you know: "Olive the other reindeer, used to laugh and call him names."

What do you give a reindeer with an upset tummy?
Elka Seltzer.

What has antlers, pulls Santa Claus and a sleigh, and is made of cement?
I don't know.
A reindeer.
What about the cement?
Oh, I just threw that in to make it hard.

REPTILES

What powerful reptile is found in the Sydney Opera House?
The Lizard of Oz.

A train full of tortoises crashed into a bus crowded with terrapins.
The local news said it was a turtle disaster.

Why did the tortoise go to assertiveness classes?
To bring him out of his shell.

Why did the turtle cross the road?
To get to the Shell station.

Where did the turtle buy a new shell?
From the hard-wear store.

A family of tortoises went into a café for some ice cream. They sat down and were about to start when Father Tortoise looked outside and said, "Oh dear, it looks like it's about to rain. Junior, would you mind popping home to fetch my umbrella?"

So off went Junior for Father's umbrella, but ten hours later he still hadn't returned. Mother Tortoise turned to Father Tortoise and said, "I think we ought to eat Junior's ice cream before it melts."

And a voice from the door said, "If you do that, I won't go!"

What do you call a sick crocodile?
An illigator.

A tourist was being led through the swamps of Florida. "Is it true," he asked, "that an alligator won't attack you if you are carrying a flashlight?"

"That depends," replied the guide, "on how fast you carry the flashlight!"

Why did the lizard go on a diet?
He weighed too much for his scales.

A boy was on vacation in Florida when he was attacked by an alligator in the backyard of their cabin.

"Mom!" he cried. "An alligator's bitten off my finger!"

"Which one?" called his mother from inside the cabin.

"I don't know," said the boy. "All alligators look the same to me!"

What is a chameleon's favourite saying?
A change is as good as a rest.

What kind of tiles can't you stick on walls?
Reptiles.

Why did all the lizards run from the house when they heard the music player?
Because it was a gecko blaster.

Why is turtle wax so expensive?
Because turtles have such tiny ears.

As the heavens opened, one turtle turned to the other and said, "Don't you just love the sound of rain on your roof?"

A man was on holiday in the depths of Louisiana, where he tried to buy some alligator shoes. However, he was not prepared to pay the high prices, and after having failed to haggle the vendor down to a reasonable price level, ended up shouting, "I don't give two hoots for your shoes, man. I'll go and kill my own croc!"

The shopkeeper replied, "By all means, just watch out for those two men who are doing the same."

So the man went out into the swamp, and after a while saw two men with spears, standing still in the water. "They must be the two men the shopkeeper told me about," he thought. Just at that point he noticed an alligator moving in the water towards one of them. The guy stood completely passive as the gator came ever closer.

Just as the beast was about to swallow him, he struck home with his spear and wrestled the gator up on to the beach, where several were already lying dead. Together the two guys threw the alligator on to its back, and one of the men exclaimed, "Darn! This one isn't wearing shoes either!"

What do you call a crocodile's hiss?
An alarm croc.

Deep within a forest a little turtle began to climb a tree. After hours of effort he reached the top, jumped into the air waving his front legs and crashed to the ground. After recovering, he slowly climbed the tree again, jumped, and fell to the ground.

The turtle tried again and again while a couple of birds sitting on a branch watched his sad efforts. Finally, the female bird turned to her mate.

"Dear," she chirped. "I think it's time to tell him he's adopted."

What reptile always makes people laugh?
A stand-up chameleon.

RHYMES

What do you call a cat that tells jokes?
A witty kitty.

What do you call a rabbit that tells jokes?
A funny bunny.

What do you call a joke told by a small orange?
Satsuma humour.

What do you call it when you lease false teeth?
A dental rental.

What do you call a blonde from central Germany?
A flaxen Saxon.

What do you call a crustacean in the Mafia? **A lobster mobster.**

What do you call someone who lives underground?
A cellar dweller.

What do you call a relaxed stringed instrument?
A mellow cello.

What do you call a black Eskimo dog?
A dusky husky.

What do you call a happy Lassie?
A jolly collie.

What do you call an evil pastor?
A sinister minister.

What is another name for a Trojan horse?
A phoney pony.

What do you call a quiet argument?
A sedate debate.

What do you call a friend who falls into a puddle?
A muddy buddy.

What do you call a humdrum tile design?
A prosaic mosaic.

What do you call a spaghetti expert?

A pasta master.

What do you call a swelling on the foot of a shallot?
An onion bunion.

What do you call a cruise ship restaurant?
A liner diner.

What do you call a fruity dance?
A mango tango.

What do you call a shoe wrecker?
A sandal vandal.

What do you call the ceramics' sweepstakes?
A pottery lottery.

What do you call a bad flower crop?
A dahlia failure.

What do you call a disobedient stone?
A rebel pebble.

What do you call it when you sleep like a log?
Lumber slumber.

What do you call a kangaroo that would like to become smaller?
A wannabe wallaby.

What do you call a young cat that's in love?
A smitten kitten.

What do you call a newlywed woman who gets sunburned on her honeymoon?
A fried bride.

What do you call choristers' vestments?
Choir attire.

What do you call tomorrow's fruit?
Mañana banana.

What do you call a disc jockey's nightwear?
A DJ's PJs.

What do you call a frozen means of transport?
An icicle bicycle.

What do you call a dapper pachyderm?
An elegant elephant.

What is another name for the White House?
The President's residence.

What do you call a macaque that loves soul music?
A funky monkey.

What do you call a small fish that likes a Canadian rock band?
A Nickelback stickleback.

What do you call a fruit from the capital of Cuba?
A Havana banana.

What do you call the language of an Australian dog?
Dingo lingo.

What do you call a bees' dance?
A hive jive.

What do you call a snake dance?
A mamba samba.

What is another name for a superior pullover?
A better sweater.

What do you call a Norseman riding a Harley-Davidson?
A biking Viking.

What do you call a good time at a convent?
Nun fun.

What do you call something used by an artistic stoat?
A weasel easel.

What do you call a fondly remembered item from 150 million years ago?
A Jurassic classic.

What do you call an agreeable game bird?
A pleasant pheasant.

What do you call a wind instrument that has been made homeless?
An oboe hobo.

What do you call a less effective orator?
A weaker speaker.

What do you call a cheese on a sleigh?
A Cheddar sledder.

What do you call a clergyman with wrinkled skin?
A creased priest.

What do you call a large rodent that's running a high temperature?
Beaver fever.

What is another name for a marsupial that's late?
An overdue kangaroo.

What is another name for a serious newspaper article?
A solemn column.

What do you call a large ungulate that has hit the bottle?
A wino rhino.

What do you call overweight birds?
Obese geese.

What do you call a dog that works as a lawyer?
A legal beagle.

What do you call a fairly angry root vegetable?
A maddish radish.

What do you call the captain of a sailing vessel?
A clipper skipper.

What is another name for a wooden headrest?
A willow pillow.

What do you call a small dog that is more cheerful than it used to be?
A merrier terrier.

What is another name for a bovine argument?
A cattle battle.

What do you call the strength of a small crustacean?
Prawn brawn.

What do you call a newspaper

devoted to specialist eyewear?
A monocle chronicle.

What do you call a frightening songbird?
A scary canary.

What do you call a red sled?
A rouge luge.

What do you call danger in an Italian city?
Venice menace.

What do you call a damp pooch?
A soggy doggy.

What do you call a bloodthirsty tale?
A gory story.

What do you call an iguana that casts spells?
A lizard wizard.

What do you call a voracious lamb eater?
A mutton glutton.

What do you call an aggressive sheep?
A woolly bully.

What do you call two lithe people?
A supple couple.

What do you call an impassioned retainer?
A fervent servant.

What do you call an impertinent flower child?
A lippy hippie.

What do you call a cook who can't hear?
A deaf chef.

What do you call a play about Andean animals?
A llama drama.

RIDDLES

What's pink and close to silver?
The Lone Ranger's bum.

Did you hear about the guy that lost his left arm and leg in a car crash?
He's all right now.

How do crazy people go through the forest?
They take the psycho path.

What has four legs, is big, green, fuzzy, and if it fell out of a tree would kill you?
A pool table.

What were Tarzan's last words?
Who greased the vine!

Where did the sick ship go?
To the dock.

Who gets the sack the minute they start work?
A postman.

What does a king do when he burps?
He issues a royal pardon.

You are sitting in a pitch dark car. The doors and windows are shut and all you have is a

chisel and a saw. How do you get out?
Open the door.

What goes zzub, zzub, zzub?
A bee flying backwards.

What is yellow and stupid?
Thick custard.

What is black and white and has sixteen wheels?
A zebra on roller skates.

What did the big telephone say to the little telephone?
You're too young to be engaged.

What did the big chimney say to the small chimney?
You're too young to smoke.

What did the pencil sharpener say to the pencil?
Stop going in circles and get to the point.

Why did the boy take toilet paper to the party?
Because he was a party pooper.

What colour is the wind?
Blew.

Why is the letter T like an island?
Because it's in the middle of water.

Why did the man stamp on his watch?
Because he had time to kill.

Why do giraffes have such long necks?

Because their feet smell.

What's renewable, derived from wind, sun, tides, waves and biofuels, and has just three letters?
N-R-G.

Forwards it's heavy, backwards it's not. What is it?
A ton.

Why did the man feel stuck with his debt?
Because he couldn't budge it.

How do you address a female health inspector?
Hi Jean.

Why was the chimney ill?
It caught flue

What do lawyers wear to court?
Lawsuits.

What happened to the man who fell into an upholstery machine?
He is fully recovered.

How many aerosol deodorants do you need to make a big stink?
Just a phew.

Why is it hard to keep a secret in the winter?
Because your teeth chatter.

What parts of the river can be eaten?
The sauce and the currants.

What has two legs, one wheel and stinks?
A wheelbarrow full of manure.

What is wind?
Air in a hurry.

What stays hot in the fridge?
Mustard.

What did one virus say to the other?
Stay away! I think I've got penicillin.

What did Geronimo cry as he jumped out of the airplane?
Me!!!!

Why is a toupée like a secret?
Because you keep it under your hat.

What has a mouth and a fork, but never eats?
A river.

What's the quickest way to make anti-freeze?
Hide her clothes.

Why can't a bike stand up for itself?
Because it's two tyred.

What goes up when the rain comes down?
An umbrella.

What goes into the water pink and comes out blue?
A swimmer on a cold day.

If a Red Indian falls into the Black Sea, what does he become?
Wet.

How did the girl's father know she hadn't had a bath?
She forgot to wet the soap.

What is the centre of gravity?
V.

Why is the sky so high?
So that birds don't bump their heads.

What can fall on water without getting wet?
A shadow.

Why did the girl who wanted to be a singer just sit around all day doing nothing?
She was auditioning for American Idle.

What can run across the floor, but has no legs?
Water.

What happened when the glassblower inhaled?
He got a pane in the stomach.

What do you get hanging from trees?
Sore arms.

What did one oil slick say to the other oil slick?
Oil see you again.

What's wet, black, floats on water and shouts "knickers!"?
Crude oil.

What's wet, black, floats on water and shouts "underwear!"?
Refined oil.

What's hot and moves at one hundred miles per hour?
A person running a temperature.

What's worn over a school shirt and bursts into flames easily?

A blazer.

What is a myth?
A female moth.

Who sings and helps insulate the home from draughts?
Julio Doubleglasias.

What contest do aerosol deodorants enter?
The Eurovision Pong Contest.

What's black and white and makes a lot of noise?
A zebra with a drumkit.

What's grey, yellow, grey, yellow, grey, yellow, grey, yellow, grey, yellow?
An elephant rolling down a hill with a daisy in its mouth.

Have you heard the one about the millionaire who hated washing?
He was filthy rich.

What do you call an unemployed jester?
Nobody's fool.

Which Disney film features lots of swearing and cursing?
101 Damnations.

What happened when the waltzers broke down at a theme park?
They had to hire a spin doctor.

If you peel my skin off, I won't cry, but you will. What am I?
An onion.

Why was six afraid of seven?

Because seven eight nine.

Why couldn't the man make up his mind about laying a new lawn?
Because it was a turf decision.

Why did the man put his money in the freezer?
Because he wanted cold hard cash.

What did the baby porcupine say to the cactus?
Is that you, Mummy?

What is black and white and sleeps a lot?
A snoozepaper.

What did one plate say to the other plate?
Lunch is on me.

What did one toilet say to the other toilet?
You look a bit flushed.

Why did the man destroy his piano?
He was looking for his keys.

Why did Piglet look in the toilet?
He was looking for Pooh.

What do people do in clock factories?
They make faces all day.

Why did the tap dancer retire?
He kept falling in the sink.

Why did the boy stand on his head?
So that he could turn things over in his mind.

What is so fragile that even saying its name can break it?
Silence.

If you were surrounded by ten lions, ten tigers, ten elephants, ten kangaroos and ten hippopotamuses, what would you do?
Step off the carousel.

What's got a trunk, lots of keys and four legs?
A piano up a tree.

What is a zebra?
Twenty-six sizes larger than an A bra.

What do you have when sitting, but lose when you stand up?
Your lap.

When is a door not a door?
When it's ajar.

What gets wetter as it dries?
A towel.

What's black and white, black and white, black and white, black and white?
A penguin rolling down a hill.

What's black and white and laughing?
The penguin who pushed him.

Did you hear about the dyslexic agnostic schizophrenic?
He was in two minds about whether there's a dog.

What's brown and sticky?
A stick.

Who wore the first shell suit? **Humpty Dumpty.**

What else is brown and sticky?
Another stick.

What's pink and fluffy?
Pink fluff.

What's blue and fluffy?
Pink fluff holding its breath.

What is dark but made out of light?
A shadow.

What's the definition of a will?
(It's a dead giveaway)

If April showers bring rain, what do May flowers bring?
Pilgrims.

How do you make seven even?
Remove the "s".

What works only when it's fired?
A rocket.

What's sweet, cold, heavy, has lots of wheels and drives along the road with a stick poking out?
An articulated lolly.

What happened when the bicycle salesman broke his leg?

He couldn't peddle his wares.

What bow can't be tied?
A rainbow.

What starts with T, ends with T and is full of T?
A teapot.

If a dictionary goes from A to Z, what goes from Z to A?
A zebra.

What did the window say to the door?
What are you squeaking about, I'm the one with the pane.

What did the hat say to the scarf?
You hang around while I go on ahead.

What is green and has wheels?
Grass. I lied about the wheels.

What is green and goes to a summer camp?
A Brussel Scout.

What did the carpet say to the floor?
It's okay, I'll cover you.

What is white when it's dirty and black when it's clean?
A blackboard.

Why are giraffes so slow to apologize?
Because it takes them a long time to swallow their pride.

Why is a shoemaker like a church minister?
Both try to save soles.

What did the actress think when she saw her first strands of grey hair?
She thought she'd dye.

Who earns a living by driving his customers away?
A taxi driver.

What starts with E, ends with E but usually only has one letter?
An envelope.

What flowers grow on your face?
Tulips.

What is a lumberjack's favourite month of the year?
Septimber.

Why did the little girl put lipstick on her head?
She wanted to make up her mind.

What do you get when you cross a porcupine with a balloon?
Pop.

What city has no people?
Electricity.

Why are igloos round?
So that polar bears can't hide in the corners.

Why did it take three burly policemen to help the old lady across the street?
Because she didn't want to go.

What's grey and squirts jam at you?
A mouse eating a doughnut!

Why did the baker stop making doughnuts?
He got sick of the hole business.

Why were the suspenders sent to jail?
For holding up a pair of trousers.

What nails do carpenters hate to hit?
Fingernails.

What do you call a very popular perfume?
A best-smeller.

How do you know when a fir tree is in love?
It pines every day.

What's white and fluffy and beats its chest?
A meringue-utan.

What is at the end of everything?
The letter G.

What does the winner of the race lose?
His breath.

What's worse than raining cats and dogs?
Hailing taxis.

What happened when the fence builders became upset with their working conditions?
They started to picket.

What did the light say when it was turned off?
I'm delighted.

Why did the calendar think it was about to die?
Because its days were numbered.

Why did the Dalmatian refuse to bathe in the dishwasher detergent?
He didn't want to come out spotless.

Why did the electrician lose his temper?
Because he had a short fuse.

What word is always pronounced incorrectly?
Incorrectly.

Why did the shoe cry?
It bit its tongue.

How many birthdays does the average man have?
Just one!

What is the strongest animal in the world?
A racehorse because it can take hundreds of people for a ride at once.

Why did the woman go out in the rain with her purse open?
She was hoping for some change in the weather.

What do cars, trees and elephants all have in common?
They all have trunks.

What did the pencil say to the paper?
I dot my i's on you.

What kind of coat goes on wet and never has buttons?
A coat of paint.

Why couldn't the lifeguard save the hippie from drowning?
He was too far out.

What did the bug say when it hit the windshield?
I don't have the guts to do that again.

Why is it hard to carry on a conversation with a goat?
Because they're always butting in.

What kind of building is the tallest in the world?
A library; it has the most stories.

Who serves ice cream faster than a speeding bullet?
Scooperman!

How do angels greet each other?
They say halo.

What occurs once in a minute, twice in a moment, but never in a thousand years?
The letter M.

Why was the dry cleaner depressed?
Because he couldn't iron out all of his problems.

What kind of driver never gets a speeding ticket?
A screwdriver.

What bone keeps getting longer and shorter?
A trombone.

Why did the brain cell try to go to the other side of the brain?
I don't know. It hadn't really crossed my mind.

What do you give a man who has everything?
Antibiotics.

What's the longest word in the English language?
Smiles – because there's a mile between the first and last letters.

What kind of clothing last the longest?
Underwear – it's never worn out.

What happened to the man who put on a clean pair of socks every day?
By the end of the week he couldn't get his shoes on.

What's brown, has a hump and lives at the North Pole?
A lost camel.

What did one volcano say to the other volcano?
I lava you.

What is better than a dog that can count?
A spelling bee.

What did the tree say to the woodcutters?
Leaf me alone!

Did you hear the joke about the playing cards?
It's no big deal.

What would you get if you crossed a giraffe with a rooster?
An animal that wakes up people who live on the top floor.

What makes a chess player happy?
Taking a knight off.

Why does a ballerina wear a tutu?
Because a one-one's too small and a three-three's too big.

What do you get if you cross a sheep and a porcupine?
An animal that knits its own sweaters.

What bowl can you wash thousands of times, but it's still not clean enough to eat out of?
A toilet bowl.

Do you think it's hard to spot a leopard?
No they come that way.

What happened to the man who couldn't keep up his payments to the exorcist?
He got repossessed.

What kind of shot do you give a sick car?
A fuel injection.

Where is the best place to have a bubble-gum contest?
On a choo-choo train.

Where do polar bears keep their money?

Now you see it, now you don't. What is it?

A black cat on a zebra crossing.

In a snow bank.

What did the postcard say to the stamp?
Stick with me kid, and we'll go places.

Why didn't the clock work?
Because it needed a hand.

In what way is a bell obedient?
It makes a noise only when it is tolled.

What's full of holes but still holds water?
A sponge.

What happened to the butcher who backed into a meat grinder?
He got a little behind in his work.

When is a river like the letter T?
When it has to be crossed.

Why did the little girl bury her flashlight?
Because its batteries were dead.

What's the easiest house to pick up?
A light house.

What kind of wood gets scared?
Petrified wood.

What plant goes round in circles?
A lupin.

What do you call someone who keeps talking when no one is listening?
A teacher.

Why is an empty purse always the same?
Because there's never any change in it.

Why did the cowboy fire bullets at the fast-flowing river?
He was trying to shoot the rapids.

Why is it a bad idea to write a letter on an empty stomach?
Because it's much better to write on paper.

What is the one thing everybody in the world is doing at the same time?
Growing older.

What did the fireman say when the church caught fire?
Holy smoke!

When are your eyes not eyes?
When the wind makes them water.

Which burns longer, the candles on a girl's birthday cake or the candles on a boy's birthday cake?
Neither. They both burn shorter.

What do you get when you take the circumference of your jack-o-lantern and divide it by its diameter?
Pumpkin pi.

What did the dirt say when it started to rain?

If this keeps up, my name is going to be mud.

What did the angle say to his professor?
Give me my degree!

Why does a milking stool only have three legs?
Because the cow has the udder.

What is the difference between the Christmas alphabet and the ordinary alphabet?
The Christmas alphabet has Noel.

What happened to the man who shoplifted a calender at Christmas?
He got twelve months.

What do you shout to the Frenchman at the back of the race?
Camembert!

What's the purpose of origami?
Two-fold.

Did you hear the story about the smog?
You don't have to tell me, it's all over town.

How can you eat and study at the same time?
Eat alphabet soup.

How can you get out of a locked room with a piano in it?
Play the piano until you find the right key and then you can get out.

What is the best thing to take with you into the desert?
A thirst aid kit.

How do they drink water in the South?
From Dixie cups.

How do hedgehogs play leap-frog?
Very carefully.

Why did the toilet run down the hill?
To get to the bottom.

Why did the nickel jump off the building but the dime didn't?
The dime had more cents.

What gets smaller the more you put in it?
A hole in the ground.

Why is a room full of married people empty?
There isn't a single person in it.

If fish lived on land, where would they live?
In Finland.

If the green house is on the right side of the road, and the red house is on the left side of the road, where is the white house?
In Washington, DC.

How does Posh Spice keep her husband under control?
He's at her Beckham call.

What's the difference between a buffalo and a bison?
You can't wash your hands in a buffalo.

What wobbles as it flies? **A jellycopter.**

If two's company and three's a crowd, what are four and five?
Nine.

What causes baldness?
Lack of hair.

What did one car say to the other?
You look familiar. Haven't we bumped into each other before?

What did one faucet say to the other faucet?
You're a big drip.

When is it not a good idea to keep your feet on the ground?
When you're putting on pants.

What has wheels and flies?
A garbage truck.

What did one girl calendar say to the other girl calendar?
I have more dates than you do.

What is it that even the most careful person overlooks?
His nose.

What did one invisible man say to the other invisible man?
It's nice not to see you again.

Why did the Invisible Man look in the mirror?
To make sure he still wasn't there.

What did one magnet say to the other magnet?
I find you very attractive.

What's brown and sounds like a bell?
Dung.

What did one windshield wiper say to the other windshield wiper?
Isn't it a shame we seem to meet only when it rains?

What did the big carburettor say to the little carburettor?
Don't inhale so fast or you'll choke.

What did the book say to the librarian?
Can I take you out?

What did the boy Frankenstein say to the girl Frankenstein?
You are so electrocute.

What did the shirt say to the pants?
Meet me at the clothesline. That's where I hang out.

What did the stocking with the hole say to the shoe?
Well, I'll be darned!

What's a wok?
Something you throw at a wabbit.

What happened when the man leaped off a 200-foot-high cliff?

He jumped to a conclusion.

What did the wig say to the head?
I've got you covered.

What do hill people use to cook their food on?
A mountain range.

What do you call someone who carries a dictionary in his jeans?
Smarty pants.

What sound do you get if you hit a counterfeit penny with a hatchet?
A phony axe cent.

Where do parasites live?
In Paris.

What is a ship for good writers?
Penmanship.

What's pink and looks like a watering can?
A pink watering can.

What's yellow and 1,454 feet tall?
The Empire State Banana.

If two wrongs don't make a right, what do two rights make?
A u-turn.

What is an ocean?
Where buoy meets gull.

Why did the lumberjack hand pieces of wood to the bank manager?
He wanted to open a shavings account.

Why did the Buddhist refuse Novocain during root canal surgery?

He wanted to transcend dental medication.

Why are tall people more lazy?
Because they lie longer in bed.

Why did the clown buy an extra large shirt?
So that he could get used to performing in the Big Top.

What did the boots say to the cowboy?
You ride, I'll go on foot.

Why did the beach crumble beneath the jetty?
Pier pressure.

What is an ultimate?
The last person you marry.

What is black and white and red all over?
A blushing penguin.

What is black and white and red all over?
A newspaper.

What is black and white and red all over?
A skunk with diaper rash.

What is black and white and red all over?
A sunburned zebra.

What is green and pecks on trees?
Woody Wood Pickle.

What is the correct height for people to stand?
Over two feet.

What's the definition of parity?
Two identical parrots.

What kind of clothing does a pet wear?
A petticoat.

What can you catch but not throw?
Your breath.

What is hairy and coughs?
A coconut with flu.

How do you stop a cold getting to your chest?
Tie a knot in your neck.

Why was the TV documentary about the navy so popular?
It got the best ratings.

What lottery did the broom win?
The sweepstakes.

What kind of truck is always a "he" and never a "she?"
A mail truck.

What letter stands for the ocean?
The letter C.

What has a bottom at the top?
Your legs.

What part of a clock is always old?
The second hand.

What goes "Clip"?
A one-legged horse.

What radio has a crewcut?
A short-wave radio.

Which two words in the English language have the most letters?
Post Office.

What would happen if you swallowed your knife and fork?
You would have to eat with your hands.

What would you call the life story of a car?
An autobiography.

Why shouldn't you go into the shower with Pokemon?
Because he might Pikachu.

When are people smartest?
During the day, because when the sun shines everything is brighter.

What are hippies for?
Holding up your leggies.

When do the leaves begin to turn?
The night before an important test.

Why didn't the man get wet despite losing his umbrella?
Because it wasn't raining.

When do your car's brakes work best?
In the morning when its brakefast time.

When is an army like a sales clerk making out a bill?
When it is ready to charge.

Why don't human cannonballs keep their jobs very long?
Because as soon as they start they get fired.

Where can you always find diamonds?
In a deck of cards.

Why don't mountains get cold in winter?
They wear snow caps.

Where does Friday come before Thursday?
In the dictionary.

Why are Boy Scouts chubby?
Because scouting rounds a guy out.

Why can you always believe a ruler?
Because it is on the level.

What happened when the woman's underwear fell in the vat at a beermaker's?
A scandal was brewing.

Why did the girl sit on her watch?
She wanted to be on time.

What did the toothbrush want to be when he grew older?
A broom.

Why did the girl tear the calendar?
Because she wanted to take a month off.

How many successful jumps must a skydiver make before he graduates?
All of them.

Why did the sword swallower swallow an umbrella?
He wanted to put something away for a rainy day.

Why did the man keep a ruler on his newspaper?
Because he wanted to get the story straight.

Why do hurricanes travel so fast?
Because if they travelled slowly, we'd have to call them slow-i-canes.

Why do people laugh up their sleeves?
That's where their funny bones are.

Why is a book like a king?
Because they both have pages.

Why shouldn't you carry two half dollars in your pocket?
Because two halves make a whole, and you could lose your money through it.

What is the cheapest time to call your friends long distance?
When they're not home.

When doesn't a telephone work underwater?
When it's wringing wet.

How did the steelworker go to the wrong factory?
He lost his bearings.

Why couldn't the bankrupt cowboy complain?
Because he'd got no beef.

How do you know when a chair doesn't like you?
When it can't bear you.

How can you double your money?

Eeeek!

FLOAT

What happened to the Dutch girl who wore inflatable shoes?
Sadly, she popped her clogs.

Look at it in a mirror.

How do you file a nail?
Under the letter N.

How do you make a lemon drop?
Hold it and then let go.

When prices are going up, what remains stationary?
Writing paper and envelopes.

How can you get your name in lights the world over?
Change it to Emergency Exit.

On what nuts can you hang pictures?
Walnuts.

What are southern fathers called?
Southpaws.

What can you hold without touching it?
A conversation.

What did one broom say to the other broom?
Have you heard the latest dirt?

What did Tennessee?
He saw what Arkansas.

What did the big watch hand say to the small watch hand?
Got a minute?

What else did the big watch hand say to the small watch hand?
Don't go away, I'll be back in an hour.

What did the girl watch say to the boy watch?

Keep your hands to yourself!

What did the electric plug say to the wall?
Socket to me!

Why did the man always fly off the handle?
Because he had a screw loose.

Name three things that have eyes but can't see.
Needles, storms and potatoes.

What is a parrot?
A wordy bird.

What is one of the hardest subjects?
The study of rocks.

What is another name for a telephone booth?
A chatterbox.

What do the bathroom doors at a funeral parlour say?
His and Hearse.

What is bought by the yard and worn by the foot?
A carpet.

What is ice?
Skid stuff.

Why can't you keep secrets in a bank?
Because of all the tellers.

What is the left side of an apple?
The part that you haven't eaten.

How does a broom act?
With sweeping gestures.

Why do gardeners plant bulbs?
So that worms can see underground.

What do you say if you see three holes in the ground?
Well, well, well.

What kind of bird is like a letter?
A jaybird.

What kind of meat doesn't stand up?
Lean meat.

Why did the girl have a horse on her head?
Because she wanted a pony tail.

How did the teenager know he had bad acne?
His dog called him Spot.

What pet is always found on the floor?
A carpet.

Where do geologists go for entertainment?
To a rock concert.

What ring is square?
A boxing ring.

What time is it when a clock strikes thirteen?
Time to get it fixed.

What wears shoes but has no feet?
The sidewalk.

When is a chair like a fabric?
When it's sat in.

How could a cowboy ride into town on Friday, stay two nights, and ride out on Friday?
Friday is the name of his horse.

Why couldn't the guy get a job as a milkman?
He didn't have the bottle.

Where do baby plants go to school?
To a nursery.

Why did the cowboy ride his horse?
Because the horse was too heavy to carry.

Why did the man put a clock under his desk?
He wanted to work overtime.

Why did the man throw a clock out of the window?
He wanted to see time fly.

Why did the window pane blush?
It saw the weather-strip.

Why do mummies tell no secrets?
Because they keep things under wraps.

Who makes suits and eats spinach?
Popeye the Tailorman.

Why shouldn't you believe a person in bed?
Because he is lying.

How can you tell if you are cross-eyed?
When you see eye-to-eye with yourself.

What did the mother buffalo say to her child as he left for school?
Bison.

How do you know that army sergeants have a lot of headaches?
Because they always yell, "Tension!"

Why did God make only one Yogi Bear?
Because when he tried to make a second one he made a Boo-Boo.

Why were all the ink spots crying?
Their father was in the pen.

How did the barber win the race?
He took a short cut.

Why did the booger cross the road?
Because he was being picked on.

What did one casket say to the other casket?
Is that you coffin?

Which movie featured Sister Bernadette as a crack US fighter aircraft pilot?
Top Nun.

What's taken before you get it?
Your picture.

Why are birthdays good for you?
The more you have, the longer you live.

What is half of infinity?
Nity.

Why don't anteaters get sick?
Because they're full of anty-bodies.

Why was the man born to be a pessimist?
His blood type was B Negative.

What do you call an Italian feline trying on clothes?
Catalina dressing.

What did the digital watch say to his mom?
Look, Mom, no hands!

How was the blind carpenter able to see?
He picked up his hammer and saw.

Why did the willow weep?
He was unpoplar.

If you don't feel well, what do you probably have?
A pair of gloves on your hands.

If you fell off a ladder, what would you fall against?
Against your will.

What is the guillotine?
A French chopping centre.

What do cowboys call a doctor's hypodermic needle?
A sick shooter.

What do seven days of dieting do?
They make one weak.

What are never built to scale?
Prison walls.

What do you call a person who doesn't have all his fingers on one hand?

Normal. Fingers are supposed to be on two hands.

What did the log say to the lumberjack?
You give me a splitting headache.

What do you get if you put your hand in a pot?
A potted palm.

What do you get if you put your head in a washing machine?
Cleaner and brighter thoughts.

What do you have if your head is hot, your feet are cold, and you see spots in front of your eyes?
You probably have a polka-dotted sock over your head.

What does every drowning person say no matter what language he speaks?
"Glub, glub!"

What goes up but never goes down?
Your age.

What else goes up but doesn't come down?
A bear stuck in a tree.

Why do pens get sent to prison?
To do long sentences.

From which five-letter word can you take out the first, third and fifth letters and still be left with the same word?
Empty.

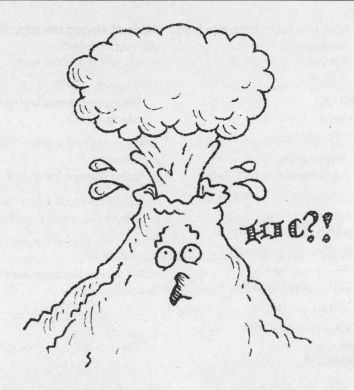

What is a volcano? **A mountain with hiccups.**

What goes, "Ho, ho, ho, bonk!"?
Santa Claus laughing his head off.

What happened when the horse swallowed a dollar bill?
He bucked.

What happened when the icicle landed on the man's head?
It knocked him cold.

What is better than presence of mind in an automobile accident?
Absence of body.

What is the best thing to take when you're run down?
The number of the car that hit you.

What is the best way to cure acid indigestion?
Stop drinking acid.

What is the famous last word in surgery?
Ouch!

What is the healthiest kind of water?
Well water.

What has tracks that arrive
before it gets there?
A train.

What is the perfect cure for
dandruff?
Baldness.

What is worse than a centipede
with sore feet?
A giraffe with a sore throat.

What is worse than a giraffe with a
sore throat?
A turtle with claustrophobia.

What is worse than a turtle with
claustrophobia?
An elephant with hay fever.

What kind of television programme
tells you who just broke an arm
or leg?
A newscast.

What nuts give you a cold?
Cachoo nuts.

What goes up a chimney down,
but won't go down a chimney up?
An umbrella.

What sickness do cowboys get
from riding wild horses?
Bronchitis.

What would happen if you
swallowed uranium?
You would get atomic ache.

When a girl slips on the ice,
why can't her brother help
her up?
**He can't be a brother and
assist her too.**

When doesn't it matter if a sailor
can't swim?
When he's not in the water.

When do you have acute pain?
**When you own a very pretty
window.**

Why wouldn't the butterfly go to
the dance?
Because it was a moth ball.

When don't you feel so hot?
When you catch a cold.

When is the best time to buy a
thermometer?
**In the winter, because then it is
lower.**

What did one candle say to the
other candle?
Are you going out tonight?

When is the vet busiest?
When it rains cats and dogs.

When they take out
an appendix, it's an
appendectomy; when they
remove your tonsils, it's a
tonsillectomy. What is it when
they remove a growth from
your head?
A haircut.

How can you get four suits for a
dollar?
Buy a pack of cards.

What happens to an air
conditioner when you pull its
plug?
It loses its cool.

Why was the man frustrated by his new job at the cemetery?
Because no matter what he said to the customers, they were always dead right.

Which eye gets hit the most?
A bullseye.

What gets closer and closer but never arrives?
Tomorrow.

Why can't a very thin person stand up straight?
Because he is lean.

Why did the germ cross the microscope?
To get to the other slide.

Why is a woman in love like a welder?
Because they both carry a torch.

Why did the man hit his hand with a hammer?
He wanted to see something swell.

Why did the secretary cut off her fingers?
She wanted to write shorthand.

How is manna from heaven like horse hay?
Both are food from aloft.

How do you make a Venetian blind?
Poke his eyes out.

Why did the timid soul tiptoe past the medicine cabinet?

He didn't want to wake the sleeping pills.

Why did the man swallow a pack of razor blades?
To sharpen his appetite.

Why was the barber arrested?
For running a clip joint.

Why do your eyes look different when you have been to an eye doctor?
Because they've been checked.

Why is a fishing hook like the measles?
Because it's catching.

Why is an eye doctor like a teacher?
They both test the pupils.

Why is Congress like a cold?
Because sometimes the ayes have it and sometimes the nos.

Why shouldn't you make jokes about a fat person?
Because it's not nice to poke fun at someone else's expanse.

You never catch cold going up in an elevator. True or false?
True. You come down with a cold, never up.

What do you call a sleepwalking nun?
Roamin' Catholic.

How long does it take for a candle to burn down?

About a wick.

Why do we put candles on top of a birthday cake?
Because it's too difficult to put them on the bottom.

Why did the tightrope walker visit his bank?
To check his balance.

What is a king's favourite kind of precipitation?
Hail.

What is a tornado's favourite game?
Twister.

What did the thermometer say to the other thermometer?
You make my temperature rise.

What did the hurricane say to the other hurricane?
I have my eye on you.

What did the lightning bolt say to the other lightning bolt?
You're shocking.

What did one tornado say to the other?
Let's twist again, like we did last summer...

Why did the man use ketchup in the rain?
Because it was raining cats and hot dogs.

What type of lightning likes to play sports?
Ball lightning.

What type of sense of humour does a dust storm have?
A very dry sense of humour.

What did the shy pebble say?
I wish I was a little boulder.

What animals talk longest on the telephone?
Yakety-yaks.

Why are manhole covers round?
Because manholes are round.

What is bright red and dumb?
A blood clot.

What has eighteen legs and catches flies?
A baseball team.

Why is Easter like whipped cream and a cherry?
Because it's always on a sundae.

What's the richest kind of air?
A billionaire.

What is a specimen?
An Italian astronaut.

What did the mountain climber name his son?
Cliff.

Why did the lady and her attorney seek a scarlet frock as part of her settlement?
Because she wanted a red dress for her grievances.

What must you know to be an auctioneer?
Lots.

Which runs faster, hot or cold?
Hot. Everyone can catch cold.

What's round and has got sharp teeth?
A vicious circle.

What do you do with a wombat?
You play wom with it.

What did the zero say to the eight?
Nice belt!

What has ten letters and starts with g-a-s?
An automobile.

What did the traffic light say to the car?
Don't look, I'm changing.

Why did the traffic light turn red?
You would, too, if you had to change in the middle of the street.

What's a hospice?
About twenty litres.

Did you hear about the guy with the corduroy pillow?
It made headlines.

ROBOTS

How does a robot shave?
With a laser blade.

What do you call a robot that always takes the longest route to get somewhere?
R2 detour.

Do robots have sisters?
No, just transistors.

A robot walks into a bar, orders a drink and lays down some cash. The bartender says, "We don't serve robots."
The robot says, "Maybe not now, but someday you will."

RODENTS

What do mice do when they are at home?
Mousework.

What do you call a superb painting done by a rat?
A mouse-terpiece.

What are the most athletic rodents?
Track and field mice.

A family of mice are sitting around in the lounge. Father mouse is reading the paper while mother and the children are watching television. All of a sudden a cat rushes in. Father mouse gets a terrible fright and starts barking like a dog. The cat runs away.

Turning to the rest of his family, father mouse says, "You see now how important it is to learn a second language."

What is a mouse's favourite musical instrument?
A mouse organ.

> What is a mouse's favourite game?
> **Hide and squeak.**

How do you save a drowning mouse?
Use mouse-to-mouse resuscitation.

> What did the rat say when he saw the supermodel mouse?
> **That was a narrow squeak.**

Where do mice put their boats?
At the hickory dickory dock.

> A child pestered his mother to buy him a pet hamster. Eventually, she agreed but the child only looked after the pet for a couple of days before becoming bored with it. So the tasks of feeding the hamster, giving it fresh water and cleaning out its cage fell to the mother.
>
> One day she became so irritated by his lack of responsibility that she said to him, "How many times do you think this hamster would have died by now if I wasn't looking after it?"
>
> "Um, I don't know," replied the child. "Once?"

Why do mice need oiling?
Because they squeak.

What do rodents say when they play bingo?
Eyes down for a full mouse.

How do mice celebrate when they move home?
With a mouse-warming party.

> When did Tom get when he locked Jerry in the freezer?
> **Mice cubes.**

What is small and furry and smells like bacon?
A hamster.

> Where do squirrels go when they have nervous breakdowns?
> **To the nut house.**

What happened to the miserly squirrel?
He never found a mate because he insisted on a prenutshell agreement.

> What has six eyes but cannot see?
> **Three blind mice.**

What is small, furry and great at sword fighting?
A mouseketeer.

> A carpet layer had just finished installing a carpet for a lady. He stepped out for a smoke, only to realize he'd lost his cigarettes. In the middle of the room, under the carpet, was a bump.
>
> "No sense pulling up the entire floor for one pack of

Which mouse was a Roman emperor? **Julius Cheeser.**

cigarettes," he said to himself. He proceeded to get out his hammer and flattened the hump.

As he was cleaning up, the lady came in. "Here," she said, handling him his pack of cigarettes. "I found them in the hallway. Now, if only I could find my pet hamster…"

What is grey, has four legs and a trunk?
A mouse going on vacation.

What did the beaver say to the tree?
It's been nice gnawing you.

What is brown, has four legs and a trunk?

A mouse coming back from vacation.

How do you catch a squirrel?
Climb up a tree and act like a nut.

Where do hamsters come from?
Hamsterdam.

Hickory hickory dock.
The mice ran up the clock.
The clock struck one.
But the rest got away with minor injuries.

A woman wanted to buy a coat made from squirrel fur. "I have only one concern," she told the store manager. "Will it be all right in the rain?"

"Certainly, madam," said the manager. "After all, you never see a squirrel with an umbrella, do you?"

What happened when the mouse fell into a bathtub?
He came out squeaky clean.

Which rodents were American TV crimefighters?
Miami Mice.

What goes dot, dot, dash, squeak?
Mouse code.

What goes squeak, squeak, bang?
A mouse in a minefield.

ROMANCE

A girl asks her boyfriend, "Do you love me?"
"Of course," he replies.
"Then whisper something soft and sweet in my ear."
He leans close to her and quietly says, "Lemon meringue pie."

What do you get if you go on a blind date wearing football boots?
Stud up.

A girl says to her mean sister, "I wish I had a penny for every boy who's asked me out."
"Wow!" says the sister. "So you'd have enough to use a public lavatory then?"

An ugly boy says to a pretty girl, "What would it take to get you to kiss me?"
She replies, "An anaesthetic."

What happened to the girl who was engaged to a boy with a wooden leg?
She broke it off.

A boy asks his friend, "Why is your face all scratched?"
"My girlfriend said it with flowers."
"How romantic."
"Not really, she hit me round the head with a bunch of thorny roses."

A boy said to his girlfriend, "I'm not rich like Jack, don't have a mansion like Russell or have a Porsche like Martin, but I do love you and want to marry you."

She replied, "I love you, too, but what was that you said about Martin?"

One man says to another, "My daughter has recently married an Irishman."

"Oh, really?"

"No, O'Reilly."

Why did the young man break off his relationship with a telephone operator?
She had too many hangups.

A woman asked her friend, "Where are you off to?"

"To see the doctor," her friend replied. "I don't like the look of my husband."

"Can I come with you? I can't stand the sight of mine."

What happened after the jigsaw split up with his girlfriend?
He was in pieces.

Why was the Irish girl disappointed with the engagement ring from her boyfriend?
Because it was a sham rock.

How did the telephones get married?
In a double ring ceremony.

A lady asked her friend, "I suppose you carry a memento of some sort in that locket of yours?"

Her friend said, "Yes, a strand of my husband's hair."

"But your husband's still alive!"

Her friend replied, "Yes, but his hair's gone."

A girl said to her boyfriend, "You remind me of a pepper pot."
He said, "I'll take that as a condiment."

Two friends were getting ready to go to a nightclub. One of them had a wooden eye. He said, "If anyone in there says anything about my wooden eye, I'm going to snap."

As soon as they entered the club, he went up to a girl and asked her if she wanted to dance.

She said, "I'd be daft not to, wouldn't I?"

A woman said to her friend, "My husband is a man of many parts."

Her friend remarked, "Pity they weren't put together properly."

A young man was in love with two women and could not decide which one to marry. In an attempt to solve his dilemma, he went to a marriage counsellor. When asked to list the virtues of his two loves, the young man revealed that one made delicious pancakes and the other was a talented poet.

"I see your problem," said the counsellor. "You can't decide whether to marry for batter or verse."

A man said to his friend, "I've just bought my wife a bottle of eau de toilette for fifty dollars."

His friend replied, "You could have had some from my toilet for nothing."

What happened to that couple who met in a revolving door? **They're still going round together.**

A stupid girl is in the cinema with her boyfriend. She begins to feel quite peckish so her boyfriend goes to get some snacks. He comes back with some M&Ms. The girl takes them, opens the packet and begins to eat them but picks out all the brown ones.

Her boyfriend asks, "Why are you picking out all the brown ones?"

The girl replies, "I'm allergic to chocolate."

A young man says to his girlfriend's father, "I've come to ask for your daughter's hand in marriage."

The prospective father-in-law replies, "Well, you'll have to take the rest of her, too, or the deal is off."

A boy told his sister, "Girls whisper that they love me."

His sister answered, "Well they'd hardly say it out loud now, would they?"

A girl said to her friend, "My

brother fell in love with his wife the second time he met her. He didn't know how rich she was the first time."

Two ladies were gossiping about a mutual friend. The first lady said, "She was two thirds married once."

"What do you mean?" her friend asked.

"Well, she turned up, the minister turned up, but the groom didn't."

Feeling sorry for himself, a husband confessed to his wife, "Sometimes I think I'm nothing but an idiot."

His wife held his hand tenderly and said, "Don't worry, darling. Lots of people feel like that. In fact, virtually everyone I know thinks you're an idiot!"

A thief and his girlfriend were walking down Main Street when she spotted a beautiful diamond ring in a jewellery store window.

"Wow, I'd sure love to have that!" she said.

"No problem, baby," said the thief, and he threw a brick through the glass and grabbed the ring.

A few blocks later, his girlfriend was admiring a leather jacket in another shop window.

"What I would give to own that!" she said.

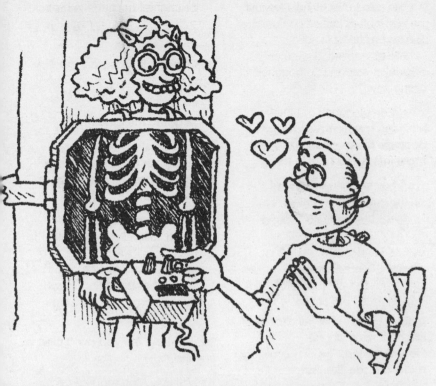

Did you hear about the X-ray technician who married one of his patients?
Everybody wondered what he saw in her.

"Sure thing, darling," said the guy, and he threw another brick through the window and snatched the jacket.

Finally, turning for home, they passed a Mercedes car dealership.

"Boy, I would do anything for one of those!" she said dreamily.

"Forget it!" the guy moaned. "Do you think I'm made of bricks?"

Why do they call her an after dinner speaker?
Because every time she speaks to a man she's after a dinner.

Once there was a girl who desperately wanted a boyfriend. Her mother wanted to help her, so she set up a blind date for her daughter.

When the girl got back from the date she said, "That was the worst night of my life!"

"Why is that?" her mother asked.

"He owns a 1938 Rolls-Royce!"

Her mother looked confused, "Isn't that a good thing?"

The girl replied, "He's the original owner and he bought it brand new!"

Why is an archaeologist the best husband a woman can have? **Because the older she gets, the more interested he is in her.**

A boy told his girlfriend at the end of the evening, "I'm sorry, but I just can't leave you, darling."

"Do you love me that much?" she asked.

"It's not that," he said. "You're standing on my foot!"

A boy told his pal, "I got a lovely kitten for my girlfriend." **His pal replied, "I wish I could make a trade like that."**

Mr Clemens was vacationing on a riverboat casino on the Mississippi with his wife.

By the second day, they were already fighting.

"Your dresses are too tight," he screamed. "You look like a tramp!"

"Oh," she replied. "You want to see me in something long and flowing? If you find something long and flowing, let me know and I'll get in it."

He pointed to the Mississippi River and said, "That's long and flowing!" and he pushed her into the river.

Wife: I'll cook you dinner. What would you like? **Husband: A life insurance policy.**

Why did the polygamist cross the aisle? **To get to the other bride.**

Girl: Now that we are engaged I hope you'll give me a ring. **Boy: Of course. What's your phone number?**

First boy: My girlfriend has beautiful long hair all down her back. **Second boy: What a pity it's not on her head!**

First boy: I can marry anyone I please. **Second boy: But you don't please anyone.**

The Invisible Man married an invisible woman. The kids were nothing to look at.

"Sir, I'd like your daughter for my wife." **"Can't she get one of her own?"**

How does a man know that he can count on his wife? **When she wears beads.**

Kurt was going out with a nice girl and finally decided to propose to her.

"Will you marry me, darling?" he asked.

Lisa smiled coyly and said,

"Yes, if you'll buy me a mink."

Kurt thought for a moment and then replied, "Okay, it's a deal, on one condition."

"What is that?" Lisa asked.

Kurt replied, "You'll have to clean its cage."

Two brooms were hanging in the cupboard and after a while they got along so well that they decided to get married. The bride broom looked beautiful in her white dress while the groom broom looked extremely suave in his tuxedo.

At the reception the bride broom was asked whether any baby brooms were on the horizon.

"It's far too soon to be talking about things like that," said the bride broom. "We haven't even swept together!"

First girl: Julie's boyfriend told her he'd lost all his money.
Second girl: What did she say?
First girl: I'll miss you, darling.
First boy: Your girlfriend has a big mouth.
Second boy: How do you mean?
First boy: When she yawns her ears vanish.

A young girl says to her friend, "When I grow up I'm going to marry the boy next door."

"Why?" her friend asks.

"I'm not allowed to cross the road."

Why did the husband want to be buried at sea?
To stop his wife dancing on his grave.

A young man had a girlfriend called Lorraine who was very pretty and he liked her a lot.

One day he went to work to find that a new girl had started. Her name was Janice Clearly and she was absolutely gorgeous. He became quite besotted with her and after a while it became obvious that she was interested in him, too.

But this guy was a loyal man and he wouldn't get involved with anyone else while he was still going out with Lorraine. So he decided that there was nothing for it but to break up with Lorraine and start dating Janice Clearly. He planned several times to tell Lorraine but couldn't bring himself to do it. One day they went for a walk along the river bank when Lorraine suddenly slipped and fell in to the river. The current carried her off and she drowned.

The guy stopped for a moment by the river and then ran off smiling and singing, "I can see Clearly now Lorraine has gone."

What's the wife of a hippy called?
Mississippi.

First man: My wife is one in a million.

Second man: Really? I thought she was won in a raffle.

They're the perfect match, he's a history teacher and she likes dates.

They're the perfect match, she likes jogging and he's on the run from the law.

They're the perfect match, she works in the chip shop and there is something fishy about him.

They're the perfect match, she's a geologist and he's on the rocks.

A man was relaxing on the sofa watching television when he heard his wife's voice in the kitchen. "What would you like for dinner, sweetie? Do you want chicken, beef or lamb?"

Surprised, he answered, "Thanks! I'd like chicken."

His wife replied, "You're having soup. I was talking to the cat."

When plus and minus got married they had an addition to the family. The thing is, though, he turned out to be a problem child.

First woman: Don't you think that man over there is the ugliest person you've ever seen?
Second woman: He's my husband.
First woman: Oh dear, I am sorry.
Second woman: You're sorry?!

A woman woke her husband in the middle of the night and said, "There is a burglar in the kitchen eating my homemade steak and kidney pie."

"Oh dear," said her husband. "Who should I call, the police or an ambulance?"

A man who lived in an apartment block wanted to check whether or not it was raining outside, so he opened the window and held out his hand. But as he did so, a glass eye fell into his palm. Looking up to see where it had come from, he saw a woman looking down from an apartment on the top floor.

"Is this yours?" he asked, holding the glass eye.

"Yes," she replied. "Could you bring it up?"

He took the glass eye up to the woman's apartment, and she was so grateful for its safe return that she offered him a drink. Then she asked him whether he would like to stay for dinner, and he accepted the invitation. They had a lovely meal, at the end of which she suddenly leaned over and kissed him.

The man was taken aback and asked, "Do you behave like this with every man you meet?"

"No," she said. "Only those who catch my eye."

SCHOOL

Pupil: I don't think I deserved zero on the test.
Teacher: I agree, but that's the lowest mark I could give you.

Pupil: My teacher was mad with me because I didn't know where the Rockies were.
Mother: Well next time remember where you put things.

Mother: Did you enjoy the school outing, dear?
Daughter: Yes, and we're going again tomorrow.
Mother: Why's that?
Daughter: To try and find the kids we left behind.

Mother: How do you like your new teacher?
Son: I don't.
Mother: Why not?
Son: She told me to sit up front for the present and then she didn't give me one.

Mother: What was the first thing you learned in class?
Daughter: How to talk without moving my lips.

Why did the jellybean go to school?
Because he wanted to be a smartie.

Son: The art teacher doesn't like what I'm making.
Father: Why, what are you making?

Son: Mistakes.

Teacher: I want to talk to you about two words I wish you wouldn't use so often in class. One is "great" and the other is "lousy".
Pupil: Certainly, sir. What are they?

Teacher: Please don't whistle while studying!
Pupil: I'm not studying, just whistling.

Teacher: What is a comet?
Pupil: A star with a tail.
Teacher: Can you name one?
Pupil: Lassie.

A seventh grade biology teacher arranged a demonstration for his class.

He took two earthworms and in front of the class he dropped the first worm into a beaker of water where it fell to the bottom and wriggled about. He then dropped the second worm into a beaker of ethyl alcohol and it immediately shrivelled up and died.

Finally, he asked the class if anyone knew what this demonstration was intended to show them.

A boy in the second row immediately shot his arm up and said:

"You're showing us that if you drink alcohol, you won't have worms!"

Teacher: Can you give me an example of how to use the word "politics" in a sentence?
Pupil: My parrot swallowed a watch, and now Polly ticks.

Teacher: You try my patience!
Pupil: No, sir, you had better try mine. There's more of it!

An inflatable boy goes to an inflatable school and one day he finds himself having a really bad day. Bored with the lesson, he gets up and walks out of the inflatable classroom but, while walking down the corridor, he sees the inflatable headmaster approaching him.

The inflatable boy pulls out a pin and punctures the inflatable headmaster before running out of the inflatable school gates. Just as he gets past the gates, he thinks about how much he hates school and once more pulls out his pin and pokes it into the inflatable school. He then runs as fast as his inflatable legs allow, all the way home and races into his inflatable bedroom.

A couple of hours later, his inflatable mother is knocking at his bedroom door and with her are the inflatable police. Panicking, the inflatable boy yet again pulls out the pin and jabs it into himself. Later on that evening, he wakes up in an inflatable hospital and, in the bed next to him, he sees the inflatable headmaster.

Shaking his deflated head, more in sorrow than in anger, the headmaster says, "You've let me down, you've let the school down, but worst of all, you've let yourself down."

Teacher: Why does the Statue of Liberty stand in New York harbour?
Pupil: Because it can't sit down.

Teacher: If one plus one is two and two plus two equals four, what is four plus four?
Pupil: That's not fair! You answer the easy ones and leave us with the hard one.

When a teacher closes his eyes, why should it remind him of an empty classroom?
Because there are no pupils to see.

Teacher: That's an interesting pair of socks you have on. One red and one blue.
Pupil: Yes, Miss. And I've got another pair at home just like it!

Why did the teacher put the lights on?
Because the class was so dim.

The teacher asked Simon to say his name backwards.
He said, "No mis."

Two students who were studying English went to Honolulu on holiday. Soon they began to argue about the correct way to pronounce the word Hawaii.

One student insisted that it's Hawaii, with a "w" sound.

The other student said it was pronounced "Havaii", with a "v" sound.

Finally, they saw a man on the beach whom they knew had lived on the islands for many years and asked him which was correct.

The old man said, "It's Havaii." The student who was right was very happy, and thanked the old man.

The old man replied, "You're velcome."

Every day over a period of several months a small boy brought raisins into school for his teacher, but then suddenly he stopped. After a few days without raisins, the teacher asked the boy why he had stopped bringing raisins for her. He explained, "My rabbit died."

Over the course of several days, a student teacher was seen coming out of the school restroom with a marker pen in his hand. On the walls of the restroom were rude expressions and graffiti. It was very bad.

Finally, the headmaster called the student teacher into his office and told him that it was terrible to write those things on the walls.

The student teacher said, "I'm not the one writing all these things. I'm just correcting the grammar."

First student: Great news, teacher says we have a test today come rain or shine.
Second student: What's so great about that?
First student: It's snowing outside.

What kind of food do mathematics teachers eat?
Square meals.

Teacher: Why are you doing your multiplication on the floor?
Pupil: You told me to do it without using tables.

One day an English grammar teacher was looking ill.

A student asked, "What's the matter?"

"Tense," answered the teacher, describing how he felt.

The student paused, then continued, "What was the matter? What has been the matter? What might have been the matter?"

Teacher: Where's your homework?
Pupil: I made it into a paper plane and someone hijacked it.

Father: How do you like going to school?
Son: The going bit is fine, as is the coming home bit, but I'm not too keen on the time in-between.

Little Johnny was busy doing his homework. As his mother approached she heard him repeat, "One and one, the son-of-a-witch is two. Two and two, the son-of-a-witch is four. Three and three..."

His mother interrupted, asking where he had learned this way of doing sums. Little Johnny remarked that his teacher had taught him.

His mother was upset and told him to stop the homework. The next day she stormed into little Johnny's classroom and confronted his teacher about her bizarre method of teaching arithmatic.

The teacher was flabbergasted. She said that she couldn't understand why little Johnny had said what he did. Then suddenly, she exclaimed, "Oh, I know! Here in school we say, one and one, the sum-of-which is two."

Teacher: Are you good at math?
Pupil: Yes and no.
Teacher: What do you mean?
Pupil: Yes, I'm no good at math.

Teacher: Now class, whatever I ask, I want you all to answer at once. How much is six plus four?
Class: At once.

Teacher: Why are you the only child in the classroom today?
Pupil: Because I was the only one who didn't have school dinner yesterday!
Teacher: Why weren't you at school yesterday?
Pupil: Our cow was on heat, so I had to take her to the bull.
Teacher: Surely your father could have done that?
Pupil: No, it has to be the bull.

Teacher: This essay you've written about your pet dog is word for word exactly the same essay as your brother has written.
Pupil: Of course it is. It's the same dog!

A Sunday School teacher was having trouble opening a combination lock on the church safe. Eventually, she went to the minister's room and asked for help.

The minister started to turn the dial, but after the first three numbers he paused and stared blankly for a moment. Then he looked heavenward, mouthed something in silence, looked back at the safe, dialled the last two numbers and successfully opened the lock.

The teacher gushed, "I'm so impressed by your faith, minister. The power of prayer was never better illustrated."

"Not really," he answered. "You see, I can never remember the combination either. That's why I wrote the number on a piece of paper and stuck it to the ceiling."

Why was the *Lord of the Rings* author told off at school?
For Tolkien in class.

Teacher: If I had nine oranges in one hand and eight oranges in the other hand, what would I have? **Pupil: Big hands.**

An elementary school student asked his teacher if a person should be punished for something he hadn't done.

"No," said the teacher. "Of course not!"

"Good," said the boy. "Because I haven't done my homework."

Why was the little boy teacher's pet?
Because she kept him in a cage at the back of the class.

Father: How were the exam questions?
Son: Easy.
Father: Then why are you looking so unhappy?

Son: The questions didn't give me any trouble – but the answers did.

Father: How are your exam results?
Son: They're under water.
Father: What do you mean?
Son: They're below C level.

Son: Dad, will you do my homework for me tonight?
Father: No, son, it wouldn't be right.
Son: Well, you could try.

Father: Why are your school marks so bad? You weren't absent on the day of the test, were you?
Son: No, but the boy who sits

next to me was.

Teacher: When was Rome built?
Pupil: At night.
Teacher: Why did you say that?
Pupil: Because my dad always says that Rome wasn't built in a day!

Teacher: Can anyone tell me how many seconds there are in a year?
Pupil: Twelve. The second of January, the second of February...

Teacher: Does anyone know which month has twenty-eight days?
Pupil: All of them.

Mother: What did you learn in school today
Son: How to write
Mother: What did you write?
Son: I don't know, they haven't taught us how to read yet.

First boy: Can you come out to play after school?
Second boy: No, sorry. I promised my dad that I would stay in and help him with my homework.

A boy at school asked his teacher, "May I use the bathroom?"
The teacher replied, "No, not unless you say your ABCs."
The boy said: "a b c d e f g h i j k l m n o q r s t u v w x y z."
The teacher asked, "Where's the p?"
The boy replied, "Running down my leg!"

"What's your father's occupation?" the school secretary asked a young boy on the first day of the new academic year.
"He's a magician," replied the boy.
"How interesting! What's his favourite trick?"
"He saws people in half," said the boy.
"Gosh!" exclaimed the secretary. "Have you any brothers or sisters?"
"Yes. One half-brother and two half-sisters."

Teacher: This is the third time I've had to tell you off this week! What have you got to say about that?
Pupil: Thank heavens it's Friday.

Teacher: Didn't you hear me call you?
Pupil: But you said not to answer you back.

Teacher: Didn't you promise to behave in class?
Pupil: Yes, Miss.
Teacher: And didn't I promise to punish you if you were naughty?
Pupil: Yes, but since I broke my promise, you don't have to keep yours.

Teacher: What's the definition of a polygamist?
Pupil: A parrot with more than one wife.

Teacher: If there are four birds on a fence and you shot one, how many would be left?
Pupil: None.
Teacher: No, the correct answer is three.
Pupil: But, Miss, if you shot one, the other three would fly away.

What tables don't you have to learn?
Dinner tables.

Why did the teacher jump into the lake?
Because she wanted to test the waters.

Teacher: What do you know about the Dead Sea?
Pupil: Dead? I didn't even know it was ill.

Why was the headmaster worried?
There were too many rulers in school.

Why did the pupils think their school was haunted?
Because the principal was always going on about the school spirit.

One morning, before school, a young boy said to his father, "Dad, I don't want to go to school today."

"Why not?" his father asked, concerned that his son was ill or unhappy at school.

The boy said, "Well, one of the chickens on the school farm died last week and we had chicken soup for lunch the next day. Then three days ago one of the pigs died and we had roast pork the next day."

The boy's father looked confused, "But why don't you want to go today?"

The boy replied, "Because our English teacher died yesterday."

Teacher: I wish you would pay a little attention.
Pupil: I'm paying as little as I can!

Teacher: I'd like to go through one whole day without telling you off!
Pupil: You have my permission.

Teacher: I'm glad to see your writing has improved.
Pupil: Thank you, Miss.
Teacher: Because now I can see how bad your spelling is.

A small girl arrived home from school and told her mother, "Our teacher has a bad memory. For three days she asked us how much is two and two. We told her it was four, but she still doesn't know. Because today she asked us again!"

Teacher: I want you to tell me the longest sentence you can think of.
Pupil: Life imprisonment.

Son: I failed every subject except for algebra.
Mother: How did you keep from failing that?
Son: I didn't take algebra.

Mother: Why are you home

from school so early?

Son: I was the only one who could answer a question.

Mother: Oh, really? What was the question?

Son: Who threw the eraser at the principal?

The teacher asked little Johnny if he knew his numbers.

"Yes, I do," he said. "My dad taught me."

"Good," said the teacher. "So what comes after four?"

"Five."

"And what comes after seven?"

"Eight."

"And what comes after ten?"

"The jack."

A young boy was at his first day at a new school. The teacher asked him, "If I had six coconuts and I gave you three, how many would I have left?"

"I don't know," said the boy. "At my old school we did all our sums in apples and oranges."

Teacher: Johnny, you know you can't sleep in my class.

Pupil: I know, Miss. But maybe if you were a little quieter, I could.

Teacher: That's quite a cough you have there. What are you taking for it?

Pupil: I don't know, Miss. How much will you give me?

Teacher: Why are you late?

Pupil: Because of the sign.

Teacher: What sign?

Pupil: The one that says "School Ahead. Go Slow". So I did!

Teacher: Why are you picking your nose in class?

Pupil: My Mom won't let me do it at home.

Teacher: Why have you got cotton wool in your ears? Have you got an infection?

Pupil: Well, Miss, you keep saying that things go in one ear and out the other, so I'm trying to keep them in.

Why shouldn't you put grease on your hair the night before an important school test?

If you did, everything might slip your mind.

A young girl by the name of Rosemary worked really hard at school in the hope that she would one day be as clever as her classmates. As she was not naturally gifted, study did not come easy to her and there were occasions when everything seemed too much. So she constantly needed reassurance from her teacher.

One day she asked the teacher, "Do you think I will ever be as smart as my friends?"

The teacher responded encouragingly, "You will be partially sage, Rosemary, in time."

Father: Let me see your school

report.
Son: I haven't got it.
Father: Why not?
　　Son: My friend has borrowed it. He wants to scare his parents!

After seeing their thirteen-year-old son finish bottom of the class in every subject, his parents decided to send him to a private tutor. A month later, they asked the tutor how the boy was doing.

"He's getting straight As," said the tutor.

"That's great," said the relieved parents.

"Mind you," added the tutor, "his Bs are still a bit wonky."

Teacher: This note from your father looks like your handwriting.
Pupil: That's because he borrowed my pen.

A science teacher was irritated that one of his students was late for his class for the third time in a week. So as soon as the boy sat down, the teacher made a point of asking him, "Jenkins, what's the chemical formula for sulphuric acid?"

"I don't know, sir," replied the boy.

"Well, Jenkins," said the teacher sternly, "perhaps if you came to class on time you would know."

"I doubt it," replied the boy, "because I never pay attention anyway!"

Why don't you see any giraffes in elementary school?
Because they're all in high school.

Why did the teacher wear sunglasses?
Because his class was so bright.

Teacher: What do you get if you add 4,657 and 7,854, then subtract 678 and divide the answer by 62?
Pupil: A headache.

At a school careers evening, a fifteen-year-old boy was asked what he wanted to do when he left school. He replied, "I want to be a stamp collector."

The careers advisor was sceptical. "What about banking? There's plenty of money to be made in banking."

"No, I want to be a stamp collector."

"Or how about teaching? There's always a shortage of teachers."

"No," the boy insisted. "I want to be a stamp collector."

"Or journalism?" persisted the careers advisor. "That can lead to all manner of opportunities – public relations, radio, television…"

"No, I want to be a stamp collector."

The careers advisor threw up his hands in despair and cried, "But don't you see, philately will get you nowhere!"

Did you hear about the cross-eyed teacher?
He couldn't control his pupils.

Teacher: What family does the octopus belong to?
Pupil: Nobody I know.

Why is math always sad?
Because it has too many problems.

Teacher: Be sure you go straight home after school.
Pupil: I can't. I live round the corner.

Boy: Dad, can you help me find the lowest common denominator in this problem please?
Father: Don't tell me that they haven't found it yet. I remember looking for it when I was a boy.

Father: Are you in the top half of your class?
Son: No, I'm one of the students who make the top half possible.

"Mary!" shouted the teacher to the pupil who was daydreaming. "If India has the world's second largest population, oranges are $1.50 for six, and it costs $8 for a day return to Pittsburgh, how old am I?"

"Twenty-eight," replied Mary instantly.

"Why did you say that?" asked the teacher.

"Well," said Mary, "my brother's fourteen and he's half mad!"

SCIENCE

Why did the scientist install a knocker on his door?
He wanted to win the no bell prize.

Why was there thunder and lightning in the laboratory?
The scientists were brainstorming.

Science teacher: What is Ba + Na2?
Pupil: Banana.

Why do scientists look for things twice?
Because they re-search everything.

What happened to the mad scientist who created a liquid that could burn through any material?
He spent the rest of his life trying to invent something to hold it in.

The science teacher asked her class whether anyone could remember the chemical formula for water.

"Yes," said one pupil brightly. "It's HIJKLMNO."

"It's what?" snapped the teacher.

"Well, you told us last week it was H to O."

What kind of aftershave do genetic scientists wear?
Eau de clone.

A Russian scientist and a scientist from the Czech Republic had spent their lives studying the grizzly bear. Each year they asked their respective governments to allow them to go to Yellowstone National Park to study the bears. Finally, their request was granted, and they immediately flew to the park.

They reported to the ranger station but the chief ranger told them that it was the grizzly mating season and it was too dangerous to go out and study the animals. They pleaded that this was their only chance, and finally the ranger relented.

The Russian and the Czech

were given mobile phones and told to report in every day. For several days they called in, and then nothing was heard from the two scientists. The rangers mounted a search party and found the camp completely ravaged, with no sign of the missing men. Following the trails of a male and a female bear, they finally caught up with the female.

Fearing an international incident, they decided they must kill the animal to find out if she had eaten the scientist. They killed the female and opened the stomach to find the remains of the Russian.

One ranger turned to the other and said, "You know what this means, don't you?"

The other ranger responded, "I guess it means the Czech's in the male."

Science professor: Now what can you tell me about atoms and mass?
Student: I didn't even know they were Catholic!

SHAGGY DOG STORIES

Ted and his girlfriend Alice lived in Texas, but Ted had always wanted to see the amazing natural sky illumination known as the northern lights. Alice was less enthusiastic but decided that a few days in Canada would at least be a nice break from Houston.

So they drove all the way up to Canada. By the time they arrived, Ted was beside himself with excitement. The northern lights were fantastic – the greatest light show he had ever seen. The whole sky was ablaze with colour. Ted jumped out of the car and took in the wonder of it all, but his girlfriend stayed in the vehicle reading a magazine. Ted couldn't believe her lack of interest. So eventually he went over to her and said, "What's the matter? Does the aurora bore ya, Alice?"

A major highway had a toll bridge spanning a river. Cars and trucks had to stop at a toll booth and pay a fee to a collector who would then raise the gate to allow the vehicle to cross the bridge. However, the job was not without incident. From time to time, a wide truck would smash into one of the toll booths, forcing the collector to close his booth and move to a new one while repairs were carried out.

One of the collectors, George,

had his own special method of dealing with damage to his booth. Whenever a truck or car smashed into it, he would gather up all the little pieces of brickwork, re-assemble them, and in no time at all his toll booth would be open again and ready for business. His fellow collectors were puzzled about how it was that a crash caused George only minor inconvenience.

"I don't understand," said one. "How is that whenever a truck smashes into my toll booth I have to call a crew to repair it, but you seem to be able to re-assemble yours yourself in just a few hours?"

"It's simple," said George. "I use Toll Gate Booth Paste."

A man was driving down the road when his car broke down near a monastery. He went to the monastery, knocked on the door, and said, "My car broke down. Do you think I could stay the night?"

The monks graciously accepted him, gave him dinner, even fixed his car. As the man tried to fall asleep, he heard a strange sound. The next morning, he asked the monks what the sound was, but they said, "We can't tell you. You're not a monk." The man was disappointed but thanked them for their hospitality and went on his way.

Some years later, the same man broke down in front of the same monastery. The monks accepted him, fed him, even fixed his car. That night, he heard the same strange noise that he had heard years earlier. The next morning, he asked what it was, but the monks replied, "We can't tell you. You're not a monk."

The man said, "Listen, I'm dying to know what that sound is. If the only way I can find out is to become a monk, how do I become a monk?"

The monks replied, "You must travel the earth and tell us how many blades of grass there are and the exact number of sand pebbles. When you find these numbers, you will become a monk."

The man set about his task. Forty-five years later, he returned and knocked on the door of the monastery. He announced, "I have travelled the earth and have found what you have asked for. There are 145,236,284,232 blades of grass and 231,281,219,999,129,382 sand pebbles on the earth."

The monks replied, "Congratulations. You are now a monk. We shall now show you the way to the sound." The monks led the man to a wooden door, where the head monk said, "The sound is right behind that door."

The man reached for the knob, but the door was locked. He asked for the key, the monks gave him it and he opened the door. Behind the wooden door was another door made of stone. The man demanded the key to the stone door. The monks gave him the key and he opened it, only to find a door made of ruby. He demanded another key from the monks, who provided it. Behind that door was another door, this one made of sapphire. So it went on until the man had gone through doors of emerald, silver, topaz and amethyst.

Finally, the monks said, "This is the last key to the last door." Greatly relieved, the man slowly unlocked the door, turned the knob, and behind that door he was amazed to find the source of that strange sound.

But I can't tell you what it is, because you're not a monk.

_____

Back in the days of the Wild West, Dodge City was just about the toughest place in America. Yet along with the saloons and gambling dens the town also boasted a lively little theatre group.

One year, the group was due to put on a version of Swan Lake, but on the day of the dress rehearsal it was discovered that moths had got into the tutus. The outfits were damaged beyond repair but luckily the producer heard of a company in Kansas City that had some spare tutus. The proprietor promised to send the garments over on a special train.

Back at Dodge, everyone was rushing around making last-minute preparations for the show but someone needed to go to the station to fetch the tutus. Eventually, Butch, the biggest, meanest hombre in town, offered to go.

Butch had no sooner arrived at the station and taken a seat than the station master timidly asked whether he might be of any assistance.

"Nah," growled Butch. "I'm fine. I'm just waiting for the tutu train."

_____

An Indian chief was feeling very sick, so he summoned the medicine man. After a brief examination, the medicine man took out a long, thin strip of elk hide and handed it to the chief with instructions to bite off, chew and swallow one inch of the leather every day.

Three weeks later, the medicine man returned to see if the chief was feeling any better. The chief shrugged and said, "The thong is ended, but the malady lingers on."

_____

On holiday in France, an American man bumped into an Egyptian. They began to make small talk, and after the discussion had been carrying on for a little while, the Egyptian decided to pull out his wallet and show pictures of his family to the American.

When the American saw the picture of the Egyptian's family, he was shocked. "Hey, that looks like my son," he said, referring to one of the Egyptian's children. "That looks just like my Juan!"

The Egyptian explained, "About fifteen years ago, I went to Mexico to drill for oil. While I was there, my wife and I decided to adopt a young boy. We named him Amal and he's grown up with us."

The American said, "Well, about fifteen years ago, my wife and I were stationed at the Mexican embassy. We adopted Juan and now he's in high school. I wonder if your boy and mine are twins?"

Sure enough, the boys had the same birthday and they agreed that the two boys must have been twins. After the holiday ended, they agreed to meet in Los Angeles and have a big reunion. Of course, the news media received word of this and were eagerly anticipating the arrival of the young boy from Egypt.

However, to the disappointment of the crowd that had assembled, it was announced that the plane would be over four hours late.

Juan's mother said to the media, "You might as well go home. There's no point in waiting here."

"Why would we want to do that?" asked a reporter.

"Well," she replied, "they're identical twins. If you've seen Juan, you've seen Amal."

_____

Gene Kelly made *An American In Paris* in the studios in Hollywood. The next year he decided to make a film that would be shot on location in Paris. So he went there with the camera crew, and the first scene called for Kelly to ring the bell in the belfry at Notre Dame Cathedral. He pulled on the rope and pulled and pulled and got carried away, failing to notice that the bell had come loose from its casters. It fell out of the belfry, pulling the rope, with Gene Kelly still hanging on, into the river below.

Improvizing as best he could under the circumstances, Kelly trod water and kept on pulling the rope. The director in the belfry heard a ringing, gurgling sound below and called down with his megaphone to ask what was going on. Kelly replied, "I'm ringing in the Seine! I'm ringing in the Seine!"

_____

A man ran an ice delivery service. Most of his customers were bar owners. One day, he was on the way to making his last delivery – to Sue's Bar – when he passed Jane's Joint. As he did so, Jane flagged him down and said breathlessly, "I'm sorry, I forget to order any ice this week. Is there any spare you could let me have?"

"Sorry," said the driver. "I only have ice for Sue."

Penny was a hard-working, conscientious girl, whose dream in life was to go on an ocean cruise around the world. So she scrimped and saved until finally she had enough money to book a ticket on a luxury liner.

It was a wonderful experience on board the liner until one night, after they had been at sea for a week, Penny was walking back to her cabin, when the heel on her left shoe broke throwing her off balance. At that precise moment, the ship also lurched to port, pitching Penny overboard. Members of the crew jumped into a lifeboat and after about five minutes they found her. Hauling her aboard, the ship's crew realized that it was too late; poor Penny was dead.

Under normal circumstances, the crew would have performed a burial at sea, but Penny had taken the precaution of writing a will. In it, she specified that she wanted her body cremated and kept in a jar above her parents' fireplace. Her wishes were fulfilled, which just goes to show that a Penny saved is a Penny urned.

A middle eastern king was down on his money and began to sell off his valuables. The last of these was the Star of the Euphrates, at that time the most valuable diamond in existence. He went to a pawnbroker who offered him 100,000 rials for it.

"Are you crazy?" said the king. "I paid one million rials for this gem! Don't you know who I am?"

The pawnbroker replied in song, "When you wish to pawn a star, makes no difference who you are."

Some friars wanted to do more for their flock but their vow of poverty, simple lifestyle and lack of gainful employment meant that their supply of available funds was, to say the least, meagre. Nevertheless, they put their collective heads together and came up with the idea of opening a small florist shop. They reasoned that they could grow most of the flowers on the church grounds, and what they couldn't grow, they could probably pick from the surrounding countryside.

Everyone liked to buy flowers from the men of God and their little business flourished – so much so that the rival florist across town thought the competition was unfair. He asked the good fathers to close their little shop, but their flower business was providing them with much-needed funds for their good works and they refused. Time and again he begged the friars to shut up shop but his pleas fell on deaf ears.

As his business continued to fall off, the florist was plunged toward bankruptcy and in desperation he hired Hugh MacTaggart, the roughest and most vicious thug in town, to "persuade" the good friars to close. Being a man of few morals, Hugh had no ethical problems with his task and promptly gave the friars a thorough beating and trashed their store. He departed with a stern warning that he'd be back if they didn't close the shop. Terrified, the friars did so immediately, proving yet again that only Hugh can prevent florist friars.

There was a snake called Nate. His purpose in life was to stay in the desert and guard the lever. This lever was no ordinary lever. It was the lever that if moved would destroy the world. Nate took his job very seriously. He let nothing get close to the lever.

One day he saw a cloud of dust in the distance. He kept his eye on it because he was guarding the lever. The dust cloud continued to move closer to the lever. Nate saw that it was a huge boulder and it was heading straight for the lever.

Nate thought about what he could do to save the world. He decided if he could get in front of the boulder he could deflect it and it would miss the lever. Nate slithered quickly to intersect the boulder, which ran him over and crushed him to death. But his brave action did indeed deflect the huge rock, leaving history to conclude that it was better Nate than lever.

The story of Mary Poppins as a nanny is well known. Less well-known is her subsequent tale. She travelled to Hollywood, where she opened a shop on Sunset

Boulevard as a fortune-teller. Of course, we already know she had supernatural powers, so it's no surprise that she was quite skilled in fortune-telling, and her reputation grew rapidly.

She continued to tell fortunes, and found that in particular, she always received a very strong premonition whenever someone was about to have an onset of bad breath. Her predictions of this turned out to be accurate 100 per cent of the time. In order to publicize her success at this, she had a large sign placed above her door, which read: Super California Mystic Expert Halitosis.

A botanist was trying to research some details about a particular kind of fern, so he sent a request to all his colleagues, asking them to send him any information they had about it.

Unfortunately, he didn't word his request very well, and all the botanists he'd contacted thought he was looking for details about any ferns, rather than just the one species. So within a few hours of sending it out, his fax machine was buzzing with piles of useless documents about all kinds of ferns – there were tree ferns and wood ferns, ostrich ferns and cinnamon ferns but very few about the particular type he wanted.

So he sent another message to

everyone: If it ain't bracken, don't fax it.

A piece of road walks into a bar and declares to all the occupants, "I'm the hardest bit of tarmac in the whole of this town!"

The piano player stops and the bar goes deadly silent. After a brief pause, all eyes drop, the pianist returns to playing and the piece of road pulls up a bar stool and settles down to a beer.

Five minutes later, a piece of dual carriageway throws open the bar door. Once again, the bar goes silent but for the creaking of the slow-moving overhead fans.

The dual carriageway declares, "I'm the toughest piece of tarmac you'll ever see this side of the border!"

The piece of road slowly turns and locks eyes with the piece of dual carriageway. The tension mounts, other drinkers scatter and take cover.

At that precise moment, in walks a piece of freeway, which says, "I'm the toughest bit of tarmac in the whole country and I'll take you both on!"

And there they stood staring at each other for what seemed like an eternity.

Once again, the door opens and into the middle of the stand-off walks a strange-looking piece of coloured tarmac with a blue stripe.

The other three turn their backs to the door, sit down at the bar and stare sheepishly into their drinks.

The bartender goes up to the three of them and asks what the problem is.

"Shhhh!" says the dual carriageway. "Watch what you say, that guy's a real cycle path."

Once upon a time there were two old hillbillies living in the wilds of Montana. They were called Jed and Clarence, and they lived on opposite sides of the river and hated each other with a vengeance.

Every morning, just after sunrise, Jed and Clarence would go down to their respective sides of the river and yell abuse at each other.

"Jed!" Clarence would shout. "You better thank your lucky stars I can't swim or I'd swim this river and whup your butt!"

"And Clarence!" Jed would holler back. "You better thank your lucky stars I can't swim or I'd swim this river and whup your skinny butt!"

This happened every morning for twenty years. Eventually, the army built a bridge over the river, but it made no difference. Every morning for another five years, Jed and Clarence continued to yell insults across the river.

Finally, Jed's wife could take no more. She told her husband, "Every day for twenty-five years, I've had to listen to you saying you're gonna whup Clarence's butt. There's the bridge! Why don't you show that you're more than just all talk?"

Jed thought about this for a moment, and then said, "Woman, you're right. I'm gonna go down to that bridge, I'm gonna cross that bridge and I'm gonna whup Clarence's butt!"

So Jed walked out the door of his house and down to the river. He stepped on to the bridge, walked halfway across, then looked up. Suddenly he turned tail and ran screaming back to the house. He slammed the door, bolted the windows and grabbed his shotgun. Still panting breathlessly, he hid under his bed.

"Jed!" cried his wife. "What's happened to you? I thought you were gonna whup Clarence's butt!"

"I was, woman, I was," replied a quivering Jed.

"What in tarnation is the matter?" demanded his wife. "You ain't never run from no man in your life!"

"Well," spluttered Jed, "it was like this. I went down to the bridge, I stepped on to the bridge, I walked halfway across the bridge, and then I looked up…"

"And?" said his wife impatiently.

"There was this sign on the bridge," gasped Jed. "It said

'Clarence: 13 feet 6 inches'. I tell you, he ain't never looked that big from this side of the river!"

_____

An Indian chief had three wives, each of whom was pregnant. The first wife gave birth to a boy and the chief was so delighted that he built her a tepee made out of deer hide.

A few days later, the second wife gave birth, also to a boy. The chief was very happy and built her a tepee made out of antelope hide.

A week later, the third wife gave birth, but this time the chief kept the details a secret. In gratitude he built this wife a two-storey tepee made out of hippopotamus hide. The chief then challenged the rest of the tribe to work out what had happened.

Many tried but were unsuccessful. Finally, a young brave confidently announced that the third wife had given birth to twin boys.

"That's right," said the chief. "How did you figure it out?"

"It's elementary," replied the brave. "The value of the squaw of the hippopotamus is equal to the sons of the squaws of the other two hides."

_____

Old Edna had two claims to fame. She could tell fortunes and she was a midget. The local authorities frowned on her because they thought that fortune-telling was fraudulent. They had her arrested and she was placed in a holding cell. Since she was so small she was able to squeeze between the bars of her cell and escape. This so incensed the judge that he ordered the local newspaper to print an article about her. The following was printed in the paper the next day: Small medium at large.

_____

An architect was very famous because he always ordered exactly enough materials for every project. He was very popular because he could construct buildings at the lowest possible cost.

After ten years of perfect building, one of his men came to him when they had finished a forty-storey building.

"I have some bad news," the man said. "We have one brick left over."

"Oh no!" the architect exclaimed. "My ten-year record of perfection is broken!"

Do you know what he did with the brick?

He threw it away.

_____

When a very tired man got on a crowded bus one afternoon, he could not find an empty seat. A small dog was sitting on one seat, so he asked the lady with the dog to put the dog on her lap. The lady refused and they got into a big argument. Finally, the driver stopped the bus and told the lady to put the dog on her lap.

When the man sat down, he took a pickle out of his pocket and began noisily sucking on it. When the lady told him the sound and the smell were irritating, he told her she should have thought about being nice when he had asked her to move the dog.

They began another argument and the lady threw the pickle out the window. The man then threw the dog out the window. Just then the bus stopped and the dog stood in line to get back on. Guess what the dog had in its mouth?

The brick.

———————

Lucy was visiting France, and while in Paris she decided to take a guided tour around the beautiful cathedral on the banks of the river Seine. As she was being shown around the building, all of a sudden she spotted a sandwich box lying on the floor.

She picked it up, and handed it to the guide. He was very apologetic, and hurried off with it. After a few minutes, Lucy could hear him calling up the bell tower, "Quazimodo! You left your sandwich box lying around again!"

When the guide returned, he apologized once more and when Lucy asked him about the sandwiches, he said, "Don't worry about it, it's just the lunchpack of Notre Dame."

———————

In days of old, when Genghis Khan's men were running amok over Asia, they set their sights on more distant shores. These warriors were known as Khan's Men or just Khans. When they had conquered all the way to the water's edge, they built boats, gathered their loot, and bravely went to sea. By a sad twist of fate, they landed on an island of lepers, which resulted in most of the crew being infected. Hastily leaving that island, they set sail again, but by the time they reached Ireland, few had survived. Leaving the boats, they set forth, but were soon set upon by the natives for the riches they carried in pots.

The Khans were very ill, but ever resourceful, they hid on the island and awaited rescue, as a result of which the locals never did get their hands on the treasure.

And that's how the story of the little people got started in Ireland – the leper Khans and their pots of gold. Cunning though diseased, the Khans were never fooled by those who tried to trick them out of their pots of gold by swapping them for an empty pot – which gave us the saying a leper won't change his pots.

———————

After leading an invasion of England, a feared Viking explorer returned to his homeland, only to find that his name was missing from the town's electoral register. His wife immediately complained to the local civic official who apologized profusely, saying, "I must have taken Leif off my census."

––––––––––

Following disappointing annual profits, the management at an English potato crisp factory decided to introduce new working practices. Part of the manufacturing process involved transporting the crisps around the factory in purpose-made metal bins. For decades, the materials for the bins had been supplied by a local sheet-metal manufacturer, with final construction carried out by the crisp factory workers themselves. With their neatly soldered seams, these hand-crafted bins were much admired, so the management's decision to replace them with cheap, ready-made plastic models met with an angry response.

Fearing that some men would be made redundant as a result of the changes, the factory workers voted to go on strike. In an attempt to drum up national support, the strike leaders organized a rally, with a march taking place from the factory to the rally site.

To lift the workers' spirits as they marched with their banners, they sang heartily, "Onward crisp bin solderers…"

––––––––––

A debt collector knocked on the door of a country family who made their living weaving cloth.

"Is Jack home?" he asked the woman who answered the door.

"I'm sorry," the woman replied, "Jack's gone for cotton."

A few weeks later the collector tried again. "Is Jack here today?"

Once again the answer was, "No, sir, I'm afraid he has gone for cotton."

When he returned for the third time and Jack was still nowhere to be seen, the debt collector complained, "I suppose Jack has gone for cotton again?"

"No," the woman answered sadly, "Jack died a few days ago."

Suspicious that the woman was being deliberately evasive, the collector decided to go down to the cemetery and investigate. But sure enough, there was poor Jack's tombstone, with this inscription: "Gone, but not for cotton".

––––––––––

After a heavy day's digging at the archaeological site in Norway, researchers uncovered a priceless statue of the ancient Norse thunder god. It was a wondrous piece of artwork. He had bulging muscles, an imposing stance, and of course his famous giant hammer. But most important of all, the eyes in his fierce-looking face were made of two giant rubies that glittered a brilliant red.

The two leading archaeologists on the dig were both determined that they should be the one to have their name listed against the discovery, and pretty soon the argument was intensifying to the point where the rest of the team, despite being exhausted after the day's work, started to gather round to watch.

The two of them continued

squabbling for some time, and they provided the others with a great source of amusement for the evening, and by the time they finally gave up and called a truce, everyone else was feeling quite refreshed by the entertainment.

As the crowd dispersed, one junior digger turned to his friend, and said, "Well, that was a fight for Thor eyes."

The saloon in a Wyoming town was packed with people on a Saturday night. There was dancing, singing and gambling, and everyone was having a great time. Then at the height of the revelry a man burst through the swing doors and yelled, "Look out, everybody! Big Seth's-a-comin'!"

The saloon emptied in an instant. Most people piled out through the doors while others frantically climbed out of windows, often trampling each other underfoot in their haste to escape. In their place was an eerie silence, broken only by the faint sound of the bartender cleaning glasses behind the bar.

A few minutes later, a cloud of dust appeared in the distance. As the cloud grew nearer, it became apparent that it was caused by two buffalo being ridden by a colossus of a man. He was over seven feet tall, built like a brick outhouse, with black teeth, scars down his face and fists the size of bowling balls. Leading the buffalo was a large mountain lion on a leash.

The two buffalo pulled up outside the saloon. The man dismounted, tied the lion and the buffalo to a hitching post and strode into the saloon, the wooden floorboards creaking under his sheer weight. Spitting out a wad of gum and crushing a leftover glass with his bare hands, he walked over to the bar. The bartender began shaking nervously and tried to hide behind the bar, but the man spotted him. Pounding his fist on the bar top with such force that three bottles shattered from the reverberation, he demanded, "Whiskey!"

By now the bartender was so freaked out that he couldn't concentrate and accidentally poured the man a bourbon. The man spat it out instantly and repeated his demand for whiskey.

The bartender handed him the whiskey barrel. The man broke the barrel over his knee, gulped down half the contents, wiped his mouth on a tablecloth and drank the other half. The bartender asked timorously, "Would you like some more? It's on the house."

"Nah," said the giant. "I don't have time for another. I gotta get out of this place."

"W-w-w-why's that?" asked the bartender.

The man turned on his heels

and, starting to shake like a leaf, replied, "Cos Big Seth's-a-comin'!"

———————

Several years ago, Andy was sentenced to prison. During his stay, he got along well with the guards and all his fellow inmates. The warden knew that, deep down, Andy was a good person. So, the warden made arrangements for Andy to learn a trade while doing his time.

Some three years later, Andy was recognized as one of the best carpenters in the local area. Often, he would be given a weekend pass to do odd jobs for citizens of the community. And he always reported back to prison by early Sunday evening. Andy was a model inmate.

One day, the warden considered remodelling his kitchen, but he lacked the skills to build a set of kitchen cupboards and a large counter top. So he called Andy into his office and asked him to do the job for him.

To the warden's surprise, Andy simply refused to help.

The warden said, "But you're an expert, Andy, and I really need your help."

Andy replied, "Well, warden, I'd really like to help you, but counter fitting is what got me into prison in the first place."

———————

Noah is waiting by his ark for all the animals that God has promised will squeeze into the boat that he's built.

And then he sees them, great numbers of beasts all converging on where he's standing. So he lowers the gang-plank, and watches as the animals start filing on board, two-by-two.

And as they go into the ship, Noah can be heard passing comments on each animal that goes by. "Hmmm, two horses," he says. "They don't taste very nice, but they're edible," and, "Ooh! Two sheep. I love roast lamb."

And so it goes on. For each pair of animals that Noah counts going on board, he says something about what they're like to eat. Eventually, Noah's son can stand it no longer and goes to his mother to ask why he does it.

She answers, "Well, there's Noah counting for taste."

———————

There were two brothers, Simon and Garth Brown. They had a dog called Walter, and they loved to take the dog Walter to their Uncle Charlie's mansion at the edge of town.

But one day, as they arrived at the mansion, they were surprised to find that the gates were locked and they couldn't get in. Fortunately, just then, Uncle Charlie's tall chauffeur appeared at the mansion door and began walking toward the trio at the gates.

However, the dog Walter took a sudden dislike to the tall chauffeur, and began barking and growling, making a huge noise. Neighbours leaned out of the windows of their mansions and asked what the noise was.

One of the neighbours replied, "Simon and Garth's uncle's big chauffeur's troubled Walter."

David was a chef for a large catering company. He enjoyed his work with the other chefs, but often liked to relax by going to the zoo. He particularly enjoyed the three-toed sloth, which absolutely fascinated him. He would stand and watch the creature for hours, just hanging there, occasionally making the tiniest movement. He found it incredibly relaxing. So relaxing, in fact, that when a friend from the catering company complained that work was stressing him out, he suggested they go to the zoo to watch the sloth and relax. This caught on among the chefs, and soon more and more of them would go to watch the sloth.

Eventually, David and his company were offered the opportunity to provide outdoor catering at the zoo. Pans and stoves were set up by the sloth's enclosure and the chefs got to work cooking food for all the visitors.

Suddenly, without warning, the sloth lost its grip on the vine from which it had been hanging. It hit the ground heavily and rolled out of its enclosure and fell into one of the pans of water. To the horror of the gathered chefs, the water began to bubble and steam furiously, until the sloth was well and truly cooked.

David suddenly realized what had happened. "Oh, no!" he shouted. "We should have known better! Everyone knows too many cooks boil the sloth!"

Two men were out hunting in the woods. One of them was a fanatic who went hunting as often as he could. The other was his friend: a peaceful, nature-loving fellow, who didn't really want to hurt anything.

They had been out in the woods for some time, when they picked up the tracks of a deer. They soon caught up with it, and when they saw it, it was obvious why it had been so easy to sneak up on: the animal had a terrible infection over its left eye, and couldn't even see out of it.

The hunter started to take aim with his shotgun, but his friend begged him to stop.

He said, "Can't you see that's a bad-eye deer?"

Steven Spielberg was discussing his new project – an action

docudrama about famous composers starring top movie stars. Sylvester Stallone, George Segal, Bruce Willis and Arnold Schwarzenegger were all present. Spielberg needed the box office appeal of these superstars, so he was prepared to allow them to select whichever famous composer they wanted to portray.

"Well," started Stallone, "I've always admired Mozart. I would love to play him."

"Chopin has always been my favourite, and my image would improve if people saw me playing the piano," said Willis. "I'll play him."

"I've always been partial to Strauss and his waltzes," said Segal. "I'd like to play him."

Spielberg was very pleased with these choices. Then, looking at Schwarzenegger, he asked, "Who do you want to be, Arnold?"

So Schwarzenegger replied, "I'll be Bach."

Once upon a time in a purple universe there was a purple planet and on this purple planet was a purple land with purple houses where purple villagers lived.

Near to the purple village was a purple hilltop, and on this purple hilltop was a purple palace. Past the purple gates of the purple palace and up the purple path, through the grand purple doors, guarded by purple knights, sat a purple king in a purple throne room on a purple throne next to his purple queen.

One day the purple king held a meeting for the purple people of purple in his purple meeting room in his purple palace. He said to the purple people of purple, "Purple people of purple, I will give the greatest reward in the history of this purple planet to the purple person who makes me the tastiest purple beer in the entire purple world."

One purple villager decided that he would make the tastiest purple beer in the entire purple world, so he left the purple meeting room through the purple doors, past the purple gates, down the purple path to his purple cottage, down his purple stairs leading to his purple cellar, where his purple beer-making machine was housed, and brewed the tastiest purple beer in the entire purple world. When he was satisfied that it was indeed the tastiest purple beer in the entire purple world, he left his purple cottage, ran up the purple street to the purple king's purple palace, through the purple gates, past the purple doors to the purple throne room and presented the tastiest purple beer in the entire purple world to the purple king who was sitting on his purple throne next to his purple queen.

The purple king took a sip of the purple beer from the purple glass but immediately spat it out on to the purple carpet that covered the purple floor of the purple throne room of his purple palace. "Yuk!" he groaned. "That's the most disgusting purple beer in the entire purple world. But, purple person, because I'm a fair purple king, I will give you one more chance to make the tastiest purple beer in the entire purple world."

So once again the purple person of this purple land left the purple palace, went down the purple street to his purple cottage, down his purple stairs to his purple cellar, where his purple beer-making machine was housed, and brewed what he hoped would be the tastiest purple beer in the entire purple world. When he was satisfied that it was indeed the tastiest purple beer in the entire purple world, he left his purple cottage, ran up the purple street through the purple gates of the purple palace, past the purple guards and into the purple throne room where the purple king sat on his purple throne next to his purple queen. The purple person presented the purple beer and the purple king sipped the purple beer from the purple glass but immediately spat it out on to the purple carpet that covered the purple throne room of the purple palace.

"Ughh!" screamed the purple king. "That purple beer is even worse than your last purple beer! Purple person, you have disrespected this purple kingdom and everything purple that this purple land represents. Purple guards, take this purple person to the purple dungeons!"

So the purple guards led the purple person across the purple throne room, through the purple hall to a purple door that led to purple stairs, which descended to the purple dungeons. When they reached the purple dungeons, the chief purple guard took out a purple key, put it in the purple lock, opened the purple door, turned to the purple prisoner and told him, "Indigo…"

One day in the jungle a chimpanzee made some tools to eat his dinner. Among the tools was a flat stick sharpened along one edge, which the chimp used to cut his food. The other was a stick with four smaller sticks attached to the end, each sharpened to a point. The chimp used this tool to spear his food and place it in his mouth. The chimp was justifiably proud of his inventions, which he called his one-point tool and his four-point tool.

One day he awoke to find that the four-point tool was missing. The chimp was distraught. He ran around the jungle trying to find his precious tool.

First he came upon the lion.

"Lion, lion!" he cried. "Have you seen my four-point tool?"

"No," replied the lion. "I have not seen your four-point tool."

Then the chimp came upon the gorilla.

"Gorilla, gorilla!" he cried. "Have you seen my four-point tool?"

"No," replied the gorilla. "I have not seen your four-point tool."

Then the chimp came upon the jaguar.

"Jaguar, jaguar!" he cried. "Have you seen my four-point tool?"

"Yes," replied the jaguar. "I have seen your four-point tool."

"Well where is it?" asked the chimp.

"I ate it," the jaguar said.

"Why would you do that?" cried the chimp.

"Because," replied the big cat, "I am a four-point tool eater Jaguar."

Many years ago, a fisherman and his wife had twin sons, but they didn't know what to name them. The husband said, "Let's be patient. If we wait long enough, the names will simply occur to us." After several weeks, they noticed something peculiar about the children. When left alone, one boy would face the sea, and the other would face inland.

"Let's call the boys Toward and Away," suggested the fisherman, and his wife agreed.

Years passed, and one day the fisherman told his adult sons, "It's time that you learned how to make a living from the sea." The fisherman and his sons provisioned their ship and set sail for a three-month voyage. At the voyage's end, the fisherman returned alone.

"What happened?" his wife cried.

"We were barely one day out to sea," the fisherman explained solemnly, "when Toward hooked a great fish. Toward fought long and hard, but the fish was great and strong. For an entire week they wrestled upon the waves, yet eventually the great fish started to win the battle, and Toward was pulled over the side. He was swallowed whole, and we never saw either of them again."

"Oh dear!" the wife cried. "What a huge fish that must have been! What a terrible fish! What a horrible fish!"

"Yes, it was," said the fisherman, "but you should have seen the one that got Away."

In a land of primitive tribes and grass huts lived one tribe that was very warlike. They won numerous battles and took control of many other tribes.

One of their victory customs was to take the most prized possession of the vanquished tribe's chief.

Once, after a particularly fierce battle, they defeated a rich tribe, whose king had a much-prized solid gold throne.

The warlike tribe seized the throne and put it in the loft in their own chief's house. Unfortunately, the throne was much too heavy to be kept in a loft in a grass house, and it fell right through the ceiling on to the chief, killing him instantly.

The moral of this story is that people who live in grass houses shouldn't stow thrones.

A man was sitting by his car at the side of the road looking unhappy. A passer-by saw his glum face and asked what the problem was.

"I've locked myself out of my car," replied the man.

"That's not a problem," said the passer-by. "Step out of the way, and let me have a look."

The motorist was a bit perplexed, but decided there was no harm in letting the man try. So the passer-by turned around, and rubbed his legs slowly up and down the driver's door. Suddenly, the lock opened and the man turned and opened the car door.

"That's amazing!" said the motorist. "How did you do it?"

"It's easy," replied the pedestrian. "I'm wearing khaki trousers."

Carlos the ice-cream man's van is parked at the side of the road, lights flashing and music playing. A long queue of excited kids stretches down the street. But there's no sign of Carlos.

A policeman walking down the road wonders what is going on. Where is Carlos? Why is he not dishing out the ice cream?

He goes over to the van and peers over the high counter. On the floor he spots Carlos lying very still covered in chocolate sauce, strawberry sauce, nuts and sprinkles.

"Get back, kids," the officer shouts. He moves away so that the children cannot overhear him and gets on the radio to the station.

"Sergeant, you'd better get a team down here quick," he says. "It's Carlos the ice-cream man. He's topped himself."

Alfred Lord Tennyson went to Africa on safari. While there he became separated from the rest of his party and was eaten alive by Laurie, a lion that was the mascot of a local village chieftain. But after swallowing Tennyson, the big cat was stricken with a severe case of indigestion and brought him back up again. Against all the odds, Tennyson had survived.

News of the attack on Tennyson spread like wildfire. After wandering dazed through the jungle for a few hours, he limped into the village seeking help, and told the chieftain what had happened.

"Ah," said the chieftain, "you must be the poet Laurie ate."

———————

A piece of string walks into a bar and orders a beer. The bartender throws it out saying, "We don't serve string in here."

The string goes outside, ties itself into a knot and backcombs its hair. It walks back into the bar and orders a beer.

The bartender says, "Aren't you that piece of string I threw out earlier?"

The piece of string replies, "No, I'm a frayed not."

———————

A British couple on holiday in Greece stepped out of their hotel on the first night and explored the town looking for somewhere to eat. There were dozens of restaurants and outside each one a waiter was poised ready to pounce. As soon as the couple showed the slightest interest in a particular menu, the waiter of that establishment would try to persuade them to dine there. But the couple resented the sales push and continued on their way.

After nearly an hour of

searching for a good restaurant, they were starting to feel tired and hungry. They reached a street corner on which there were three restaurants and decided to choose one of them.

The moment they glanced at the menu outside the first restaurant, a little waiter appeared and offered them a table. They said they hadn't decided yet and wanted to study the menus at the other two restaurants.

At the second restaurant, another little waiter – no more than five feet tall – tried to induce them inside, but again they said they were undecided and wanted to study the menu at the third restaurant.

When they looked at the menu outside the third restaurant, a much taller waiter appeared. But there was something strange about him. His body and legs were no longer than those of the other two waiters but his shoes had been built up to make him look taller and more imposing. The husband was immediately suspicious of him.

"I don't think we should eat here," he said.

"Why not?" asked the wife.

"Because you know what they say – beware of Greeks wearing lifts."

A young boy had a job bagging groceries at a supermarket. One day the store decided to install a machine for squeezing fresh orange juice. The young lad was most intrigued by this and asked if he could be allowed to work the machine. The manager refused, but the youngster couldn't understand why.

The store manager explained, "Sorry, kid, but baggers can't be juicers."

Artie gets tired of working so hard and not getting anywhere, and seeing all these guys in the Mafia in their fine three-piece suits and fancy cars, decides that he, too, has to join the Mafia.

He goes up to one of the guys and says, "I want to join the Mafia."

The guy answers, "Have you ever killed anyone for money?"

Artie answers, "No."

The guy says, "Well, you've either got to be born into the Mafia, or you've got to kill somebody for money."

So Artie says, "How much will you pay me if I kill someone?"

"I'm not going to pay you," replies the guy.

Artie says, "Please, just pay me a dollar so I can get in."

The guy says, "Okay, I'll tell you what. You kill somebody, tell me about it, and if I see it in the morning paper, I'll pay you a dollar."

Artie thanks the man and heads off on his mission. He goes to Ralph's Supermarket, sees an old lady pushing a cart, and deciding that she's lived a full life, goes up to her, grabs her round the neck and chokes her to death.

The bag boy sees him, and chases after him. Artie realizes that he can't outrun the bag boy, turns around, grabs the bag boy by the neck and chokes him to death.

The next day, the local newspaper's front page headline reads: Artie Chokes Two For a Dollar at Ralph's.

One night, the Potato family sat down to dinner, Mother Potato and her three daughters. Midway through the meal, the eldest daughter spoke up. "Mother Potato," she said, "I have an announcement to make."

"And what might that be?" said Mother, seeing the obvious excitement in her eldest daughter's eyes.

"Well," replied the daughter, with a proud but sheepish grin, "I'm getting married!"

The other daughters squealed with surprise as Mother Potato exclaimed, "Married! That's wonderful! And who are you marrying?"

"I'm marrying a Russet!"

"A Russet!" replied Mother Potato with pride. "Oh, a Russet is a fine tater, a fine tater indeed!"

As the family shared in the eldest daughter's joy, the middle daughter spoke up. "Mother, I, too, have an announcement."

"And what might that be?" asked Mother Potato encouragingly.

Not knowing quite how to begin, the middle daughter paused, then said with conviction, "I, too, am getting married!"

"You, too!" Mother Potato said with joy. "That's wonderful! Twice the good news in one evening! And who are you marrying?"

"I'm marrying an Idaho!" beamed the middle daughter.

"An Idaho!" said Mother Potato with joy. "Oh, an Idaho is a fine tater, a fine tater indeed!"

Once again, the room came alive with laughter and excited plans for the future, when the youngest Potato daughter interrupted. "Mother! Mother Potato! Um, I, too, have an announcement to make."

"Yes?" said Mother Potato with great anticipation.

"Well," began the youngest Potato daughter with the same sheepish grin as her eldest sister before her. "I hope this doesn't come as a shock to you, but I am getting married, as well!"

"Really?" said Mother Potato with sincere excitement. "All of my lovely daughters married! What wonderful news! And who, pray tell, are you marrying?"

"I'm marrying John Motson."

"John Motson?" Mother Potato scowled suddenly. "But he's just a common tater!"

Driving to work, a man had to swerve to avoid a box that fell out of a truck in front of him. Seconds later, a policeman pulled him over for reckless driving. Fortunately, another officer had seen the carton in the road and he stopped the traffic and recovered the box. It was found to contain large upholstery tacks.

"I'm sorry, sir," the first police officer told the driver, "but I am still going to have to write you a ticket."

Amazed, the driver asked what offence he was supposed to have committed.

The officer replied, "Tacks evasion."

Joe and Frank were at work in their office and noticed that someone had put up a suggestion box with some blank cards next to it. Both decided that this was a great idea, and each took a card to fill out.

Joe wrote: "The office workers should all be given raises!"

When he looked at Frank's card, it said: "Can we all have raises, and keys to the executive washroom, and personal secretaries, and new company cars, and new coffee cups, and longer lunch breaks, and an extra three weeks' vacation each year, and a holiday on St Patrick's day, and Columbus day, and Martin Luther King's birthday?"

Joe said, "Frank, that isn't the right way of getting things changed around here. You shouldn't put all of your begs in one ask-it."

Two young men were out in the woods on a camping trip, when they came upon a great trout brook. They stayed there all day, enjoying the fishing, which was superb.

At the end of the day, knowing that they would soon be graduating from college, they vowed that they would meet again in twenty years at the same place and renew the experience.

Twenty years later as planned, they met and travelled to a location close to that very spot where they had enjoyed such a wonderful day all those years before. They walked into the woods and before long came upon a brook. One of the men said to the other, "This is the place!"

The other replied, "No, it's not."

The first man said, "Yes, it is. I recognize the clover growing on the bank on the other side."

To which the other man replied, "Don't be silly, you can't tell a brook by its clover."

A local police officer had just finished his shift one cold November evening and was at home with his wife. "You just won't believe what happened this evening," he said. "In all my years on the force I've never seen anything like it."

"Oh yes, dear, what happened?" his wife asked.

The officer replied, "I came across two guys down by the canal. One of them was drinking battery acid and the other was eating fireworks."

"Drinking battery acid and eating fireworks! What did you do with them?"

The officer said, "Oh, that was easy. I charged one and let the other off."

———————

A man was famous the world over for growing tulips. People used to travel for hundreds of miles to ask him the secret of how he managed to obtain such magnificent blooms from the bulbs but he remained extremely cagey, insisting, "I simply plant the bulbs and they all happen to come up perfect."

Such was the interest in discovering the tulip grower's recipe for success that one of his friends decided to get him drunk in the hope that he might spill the beans. After plying the tulip grower with wine, the friend popped the question, "So come on, you can tell me, what is it that you grow your tulips in?"

His tongue loosened, the grower replied, "I use hamsters."

"What do you mean?" asked the friend. "How can hamsters help you produce such beautiful tulips?"

"Well, you see," said the grower, "I have another farm where I breed hamsters – not just a few but thousands. Hamsters only live for a few years, and when they die, I put them into a special machine that mashes them into pulp. I then add sugar to turn the pulp into a jam, and that is what I spread over the fields before I plant the bulbs. It's an old Dutch recipe – tulips from hamster jam."

———————

Bob Hill and his new wife Betty were on holiday in Salzburg, in Austria. They were driving in a rental car along a rather deserted highway. It was late and raining very hard. Bob could barely see twenty feet in front of the car.

Suddenly, the car skidded. Bob attempted to control it, but to no avail. The car swerved and smashed into a tree.

Moments later, Bob shook his head to clear the fog. Dazed, he looked over at the passenger seat and saw his wife unconscious, with her head bleeding. Despite the rain and unfamiliar countryside, Bob knew he had to carry her to the nearest phone.

Bob carefully picked up his wife and began trudging down the road. After a short while, he saw a light. He headed toward the light, which was coming from an old, large house. He approached the door and knocked.

A minute passed before a woman opened the door. Bob said, "Hello, my name is Bob Hill, and this is my wife Betty. We've been in a terrible accident, and my wife has been seriously hurt. Can I please use your phone?"

"I'm sorry," replied the woman, "but we don't have a phone. However, my husband is a doctor. I will get him for you."

Bob brought his wife inside, and the doctor came down to look at her. "It is many miles to the nearest clinic," he said, "but I will see what I can do."

Bob carried Betty through to a spare bedroom before collapsing from exhaustion and his own injuries.

After conducting a brief examination, the doctor looked worried and told his wife that he didn't think the couple would survive. Sure enough, they died a few hours later.

The Hills' deaths upset the doctor greatly. Wearily, he went to his conservatory where he kept his grand piano, for it was there that he had always found solace. He began to play, and a stirring, almost haunting, melody filled the house.

Meanwhile, his wife was tidying the spare room, with the Hills still in it. Suddenly, out of the corner of her eye she caught a movement, and she noticed the fingers on Betty's hand twitch. Stunned, she watched as Bob's leg then moved slightly. She stared in amazement as the couple slowly regained consciousness and sat up.

Unable to contain herself, she ran to the conservatory, burst in and shouted joyously to her husband, "The Hills are alive with the sound of music!"

———————

Three creatures were arguing about who was the best. The first, a hawk, maintained that he was the best because he had great eyesight, could fly at speed and swoop on his prey from tremendous heights.

The second, a lion, insisted that he was the best because he was so strong – no other animal in the jungle would dare challenge him.

The third, a skunk, pointed out that he needed neither the power of flight or brute strength to see off an adversary.

As the three continued to debate the issue, a grizzly bear came along and swallowed them all – hawk, lion and stinker.

A man was working on the buses and collecting tickets. As he rang the bell for the driver to set off, a woman desperately tried to get on the bus. However, she had just one foot on board when the driver moved away. The woman fell from the bus and was killed.

At the subsequent trial the man was sent down for murder, and, because it was Texas, he was sent to the electric chair. On the day of his execution he was sitting in the chair when the executioner granted him a final wish.

"Well," said the man, "is that your packed lunch over there?"

"Yes," answered the executioner.

"Please can I have that green banana?"

The executioner gave the man his green banana and waited until he'd eaten it. When the man had finished, the executioner flipped the switch, sending hundreds of volts through him. When the smoke cleared, the man was still alive. The executioner couldn't believe it.

"Can I go?" the man asked.

"I suppose so," said the executioner. "That's never happened before."

The man left and eventually got his job back on the buses, selling tickets. Once again he rang the bell for the driver to go when people were still getting on. As a result of his recklessness, a woman fell under the wheels and was killed.

The man was again convicted of murder and sent to the electric chair.

The executioner was determined to do it right this time, so he rigged the chair up to the electric supply for the whole of the town. The man was again seated in the chair.

"What is your final wish?" asked the executioner.

"Can I have that green banana in your packed lunch?" said the condemned man.

The executioner sighed and reluctantly gave up his banana.

The man ate the banana and the executioner flipped the switch. Thousands of volts coursed through the chair, blacking out the town. When the smoke cleared, the man was still sitting there, smiling, in the chair. The executioner couldn't believe it and let the man go.

The man got his job back on the buses, selling tickets. Yet again he made the mistake of ringing the bell for the driver to go while passengers were still getting on, this time killing three of them. He was sent to the electric chair again.

The executioner rigged up all of the state's electricity to the chair, determined to get his man this time. The man sat down in the chair smiling.

"What's your final wish?" asked the executioner.

"Well," said the man, "can I have that green banana out of your packed lunch?"

The executioner handed over

his banana and the man ate it all, skin included.

The executioner pulled the handle and millions of volts surged through the chair, blacking out the whole of Texas. When the smoke rose, the man was still sitting there alive without even a burn mark.

"I give up," said the executioner. "I don't understand how you can still be alive after all that." He stroked his chin. "It's something to do with that green banana, isn't it?" he asked.

"No," said the man, "I'm just a bad conductor."

A sealife centre prided itself on its performing animals – killer whales, dolphins and sea lions – but had struggled to find a suitably spectacular routine for the otters. So one of the keepers was given the job of trying to teach an otter to walk backwards, but after three months he was still not having any success. Eventually, in despair, he asked another keeper to see if he could train the otter. Amazingly, within two days the otter was walking backwards.

"How did you do it?" asked the first keeper. "How did you manage to get the otter to walk backwards?"

"It was easy," replied the second keeper. "You just put one foot in front of the otter."

A man was getting a haircut prior to a trip to Rome. He mentioned the trip to the barber who responded, "Rome? Why would anyone want to go there? It's crowded and dirty and full of Italians. You're crazy to go to Rome. So, how are you getting there?"

"We're taking British Airways," the man replied. "We got a great rate."

"British Airways?" said the barber. "That's a terrible airline. Their planes are old, their flight attendants are useless, and their flights are always delayed. So, where are you staying in Rome?"

"We'll be at the downtown International Marriott."

"That dump! That's the worst hotel in the city. The rooms are small, the service is surly and they're overpriced. So, what will you be doing when you get there?"

"We're going to go to see the Vatican and we hope to see the Pope."

"That's rich!" laughed the barber. "You and a million other people trying to see him. He'll look the size of an ant. Boy, good luck on this lousy trip of yours! You're going to need it."

A month later, the man again came in for his regular haircut. The barber asked him about his trip to Rome.

"It was wonderful," explained the man. "Not only were we on one of British Airways' brand new planes, but it was overbooked and they bumped us up to first class. The food and wine were wonderful, and the stewardesses were very attentive and helpful. The flight was bang on time, so we didn't miss a minute of our trip. The hotel was great, they'd just finished a twenty-five million dollar refurbishment and now it's the finest hotel in the city. They, too, were overbooked, so they apologized and gave us the presidential suite at no extra charge!"

"Well," muttered the barber, "I bet you didn't get to see the Pope?"

"Actually, we were quite lucky, because as we toured the Vatican, a Swiss Guard tapped me on the shoulder and explained that the Pope likes to meet some of the visitors personally, and if I'd be so kind as to step into his private room and wait, the Pope would come to greet me. Sure enough, five minutes later the Pope walked through the door and shook my hand! I knelt down as he spoke a few words to me."

"Really?" asked the barber. "What did he say?"

"He said, 'Where did you get that lousy haircut?'"

A nineteenth-century English landlady had a couple of struggling poets for tenants. When the pair fell behind with their rent, she tried to evict them but when that failed, she took drastic action and decided to murder them.

She baked a large scone, inserted some arsenic and invited them down for tea. The hungry poets devoured the scone and within an hour both were dead.

However, the landlady's hopes of getting away with murder were shortlived and she was quickly arrested. Feigning innocence, she demanded to know what crime she was being charged with.

The police officer told her, "It seems, madam, that you have killed two bards with one scone."

Mary Poppins was travelling home, but due to worsening weather, she decided to stop at a hotel for the night. She approached the receptionist and asked for a room.

"Certainly madam", she replied courteously.

"Is the restaurant still open?" asked Mary.

"I'm afraid not," came the reply. "But room service is available all night. Would you care to select something from this menu?"

Mary smiled, took the menu and perused it. "I would like cauliflower cheese please," said Mary.

"Certainly madam," he replied.

"And can I have breakfast in bed?" asked Mary politely. The receptionist nodded and smiled.

"In that case, I would love a couple of poached eggs, please," Mary said. After confirming the order, Mary signed in and went up to her room for the night.

The night passed uneventfully and next morning Mary came down early to check out. The same guy was still on the desk.

"Morning madam. Did you sleep well?"

"Yes, thank you," Mary replied.

"Was the food to your liking?"

"Well, I have to say the cauliflower cheese was delicious, I don't think I have had better. It was a shame about the eggs, though. They really weren't that nice at all," replied Mary truthfully.

"Oh. Well, perhaps you could contribute these thoughts to our Guest Comments Book. We are always looking to improve our service and would value your opinion," said the receptionist.

Mary checked out, then scribbled a comment into the book. Waving goodbye, she left to continue her journey.

Curious, the receptionist picked up the book to see the comment Mary had written.

"Super cauliflower cheese but eggs were quite atrocious."

A guy spent five years travelling all around the world, making a documentary on native dances. At the end of this period, he had every single native dance of every indigenous culture in the world on film – or so he thought. He wound up in Australia, in Alice Springs, so he popped into a pub for a well-earned beer.

He got talking to one of the local Aborigines and told him about his project. The Aborigine asked the guy what he thought of the Butcher Dance.

"Butcher Dance?" he said, confused. "What's that?"

"What?" asked the Aborigine. "You didn't see the Butcher Dance?"

"No, I've never heard of it," said the documentary maker.

"Mate, you're crazy," the Aborigine replied. "How can you say you filmed every native dance if you haven't seen the Butcher Dance?"

"Umm. I got a Corroborree on film just the other week. Is that what you mean?"

"No, no. The Butcher Dance is much more important than the Corroborree."

"Well how can I see this Butcher Dance then?"

"Mate, the Butcher Dance is way out in the wilderness. It'll take you many days of travel to go see it."

"Look, I've been everywhere from the forests of the Amazon, to deepest darkest Africa, to the frozen wastes of the Arctic filming these dances. Nothing will prevent me from recording this one last dance."

"Okay, mate," the Aborigine replied, shrugging. "You drive north along the highway toward Darwin. After 197 miles, you'll see a dirt track veer off to left. Follow the dirt track for 126 miles till you see a huge dead gum tree – the biggest tree you've ever seen. Here you gotta leave your car, because it's much too rough for driving. You strike out due west into the setting sun. Walk three days till you hit a creek. You follow this creek to the northwest. After two days you'll find where the creek flows out of some rocky mountains, but it's much too difficult to cross the mountains there. So you head south for half a day until you see a pass through the mountains. The pass is very difficult and very dangerous. It'll take you two, maybe three, days to get through it. On the other side, head northwest for four days until you reach a huge rock – twenty feet high and shaped like a man's head. From the rock, walk due west for two days, and then you'll find the village. You'll be able to see the Butcher Dance there."

So the guy grabbed his camera crew and equipment and headed out. After a couple of hours, he found the dirt track. The track was in a shocking state, and he was forced to crawl along at a snail's pace. Consequently, he didn't

reach the tree until dusk, and was forced to set up camp there for the night.

He set out bright and early the following morning. His spirits were high, and he was excited about the prospect of capturing on film this mysterious dance that he had never heard mention of before. True to the directions he had been given, he reached the creek after three days and followed it for another two, until he reached the rocky mountains.

The merciless sun was starting to take its toll, and the spirits of both himself and his crew were starting to flag; but wearily they trudged on, finally finding the pass through the mountains. Nothing would prevent him from completing his life's dream. The mountains proved to be every bit as treacherous as their guide had said, and at times they despaired of ever getting their bulky equipment through. But after three and a half days of back-breaking effort, they finally forced their way clear and continued their long trek.

When they reached the huge rock, four days later, their water was running low, and their feet were covered with blisters, but they steeled themselves and headed out on the last leg of their journey. Two days later they virtually staggered into the village. To their relief, the natives welcomed them and fed them and gave them fresh water, and they began to feel like new men. Once he recovered enough, the guy went before the village chief and told him that he had come to film the Butcher Dance.

"Oh mate," he said. "Very bad you come today. Butcher Dance last night. You too late. You miss dance."

"Well, when do you hold the next dance?"

"Not till next year."

"Well, I've come all this way. Couldn't you just hold an extra dance for me tonight?"

"No, no, no!" the chief exclaimed. "Butcher Dance very holy. Only hold once a year. You want see Butcher Dance, you come back next year."

Understandably, the guy was devastated, but he had no other option but to head back to civilization and return home.

The following year, he headed back to Australia and, determined not to miss out again, set out a week earlier than before. He was quite willing to spend a week in the village before the dance was performed in order to ensure he was present to witness it.

But right from the start, things went wrong. Heavy rains that year turned the dirt track to mud, and the car got bogged down every few miles. Finally, they had to abandon their vehicles barely halfway to the tree and

slog through the mud on foot. They reached the creek and the mountains without any further problems, but halfway through the mountain pass, they were struck by a fierce storm that raged for several days, during which they were forced to cling forlornly to the mountainside until it subsided.

Then, before they had travelled a mile out from the mountains, one of the crew badly sprained his ankle, slowing down the rest of their journey. Eventually, having lost all sense of how long they had been travelling, they staggered into the village at the stroke of noon.

"The Butcher Dance!" the man gasped. "Please don't tell me I'm too late to see it!"

The chief recognized him and said, "No, white fella. Butcher Dance performed tonight. You come just in time."

Relieved beyond measure, the crew spent the rest of the afternoon setting up their equipment and preparing to capture the night's ritual on celluloid. As dusk fell, the natives started to cover their bodies in white paint and adorn themselves in all manner of birds' feathers and animal skins. Once darkness had settled fully over the land, the natives formed a circle around a huge roaring fire. A deathly hush descended over performers and spectators alike as a wizened old figure with elaborate swirling designs covering his entire body entered the circle and began to chant.

"What's he doing?" the documentary maker whispered to the chief.

"Hush," the chief replied. "You first white man ever to see most sacred of our rituals. Must remain silent. Holy man, he asks that the spirits of the dream world watch as we demonstrate our devotion to them through our dance, and, if they like our dancing, will they be so gracious as to watch over us and protect us for another year."

The chanting of the holy man reached a stunning crescendo before he removed himself from the circle. The rhythmic pounding of drums boomed out across the land, and the natives began to sway to the stirring rhythm. The documentary maker himself became caught up in the fervour of the moment. This was it. He realized beyond all doubt that his wait had not been in vain. He was about to witness the ultimate performance of rhythm and movement ever conceived by mankind.

The chief strode to his position in the circle and, in a big booming voice, started to sing, "You butch yer right arm in, you butch yer right arm out, in, out, in, out, you shake it all about…"

An elderly woman was walking along the street on her way home from the supermarket. Her bag of groceries was especially heavy that day, and as she passed Martin Hale's Used Cars, she got an idea that she could drive herself to the store and save a lot of time and aching muscles. She walked into the car dealership and happened to be served by the owner himself. He asked her what kind of car she wanted and she replied, "Well, I can't remember the name exactly, but it has something to do with hate or anger."

The owner thought for a moment, then said, "Oh yes, you want a Plymouth Fury. We have a couple on the lot. What colour do you prefer?"

The lady had some trouble explaining the exact colour to him, so she reached into her shopping bag, took out an ear of corn, stripped down the shucks and said, "I want this colour."

Mr Hale replied, "I'm sorry, but we don't have any in this colour. Could I show you a nice blue one?"

"No," said the woman. "I want this colour."

"But they didn't make that colour!" explained the owner. "Maybe a cherry red one would suit you?" he suggested, obviously worried about losing a sale.

By this time, the old lady was really mad. She started throwing things at Martin Hale and chased him out of the office and into the lot. One of the salesmen, coming into the office from the back door, noticed the disruption and asked the secretary what the old woman was so upset about.

The secretary replied, "Apparently, Hale hath no Fury like the woman's corn."

A research group was engaged in a study of longevity in sea creatures and had recently focused their attention on a particular species of porpoise, which they studied from their floating laboratory off the coast of Baja Mexico. They came to believe that, if fed just the right combination of nutrients, this particular porpoise could, in theory, live forever.

To put this to the test, they studied the world's flora and fauna to see if any naturally occurring creature would fit the bill. They finally narrowed the selection down to an unusual species of mynah bird, and they sent a team of researchers off to gather a specimen.

It turned out that the mynah bird in question was quite rare, living only in a single tree in Kenya. The research team finally arrived at the tree to capture a bird, only to find that the tree was surrounded by a pride of very hungry lions, precluding any reasonable attempt to approach and climb the tree.

A suggestion was made that the lions might be manageable if they could be fed, and a couple of fat cape buffalo were captured and offered to the lions. The hungry lions devoured the hapless beasts and lay down upon the grass to digest their meal.

One of the researchers then gingerly tiptoed past the lions, climbed the tree, and had little difficulty capturing one of the mynah birds. He climbed back down the tree and had just walked past the lions to rejoin the group when a game warden appeared and arrested him for transporting mynahs across sated lions for immortal porpoises.

A boy was on his way to school one morning when he saw the words "Red Ruby" written on a wall. He had no idea what they meant, so when at the end of the first lesson of the day the teacher asked if there were any questions, the boy raised his hand.

"What is Red Ruby?" he asked.

The teacher immediately flew into a rage and sent him to the principal.

The principal wanted to know why the boy had been sent to him. The boy explained, "When I was on my way to school today, I saw some words written on a wall and I didn't know what they meant. So when the teacher asked if there were any questions, I asked her what they meant, and she yelled at me and sent me here."

"What are the words?" asked the principal.

"'Red Ruby'," answered the boy.

The principal immediately freaked out and expelled him on the spot.

At home his mother asked him why he had been expelled. He said, "When I was on my way to school today, I saw some words written on a wall and I didn't know what they meant. So when the teacher asked if there were any questions, I asked her what they meant, and she yelled at me and sent me to the principal's office. When I got there, he asked me what had happened and I told him everything, and he asked me what the words were and when I told him, he freaked out and expelled me."

"What are the words?" asked his mother.

"'Red Ruby'," answered the boy.

His mother immediately yelled at him to go up to his room and wait for his father to get home.

When his father got home he said to the boy, "So I hear you got into a lot of trouble today? Tell me what happened."

So the boy said, "When I was on my way to school today, I saw some words written on a wall and I didn't know what they meant. So when the teacher asked if there were any questions, I asked her what they meant, and she

yelled at me and sent me to the principal's office. When I got there, he asked me what had happened and I told him everything, and he asked me what the words were and when I told him, he freaked out and expelled me. When I got home, Mom asked me what had happened and I told her everything, and she asked me what the words were. When I told her, she sent me up here to wait for you."

"Well, son, what are the words?" asked the father.

"'Red Ruby," answered the boy.

His father exploded and kicked him out of the house.

As the boy was wandering the streets, he ran into some friends. They said, "Hey, what's going on? We heard you got expelled and your dad kicked you out."

So the boy said, "When I was on my way to school today, I saw some words written on a wall and I didn't know what they meant. So when the teacher asked if there were any questions, I asked her what they meant and she yelled at me and sent me to the principal's office. When I got there, he asked me what had happened and I told him everything, and he asked me what the words were and when I told him, he freaked out and expelled me. When I got home, my mom asked me what had happened and I told her everything, and she asked me what the words were. When I told her, she sent me up to my room to wait for my dad. He asked me what happened and after I told him everything he asked me the words and when I told him he kicked me out."

"Wow! What are the words?" asked the friends.

"'Red Ruby,'" answered the boy.

His friends immediately started beating him up until a hobo came by and scared them off.

The hobo said, "I just saved your life. Why were they all beating you up?"

The boy said, "When I was on my way to school today, I saw some words written on a wall and I didn't know what they meant. So when the teacher asked if there were any questions, I asked her what they meant and she yelled at me and sent me to the principal's office. When I got there, he asked me what had happened and I told him everything, and he asked me what the words were and when I told him, he freaked out and expelled me. When I got home, my mom asked me what had happened and I told her everything and she asked me what the words were. When I told her, she sent me up to my room to wait for my dad. He asked me what happened and after I told him everything he asked me the words and when I told him, he kicked me out. I ran into my friends and they asked me why

I had been expelled and kicked out of my house and I told them everything, and then they asked what the words were. When I told them, they beat me up."

"So what are the words?" asked the hobo.

"I don't know if I should say," answered the boy.

"Come on, I just saved your life," said the hobo. "Don't be ungrateful."

"Very well," said the boy. "The words were 'Red Ruby'."

The hobo freaked out and started beating the boy up until a cop came along to break it up.

The cop asked the boy what happened. The boy said, "When I was on my way to school today, I saw some words written on a wall and I didn't know what they meant. So when the teacher asked me if there were any questions, I asked her what they meant and she yelled at me and sent me to the principal's office. When I got there, he asked me what had happened and I told him everything, and he asked me what the words were and when I told him, he freaked out and expelled me. When I got home, my mom asked me what had happened and I told her everything, and she asked me what the words were. When I told her, she sent me up to my room to wait for my dad. He asked me what happened and after I told him everything he asked me the words and when I told him, he kicked me out. I ran into my friends and they asked me why I had been expelled and kicked out of my house and I told them everything, and then they asked what the words were. When I told them, they beat me up. The hobo came by and scared them off and then he asked me what had happened and I told him everything. Then he asked what the words were and when I told him, he began beating me up.

"What were the words?" asked the cop.

"'Red Ruby," answered the boy.

The cop put the boy into handcuffs and took him to jail.

The next day the boy appeared before a judge. The judge asked him for his story. The boy said, "When I was on my way to school yesterday, I saw some words written on a wall and I didn't know what they meant. So when the teacher asked me if there were any questions, I asked her what they meant and she yelled at me and sent me to the principal's office. When I got there, he asked me what had happened and I told him everything, and he asked me what the words were and when I told him, he freaked out and expelled me. When I got home, my mom asked me what had happened and I told her everything, and she asked me what the words were. When I told her, she sent me up to

my room to wait for my dad. He asked me what happened and after I told him everything he asked me the words and when I told him, he kicked me out. I ran into my friends and they asked me why I had been expelled and kicked out of my house and I told them everything, and then they asked what the words were. When I told them, they beat me up. A hobo came by and scared them off, then he asked me what had happened and I told him everything. Then he asked what the words were and when I told him, he began beating me up. Then a cop came by and broke it up and after I had explained the story to him he asked what the words were and when I told him, he handcuffed me and took me to jail."

"What were the words?" asked the judge.

The boy said, "Haven't you been paying attention? I'm not going to tell you because they keep landing me in trouble."

The judge warned him that he would get into even more trouble if he didn't reveal the words.

So the boy reluctantly said, "Red Ruby."

The judge was appalled and sentenced the boy to ten years in jail.

The cons in jail were curious about their new cellmate, so they asked him what he was in for. The boy said, "When I was on my way to school one day, I saw some words written on a wall and I didn't know what they meant. So when the teacher asked if there were any questions, I asked her what they meant and she yelled at me and sent me to the principal's office. When I got there, he asked me what had happened and I told him everything, and he asked me what the words were and when I told him, he freaked out and expelled me. When I got home, my mom asked me what had happened and I told her everything, and she asked me what the words were. When I told her, she sent me up to my room to wait for my dad. He asked me what happened and after I told him everything he asked me the words and when I told him, he kicked me out. I ran into my friends and they asked me why I had been expelled and kicked out of my house and I told them everything, and then they asked me what the words were. When I told them, they beat me up. A hobo came by and scared them off, then he asked me what had happened and I told him everything. Then he asked what the words were and when I told him, he began beating me up. Then a cop came by and broke it up and after I had explained the story to him he asked what the words were and when I told him, he handcuffed me and took me to jail. The next day I had to go

to court and the judge asked me what happened and I told him everything and then he asked me the words and when I told him, he gave me ten years."

His cellmates were amazed at the story and wanted to know what the words were.

Taking a deep breath, the boy answered, "Red Ruby." He spent the next ten years getting beaten up.

The day he was released from jail he met a beautiful woman. She said, "You look like you've had a rough time. What happened?"

So the man said, "When I was on my way to school one day, I saw some words written on a wall and I didn't know what they meant. So when the teacher asked me if there were any questions, I asked her what they meant and she yelled at me and sent me to the principal's office. When I got there, he asked me what had happened and I told him everything, and he asked me what the words were and when I told him, he freaked out and expelled me. When I got home, my mom asked me what had happened and I told her everything, and she asked me what the words were. When I told her, she sent me up to my room to wait for my dad. He asked me what happened and after I told him everything he asked me the words and when I told him, he kicked me out. I ran into my friends and they asked me why I had been expelled and kicked out of my house and I told them everything, and then they asked what the words were. When I told them, they beat me up. A hobo came by and scared them off, then he asked me what had happened and I told him everything. Then he asked what the words were and when I told him, he began beating me up. Then a cop came by and broke it up and after I had explained the story to him he asked what the words were and when I told him, he handcuffed me and took me to jail. The next day I had to go to court and the judge asked me what happened and I told him everything, and then he asked me the words and when I told him, he gave me ten years. All of my cellmates asked me what the words were and I took a deep breath and told them. I have spent the last ten years getting beaten up."

"That is so awful!" exclaimed the beautiful woman. "What were the words?"

"Do you think I'm stupid?" exploded the man. "I'm not going to tell you the words. They've brought me nothing but grief for more than ten years!"

"Oh, come on," purred the beautiful woman. "I won't do anything to you."

Against his better judgement the man relented. "Okay," he said.

"The words were 'Red Ruby'."

"Red Ruby?" asked the beautiful woman, her eyes ablaze with passion. "You see that hotel across the street? Meet me there in one hour and I will tell you the meaning of 'Red Ruby'."

The man was ecstatic. He was finally going to learn what 'Red Ruby' meant after all this time. An hour later, he set off across the street in eager anticipation, but as he stepped off the kerb he was hit by a bus and killed.

The moral of the story – look both ways before crossing the street.

SHEEP

Why did the sheep fall over the cliff?
He didn't see the ewe turn.

What do you call a sheep with no legs?
A cloud.

What did the well-mannered sheep say to his friend at the field gate?
After ewe.

What do you get if you cross a sheep with a rainstorm?
A wet blanket.

What do you get if you cross a lamb with a spaceship?
The Star-sheep Enterprise.

Why did the sheep cross the road? **To get to the baa baa shop.**

Did you hear about the snobby lamb?

He thought he was a cutlet above the rest.

One Christmas, two businessmen built a skating rink in the middle of a pasture. A shepherd leading his flocking tried to take a short cut across the rink but the sheep were afraid of the ice and wouldn't cross it.

As the shepherd desperately tried to tug the sheep to the other side, one businessman turned to the other and said, "Look. That guy is trying to pull the wool over our ice."

What sort of food can you get in a pub run by sheep ?

Baaa meals.

Why do white sheep eat more than black ones?
Because there are more of them.

What do you get if you cross a lamb and a penguin?
A sheepskin dinner jacket.

A man needing a heart transplant was informed by his doctor that the only heart available was that of a sheep. The man wasn't at all sure about this at first but he eventually agreed and the doctor successfully transplanted the sheep's heart into the patient.

The next day, the doctor was doing his hospital rounds and asked the man how he was feeling.

The man replied, "Not baaaad!"

How do sheep keep warm in winter?
They use central bleating.

Who's afraid of Virginia Woolf?
Virginia Sheep.

Teacher: Suppose there were a dozen sheep and six jumped over a fence. How many would be left?
Pupil: None.
Teacher: None? You don't know your numbers.
Pupil: And you don't know your sheep. When one goes, they all go!

Teacher: Did you know that it takes three sheep to make one jumper?
Pupil: I didn't even know sheep could knit!

Why did the sheep smash through the shop window?
He was a ram raider.

Which sheep drives a racing car at 180 mph?
Jenson Mutton.

Once upon a time there was a really clever female sheep in Mexico, who knew how to make butter and buttermilk. One night she sneaked across the border into the United States and got a job working for a farmer, who set up a roadside stand and told her to try to sell the produce to passing motorists. Traffic was extremely heavy and inevitably the sight of a sheep making butter and buttermilk proved so distracting that there was an accident.

The police duly investigated and charged the farmer with attempting to make an illegal ewe churn on a busy highway.

SKELETONS

Why didn't the skeleton cross the road?
Because he had no body to go with.

Why are skeletons usually so calm?
Nothing gets under their skin.

What do skeletons say before a meal?
Bone appetit.

What happened when the skeletons jumped on pogo sticks?
They had a rattling good time.

Why do skeletons hate winter?
Because the cold goes right through them.

When does a skeleton laugh?
When something tickles his funny bone.

What did the skeleton have for dinner?
Ribs.

Why couldn't the skeleton do a bungee jump?
He didn't have the guts.

Who was the most famous skeleton detective?
Sherlock Bones.

What did the skeleton say to his girlfriend?
I love every bone in your body.

Who was France's most famous skeleton?
Napoleon Bone-apart.

How did the skeleton know it was going to rain?
He could feel it in his bones.

Why did the skeleton play the piano?
Because he didn't have any organs.

What do you call a stupid skeleton?
Bonehead.

Why did the skeleton stay out in the snow all night?
Because he was a numbskull.

What musical instrument does a skeleton play?
The trom-bone.

What happened to the skeleton who stood by the fire too long?
He became bone dry.

What do boney people use to get into their homes?
Skeleton keys.

What happened to the skeleton who went to a party?
Everyone used him as a coat rack.

What kind of plate does a skeleton eat off?
Bone china.

What do you call a skeleton who won't get up in the morning?
Lazybones.

What do you call a skeleton snake?
A rattler.

Why wasn't the bank robber skeleton afraid of the police?
Because he knew they couldn't pin anything on him.

What do you call a skeleton in a kilt?
Boney Prince Charlie.

A skeleton walked into a bar and said, "I'd like a beer and a mop…"

SKUNKS

Did you hear the joke about the skunk?
Never mind, it stinks.

How many skunks do you need to make a house really smelly?
Just a phew.

What do you get if you cross a skunk and a dinosaur?
A stinkasaurus.

How can you tell when a skunk is angry?
It raises a stink.

What do you get if you cross a skunk and a hot-air balloon?
Something that stinks to high heaven.

What's a skunk's favourite game in school?
Show and smell.

What do you get if you cross a skunk and a boomerang?

A bad smell that keeps coming back.

Why couldn't the skunk use her phone?
It was out of odour.

How much money does a skunk have?
One scent.

What do you get if you cross a skunk and a bear?
Winnie the Pooh.

What did the baby skunk want to be when he grew up?
A big stink.

What's a skunk's philosophy of life?
Eat, stink and be merry.

Two skunks were being chased by a bear. As the bear got closer, one of the skunks said, "Whatever shall we do?"
The other skunk replied, "Let us spray."

What's the difference between a skunk and a squirrel?
A skunk uses a cheaper deodorant.

What did one skunk say to the other?
And so do you!

Why did the skunk buy five boxes of paper tissues?
Because he had a stinking cold.

What did the judge say when the skunk was on trial?
Odour in court.

What do you get if you cross a skunk with an owl that has lost its voice?
A bird that stinks but doesn't give a hoot.

What do you call a flying skunk?
A smellicopter.

A mother skunk gave birth to twins, whom she named In and Out.

One day In was outside, so she asked her other baby, "Out, go out and find In. In's out and I want him in. I've been looking for In outside for ages. I can't find In, he is out so go out, find In and bring him in."

"What?" said Out.

His mother said, "In's out, so Out go out, find In and bring him in. I've been looking for ages and can't find In. I want In in. Out go out and bring In in, if you can find him."

So Out goes out to look for his brother In, and within seconds of leaving, he comes back with In in tow.

His mother asks, "Out, how did you find In so quickly?"

Out replies, "In stinked."

SNAKES

What snake is good with numbers?
An adder.

A snake slithers into a bar. The bartender says, "I'm sorry, but I can't serve you here."
"Why not?" asks the snake.
"Because you can't hold your liquor."

What subject do snakes like at school?
Hiss-tory.

What do you get if you cross a snake with a Lego set?
A boa constructor.

Why can't you play jokes on snakes?
Because you can never pull their legs.

What did the coach say to his losing team of snakes?
You can't venom all.

A baby snake asked its mother, "Mom, are we poisonous?"
His mother replied, "No, son, we're not poisonous."
"Thank goodness for that!" said the baby snake.
"Why do you ask?" said the mother.
The baby snake replied, "Because I just bit my tongue."

Why was the rattlesnake mad at the jewel thief?
Because he wanted his diamondback.

How do you stop a snake from striking?
Pay it decent wages.

How did the cobra find the Indian?
Charming.

What do you call a snake that operates as a police informer?
A grass snake.

What's a snake's favourite TV show?
Monty Python.

What's a serpent's favourite song?
Snake, Rattle and Roll.

A male and female python were slithering amorously down the path when they met a black mamba.
"Who's that you're with?" said the mamba to the male python. "It's my latest squeeze," replied the python.

What do you get if you cross a bag of snakes and a cupboard of food?
Snakes and larders.

What do you do if you find a cobra in your toilet?
Wait until he's finished.

What do you get if you cross a trombone and a serpent?
A snake in the brass.

What's long, green and goes hith?
A snake with a lisp.

An elderly snake went to the optician to have his eyes tested. The optician gave him a pair of glasses and sent him on his way.

Two days later, the snake returned looking thoroughly miserable.

"What's the matter?" asked the optician. "Are you having problems with your new glasses?"

"No, the glasses are fine," sighed the snake. "But I've just discovered I've been living with a garden hose for the past ten years!"

Why can't you trust snakes?
They speak with forked tongues.

What do you call an organization for people who love snakes?
A fang club.

A woman ordered a snake over the internet, but when the package arrived the box contained nothing but a feather stole. The police said the boa cons tricked her.

What did the snake say when he was offered a piece of cheese for dinner?
I'll just have a slither.

What's the best thing about venomous snakes?
They've got poisonality.

Which hand should you use to pick up a poisonous snake?
Someone else's.

What do you call a snake that's trying to become a bird?
A feather boa.

What do snakes have written on their bath towels?
Hiss and hers.

What do you get if you cross Madonna with a twenty-foot-long snake?
A singalong.

Why did the two boa constrictors get married?
Because they had a crush on each other.

A blind rabbit and a blind snake ran into each other on the road one day.

The snake reached out, touched the rabbit and said, "You're soft and fuzzy and have floppy ears. You must be a rabbit."

The rabbit reached out, touched the snake and said, "You're thick-skinned, beady-eyed and low to the ground. You must be a math teacher."

What kind of snake would you find on your car?
A windscreen viper.

Why did the viper viper nose?
Because the adder adder tissue.

Which snakes disobeyed Noah when he said, "Go forth and multiply."
The adders.

SPACE

Why did the boy become an astronaut?
Because he was no earthly good.

What do astronauts wear to keep warm?
Apollo-neck sweaters.

Where do astronauts leave their spaceships?
At parking meteors.

Two astronauts went to a bar on the moon, but they left after a few minutes.
You see, it had no atmosphere.

Which astronaut wears the biggest helmet?
The one with the biggest head.

How do spacemen pass the time on long trips?
They play astronauts and crosses.

Why did the astronomer hit himself on the head in the afternoon?
He wanted to see stars during the day.

An astronomer was studying the stars in the night sky through a telescope. In particular, he was trying to locate the brightest star of all but kept focusing on other stars by mistake. Eventually, he stood up in frustration, looked to the heavens and yelled, "You cannot be Sirius!"

Four astronauts were in a spaceship. They had eight cigarettes but no matches. How did they light their cigarettes?
They threw one cigarette overboard and that made the spaceship a cigarette lighter.

Where does Dr Who buy his ham and cheese?
At a dalek-atessen.

Why are astronauts successful people?
Because they always go up in the world.

How many ears has Captain Kirk got?
Three. The left ear, the right ear and the final front ear.

Why did Captain Kirk go into the ladies toilet?
To boldly go where no man has been before.

What do astonauts get when they're far apart?
Spaced out.

Why didn't the astronauts stay on the moon?
Because it was a full moon, and so there was no room.

Why is the moon like a dollar?
It has four quarters.

How do you know when the moon is broke?
It's down to its last quarter.

What do you do if you see a spaceman?
Park your car in it, man.

How did Darth Vader know what Luke was getting for Christmas?
He felt his presents.

If athletes get athlete's foot, what do astronauts get?
Missiletoe.

Who wears a black helmet, a black cape, breathes heavily and stands in over a foot of water?
Darth Wader.

What's an astronaut's favourite drink?
Gravi-tea.

What holds the moon up?
Moonbeams.

What did the space man say when he stepped on a giant chocolate bar?
I have just set foot on Mars.

What do dentists call an astronaut's cavity?
A black hole.

What happened to the astronaut who stepped on some chewing gum?
He got stuck in Orbit.

First spaceman: I'm hungry.
Second spaceman: So am I, it must be launch time.

What do you call a loony spaceman?
An astronut!

A boy says to his father, "I want to be an astronaut when I grow up."
His father replies, "What high

hopes you have."

What makes the moon pale?
Atmos-fear.

Jupiter came down to Earth one day and decided to help two criminals to rob a bank. However, the police caught the gang and the three of them found themselves in court.

The judge sentenced the two Earthlings to fifteen years, and Jupiter was a bit shocked when he was sentenced to ten years.

"But your honour," protested Jupiter, "I didn't even take part in the robbery."

"That's all very well," said the judge, "but you helped them… Planet."

SPIES

What did the stupid spy do when he found his room was bugged?
He sprayed it with DDT.

Two spies escaped from the enemy over the Alps into neutral Switzerland during the war. As they began to feel safe, one spy started to tell the other what he had found out in enemy territory. The other advised him to speak quietly.

"Why?" asked his friend, a little puzzled. "There's nobody around for miles. I could scream and not a soul would hear us up here. Mountains can't hear."

"I wouldn't be so sure," replied the other. "Haven't you heard of mountain ears?"

What do you call a secret agent who hangs around at department stores?
A counterspy.

What do you call an underwater secret agent?
James Pond.

What do you call a magical secret agent?
James Wand.

When one of the CIA's operatives disappeared off the radar, they called in one of their top spy hunters. The CIA boss said, "This man is a master of secrecy, so he'll be tough to track down. All I can tell you is that his name is

Jones and that he's in a small town somewhere in Wales. If you think you've located him, tell him the code words: "The forecast is for mist on the hills." And if you've got the right man, he will respond: "But I hear it's sunny in the valleys."

Armed with this limited information, the spy hunter set off for rural Wales and arrived in a suitably remote small town. Reasoning that the local pub was the centre of the community, he engaged the barman in friendly conversation. After exchanging pleasantries about the picturesque countryside, eventually the spy hunter said, "Perhaps you can help me. I'm looking for a guy named Jones."

The barman laughed. "You'll have to be more specific than that, my friend, because there are hundreds of men named Jones in this area. There's Jones the bread, who runs the baker's shop across the road; Jones the meat, who is the local butcher; Jones the nail, who runs the hardware shop two doors down; not to mention Jones the bank, Jones the hotel and Jones the travel. As a matter of fact, my name is Jones, too."

Hearing this, the spy hunter figured he might as well try the code words on the barman. So he leaned over and whispered, "The forecast is for mist on the hills."

The barman replied, "Oh, you want Jones the spy! He lives at number fifty-two, halfway up the hill."

SPORTS

What do you call a boomerang that doesn't work?
A stick.

AMERICAN FOOTBALL

A guy took his girlfriend to her first football game. Afterwards he asked her how she liked the game.

"I liked it, but I couldn't understand why they were killing each other for twenty-five cents," she said.

"What do you mean?" he asked.

"Well, everyone kept yelling, 'Get the quarter back!'"

What is a cheerleader's favourite colour?
Yeller.

What position do the fattest footballers play?
Wide receiver.

Coach: Twenty teams in the league and you lot finish bottom!
Captain: It could have been worse.
Coach: How?
Captain: There could have been more teams in the league.

Coach: I thought I told you to lose weight. What happened to your three-week diet?
Player: I finished it in three days.

It was a particularly tough football game, and nerves were on edge. The home team had been the victim of three or four close calls, and they were now trailing the visitors by a touch-down and a field goal. When the official called yet another close one in the visitors' favour, the home quarterback blew his top.

"How many times can you do this to us in a single game?" he screamed. "You were wrong on the out-of-bounds, you were wrong on that last first down, and you missed an illegal tackle in the first quarter."

The official just stared.

The quarterback seethed, but he suppressed the language that might get him banned from the game. "What it comes down to," he bellowed, "is that you stink!"

The official stared for a few more seconds. Then he bent down, picked up the ball, paced off fifteen yards, and put the ball down. He turned to face the angry quarterback.

The official finally replied, "And how do I smell from here?"

First girl: What position does your brother play in the school football team?

Second girl: I heard the teacher say he was one of the drawbacks.

BASEBALL

Why is a baseball team like a pancake?
Because they both depend on the batter.

Coming home from his Little League game, Billy swung open the front door very excited. Unable to attend the game, his father immediately wanted to know what happened. "So, how did you do son?" he asked.

"You'll never believe it!" Billy said. "I was responsible for the winning run!"

"Really? How did you do that?"

"I dropped the ball."

How do baseball players stay cool?
They sit next to the fans.

What did the baseball glove say to the ball?
Catch ya later!

Why did the baseball player go to jail?
Because he was caught trying to steal second base.

A Little League coach consoled his team after they had just been whipped.

"Boys, don't get down on yourselves. You did your best and you shouldn't take the loss personally. Keep your chins up. Besides, your parents should be very proud of you boys. In fact, just as proud as the parents of the girls on the team that beat you."

Why don't matchsticks play baseball?
Because one strike and they're out.

What do you call a crab that plays baseball?
A pinch hitter.

BASKETBALL

How did the basketball court get wet?
The players kept dribbling.

What do you call two Spaniards playing basketball?
Juan on Juan.

What stories are told by basketball players?
Tall stories.

BOWLING

Where do old bowling balls end up?
In the gutter.

BOWLS

If you have a referee in football, what do you have in bowls?
Cornflakes.

BOXING

What did the boxer have written on his gravestone?
You can stop counting, I'm not getting up.

Who was the last person to box Rocky Marciano?
His undertaker.

CHESS

All the world's top chess players show up at a hotel for an important international tournament. They spend the first hour hanging around the lobby, telling each other of their recent victories. They get progressively louder and louder as they try to outdo their competitors. Other guests at the hotel look on disapprovingly at the noisy group and some complain to the manager. Eventually, the hotel manager gets tired of hearing them. He throws them out of the lobby and tells them to go to their rooms.

"If there's one thing I can't stand," he says, "it's chess nuts boasting by an open foyer."

CRICKET

The small village cricket ground was crowded. Everyone had come to see the two Australian fast bowlers who were guests on the visiting team.

The village captain won the toss and decided to bat, which was a poor decision on his part. In the first over one fast bowler took all six wickets. The second over produced one run and the fall of the remaining four wickets.

"It must be disappointing for the crowd," said one of the village players.

"Yes," agreed the captain. "But at least they got a run for their money."

It hadn't rained for months and the Indians were worried about the drought.

"Let us do the English Rain Ritual," said one Indian.

"What is that?"

"When I was in England, I saw two men in white coats hammer six sticks into the ground, then two men carrying clubs came out and stood in front of the sticks and then eleven more men came out blowing on their hands. Then one of the white coats shouted "Play", and that's when the rain came pouring down!"

A cricketer died and went to Heaven. One day he looked down to Hell, and there to his amazement he saw a cricket ground with fielders out and batsmen at the crease.

"I say," he said to St Peter, "look at that. A cricket match about to start. And you call that Hell? Why, I'd love to be playing."

"So would they," smiled St Peter. "But they haven't got a ball."

The cricket team captain was rather surprised when a horse arrived and asked for a trial. The captain suggested that the horse play in the match that was about to begin.

"What number do you bat?" he asked the horse.

"I usually open," came the reply.

So the horse opened the innings, clad in whites and wearing a brightly coloured cap at a rakish angle over one ear. Every ball he played in the first over was a boundary, four fours and two sixes.

The bowling changed and the batsman pushed the first ball he received gently to the covers and shouted "One" as he ran. The horse didn't move and the batsman was run out. As he stalked by the horse he said, "It was my call. Why didn't you run?"

"Run?" replied the horse. "Don't be daft, I can't run. If I could run, I'd be at Ascot and not playing this stupid game!"

A husband phoned the hospital to ask about his pregnant wife, but his call accidentally went through to the local cricket ground.

The husband asked, "How are things?"

The reply came, "Seven are out already, there could be another one out any minute, and the first one was a duck!"

DARTS

Two men were playing darts in a competition. The second player was left with 100 to win. His first dart went in the treble twenty and his second dart was a single twenty, leaving him double ten for the match. He took careful aim but his final throw hit the wire and rebounded into the head of a nun who was sitting in the front row, killing her instantly.

The match announcer boomed out the score: "One nun dead and eighty."

What happened when the man said he didn't understand darts?
His friend explained some of the finer points.

FISHING

The local angling club was having its annual dinner and presentation of trophies. When the members arrived, they were surprised to see all the chairs spaced several feet apart. One of them said to the caterer, "That's a strange way to arrange seats for a party."

The caterer explained, "We always do it like that so that members can do full justice to their fish stories."

Two fishermen were talking on the riverbank. One said, "I love fishing. The fresh air. The solitude. Man against nature. Tell me, why do you fish?"
The other replied, "My daughter's learning the violin."

GOLF

Fred Flintstone and one of his buddies from work, Rex Rock, decided to knock off early one day and have a round of golf. They hadn't played at the Dinosaur Graveyard Golf Course for a while, so they thought they would give it a try.

A unique feature of the course was its hazards. Instead of the standard sand traps, water and trees, this course, as its name suggested, was littered with the carcasses of prehistoric beasts.

Rex, in particular, struggled to come to terms with the layout of the course. He endured a torrid time, hooking one shot, slicing the next, and was soon trailing Fred by more than a dozen shots. He couldn't wait for the round to end.

On the 17th hole he overhit his approach shot to the green and his ball landed in the cranial cavity of a Tyrannosaurus skull.

"Look at that lie!" grumbled Rex. "How am I supposed to play a shot from there?"

"Just quit yer complaining," said Fred, "and hit the ball off the T, Rex."

Why are old socks good for golf?
Because they have eighteen holes.

What is a golfer's favourite meal of the day?
Tee time.

Why did Tarzan spend so much time on the golf course?
To perfect his swing.

Why did the golfer wear two pairs of pants?
In case he got a hole in one.

The golfing world is celebrating a new invention that promises to revolutionize the sport. The new device that is receiving so much attention is called the bee nut. It is a fastening attachment that allows players to adjust the head on their club to any angle, thus saving the need to carry a bagful of clubs. Thus, for example, players can use the same club to putt with as they use to get out of a sand trap.

Golf clubs with this modification are selling quickly, and players everywhere are taking golfing picnics, so they can try their new bee-nut putter sand-wedge.

GYMNASTICS

What season is it when you are on a trampoline?
Spring time.

What did the trampolinist say?
Life has its ups and downs but I always bounce back.

How does a physicist exercise?
By pumping ion.

HORSE RACING

A champion jockey is about to enter an important race on a new horse. The horse's trainer meets him before the race and says, "All you have to remember with this horse is that every time you approach a jump, you have to shout 'alleee oop!' really loudly in the horse's ear. Providing you do that, you'll be fine."

The jockey thinks the trainer is mad but promises to shout the command. The race begins and they approach the first fence. The jockey ignores the trainer's ridiculous advice and the horse

What's the difference between a racehorse and a duck?
One goes quick, the other goes quack.

crashes straight through the jump.

They carry on and approach the second fence. The jockey, somewhat embarrassed, whispers "alleee oop" in the horse's ear. The same thing happens, the horse crashes straight through the middle of the jump.

At the third hurdle, the jockey thinks, "It's no good, I'll have to do it," and yells "alleee oop!" really loudly. Sure enough, the horse sails over the jump with no problems. This continues for the rest of the race, but due to the earlier problems the horse finishes third.

The trainer is fuming and asks the jockey what went wrong. The jockey replies, "Nothing is wrong with me, it's this stupid horse. What is he, deaf or something?"

The trainer replies, "Deaf? Deaf? He's not deaf, he's blind!"

Why are clouds like jockeys?
Because they hold the reins.

A woman was considering buying a decrepit old thoroughbred but wanted a vet's opinion of the horse before finalizing the deal. When the vet had completed his examination, she asked, "Will I be able to race him?"
The vet looked at the woman and then at the horse. "Sure," he replied. "And you'll probably win!"

Why did the racehorse go behind the tree?
To change his jockeys.

Why was the racehorse named Bad News?
Because bad news travels fast.

A jockey was riding the favourite at a race meeting, and was well ahead of the field.

His horse rounded the final corner, when suddenly the jockey was hit on the head by a turkey and a string of sausages.

He managed to keep control of his mount and pulled back into the lead, only to be struck by a box of Christmas crackers and a dozen mince pies as he went over the last fence.

With great skill he managed to steer the horse to the front of the field once more when, on the run in, he was struck on the head by a bottle of sherry and a Christmas pudding. Thus distracted, he succeeded in coming only second.

He immediately went to the race stewards to complain that he had been seriously hampered.

ICE SKATING

What's the hardest thing about learning to ice skate?
The ice.

What's brown and sweet and glides around an ice rink?
Bourneville and Dean.

MARTIAL ARTS

What happened to the army karate champion?
The first time he saluted he nearly killed himself.

Did you hear about the sick martial arts teacher?
He had kung flu.

POOL AND SNOOKER

Two owls were playing pool.
One said, "Two hits."
The other said, "Two hits to who?"

Did you hear about the underwater snooker player?
He was a pool shark.

SOCCER

What's the chilliest ground in the Premiership?
Cold Trafford.

How did the soccer pitch end up as a triangle?
Somebody took a corner.

What part of a football pitch smells nicest?
The scenter spot.

What do a footballer and a magician have in common?
Both do hat tricks.

Why did the footballer hold his boot to his ear?
Because he liked sole music.

What do soccer players drink?
Penaltea.

What do you call a person who shouts all the way through a football match ?
A foot bawler.

Why can't Cinderella play soccer?
Because she's always running away from the ball.

A soccer referee walked into a bar. The bartender thought, "It's all going to kick off now!"

Why did a soccer player take a piece of rope on to the pitch?
He was the skipper.

Which Greek philosopher was great at football?
Soccerates.

What do you call an overweight vicar who plays football?
The roly-poly-holy-goalie!

What lights up a football stadium?
A football match.

Which soccer team loves ice cream?
Aston Vanilla.

What is a goalkeeper's favourite snack?
Beans on post.

Where do football directors go during a dull match?
The bored room.

What's the difference between Accrington Stanley and a tea bag?
The tea bag stays in the cup longer.

Which Argentinian footballer was a fluorescent colour?
Dayglow Maradona.

Why do managers take suitcases to away games?
Because they need to pack the defence.

Why were the two managers sitting around sketching crockery before the start of the game?
Because it was a cup draw.

Why did the struggling soccer manager shake the club cat?
To see if there was any more money in the kitty.

Why was the goal post fed up?
Because of the cross bar.

What part of a football ground is never the same?
The changing rooms.

What should a soccer team do if the pitch is flooded?
Bring on their subs.

What did the football say to the footballer?
I get a kick out of you.

Why do artists never win when they play soccer?
Because they keep drawing.

A soccer match was short of a referee so one of the team's captains walked into the pub and asked if there was a referee present.

One man stepped forward and said, "I'm a referee."

"Have you stood before?" asked the captain.

"Of course I have, and my three friends here will vouch for that," was the reply.

"Thank you for offering, but I don't think we'll accept."

"You don't think I'm a referee?"

"Quite frankly I don't, because I've never heard of a referee having three friends."

What did the footballer say when he accidentally burped during a game?
Sorry, it was a freak hic.

What do you get if you drop a piano on a soccer team's defence?
A flat back four.

What do you get if a soccer team's defence goes to Ikea?
A flat-pack four.

What position did the obese footballer play?
Centre-forward.

What happened when a team of brooms played a team of brushes?
They all wanted to be the sweeper.

Soccer manager: Our new striker cost twenty million, and I call him our wonder player.
Fan: Why's that?
Manager: Because every time he plays, I wonder why I signed him!

Referee: I'm sending you off.
Player: What for?
Referee: The rest of the match!

The Seven Dwarfs were in a cave when the roof suddenly collapsed. Snow White ran to the entrance and yelled down to them.

From the dark depths of the cave a voice cried out, "West Ham are the best team in Europe."

Snow White said, "Well, at least we know Dopey's alive!"

Once upon a time there was a big soccer match between the insects and the animals. The entire jungle turned out to watch in the expectation of a comfortable victory for the animals. With the giraffe winning everything in the air and the cheetah sprinting down the wing, the animals led 1–0 at halftime.

It was then that the insects' coach decided to make a change. He took off the dung beetle, who was having a stinker, and brought on the earwig, wearing a shirt with the number 0 on the back, because it was the only one that would fit him. Anyway, the earwig was a revelation, and with the bee buzzing in midfield and the moth managing to keep away from the floodlights, the insects fought back.

With ten minutes left, the earwig equalized. Then, in the final minute, the spider weaved his way down the left and crossed the ball for the earwig to score a sensational winning goal. All the insect supporters went wild and burst into the familiar chorus of earwig 0 earwig 0 earwig 0 earwig 0 earwig 0 earwig 0…

SWIMMING

Why did the swimmer keep doing the backstroke?
Because he'd just had his lunch and didn't want to swim on a full stomach.

What is a swimmer's favourite sport?
Pool.

TENNIS

A woman bought a tennis racket as a present for her son but when he tried it out, the strings were too tight, so she took it back to the shop to have it restrung.

Three days later, the racket was delivered back to her house but to her horror she saw that all the strings had been removed. It was nothing but the frame.

So she marched round to the shop to complain. "That tennis racket I bought the other day. Now it's got no strings! Why have you taken them all out?"

"Well, madam," explained the shop manager, "you see, we operate on a no-returns basis."

Why is tennis the noisiest game?
Because you can't play it without raising a racket.

Why do waiters enjoy playing tennis?
Because they are good at serving.

Why couldn't the tennis player boil a kettle?
She'd lost all her matches.

Why shouldn't you marry a tennis player?
Because love means nothing to them.

First man: All tennis players are witches.
Second man: What are you talking about?
First man: It's true. Remember Goran? Even he's a witch.

TRACK AND FIELD

Who was the fastest runner?
Adam. He was first in the human race.

How do you start a jelly race?
Get set.

A kitchen knife and a spoon had a race. Who won?
Neither. It ended in a drawer.

Why does someone who runs marathons make a good student?
Because education pays off in the long run.

At the Olympic Games, a girl bumps into a man carrying an eight-foot-long metal stick.

"Excuse me," says the girl to the man. "Are you a pole vaulter?"

"No," says the man. "I'm German, but how did you know my name is Walter?"

What is harder to catch the faster you run?
Your breath.

Why was the electrician disqualified from the race?
He made a short circuit.

Did you hear about the two fat men who ran the New York Marathon?
One ran in short bursts, the other in burst shorts.

What athlete is warmest in winter?
A long jumper.

What is a runner's favourite subject at school?
Jog-raphy.

What happens to athletes wearing bad footwear?
They suffer the agony of defeat.

TEETH

Why do you forget a tooth as soon as the dentist extracts it?
Because it goes right out of your head.

What award does the Dentist of the Year receive?
A little plaque.

Where does a dentist get gas for his car?
At a filling station.

Why did the king go to the dentist?
To get his teeth crowned.

Why do dentists seem moody?
Because they always looks down in the mouth.

What do you call a dentist in the army?
A drill sergeant.

Why did the boy wear a belt on his teeth?
He couldn't find his braces.

What time did the man go to the dentist?
Tooth hurty.

What did the judge say to the dentist?
Do you swear to pull the tooth, the whole tooth, and nothing but the tooth?

Why did the schoolboy bite the dentist?
Because he got on his nerves.

A man coughed violently, causing his false teeth to shoot across the room and smash into a wall. "Oh dear," he exclaimed. "What am I going to do? I can't afford a new set."

"Don't worry," said his friend. "My brother will be able to get a set for you."

The next day, the friend came back with a set of false teeth, which fitted the man perfectly.

"These are wonderful," said the man. "Your brother must be a really good dentist."

"Oh, he's not a dentist," replied the friend. "He's an undertaker."

Why did the tree to go to the dentist?
To get a root canal.

What game do you play if you don't take care of your teeth?
Tooth or Consequences.

What's red and bad for your teeth?
A brick.

Patient: Do you extract teeth painlessly?
Dentist: Not always. The other day I nearly disclocated my wrist.

"Open wider, please," said the dentist as he began examining the patient. "My goodness! You've got the biggest cavity I've ever seen – the biggest cavity I've ever seen."

"Okay, doc," replied the patient. "I'm scared enough without you saying things like that twice."

"I didn't," said the dentist. "That was the echo!"

What did one tooth say to the other tooth?
There's gold in them fills!

Why is 4,840 square yards like a bad tooth?
Because it is an acre.

What do you call an old dentist?
A bit long in the tooth.

What two letters of the alphabet are bad for your teeth?
D K.

What did the dentist say when

his wife baked a cake?
Can I do the filling?

Dentist: Open wide.
Patient: Is that wide enough?
Dentist: Yes, please don't open your mouth any wider. When I pull your tooth I expect to stand outside.

Patient: Tell me honestly. How am I?
Dentist: Your teeth are fine, but your gums will have to come out.

What has teeth but cannot bite?
A comb.

Why didn't the dentist enjoy his date with the manicurist?
Because they fought tooth and nail.

What did one tooth say to the other?
Get your cap on. The dentist is taking us out tonight.

TRANSPORT

A drunk driver going the wrong way along a one-way street was pulled over by a police officer.
"Didn't you see the arrows?" asked the officer.
"Arrows?" said the driver. "I didn't even see the Indians!"

A nervous passenger on an airplane asked the flight attendant, "How often do

planes of this type crash?"
The flight attendant replied, "Only once, madam."

Why did the Mexican engineer always drive his train backwards?
He had a loco motive.

What did Batman say to Robin before they got in the car?
Robin, get in the car.

Why did the pilot crash into the house?
Because the landing lights were on.

When is a car not a car?
When it turns into a driveway.

Which bus crossed the Altantic?
Columbus.

Train passenger: Guard! How long will the next train be?
Guard: About six carriages, sir.

Where do sick steamships go?
To the dock.

A passenger on a luxury cruise ship spotted a bearded man on a small, remote island, shouting something inaudible and desperately waving his arms. The passenger sought out the captain and asked, "Who is that man?"
"I don't know," said the captain, "but every year when we pass, he does that."

How did the driver get a puncture?
He didn't see the fork in the road.

How do locomotives hear?
Through the engineers.

Why was the boy confused while writing a school project on the train?
He kept losing track of what he had done.

There were 99 people in a boat and then it overturned. How many were left?
66.

Why were the inventors of the aeroplane correct in thinking they could fly?
Because they were Wright.

An elderly female passenger asked the station master, "Can I take this train to London?"
The station master replied, "I think it might be a bit heavy for you, madam!"

What form of transport is easily understood?
An articulate truck.

Passenger: Does this bus stop at the river?
Bus driver: If it doesn't, there'll be a very big splash!

What happened to the road-safety-conscious girl who always wore white at night?
Last winter she was knocked down by a snow plough.

Visiting his brother in a neighbouring county, an old hillbilly was fascinated by the railroad. He had never seen a train before and so when one came whistling and steaming down the track toward him, his brother had to drag him to safety at the last minute.

"You could have been killed!" said the brother. "It was a good thing I happened to be around."

The brother took the shaken hillbilly back to his cabin to recover. The brother put a kettle on the stove to make some tea and then went outside to chop some wood. He returned to find the hillbilly raining blows on the kettle with the butt of a shotgun.

"Why are you smashing my kettle?" demanded the brother.

"These darned things are dangerous," said the hillbilly. "I'm killin' this one before it gets a chance to grow up!"

A man went to the ticket office in London and said, "I'd like to get a train to Paris."

The clerk said, "Eurostar?"

"Well, I was on telly once," replied the man, "but I'm no Jim Carrey."

Why didn't any of the children take the bus to school?
Because it wouldn't fit through the front door.

Pilot: Tower, please call me a fuel truck.

Tower: Roger, you are a fuel truck.

Tower: What's your height and position?
Pilot: I'm six-foot tall and I'm sitting front left.

What kind of dancing do cars like?
Brake dancing.

Customer: How come this car is covered with dents? You said it had one careful owner.
Car salesman: The others weren't so careful.

What kind of ship never sinks?
Friendship.

First boy: What sort of car has your dad got?
Second boy: I can't remember the name. I think it starts with T.
First Boy: Really? Ours starts with gas.

A boy sat on a bus chewing gum and staring vacantly into space. After a while the old woman sitting opposite him said, "It's no use talking to me, young man. I'm stone deaf!"

Why did the trucker drive his truck over the cliff?
Because he wanted to try out the air brakes.

A man whose son had just passed his driving test arrived home to find that the boy had driven his car right into the dining room.

"How did you manage to do that?" he raged.
"Easy, Dad. I came in through the kitchen and turned left."

A woman boarded the bus with her teenaged son but tried to get away with paying only one fare. However, the driver insisted that she pay for the boy, too.
"But children under age six ride free," the mother protested.
"I know," said the driver, "but he doesn't look a day under fourteen."
The mother said, "Can I help it if he worries a lot?"

A man walked up to the airport ticket desk and asked for a round-trip ticket.
"Where to?" asked the ticket clerk.
"Back to here, of course," replied the man.

Why did the child study in the airplane?
He wanted a higher education.

Bus passenger: I'd like a ticket to New York, please.
Ticket seller: By Buffalo?
Bus passenger: Of course not. I'm in the bus queue, aren't I?

Passenger: Does this bus go to Birmingham?
Driver: No.
Passenger: But it says

Birmingham on the front.
Driver: There's an advertisement for baked beans on the side, but we don't sell them.

Passenger: Will this bus take me to Chicago?
Driver: Which part?
Passenger: All of me, of course!

Bus passenger: Driver, do you stop at the Savoy Hotel?
Bus driver: Not on my salary!

Bus passenger: Driver, this bus was very slow!
Bus driver: I expect we'll pick up speed, madam, now you're getting off.

Why is an old car like a baby playing?
Because it goes with a rattle.

The neighbour was furious when the teenaged cyclist nearly rode into him.

"Don't you know how to ride that thing yet?" he roared.

"Yes," said the boy, peering back over his shoulder as he rode off. "It's the bell I can't work yet!"

Motorist: When you sold me this car, you told me it was rust-free. But the underneath is covered in rust.
Car dealer: Yes, sir, the car is rust-free. We didn't charge you for the rust, did we?

What means of transportation gives people colds?
A choo-choo train.

The navigator of an ocean liner was steering the ship through dense fog. Suddenly, he turned to the captain and said, "I think our compass may be faulty, captain."

"What makes you think that?" asked the captain.

The navigator replied, "Because we've just been overtaken by a number 53 bus!"

Which musical is about a train conductor?
My Fare, Lady.

Who did the Cycling Association appoint to talk to the media?
A spokesman.

A man appeared in court on a charge of parking his car in a restricted area. Asked if he had anything to say by way of defence, the man replied, "They shouldn't put up such misleading signs."

"What do you mean?" said the judge.

"Well, the sign said: 'Fine For Parking Here'."

What happened to the wooden car with the wooden wheels and the wooden engine?
It wooden go!

What happened to the wooden car with the steel wheels and the steel engine?

It steel wooden go!

What did the jack say to the car?
Can I give you a lift?

Motorist: Does a cow have a horn?
Police officer: No, a cow has two horns.
Motorist: Then it must have been a car that ran over my aunt.

Police officer: Why were you driving on the sidewalk?
Motorist: Because it's too dangerous on the street.

Police officer: Why did you lead me on a high-speed chase?
Motorist: Because you'd catch me on a slow one.

Why was the motorist driving in circles?
He wanted to take his car for a spin.

Why did the motorist think the traffic light was cowardly?
Because it had just turned yellow.

A man said to his friend, "As I was driving to work this morning, I passed a guy in an RAC van. He was sobbing uncontrollably and looked really miserable. I thought to myself, 'That man's heading for a breakdown.'"

What happened when two tankers collided at sea, one carrying red paint, the other carrying blue paint?
The crews were marooned.

When a skinny bus driver pulled up at the bus stop, a giant of a man climbed on board and, marching straight to his seat, announced, "Big John doesn't pay." The driver thought it best not to argue.

The same thing happened the following day. The man mountain got on the bus, glared at the driver, said, "Big John doesn't pay," and went to a seat.

This went on for over two weeks, by which time the driver was starting to resent Big John's attitude. Why should Big John not pay the fare when all the other passengers had to? The driver wanted to stand up to Big John but realized that, in view of their markedly different physiques, Big John would probably just laugh at him. So the driver went to the gym and enrolled on an intensive bodybuilding course in the hope that he would soon be able to face Big John man to man.

Ten days later, the driver had spent over $400 on the bodybuilding course and his skin and bone had been replaced by an impressive array of rippling muscles. At last he felt a match for Big John and eagerly anticipated their daily encounter.

At his usual stop, the colossus boarded the bus and announced in his familiar booming tone, "Big John doesn't pay."

But this time the driver wasn't going to take it lying down. Instead he rose to his feet and said, "Oh yeah? And why doesn't Big John pay."

The giant passenger immediately reached into his inside pocket, causing the driver to fear the worst. Then he leaned ominously toward the driver's face and said, "Because Big John got bus pass."

VAMPIRES

What do you call a dog owned by Dracula?
A blood hound.

Why does Dracula have no friends?
Because he's a pain in the neck.

What did the vampire do to stop his son biting his nails?
He cut all his fingers off.

What was the Californian hippie vampire like?
He was ghoul man. Real ghoul.

What happened to the two mad vampires?
They both went a little batty.

A police officer spotted Dracula driving along the street one night.

"Hey, Dracula," he called out. "What do you think you're doing on this road?"

Dracula replied, **"Looking for the main artery, officer."**

What do you call a vampire that lives in the kitchen?
Count Spatula.

What do vampires cross the sea in?
Blood vessels.

What do vampires have at eleven o'clock every day?
A coffin break.

What did the vampire say to his vampire girlfriend?
Hello gore-juice.

What do vampire footballers have at halftime?
Blood oranges.

What do vampires like that are red and very silly?
Blood clots.

How does Dracula like to have his food served?
In bite-sized pieces.

Why did the vampire take up acting?
It was in his blood.

How do vampire footballers get the mud off?
They all get in the bat tub.

What happened when a doctor crossed a parrot with a vampire?
It bit his neck, sucked his blood and said, "Who's a pretty boy then?"

What's a vampire's favourite sport? **Batminton.**

What happened to the lovesick vampire?
He became a neck-romancer.

What do you get if you cross a vampire with a snail?
I don't know but it would slow him down.

Which vampire ate the three bears' porridge?
Ghouldilocks.

Which vampire tried to eat James Bond?
Ghouldfinger.

Why did the vampire stand at the bus stop with his finger up his nose?
He was a ghoulsniffer.

What does a vampire say when you tell him a ghoul joke?
Ghoul blimey!

Why isn't it a good idea to kiss vampires?
Because they've got bat breath.

What's Dracula's favourite dance?
The fang-dango.

When do vampires bite you?
On Wincedays.

What's a vampire's favourite drink?
A Bloody Mary.

What do vampires think of blood transfusions?
New-fangled rubbish.

What happened at the vampires' race?
They finished neck and neck.

Where did vampires go to first in America?
New-fang-land.

What do you get if you cross Dracula with Al Capone?
A fangster.

Where do Chinese vampires come from?
Fanghai.

What do vampires sing on New Year's Eve?
Auld Fang Syne.

What do vampires have for lunch?
Fangers and mash.

What happened at the vampires' reunion?
All the blood relations went.

Dracula had enjoyed a good night on the town, drinking Bloody Marys and biting the necks of unsuspecting women. Shortly before sunrise he was making his way home when something suddenly hit him on the back of the head. Looking round, he saw nothing, but on the ground was a small sausage roll.

Puzzled, Dracula continued on his way but a few moments later he felt another blow to the back of his head. Again there was no sign of an assailant but lying on the ground was a cocktail sausage. More mystified than ever, Dracula resumed his journey, only to feel another bang to the back of his head. He turned round immediately but again there was no sign of the culprit. However, as he looked down he noticed a small triangular sandwich on the ground. Distinctly unnerved, he stood motionless for a few seconds, peering into the darkness in the hope of catching a glimpse of his attacker. But there was nothing.

He had walked only a short distance farther along the road when he suddenly felt a tap on his shoulder. With a swirl of his cape, he turned in an instant and felt a sharp pain in his heart. He fell to the ground clutching his chest, which had been punctured by a small cocktail stick laden with chunks of cheese and pineapple. As Dracula lay dying, he looked up and saw a young woman.

"Who are you?" he gasped.

She replied, "I'm Buffet the Vampire Slayer."

What is Dracula's favourite fruit?
Neck-tarines.

Why did Dracula go to the dentist?
He had fang decay.

Why did he have fang decay?

He was always eating fang-cy cakes.

What is the American national day for vampires?
Fangsgiving Day.

Why are vampire families so close?
Because blood is thicker than water.

How do vampires keep their breath smelling nice?
They use extractor fangs.

What does Dracula say when you tell him a new fact?
Well, fang-cy that!

Why did the vampire attack the clown?
He wanted the circus to be in his blood.

Did you know that Dracula wants to become a comedian?
He's looking for a crypt writer.

Which flavour ice cream is Dracula's favourite?
Vein-illa.

What is the first thing that vampires learn at school?
The alphabat.

Why was the vampire so angry at leaving his cooking pot on the hob for too long?
It made his blood boil.

Why did Dracula go to the orthodontist?
He wanted to improve his bite.

Why is Hollywood full of vampires?
They need someone to play the bit parts.

Why do vampires like school dinners?
Because they know they won't get stake.

Why wouldn't the vampire eat his soup?
It clotted.

Why did the vampire sit on a pumpkin?
It wanted to play squash.

Why are vampires always exhausted in April?
Because they've just completed a long March of thirty-one days.

Did you hear about the vampire who died of a broken heart?
He had loved in vein.

What do you get if you cross a Rolls-Royce with a vampire?
A monster that attacks expensive cars and sucks out their gas tanks.

How do you join the Dracula Fan Club?
Send your name, address and blood group.

Why was the young vampire a failure?
Because he fainted at the sight of blood.

*What does a vampire stand on after taking a shower? **A bat mat.***

Why did the vampire give up acting?
He couldn't find a part he could get his teeth into.

What happened to the vampire who swallowed a sheep?
He felt baaaaaaaaaaaaad.

What's Dracula's favourite coffee?

De-coffin-ated.

What's Dracula's car called?
A mobile blood unit.

What happened when Dracula took up boxing?
He was out for the count.

Why do vampires do well at school?
Because every time they're asked a question they come up with a biting reply.

What is the vampire's favourite slogan?
Please Give Blood Generously.

Where is Dracula's American office?
The Vampire State Building.

Where do vampires keep their savings?
In blood banks.

What does the postman take to vampires?
Fang mail.

What did the vampire sing to the doctor who cured him of amnesia?
Fangs for the Memory.

Did you hear about the man who was rearranging furniture in Dracula's house?
He was doing a spot of Fang-Shui.

What's a vampire's favourite dance?
The Vaults.

Why did the vampire read the New York Times?
Because it had good circulation.

What do romantic vampires do?
Neck.

What do you call a vampire junkie?
Count Drugula.

What did the vampire call his false teeth?
A newfangled device.

What exams did the vampire look forward to at school?
Blood tests.

What did Dracula say to his new apprentice?
We could do with some new blood around here.

Why do vampires hate arguments?
Because they make themselves cross.

What happened when the vampire went to the blood bank?
He asked to make a withdrawal.

What does a vampire say to the mirror?
Terror, terror on the wall.

What's a vampire's favourite cartoon character?
Batman.

What did Dracula call his daughter?
Bloody Mary.

What type of people do vampires like?
O positive people.

What do vampires play poker for?
High stakes.

How does a vampire get through life with only one fang?
He has to grin and bare it.

What's pink, has a curly tail, and drinks blood?
A hampire.

What does Dracula do before he goes on vacation?
He cancels his daily pint of blood.

Why are vampires sometimes called simple-minded?
Because they're known to be suckers.

Was Dracula ever married?
No, he was a bat-chelor.

What do vampires gamble with?
Stake money.

What sort of group do vampires join?
A blood group.

Who do vampires fall in love with?
The girl necks door.

What happened to the woman who stole from a shop while balancing on the shoulders of a trio of vampires?
She was charged with shoplifting on three counts.

What is red, sweet and bites people?
A jampire.

What is Dracula's favourite pudding?
Leeches and scream.

Why does Dracula live in a coffin?
Because the rent is low.

Can a toothless vampire still bite you?
No, but he can give you a nasty suck!

What is it called when a vampire kisses you good night?
Necking.

What do you call a vampire that can lift up cars ?
Jack-u-la!

What do you call a vampire in a raincoat ?
Mack-u-la!

What do you call a vampire Father Christmas ?
Sack-u-la!

WAITER, WAITER...

Waiter, Waiter, will my hamburger be long?
No. It will be round and flat, sir.

Waiter, this soup tastes funny.
Then why aren't you laughing?

Waiter, there's a fly in my soup.
Please be quiet otherwise everyone will want one.

Waiter, there's a small slug in this lettuce.

I'm sorry, sir, would you like me to get you a bigger one?

Waiter, there's a caterpillar on my salad.
Don't worry, sir, there is no extra charge.

Waiter, there's a fly in my soup.
Don't worry, sir, that spider on your bread will soon get him.

Waiter, this coffee is terrible, it tastes like dirt.
Yes, sir, it was ground yesterday.

Waiter, do you have frogs' legs?
No, sir, I've always walked like this.

Waiter, bring me something to eat and make it snappy.
How about a crocodile sandwich, sir?

Waiter, why does this chicken only have one leg?
It was in a fight, sir.
Well, take it away and bring me the winner.

Waiter, is there soup on the menu?
No, madam, I wiped it off.

Waiter, this egg is bad.
Don't blame me, sir, I only laid the table.

Waiter, Waiter, I've been waiting here for nearly an hour!
So what? I've been waiting here for thirty years.

Waiter, there's a fly in my soup.
What do you expect for a dollar, a beetle?

Waiter, there's a flea in my soup.
Well tell him to hop it.

Waiter, there's a fly in my soup.
Yes, sir, he has committed insecticide.

Waiter, there's a slug in my salad.
I'm sorry, sir, I didn't realize you were a vegetarian.

Waiter, there's a fly in my soup.
Don't worry, sir, it's not hot enough to burn him.

Waiter, there's a fly in my custard.
I'll fetch him a spoon, sir.

Waiter, there's a cockroach on my steak.
They don't seem to care what they eat, do they, sir?

Waiter, there's a maggot in my soup.
Don't worry, sir, he won't last long in there.

Waiter, Waiter, do you know I've been waiting for my steak for an hour?
No, but if you hum a few bars, I might be able to sing along with you.

Waiter, a spider's drowning in my soup.
It hardly looks deep enough to drown in, sir.

Waiter, there's a slug in my salad.
Sorry, madam, no pets allowed.

Waiter, there's a wasp in my pudding.
So that's where they go in winter.

Waiter, there's a dead cockroach in my soup.
Surely you don't expect a live one at these prices?

Waiter, there's a worm on my plate.
That's not a worm, sir, it's your sausage.

Waiter, there's a fly in my wine.
Well you did ask for something with a little body in it.

Waiter, Waiter why is this piece of toast all broken?
Well, you did say toast and coffee and step on it.

Waiter, there's a fly in my soup.
Yes, sir, that's the manager, the last customer was a witch doctor.

Waiter, my lunch is talking to me.
Well you did ask for a tongue sandwich.

Waiter, there's a fly in my soup.
Yes, it's the rotting meat that attracts them.

Waiter, there's a fly in my soup.
No, sir, that's a cockroach. The fly is on your steak.

Waiter, why is a dead fly on my steak?
I don't know, sir, perhaps it died after tasting it.

Waiter, there's a spider on my plate, send me the manager.
That's no good, he's scared of them too.

Waiter, I'd like a cup of coffee with no cream.
Sorry, sir, we're out of cream. How about with no milk?

Waiter, what's this fly doing in my soup?
It looks like the backstroke, sir.

Waiter, didn't you tell me that the chef here cooked for the late heads of Europe?

Yes, sir, and that's why they're the late heads of Europe.

Waiter, do you serve snails?
Sit down, sir, we serve anyone.

Waiter, how come this fly is swimming in my soup?
Sorry, sir, I gave you too much. It should be wading.

Waiter, your thumb's in my soup.
That's okay, sir. The soup's not hot.

Waiter, there's a fly in my soup.
Sorry, sir, I must have missed it when I removed the other five.

Waiter, do you have frogs' legs?
Yes, sir.
Well hop off into the kitchen and bring my meal then please.

Waiter, are there snails on the menu?
Yes, sir, they must have escaped from the kitchen.

Waiter, what's this spider doing in my alphabet soup?
Probably trying to read, sir.

Waiter, there's a beetle in my soup.
Sorry, sir, we're out of flies today.

Waiter, this salad is frozen solid.
Yes, sir, it's the iceberg lettuce that does it.

Waiter, I'll have the steak and kiddley pie, please.
I think you mean steak and kidney?

That's what I said, diddle I?

Waiter, I can't seem to find any chicken in this chicken soup.
Well, would you expect to find angels in angel cake?

Waiter, there's a fly in my soup.
Well, throw him a doughnut – they make great lifebelts.

Waiter, Waiter, why is this burger half eaten?
I didn't have time to finish it, sir.

Waiter, there's a mosquito in my soup.
Don't worry, sir, they don't eat much.

Waiter, Waiter, what's this?
It's bean soup, sir.
I don't care what it's been. What is it now?

Waiter, there's a dead fly in my soup.
Yes, sir, it's the heat that kills them.

Waiter, your tie is in my soup.
Don't worry, sir, it's not shrinkable.

Waiter, there's a fly in the butter.
Yes, sir, it's a butterfly.

Waiter, there's a button in my salad.
It must have come off while the salad was dressing.

Waiter, waiter, what's wrong with this fish?
Long time, no sea, sir.

Waiter, there's a fly in my soup.
Don't worry, sir, I'll call the animal sanctuary.

Waiter, there is a bee in my alphabet soup.
Yes, sir, and I'm sure there is an A, a C and all the other letters, too.

Waiter, there are two flies in my soup.
That's all right, sir, have the extra one on me.

Waiter, look at this chicken! It's nothing but skin and bones.
Would you like the feathers, too, sir?

Waiter, what's this spider doing in my soup?
Drowning by the look of it, sir.

Waiter, this water is very cloudy.
No, sir, you just have a very dirty glass.

Waiter, your thumb was on my steak.
Well, you didn't want it to fall on the floor again, did you?

Waiter, there's a fly in my chicken soup.
No, sir, that's the chicken.

Waiter, this fish dish isn't as good as the one I had here last month.
That's strange, sir. It's from the same fish.

Waiter, Waiter, what's that in my soup?

I'd better call the manager, sir – I can't tell one insect from another.

Waiter, there's a spider in my salad.
Yes, sir, the chef is using Webb lettuce today.

Waiter, there's a fly in my soup.
Hold on, sir, I'll get the fly spray.

Waiter, this plate is wet.
No, that's your soup.

Waiter, could I have the steak please?
With pleasure, sir.
No with fries please.

Waiter, I can't eat this meat, it's crawling with maggots.
Quick, run to the other end of the table and grab it as it goes by.

Waiter, there's a dead fly in my soup.
Oh no, who will look after his family?

Waiter, this steak is so tough I can't even cut it. Take it away and bring me another.
I can't, sir. You've bent it.

Waiter, I can't eat this chicken. Call the manager.
It's no use. He can't eat it either.

Waiter, what is this cockroach doing on my ice-cream sundae?
Skiing, sir.

Waiter, there's a dead beetle in my soup.
Yes, sir, they're not terribly good swimmers.

Waiter, there's a fly in my soup.
Don't worry, madam, go ahead and eat it, there are plenty more.

Waiter, there's a dead fly swimming in my soup.
Don't be silly, dead flies can't swim.

Waiter, this food isn't fit for a pig.
In that case I shall take it away and bring you some that is.

Waiter, how long must I wait for that turtle soup?
Well, you know how slow turtles are, sir.

Waiter, what's the meaning of this fly in my soup?
I'm a waiter, sir, not a fortune-teller.

Waiter, there is a fly in my bean soup.
Don't worry, sir, I'll fish it out and exchange it for a bean.

Waiter, what's this bug doing in my salad?
Trying to find its way out, sir.

Waiter, what's this creepy-crawly doing in my salad?
Not him again, he's in here every night.

Waiter, there's a fly in my soup.
Okay, sir, I'll bring you a fork.

Waiter, what's this bug doing waltzing around my table !
It's the band, sir, they are playing his tune.

Waiter, there's a dead fly in my soup.
No it's not, sir. It's a piece of dirt that looks like a dead fly.

Waiter, can you get rid of this fly in my starter?
I can't do that, sir, he's not had his main course yet.

Waiter, what's this bug doing on my wife's shoulder?
I don't know, sir, but he's a friendly thing, isn't he?

Waiter, there's a fly in my soup.
That's not a fly, that's a vitamin bee.

Waiter, there's a fly in my soup.
I'm surprised, sir. I thought the chef used them all in the raisin bread.

Waiter, I thought the meals here were supposed to be like mother used to make.
They are, sir, but she couldn't cook either.

Waiter, how come the Department of Health hasn't closed this place down?
They're afraid to eat here, sir.

Waiter, there's a fly in my soup.
Just you wait until you see the main course.

Waiter, there's a wasp in my soup.
Yes, sir, it's the fly's day off.

Waiter: Sir, you haven't touched your custard. Is everything all right with it?
Customer: I'm just waiting for the fly to stop using it as a trampoline.

Waiter: And how did you find your steak, sir?
Customer: I moved this slice of tomato and there it was!

WEREWOLVES

Where do American werewolves live?
Hair-izona.

Why was the werewolf arrested in the butcher's shop?
He was chop-lifting.

How do you stop a werewolf howling in the back of a car?
Put him in the front.

What happened to the wolf that fell into the washing machine?
It became a wash and werewolf.

What did the werewolf write on his Christmas cards?
Best vicious of the season.

What do you get if you cross a hairdresser with a werewolf?
A monster with an all-over perm.

What parting gift did a mother werewolf give to her son when he left home?

Mommy, Mommy, what's a werewolf?
Don't worry about that and comb your face.

A comb.

What do you get if you cross a witch with a werewolf?
A mad dog that chases airplanes.

What happened when the werewolf chewed a bone for an hour?
When he got up he only had three legs.

What do you call a werewolf with no legs?
Anything you like – he can't chase you.

How do you know that a werewolf's been in the fridge?
There are paw prints in the butter.

How do you know that two werewolves have been in the fridge?
There are two sets of paw prints in the butter.

What does it mean if there is a werewolf in your fridge in the morning?
You had some party last night!

Did you hear about the comedian who entertained at a werewolves' party?
He had them howling in the aisles.

Did you hear about the sick werewolf?
He lost his voice but it's howl right now.

What happened when the werewolf swallowed a clock?
He got ticks.

Why did the boy take an aspirin after hearing a werewolf howl?
Because it gave him an eerie ache.

Why shouldn't you grab a werewolf by its tail?
It might be the werewolf's tail but it could be the end of you.

How do you stop a werewolf attacking you?
Throw a stick and shout fetch!

Why are werewolves thought of as quick-witted?
Because they always give snappy answers.

What do you call a hairy beast with clothes on?
A wear-wolf.

What do you call a hairy beast in a river?
A weir-wolf.

What do you call a hairy beast that no longer exists?
A were-wolf.

What do you call a hairy beast that's lost?
A where-wolf.

What did the werewolf say when he ate his mother?
Burp!

What happens if you cross a werewolf with a sheep?

You have to get a new sheep.

What would you get if you crossed a werewolf with a dozen eggs?
A hairy omelette.

What's fearsome, hairy and drinks from the wrong side of a glass?
A werewolf with hicups.

When do werewolf children stay home from school?
On howl-idays.

Doctor: I'm sorry madam, but I have to tell you that you are a werewolf.
Patient: Give me a piece of paper.

Doctor: Do you want to write your will?
Patient: No, a list of people I want to bite.

"Doctor, I've just been bitten on the leg by a werewolf."
"Did you put anything on it?"
"No, he seemed to like it as it was."

WHAT DO YOU CALL...

What do you call a man with a plank on his head?
Edward.

What do you call a man with a spade on his head?
Doug.

What do you call a man without a spade on his head?
Douglas.

What do you call a man with a car on his head?
Jack.

What do you call a woman with a bunch of holly on her head?
Carol.

What do you call a woman with a cat on her head?
Kitty.

What do you call a man with a paper bag on his head?
Russell.

What do you call a man who lies on the floor?
Matt.

What do you call a man with a seagull on his head?
Cliff.

What do you call a man with a crane on his head?
Derek.

What do you call a man with a map on his head?
Miles.

What do you call a man with a car number plate on his head?
Reg.

What do you call a man with a wig on his head?
Aaron.

What do you call a man with a doormat on his head?
Neil.

What do you call a woman with a radiator on her head?
Anita.

What do you call a woman with slates on her head?
Ruth.

What do you call a woman with a spring on her head?
April.

What do you call a man with a large blue-black-yellow mark on his head?
Bruce.

What do you call a man with some cat scratches on his head?
Claude.

What do you call a man with a stamp on his head?
Frank.

What do you call a woman with a breeze on her head?
Gail.

What do you call a woman with a tortoise on her head?
Shelley.

What do you call a woman with a twig on her head?
Hazel.

What do you call a man with a kilt on his head?
Scott.

What do you call a man with a legal document on his head?
Will.

What do you call a man who wears a coat?
Mac.

What do you call a man who wears two coats?
Max.

What do you call a man with a rabbit up his jumper?
Warren.

What do you call a woman who lies across the middle of a tennis court?
Annette.

What do you call a judge with no thumbs?
Justice Fingers.

What do you call a nun with a washing machine on her head?
Sister-Matic.

What do you call a man with a picture on his head?
Art.

What do you call a man with a pole on his head?
Rod.

What do you call two men with poles on their heads standing in the window?
Kurt and Rod.

What to do you call a man with a pole through his leg?
Rodney.

What do you call a man with a pigeon on his head?
Homer.

What do you call a man with a duck on his head?
Bill.

What do you call a man with no arms and no legs in a swimming pool?
Bob.

What do you call a man you dig up out of the ground?
Pete.

What do you call a man who comes through your letterbox?
Bill.

What do you call a man who comes through a student letterbox?
Grant.

What do you call a man pouring water into a jug?
Phil.

What do you call a man who likes doughnuts?
Duncan

What do you call a man with a rowing machine on his head?
Jim.

What do you call a man with exams on his head?
Mark.

What do you call a woman setting fire to bills?
Bernadette.

What do you call a woman wearing denim?
Jean.

What do you call a flying woman?
Rose.

What do you call a woman with a bottle on her head?
Cherie.

What do you call a woman with a lamp on her head?
Jeannie.

What do you call a Mexican man who cannot find his vehicle?
Carlos.

What do you call a woman juggling bottles of beer?
Beatrix.

What do you call a woman juggling bottles of beer and making something from clay?
Beatrix Potter.

What do you call a really small woman?
Dot.

What do you call a really happy woman?
Mary.

What do you call a singing woman?
Carol.

What do you call a man at the side of a house?
Ali.

What do you call a woman with a police car on her head?
Nina.

What do you call a girl with a frog on her head?
Lily.

What do you call a woman who knows how to get across a gap?
Bridget.

What do you call woman with a hairy top lip?
Tash.

What do you call the woman with a sunbed on her head?
Tanya.

What do you call a man with a family of foxes on his head?
Den.

What do you call a man on the top of an oil well?
Derek.

What do you call a vicar on a motorbike?
Rev.

What do you call a woman with one leg?
Eileen.

What do you call a man with a hedgehog on his head?
Spike.

What do you call a man with a toilet on his head?
John.

What do you call a woman with a window on her head?
Cilla.

What do you call a woman with diamonds on her head?
Gemma.

What do you call a woman who hires buildings on a long-term agreement?
Lisa.

What do you call a woman who completes a list of flightless birds that starts Ostrich, Emu, Kiwi?
Andrea.

What do you call a man with an insect on his head?
Anton.

What do you call a woman with shopping bags on her head?
Carrie.

What do you call a woman who's always matchmaking?
Maria.

What do you call a Pakistani police informer?
Wasim.

What do you call a woman who's always in court after damages?
Sue.

What do you call a man with a razor on his head?
Nick.

What do you call a man with a finish line on his head?
Victor.

What do you call a camel with three humps?
Humphrey.

What do you call a woman who put on weight by eating two husbands to whom she was illegally married?
Big Amy.

What do you call a man in debt?
Owen.

What do you call a man with a rubber toe?
Roberto.

What do you call a man with a cow on his head?
Pat.

What do you call a woman with a roulette wheel on her head?
Bette.

What do you call a man with a tree on his head?
Woody.

What do you call a man with lots of trees on his head?
Forrest.

What do you call a man with a man on his head?
Manny.

What do you call a man with lots of eyes on his head?
Seymour.

What do you call a man with grass on his head?
Mo.

What do you call a man with a duck on his head?
Donald.

What do you call a man with a casserole on his head?
Stu.

What do you call a woman who manufactures items for beauty contests?
Sasha.

What do you call a woman with a sheep on her head?
Baa-Baa-Ra.

What do you call a woman with a computerized piano on the side of her head?
Cynthia.

What do you call a man with a large fruit on his head?
Gordon.

What do you call a man with a karaoke machine?
Mike.

What do you call a woman with a short skirt on?
Denise.

What do you call a woman that people sit on?
Cher.

What do you call a man who swings through the jungle backwards?
Nazrat.

What do you call a woman with a nut tree on her head?
Hazel.

What do you call a woman with a boat on her head?
Maude.

What do you call a girl with a star on her head?
Stella.

What do you call a girl with a supermarket checkout on her head?
Tilly.

What do you call a woman who works in a bakers?
Bunty.

What do you call a woman with sandpaper on her head?
Sandie.

What do you call a male cat on an ocean liner?
Tom Cruise.

What do you call a dead magician?
An abracadaver.

What do you call a pretend railway?
A play station.

What do you call well-repaired holes in socks?
Darned good.

What do you call the place where the police keep rhubarb thieves?
Custardy.

What do you call Tarzan when he visits Mars?
Marzipan.

What do you call a person who falls on to you on a bus or train?
A laplander.

What do you call something purple that swings through vineyards?
Tarzan the grape man.

What do you call a man who lends his DIY tools to a neighbour?
A saw loser.

What do you call a deer with no eyes?
No idea.

What do you call a deer with no eyes and no legs?
Still no idea.

What do you call a scared biscuit?
A cowardy custard cream.

What do you call a man whose father was a Canon?
A son of a gun.

What do you call CCTV film of pedestrians?
Footage.

What do you call an educated hole in the wall?
A wisecrack.

What do you call two bananas?
A pair of slippers.

What do you call someone drilling holes in a piece of wood?
Boring.

What do you call a man with two left feet?
Whatever you like – if he tries to catch you, he'll just run round in circles.

What do you call a weekly television programme about people getting washed?
A soap opera.

What do you call a flock of birds who fly in formation?
The red sparrows.

What does the Invisible Man call his mother and father?
His transparents

What do you call a bee that is always complaining?
A grumble bee.

What do you call a school principal who makes fireworks?
A head banger.

What do you call a man that drills holes in teapots?
A potholer.

What do you call a song played on car horns?
A car tune.

What do you call an elephant that has had too much to drink?
Trunk.

What do you call the owner of a tool factory?
The vice chairman.

What do you call a zipper on a banana?
A fruit fly.

What do you call a man who rescues drowning spooks from the sea?
A ghost guard.

What do you call someone who makes half-size models of fish?
A scale modeller.

What do you call a man with a collection of fish photographs?
The Prints of Whales.

What do you call a man with a comic book on his head?
Joe King.

What do you call a man with a football pitch on his head?
Alf Time.

What do you call a Roman emperor with flu?
Julius Sneezer.

What do you call a podium that eats people?
Hannibal Lectern.

What do you call a man with a swarm of bees round his head?
A.B. Hive.

What do you call a man who is part man, part jungle cat?
Richard the Lion Half.

What do you call a man who checks the size of rabbit holes?
A burrow surveyor.

What do you call a broken down hot rod?
A shot rod.

What do you call a man who does everything in thirty seconds?
Arthur Minute.

What do you call the ring that worms leave round the bath?
The scum of the earth.

What do you call a rifle with three barrels?
A trifle.

What do you call a fish on the dining table?
A plaice mat.

What do you call a real goose?
Propagander.

What do you call a fight between film actors?
Star wars.

What do you call a man at the wheel of an ice-cream van?
A sundae driver.

What do you call a group of cars?
A clutch.

What do you call a London Underground train full of professors?

A tube of smarties.

What do you call a puzzle that is so hard it makes people swear?
A crossword.

What do you call rubber bumpers on yachts?
Shark absorbers.

What do you call a film about mallards?
A duck-umentary.

What do you call a musical instrument that is played by two teams of twenty people?
A piano forte.

What do you call a book that spies on people?
A peeping tome.

What do you call a very fast horse?
Gee gee whizz.

What do you call a pair of robbers?
A pair of nickers.

What do you call a chocolate that teases small animals?
A mole-teaser.

What do you call something that runs around your garden all day and never stops?
The fence.

What do you call a pen with no hair?
A bald point.

What do you call it when an aeroplane disappears over the horizon?
Boeing, going, gone.

What do you call a plant that's a lodger at a guest-house?
The herbaceous border.

What do you call a hearing aid made from fruit?
A lemonade.

What do you call a five-a-side soccer match played by chimney sweeps?
Soot ball.

What do you call a small parent?
A minimum.

What do you call a tall parent?
A maximum.

What do you call a traffic warden who never fines anyone?
A terrific warden.

What do you call a line of Barbie dolls?
A Barbecue.

What do you call a telephone call from one vicar to another?
A parson to parson call.

What do you call it when you pass out after eating too much curry?
A korma.

What do you call a woman who delivers puppies?
A mid-woof.

What do you call a man who is scared of Christmas?
Noel Coward.

What do you call an Arab dairy farmer?
A milk sheikh.

What do you call a snake that becomes a Canadian law officer?
Mountie Python.

What do you call a convict that dresses up as a clown?
Silicon.

What do you call a butterfingered nurse?
A medicine dropper.

What do you call a barber who cuts hair in a library?
A barbarian.

What do you call it when giraffes moving one way get mixed up with giraffes moving another way?
A giraffic jam.

What do you call a man with a double-decker bus on his head?
The deceased.

WHAT DO YOU GET IF YOU CROSS...

What do you get if you cross a tourist with an elephant?
Something that carries its own trunk.

What do you get if you cross a pig with Count Dracula?
A hampire.

What do you get if you cross a dog with a traffic warden?
A barking ticket.

What do you get if you cross a hen with some gunpowder?
An eggsplosion.

What do you get if you cross Count Dracula with Sir Lancelot?
A bite in shining armour.

What do you get if you cross a parrot with a pig?
A bird that hogs the conversation.

What do you get if you cross a thief with an orchestra?
Robbery with violins.

What do you get if you cross a Labrador with a tortoise?
A pet that goes to the shop and comes home with last week's newspaper.

What do you get if you cross a flea with a rabbit?
Bugs Bunny.

What do you get if you cross an

What do you get if you cross a vegetable with a twenty-six-mile run?
A marrowthon.

alligator with a flower?
I don't know, but I'm not going to smell it.

What do you get if you cross poison ivy with four-leaf clover?
A rash of good luck.

What do you get if you cross a telephone with an iron?
A smooth operator.

What do you get if you cross an

artist with a police officer?
A brush with the law.

What do you get if you cross an Austrian composer with a man who wears a turban?
Haydn Sikh.

What do you get if you cross a worm with an elephant?
Great big holes all over your garden.

What do you get if you cross an elephant with a fish?
Swimming trunks.

What do you get if you cross a box of matches and a giant?
The big match.

What do you get if you cross a road with a safari park?
Double yellow lions.

What do you get if you cross an overweight golfer and a pair of very tight trousers?
A hole in one.

What do you get if you cross a plumber with a field of cow pats?
The poohed piper.

What do you get if you cross an elephant and a bottle of whiskey?
A creature that's trunk and disorderly.

What do you get if you cross a flock of sheep and a radiator?
Central bleating.

What do you get if you cross a skunk and a pair of tennis rackets?
Ping pong.

What do you get if you cross an elephant with a whale?
A submarine with a built-in snorkel.

What do you get if you cross a pudding and a cow pat?
A smelly jelly.

What do you get if you cross a pig and a box of itching powder?
Pork scratching.

What do you get if you cross a bear with a freezer?
A teddy brrrrr.

What do you get if you cross a computer with a vampire?
Something new fangled.

What do you get if you cross a dog with a telephone?
A golden receiver.

What do you get if you cross a cow with a octopus?
Something that can milk itself.

What do you get if you cross a pair of dogs with a hairdresser?
A shampoodle and setter.

What do you get if you cross a shoulder bag with a mallard?
A ducksack.

What do you get if you cross a dinosaur with a dog?
Tyrannosaurus Rex.

What do you get if you cross a football team with a bunch of crazy jokers?
Madjester United.

What do you get if you cross a large computer and a beefburger?
A big mac.

What do you get if you cross an overheating large computer with a beefburger?

What do you get if you cross a soccer player and a mythical creature?
A centaur forward.

A big mac and fries.

What do you get if you cross a
mouse and a bottle of olive oil?
A squeak that oils itself.

What do you get if you cross a
jogger with an apple pie?
Puff pastry.

What do you get if you cross a
detective with a cat?
A peeping tom.

What do you get if you cross a
television programme and a group
of sheep?
A flockumentary.

What do you get if you cross a pig
and a part in a film?
A ham roll.

What do you get when you
cross a pig and a cactus?
A porky-pine.

What do you get if you cross a wireless with a hairdresser?
Radio waves.

What do you get if you cross a hairdresser and a bucket of cement?
Permanent waves.

What do you get if you cross a toadstool and a full suitcase?
Not mushroom for your holiday clothes.

What do you get if you cross Bambi with a ghost?
Bamboo.

What do you get if you cross a Frisbee with a cow?
Skimmed milk.

What do you get if you cross a dog with a vampire?
A werewoof.

What do you get if you cross a bike and a rose?
Bicycle petals.

What do you get if you cross an alligator and King Midas?
A croc of gold.

What do you get if you cross a tortoise and a storm?
An "I'm not in a hurry" cane.

What do you get if you cross a baby bird with a pod?
Chick peas.

What do you get if you cross a computer with a potato?
Micro chips.

What do you get if you cross a dog with a maze?
A labyrinth.

What do you get if you cross the moon with a monk?
A nocturnal habit.

What do you get if you cross a cow with a crystal ball?
A message from the udder side.

What do you get if you cross a crocodile with a camera?
A snapshot.

What do you get if you cross a plank of wood and a pencil?
A drawing board.

What do you get if you cross a dog with a football game?
Spot-the-ball.

What do you get if you cross a spider with a computer?
A web page.

What do you get if you cross a star with a silver cup?
A constellation prize.

What do you get if you cross a flea with some moon rock?
A lunar-tick.

What do you get if you cross a vampire and a circus entertainer?
Something that goes straight for the juggler.

What do you get if you cross a bunch of flowers with some insects?

Ants in your plants.

What do you get if you cross a bunch of flowers with a burglar?
Robbery with violets.

What do you get if you cross a bank robber with some bushes?
Armed shrubbery.

What do you get if you cross a cow and a goat?
Butter from a butter.

What do you get if you cross a philosopher with a Mafia hitman?
Someone who'll make you an offer you can't understand.

What do you get if you cross a pen with Napoleon's feet?
A footnote in history.

What do you get if you cross a ghost and an Italian restaurant?
Spook-hetti.

What do you get if you cross a Star Trek character with a pasta dish?
Spock-hetti.

What do you get when you cross a hundred pigs with a hundred deer?
Two hundred sows and bucks!

What do you get if you cross a cow with an out-of-date map?
Udderly lost.

What do you get if you cross a bat with a lonely hearts club?
A lot of blind dates.

What do you get if you cross a television soap and a rabbit colony?
Burrow Nation Street.

What do you get if you cross a pelican and a zebra?
Across the road safely.

What do you get if you cross a bee and a coach?
A buzzzz.

What do you get if you cross Cameron Diaz with Santa Claus?
A thank you from Santa.

What do you get if you cross a monster and a chicken?
Free strange eggs.

What do you get if you cross a fish and bad breath?
Halibut-osis.

What do you get if you cross a compass and a shellfish?
A guided mussel.

What do you get if you cross a school with a computer supplier?
Floppy desks.

What do you get if you cross a pig with a centipede?
Bacon and legs.

What do you get if you cross a very bent piece of wood with a spaceship?
Warp factor 7.

What do you get if you cross a

hairdresser, a storyteller and a young horse?
A pony tail.

What do you get if you cross a motorcycle and a funny story?
A Yamaha ha ha ha.

What do you get if you cross a leopard and a bunch of flowers?
A beauty spot.

What do you get if you cross a biscuit with a car tyre?
Crumbs.

What do you get if you cross a Welshman with a problem?
A Dai-lemma.

What do you get if you cross a pub and a steelworks?
An iron bar.

What do you get if you cross a shark and a parrot?
An animal that talks your head off.

What do you get if you cross a book and a pound of fat?
Lard of the rings.

What do you get if you cross a newsreader and a toad?
A croaksman.

What do you get if you cross a ghost and a newsreader?
A spooksman.

What do you get if you cross a suitcase with a hazelnut?
A nut case.

What do you get if you cross a donkey and Christmas?
Muletide greetings.

What do you get if you cross an elephant and a rhino?
'Ell if I know.

What do you get if you cross the devil and an anagram?
Santa.

What do you get if you cross a Shakespeare play and a pig?
Ham-omelette.

What do you get if you cross a Mars bar and an elk?
Chocolate moose.

What do you get if you cross a telephone with a pair of pants?
Bell-bottoms.

What do you get if you cross a skeleton, a feather and a joke book?
Rib ticklers.

What do you get if you cross pasta with a snake?
Spaghetti that winds itself around your fork.

What do you get if you cross a skeleton and a garden spade?
Skullduggery.

What do you get if you cross a skeleton and a dog?
An animal that buries itself.

What do you get if you cross a skeleton and a tumble drier?
Bone dry clothes.

What do you get if you cross teeth with candy?
Dental floss.

What do you get if you cross a madman and a bakery?
Doughnuts.

What do you get if you cross a pig and a laundry?
Hogwash.

What do you get if you cross a cake and a disco?
Abundance.

What do you get if you cross a bad-tempered witch doctor, a fizzy drink and your dad?
A bottle of pop.

What do you get if you cross SpongeBob with Albert Einstein?
SpongeBob SmartyPants.

What do you get if you cross a dog and a film studio?
Collie-wood.

What do you get if you cross a giant ape and a self-defence class?
Kong-fu.

What do you get if you cross a jet engine and a tennis racket?
A tennis rocket.

What do you get if you cross a sheep with a holiday resort?
The Baaahaaamaaas.

What do you get if you cross a chicken with a cow?

Roost beef.

What do you get if you cross a sheep and a vampire?
Were-wool.

What do you get if you cross a king and a boat?
King Canoe.

What do you get if you cross a herb and Doctor Who?
A thyme machine.

What do you get if you cross mouthwash and a bottle of HP?
Tartar sauce.

What do you get if you cross a telephone and a marriage bureau?
A wedding ring.

What do you get if you cross a joke book and a snowstorm?
Corn flakes.

What do you get if you cross a pig and a telephone?
A lot of crackling on the line.

What do you get if you cross a vampire and a plumber?
A drain in the neck.

What do you get if you cross an Italian landmark and a ghost?
The screaming tower of Pisa.

What do you get if you cross a vampire and a birthday present?
Something you wouldn't want to unwrap.

What do you get if you cross a

naked woman and the bottom of the ocean?
A deep sea Lady Godiva.

What do you get if you cross a chicken with a zebra?
A four-legged dinner with its own barcode.

What do you get if you cross a singer and a tall ladder?
Someone who can easily get the high notes.

What do you get if you cross a student and an alien?
Something from another universe-ity.

What do you get if you cross a mummy and a spaceship?
Tutankha-moon.

What do you get if you cross a gorilla and a prisoner?
A Kong-vict.

What do you get if you cross a house with a quarter pound of minced meat?
A homeburger.

What do you get if you cross a bee with a quarter pound of minced meat?
A humburger.

What do you get if you cross a sheepdog with a jelly?
The collie-wobbles.

What do you get if you cross a chef with a librarian?
Someone who cooks the books.

What do you get if you cross a donkey and an owl?
A smart ass.

What do you get if you cross a pond and a stream?
Wet feet.

What do you get if you cross a hedgehog with a giraffe?
A long-necked toothbrush.

What do you get if you cross William the Conqueror with a power station?
An electricity bill.

WHAT'S THE DIFFERENCE...

What's the difference between a train and a tree?
One leaves its shed and the other sheds its leaves.

What's the difference between the death of a barber and the death of a sculptor?
One curls up and dies and the other makes faces and busts.

What's the difference between an elephant and spaghetti?
An elephant doesn't slip off the end of your fork.

What's the difference between a crazy rabbit and a counterfeit coin?
One's a mad bunny, the other is bad money.

What's the difference between a camera and a sock?
A camera takes photos and a sock takes five toes.

What's the difference between a peeping Tom and someone who's just got out of the bath?
One is rude and nosey, the other is nude and rosy.

What's the difference between weather and climate?
You can't weather a tree, but you can climate.

What's the difference between a hill and a pill?
One is hard to get up, the other is hard to get down.

What's the difference between a boxer and a man with a cold?
One knows his blows, and the other blows his nose.

What's the difference between a bus driver and a cold?
One knows the stops, the other stops the nose.

What's the difference between a horse and the weather?
One is reined up and the other rains down.

What's the difference between Prince Charles and a tennis ball?
One is heir to the throne, the other is thrown in the air.

What's the difference between an ornithologist and a stutterer?
One's a bird watcher, the other's a word botcher.

What's the difference between a cat and a comma?
One has the paws before the claws and the other has the clause before the pause.

What's the difference between a schoolteacher and a railroad conductor?
One trains the mind, the other minds the train.

What's the difference between a schoolteacher and a train?
One says, "Spit your gum out," the other goes "Chew, chew, chew."

What's the difference between a person asleep and a person awake?
With some people it's hard to tell the difference.

What's the difference between a jeweller and a jailer?
A jeweller sells watches, and a jailer watches cells.

What's the difference between an injured lion and a wet day?
One roars with pain and the other pours with rain.

What's the difference between a frog and a cat?
A frog croaks all the time, a cat only croaks nine times.

What's the difference between an elephant and a bad student?
One rarely bites, the other barely writes.

What's the difference between a concert organizer and a crooked accountant?
One books the fiddles, the other fiddles the books.

What's the difference between a knight and Santa's reindeer?
One slays the dragon, the other is

draggin' the sleigh.

What's the difference between a thief and a church bell?
One steals from the people, the other peals from a steeple.

What's the difference between a greyhound at the start of a race and Mike Tyson's attack on Evander Holyfield?
One's champing at the bit, the other's biting at the champ.

What's the difference between a dog and a flea?
A dog can have fleas but a flea can't have dogs.

What's the difference between Santa Claus and a dog?
Santa Claus wears a whole suit, a dog just pants.

What's the difference between a lousy golfer and a lousy skydiver?
The lousy golfer goes splash then damn; the lousy skydiver goes damn then splash.

What's the difference between Joan of Arc and a canoe?
One was Maid of Orleans, the other is made of wood.

What's the difference between a soldier and a fireman?
You can't dip a fireman into your boiled egg.

What's the difference between a market gardener and a snooker player?
One minds his peas, the other minds his cues.

What's the difference between a fitness instructor and a dentist?
A dentist lets you sit down while he's hurting you.

What's the difference between a horse and a pencil?
You can lead a horse to water but a pencil must be lead.

What's the difference between a moose and an ant?
A moose has antlers but an ant doesn't have mooselers.

What's the difference between a tickle and a wise guy?
One is fun, the other thinks he's fun.

What's the difference between one yard and two yards?
A fence.

What's the difference between a guy falling from the first floor and one falling from the seventeenth floor?
The guy falling from the first floor goes, "Splat, Aaaaaaaargh" and the one falling from the seventeenth floor goes, "Aaaaaaargh, splat".

What's the difference between roast beef and pea soup?
Anybody can roast beef.

WITCHES AND WIZARDS

What do you call a motor bike belonging to a witch?
A vrrrooooooooom stick.

What's a cold, evil candle called?
The wicked wick of the north.

What is evil, ugly on the inside and green on the outside?
A witch dressed as a cucumber.

What happens if you see twin witches?
You won't be able to see which witch is witch.

What witch is useful when it's dark?
A lights witch.

Why did the witch give up fortune-telling?
There was no future in it.

What did the witch ask for when she booked into the hotel?
A broom with a view.

Did you hear about the kindly witch who took up weather forecasting?
She predicted sunny spells.

First witch: I went to the beauty parlour yesterday. I was there for three and a half hours.
Second witch: What did you have done?
First witch: Nothing. I was just there for an estimate.

A witch asked a beautician, "Do you think I'll lose my looks as I get older?"
"With any luck, yes," replied the beautician.

How can you tell when witches are carrying time bombs?
You can hear their brooms tick.

What do you give a witch at teatime?
A cup and sorcerer.

Why did the baby witch smile when she came out in blotches?
Because it was an 'appy rash.

What does a witch get if she is a poor traveller?
Broom sick.

How did the witch almost lose her baby?
She didn't take it far enough into the woods.

What name did the witch give to her cooking pot?
It was called-Ron.

Why did the stupid witch keep her clothes in the fridge?
She liked to have something cool to slip into in the evenings.

What do you call a wizard from outer space?
A flying sorcerer.

Why did the wizard wear a yellow robe to the Halloween party?
He was going as a banana.

*What is a witch with poison ivy called? **An itchy witchy.***

What kind of witch lives on a beach?
A sand witch.

Why don't witches like to ride their brooms when they're angry?
Because they're afraid of flying off the handle.

What happened to the stupid wizard who put in his false teeth back to front?

He ate himself.

What happened to the wizard who brushed his teeth with gunpowder?
He kept shooting his mouth off.

What do wizards do to get their kicks?
They drool over the pictures in *Witch* magazine.

How do you make a witch scratch?
Take away the W.

Why doesn't a witch wear a flat hat?
Because there's no point in it.

What happened when the wizard turned a boy into a hare?
He's still rabbiting on about it.

Why did the wizard wear red, white and blue braces?
To keep his trousers up.

What's the first thing that a wizard does in the morning?
He wakes up.

What subject did the witch pass in school?
Spelling.

What do wizards stop for on the motorway?
Witch-hikers.

What do you call a massive witch doctor ?
Mumbo jumbo!

ZOMBIES

What happened when a vicar saw a zombie with nothing on his neck?
He made a bolt for it.

Who do zombie cowboys fight?
Deadskins.

Do zombies like being dead?
Of corpse.

What do little zombies take to bed at night?
Their deady bears.

Why did the zombie go to hospital?
To have his ghoulstones removed.

What did the zombie's friend say when he introduced him to his girlfriend?
Good grief! Where did you dig her up from?

What's a zombie's favourite game?
Corpse and robbers.

When can't you bury people who live opposite a graveyard?
When they're not dead.

What trees do ghouls like best?
Ceme-trees.

Did you hear about the ghoul's favourite hotel?
It had running rot and mould in every room.

How can you tell if a corpse is angry?
It flips its lid.

Why are cemeteries in the middle of towns?
Because they're dead centres.

Why did the zombie go to hospital?
He wanted to learn a few sick jokes.

What did the depressed zombie say to his friend?
Mind if I pick your brain for a bit?

What do you call zombies in a belfry?
Dead ringers.

What does a zombie say when he gets a letter from his girlfriend?
It's a dead-letter day.

Where do zombies go for cruises?
The Deaditerranean.

What did the zombie get his medal for?
Deadication.

What is a zombie's favourite rock?
Tombstone.

What happened to the zombie who had a bad cold?
He said, "I'm fed up wid fuddy jokes aboud zondies."

Why was the zombie's nightclub a disaster?
It was a dead and alive hole.

Why do zombies learn Latin and Ancient Greek?
Because they like dead languages.

How do you know a zombie is tired?
He's dead on his feet.

128   *L1, 794*.
129   *L1, 800*.
130   *L1, 801*.
131   *L1, 796*.
132   *L1, 816*.
133   *L1, 796*.
134   See John Peale Bishop's letter to Edmund Wilson, 3 November 1922, quoted in Rainey, *Revisiting 'The Waste Land'*, 104.
135   *L1, 798*.
136   *L1, 803*.
137   *CPP, 77*.
138   *Facsimile*, 1.
139   Woolf, *The Diary of Virginia Woolf 2*, 178.
140   Mary Hutchinson, 'T. S. Eliot', short, unpublished, undated biographical sketch in typescript, holograph emendation, in the possession of her son Jeremy Hutchinson (quoted with his permission).
141   *L2, 124*.